University of Liverpool

Withdrawn from stock

The Economics of the European Community

The Economics of the European Community

Edited by

A M EL-AGRAA
University of Leeds

Philip Allan

First published 1980 by
PHILIP ALLAN PUBLISHERS LIMITED
MARKET PLACE
DEDDINGTON
OXFORD OX5 4SE

0 86003 028 8 hbk
0 86003 127 6 pbk

British Library Cataloguing in Publication Data

The economics of the European community.
   1. European Economic Community countries
   — Economic policy
   2. Europe — Economic integration
   I. El-Agraa, Ali M
   338.91'4   HC241.2

ISBN 0-86003-028-8
ISBN 0-86003-127-6 Pbk

Set by MHL Typesetting Limited, Coventry
Printed in Great Britain at the Camelot Press Limited, Southampton

Contents

Preface

This book is in three parts. The first gives general background information about the historical development of the EEC, its institutions, and basic statistics of member nations; also included are their potential partners in the near future and, for comparative purposes, Canada, Japan, the USA and the USSR. The second discusses the theory of customs unions and the measurement of the effects of the formation of the EEC on both the participating nations and the rest of the world. The third deals with the problems of hidden barriers to trade and of policy co-ordination and harmonisation in the specific context of the Community.

The book is aimed at students of international economics in general and at those interested in international economic integration with specific reference to Western Europe in particular. However, the policy chapters will hopefully appeal also to general economists interested in the implications of EEC membership.

A number of contributors have written chapters specially for the book. In such a venture, one can never achieve total harmonisation(!) but, as author and editor, I have endeavoured to ensure reasonable continuity.

The idea of a book on the economics of the European Community has been with me for some time. In this I have been influenced by three factors. Firstly, I specialise in international economics and am particularly interested in the field of international economic integration with specific reference to Western Europe. Secondly, there is no single book which gives adequate coverage of the impact and consequences of the EEC on both partner and non-participating countries; there are several books on the subject, but these are either outdated (on both the theoretical and policy aspects) or deal only with specialised areas of interest such as the historical, institutional, fiscal or empirical aspects. Thirdly, since 1972 Mr A.J. Jones and I have been running an undergraduate third year course at Leeds entitled 'Britain in the Common Market', which has proved not only the popularity of the topic, but also further underlined the lack of a comprehensive guide to the subject matter. All these considerations finally convinced me of the great need for a book which gives an up-to-date and comprehensive account of the European Community.

Acknowledgements

The book could not have taken its present form or structure without the help and contributions of colleagues both at the University of Leeds and elsewhere. Mr A. J. Jones, a specialist in international trade theory, has written the chapter on the theory of customs unions. Professor A. J. Brown, who was a member of the McDougall Committee which reported to the EEC Commission on the role of public finance in the Community, has contributed the chapter on the EEC budget. Professor K. M. Gwilliam, a specialist in transport economics, a member of several EEC committees on Community transport policy and currently in receipt of a grant for research in this field, has written the chapter on EEC transport policy. Dr C. D. E. Collins, who specialises in social policy and administration, has written the chapters on the history and institutions of the EEC and on social policy. Dr P. S. Goodrich, a political scientist turned accountant in the area of management studies, has written, with me, the chapter on factor mobility.

I have also drawn on the expertise of colleagues from other universities and research institutions. Professor B. T. Bayliss of Bath University, who is Director of the Institute of European Industrial Studies, has contributed the chapter on Community competition and industrial policies. Professor E. T. Nevin of the University College of Swansea, a specialist in regional policy (among other areas), has contributed the chapter on regional policy. Dr Y. S. Hu of Chatham House, who researches into EEC problems on behalf of the Federal Trust, has written the chapter on energy policy. I wish to express my gratitude to all the above.

Other Leeds colleagues have contributed to this book in an indirect way through their help in the teaching of the course 'Britain in the Common Market'. These are: Professor J. R. Crossley, a specialist in industrial relations and an EEC consultant on employment policies;

Mr G. F. Rainnie, an industrial economist who takes special interest in EEC competition and industrial policies; and Mr P. J. Mackie who is a specialist in transport economics. I am very grateful to them all for their help in running the course and for their indirect inspiration in the writing of this book.

Mr Geoffrey Denton, Reader in Economics at the University of Reading, who has been Director of the Federal Trust since 1976 and is Specialist Adviser to the House of Lords European Communities Committee, has read most of the chapters of the book and made important suggestions with regard to both its content and presentation. I owe him a special debt of gratitude.

Finally, I would like to thank all those in the office of the School of Economic Studies at the University of Leeds, and the Chairman's secretary, Mrs T.E. Brier, for their typing assistance.

University of Leeds   A.M. El-Agraa
January, 1980

To Diana

Lest it be forgotten, the European Economic Community stands for the harmonised integration of some of the oldest countries in the world with very diverse cultures and extremely complicated economic systems.

1
General Introduction

A M EL-AGRAA

The branch of international economics called international economic integration is concerned with the discriminatory removal of all trade impediments between participating nations and with the establishment of certain elements of co-operation and co-ordination between them. These elements depend entirely on the form that integration takes. Different types of integration can be envisaged:

(a) *economic integration at the single commodity level,* e.g. the European Coal and Steel Community (ECSC);
(b) *free trade areas* where member countries abolish all trade impediments between them but retain their freedom with regard to the determination of their policies *vis-à-vis* the outside world (non-participants), e.g. the European Free Trade Association (EFTA) which excludes agricultural products from its arrangements;
(c) *customs unions* which are very much like free trade areas except that member countries are obliged to conduct common external relations, for instance, they must adopt common external tariffs on imports from the outside world — the EEC is in this sense a customs union, but there is more to it as we shall see shortly;
(d) *common markets* which are customs unions that allow for free factor mobility across national member boundaries, i.e. capital, labour and enterprise should move without hindrance between the participating nations — the EEC is a common market, but again there is more to it;
(e) *complete economic unions* which are common markets that call for complete unification of monetary and fiscal policies, i.e. there is a central authority which controls these aspects so that existing nations become regions of the union;
(f) *complete political integration* where the participants become literally one nation, i.e. the central authority not only controls

1

monetary and fiscal policies, but also has a central parliament with the sovereignty of a nation's government.

The reader needs to be warned that these different types of integration should *not* be confused as *stages* in a *process* leading to a complete political union. They can be ultimate objectives in their own right as is the case in EFTA, the Central American Common Market (CACM), the East African Common Market (EACM) etc. Moreover, none of the existing arrangements falls neatly into any of these types. This is due to the fact that it is almost always necessary to have some kind of policy co-ordination in order to avoid certain problems associated with the particular type of integration. For instance, in a free trade area imports from the outside world may come through the partner country with the lowest external tariff rate; hence it is important to establish 'rules of origin' to ensure that preferential treatment is confined to commodities originating within the free trade area (see El-Agraa and Jones 1980).

The EEC

It is important for our purposes to establish the nature of the EEC in the context of the different types of international integration discussed in the previous section. Article 3 of the Treaty establishing the EEC (known as the Treaty of Rome)[1] states that for the purposes set out in Article 2:[2]

> The activities of the Community shall include, on the conditions and in accordance with the time-table provided in this Treaty:
>
> (a) the elimination, as between Member States, of customs duties and of quantitative restrictions in regard to the import and export of goods, as well as of all other measures having equivalent effect;
> (b) the establishment of a common customs tariff and of a common commercial policy towards third countries;
> (c) the abolition, as between Member States, of obstacles to freedom of movement for persons, services and capital;
> (d) the establishment of a common policy in the sphere of agriculture;
> (e) the adoption of a common policy in the sphere of transport;
> (f) the establishment of a system ensuring that competition in the common market is not distorted;
> (g) the application of procedures by which the economic policies of Member States can be co-ordinated and disequilibria in their balances of payments can be remedied;
> (h) the approximation of the laws of Member States to the extent required for proper functioning of the common market;
> (i) the creation of a European Social Fund in order to improve the possibilities of employment for workers and to contribute to the raising of their standard of living;

(j) the establishment of a European Investment Bank to facilitate the economic expansion of the Community by opening up fresh resources; and

(k) the association of overseas countries and territories with a view to increasing trade and to promoting jointly economic and social development.

(Treaty of Rome, pp. 3—4)

These elements are stated more elaborately in later Articles. For instance, Article 9 (1) states:

> The Community shall be based upon a customs union which shall cover all trade in goods and which shall involve the prohibition between Member States of customs duties on imports and exports and of all charges having equivalent effect, and the adoption of a common customs tariff in their relations with third countries.

(Treaty of Rome, p. 6)

Articles 35—37 elaborate on the CAP; Articles 48—73 on the conditions for freedom of movement for factors of production; Articles 74—84 on the Community transport policy; and Articles 99 and 100 on the harmonisation of certain taxes.

The Treaty of Rome provisions should, however, be considered in conjunction with later developments, particularly the Bremen Declaration which deals with the EEC commitment to a monetary union and the present discussion relating to a movement towards complete political integration. Hence, it can be categorically stated that *the EEC is a common market aspiring to become a complete economic and political union.*

It also needs to be mentioned that the European Community is in fact an amalgamation of three Communities: the European Coal and Steel Community; the European Atomic Energy Commission (Euratom); and the European Economic Community. (This point is explained and discussed in Chapter 2.)

The Meaning of Economic Union

The above discussion amounts to an abstract statement of the nature of the European Community as a form of economic integration. In this introductory chapter there is some need to supplement this discussion with practical or operational definitions of economic union and economic integration.

The reader may be surprised to learn that there are difficulties regarding operational definitions of these terms, but Pinder (1969), using the *Concise Oxford English Dictionary* as a reference, asserts that 'integration is the combination of parts into a whole, and union is a whole resulting from the combination of parts or members.'

Hence *'integration is the process of reaching a state of union'*. Pinder argues that it is better to make this distinction between union and integration, 'rather than to sow a seed of confusion in the discussion by defining integration as meaning both the process and the state', as Balassa (1961, pp. 1–2) does.

This distinction provides a significant choice regarding the definition of union in terms of when the combination of the parts (nations) is to be seen as a whole. According to Balassa a state of economic union is reached not only when two or more countries allow for the free movement of factors and commodities between them, but also when 'some degree of harmonisation of national economic policies' is made regarding the removal of any hidden discrimination that could exist because of them. He also distinguishes between union and complete economic integration in that the latter 'presupposes the unification of monetary, fiscal, social and counter-cyclical policies and requires the setting-up of a supra-national authority whose decisions are binding for the member states' (Balassa 1961, p. 2).

Pinder has two objections to Balassa's definitions. First, since economic union is the term generally used to describe the ultimate goal of the EEC, the act of abolishing discrimination could be seen as the limit of the EEC integration process. Secondly, the term 'complete economic integration' implies that the EEC will become a 'replica of an existing national economy' which is tightly centralised and this will preclude any discussion of what form the EEC could take.

Because of these objections, Pinder (p. 145) then defines economic integration as 'both the removal of discrimination as between the economic agents of the member countries, and the formation and application of co-ordinated and common policies on a sufficient scale to ensure that major economic and welfare objectives are fulfilled'. Hence 'economic union is a state in which discrimination has been largely removed, and co-ordination and common policies have been and are being applied on a sufficient scale'.

In order to promote meaningful discussion about the EEC, Pinder suggests that it is necessary to distinguish the abolition of discrimination by itself from the other ingredients of economic integration. For this purpose he uses his own versions of the two terms coined by Tinbergen (1954, p. 122) of 'negative integration' and 'positive integration'. For Pinder, negative integration consists only of the removal of discrimination, while positive integration consists of the establishment and adoption of co-ordinated and common policies with the object of fulfilling economic and welfare aims other than negative integration. Hence the combination of both negative and positive integration comprises economic integration, whose ultimate aim is economic union. One can therefore conceive of various forms of economic integration: those which constitute negative integration, those which constitute both negative and positive integration, those which constitute less-than-complete negative integration plus positive integration, etc. The European Community is an example of the third form since, in practice, member countries pursue their own regional policies (see Chapter 13). Pinder therefore concludes that a common market falls short of an economic union and 'without economic union will prove to be unviable' (p. 146). For technical problems related to this topic, but in a limited way, the reader is advised to consult El-Agraa (1979).

The discussion of an operational definition of economic union and economic integration was pursued further by the Federal Trust Group.[3] The outcome of the Group's deliberations was published in a short report with the title *Economic Union in the EEC* (Federal Trust 1974) and a book on a similar theme was edited by a member of the Group (Denton 1974).

The Group stressed the point that for certain members of a society the primary objective of economic union may be to facilitate or to promote the evolution of a political union (a point discussed in Chapter 2). The political union itself may be desired for intra-union or extra-union aims which may be political, strategic or both: a political union of Western Europe may be desired in order to avoid the long-sustained conflict among the participating nations or to strengthen Western Europe's bargaining position *vis-à-vis* the outside world, i.e. the USA and the USSR. However, the Group shied away from this question and devoted its attention to the problem of assessing the costs and benefits of economic union.

As the discussion regarding the UK's membership of the EEC has clearly shown (particularly at the time of the referendum), an economic union may be assessed in terms of whether or not it can result in an improvement in the economic welfare of those concerned. This welfare criterion can be expressed in terms of the usual national economic objectives of the growth in per capita output, the efficiency of reallocation and utilisation of factors of production, the stabilisation of levels of economic activity, employment and income, the equitable distribution of income, balanced regional growth and the provision of a healthy physical and social environment. The Group rightly emphasised that some of these aims may be controversial; for example, not everyone would describe the phenomenon of regional imbalance as a problem, since there may be certain societies whose development positively requires some regional imbalance (a point which is lucidly expressed by Professor Nevin in Chapter 13 on the EEC regional policy). Hence, listing aims does not serve a useful purpose; it is more meaningful to establish an order of priorities regarding such aims and to define the trade-offs which are likely to be acceptable when the aims are in conflict. Moreover, since these are points of much political debate in the individual member nations, they are very likely to be even more so in the wider context of the EEC as a whole. The Group also emphasised the point that a ranked set of economic objectives for any society needs an adequate provision of the necessary political institutions for determining them. Since these institutions are not yet adequately established at EEC level (see Chapter 2), it follows that there is a great deal of 'difficulty in arriving at a set of aims of a European economic union' (Denton 1974, p. 2).

It is therefore not surprising that the Group should conclude that the definition of economic union in the context of the EEC is an *extremely difficult* one. In the light of this conclusion the Group decided to 'let the definition emerge from the detailed accounts of problems and policies in specific areas' of enquiry. This is more or less the essence of the approach adopted in this book.

The Group then went on to discuss the relation between economic union and monetary union. In the earlier years of the development of the EEC, some took the position that economic union (in the form of co-ordination of economic policies) was a necessary pre-requisite for a successful monetary union – the so-called 'economists', of which the Dutch and the Germans were the main protagonists. There were also those who believed that monetary integration (in the form of permanently and irrevocably fixed rates of exchange) was essential for a properly functioning economic union – the so-called 'monetarists' of whom the Belgians, French and Luxembourgers were the main advocates. The Group concluded that if the position held by the 'economists' were accepted, this would amount to being content with letting the 'monetary tail wag the economic dog with vengeance. Economic union as a requirement of monetary union can only be accepted if the case for monetary union can itself be firmly based on theory and empirical evidence' (see Denton 1974, p. 3). However, this is not the place to discuss this point, since a detailed analysis is given in the chapters on European monetary integration.

It is no doubt evident that the problems of defining economic unions, political unions and monetary unions can be fascinating. Some of these problems are tackled in the specific chapters where they arise and some are not the concern of this book. The interested reader is therefore advised to consult Pinder (1969), Denton (1977), Hodges (1972) and references given there.

Areas of Economic Enquiry

The necessary areas of economic enquiry are quite apparent now that we have established the nature of the EEC. It is necessary to analyse the effect and consequences of the removal of trade impediments between the participating nations and to make an equivalent study of the establishment of the common external relations. These aspects are tackled in Chapters 4 and 5. It is also extremely important to discuss the role of competition and industrial policies and the presence of 'multinational' firms. These aspects are discussed in Chapter 6. Moreover, it is necessary to analyse the implications and consequences of a special provision for the CAP (Chapter 7), the Community transport policy (Chapter 8), the European monetary union (Chapters 9 and 10), the EEC fiscal policy (Chapters 11 and 12), the EEC regional policy (Chapter 13), the EEC energy policy (Chapter 14), the EEC social policy (Chapter 15), factor mobility (Chapter 16), and the EEC external trade relations (Chapter 17).

About This Book

This book offers, more or less, a comprehensive coverage of the theoretical issues: trade creation, trade diversion and the Cooper–Massell criticism; the domestic distortions argument; the terms of trade effects; and the scale economies argument. Moreover, the book offers a fresh look at the different attempts for an economic justification for customs union formation. A chapter is also included on the methodology and results of the measurements of the effects of the EEC formation on member nations. There is a comprehensive treatment of most of the policy considerations.

Although chapters on the EEC fisheries policy, distribution problems and political considerations may appear to be absent, these aspects have not been omitted: some elements of the fisheries policy are discussed in Chapter 18, while some of the most significant elements of the distribution problem are discussed in the chapters on the role of the Community budget, fiscal harmonisation and social policy. This is not meant to imply that these aspects are not worthy of more comprehensive consideration, as one could in fact argue that these are the most important issues in the EEC. The treatment given to them in this book is such that the significant aspects of these policies are tackled where they are particularly relevant. Moreover, with regard to some of these policies, the EEC is not yet very certain in which direction it is going to proceed in the future. The wider political considerations lie outside our scope.

Notes

1   *Treaty setting up the European Economic Community*, (Rome, 25th March, 1957), HMSO, 1967.
2   'The Community shall have as its task, by setting up a common market and progressively approximating the economic policies of Member States, to promote throughout the Community an harmonious development of economic activities, a continuous and balanced expansion, an increase in stability, an accelerated raising of the standard of living and closer relations between the Member States belonging to it.' (Article 2, p. 3).
3   The Group was established in November 1972 to study the implications of the creation of a monetary union by the members of the EEC.

References

Balassa, B., *The Theory of Economic Integration*, Allen and Unwin 1961.

Burrows, B., Denton, G.R. and Edwards, G., *Federal Solutions to European Issues*, Macmillan Press 1977.

Denton, G.R. (ed.), *Economic Integration in Europe*, Weidenfeld and Nicolson 1969.

Denton, G.R. (ed.), *Economic and Monetary Union in Europe*, Croom Helm 1974.

El-Agraa, A.M., Common markets in developing countries, in Bowers, J.K. (ed.), *Inflation, Development and Integration: Essays in Honour of A.J. Brown*, Leeds University Press 1979.

El-Agraa, A.M. and Jones, A.J., *The Theory of Customs Unions*, Philip Allan 1980, Chapter 3.

Hodges, M. (ed.), *European Integration*, Penguin 1972.

Pinder, J., Problems of European Integration, in Denton, G.R. (ed.), 1969.

Swann, D., *The Economics of the Common Market*, Penguin 1978.

Tinbergen, J., *International Economic Integration*, Elsevier 1954.

Part I

Historical, Institutional and Statistical Background

The aim of this section is to provide the reader with a general background to the EEC. Chapter 2 gives a short account of the historical development of the EEC and describes its institutions and their functioning. Chapter 3 is a general statistical survey of the major economic indicators for members of the EEC, but it also provides relevant information concerning the three potential members of the EEC and compares the state of the twelve nations with that of Canada, Japan and the USA.

2

History and Institutions
of the EEC

C D E COLLINS

The Creation of the Community

The European Community is a unique political institution. Thus political analysis dependent upon the behaviour of nation states, whether unitary or federal, or upon long-standing international organisations, is of only limited application. Furthermore, since the Community was not created as a fully mature organisation, it is still struggling towards a firmer identity and towards the creation of appropriate institutions. Not only does this mean that judgements must be tentative but, more importantly, that a discussion of its formal workings has little meaning without an understanding of the broader political context within which the Community operates. Although the emphasis in this book is on *economic* policies, which does no more than reflect the content of the Treaty of Rome, in the last analysis the objectives of the Community go beyond the economic sphere which was conceived as a means, rather than an end. In the words of the preamble of the Treaty of Rome, the European Community was to 'lay the foundations of an ever closer union among the people of Europe and by pooling resources is to preserve and strengthen peace and liberty'.[1]

The idea of creating a political unit in Europe, although we must recognise considerable uncertainty about the geographical boundaries of such a unity, is a very old one and the classic argument for it rested on the need to preserve peace in a traditionally bellicose part of the world. At both the intellectual and emotional levels there has been a constant interplay between the opposing forces of nationalism on the one hand and, on the other, the desire to create an organisation which would express the enduring sense of common history, culture, ideas and experience in Europe and which would be able to resolve antagonisms in a non-warlike manner. During the twentieth century, and particularly since 1945, there seemed greater urgency about this task.[2]

It is hardly surprising that the need to find a new way of conducting affairs should have been felt particularly acutely as the Second World War finally came to an end. The exhaustion of Europe was a fact visible to all in the form of physical devastation, a poor standard of living and immense human loss; her weakness was demonstrated by her inability to restore her economy without aid from the USA and her vulnerability soon exposed by growing mistrust about Russian policy in Europe. Under such circumstances, the pyschological barrier which had hitherto prevented effective steps towards integration in Western Europe was pierced.

There remained, however, divergent views about how to proceed and the form taken by the organisations which resulted from the early post-war years reflected several different ideas. It was in 1947 that General Marshall launched the plan of aid from the USA to revitalise the European economy, provided assistance programmes were organised on a continental and not a state basis. The following year saw the creation of the Organisation for European Economic Co-operation to control a joint recovery programme and to work for the establishment of freer trade, although limited to Western Europe only. The organisation was given substantial powers to consider and comment upon the activities of the members and has continued to be a body whose views on the handling of national economies have considerable influence and prestige. It remains an interesting example of West European integration, for although it has no supranational characteristics and in formal terms operates on unanimous voting, governments have never readily vetoed policy. The organisation has developed both means of exerting its influence and investigatory activities in fields which are highly sensitive domestically. It is also the organisation which, by doing so much to ensure European recovery, including the recreation of a West European trading area, provided the context within which a more tightly organised grouping could flourish. Its later expansion, in 1961, into the Organisation for Economic Co-operation and Development to include the USA, Canada and Japan continued, *inter alia*, to give expression to the economic interdependence of a large part of the world as a precondition for the effectiveness of the European Community.[3]

Defence considerations demanded special arrangements. The Brussels Treaty of 1948 was a pact of mutual assistance between the UK, France and the Benelux countries and in objective was neatly balanced between the perpetuation of the wartime alliance against Germany and the realisation of a newer threat from Russia. Mr Ernest Bevin, the British Foreign Secretary, speaking in the House of

Commons on 22nd January 1948, spoke of the concept of European unity and the need to preserve Europe as the heart of Western civilisation, but also of the fear of Soviet domination which made it necessary for the like-minded to draw more closely together. The realisation of the interdependence of the defence of Western Europe with wider defence concerns was marked by the signature of the North Atlantic Treaty in 1949 by the Brussels Treaty powers in association not only with the USA and Canada, but also Denmark, Norway, Portugal, Iceland and Italy. This brought a new dimension to the integrative process by recognising that Western Europe was part of a larger military grouping, but in a way which ensured that defence arrangements were handled separately from subsequent political and economic developments.

The same period saw yet another attempt to express the unity of Europe through the creation of the Council of Europe in 1949. This body has very broad political and cultural objectives, including the notable contribution to protect the individual by means of the Convention of Human Rights and Fundamental Freedoms. Its statute stresses the belief in a common political heritage based on accepted spiritual and moral values, political liberty, the rule of law and the maintenance of democratic forms of government. The Council of Europe was able to obtain wide support in Western Europe. Today it has twenty members, but it was firmly under the control of a Council of Ministers acting on the unanimity voting rule and it remains a body from which withdrawal is possible. Although it was given a Consultative Assembly, as its name implies this had no real power and it was impatience with the lack of drive towards European unification contained in these arrangements that led activists to try a new approach, which was to result in the setting up of the three European Communities.

It was not long before a means was found through offering a possible solution to certain pressing questions. A working relationship between the western alliance and West Germany had still not been established. The old Germany was in practice now divided, but the western half not yet fully accepted as an independent state, although her economic recovery had begun and with the onset of the cold war she was needed as a contributor to the prosperity and defence of the West, rather than as a burden on it. A way therefore had to be found for her re-establishment, without arousing the historic fears of her recent enemies. In short, a means of reconciliation acceptable to France was required.

The beauty of the proposal for the European Coal and Steel Community (ECSC) was its ability to appeal to so many interests in Western Europe. To the argument that it was no more than rational to treat the coal and steel industries of the area as a single whole and thus reap the benefits of a unified market operating with greater efficiency could be added the political argument that it was a means of integrating, and supervising, the essentials of war-making capacity, thus making it physically impossible for the members to go to war with each other again. It was to be the first stone in the sound and practical foundation of a united Europe creating a base of economic unity under the guidance of a strong executive. These ideas were contained in a speech delivered by M Robert Schuman, the French Foreign Minister, on 9th May 1950 which marks the formal launching of the Community idea.[4]

The sectoral approach to integration, based upon a pooling system, was familiar to many of those who had experienced the co-operative efforts of the war-time alliance. It was based upon a concept of functional integration which allowed for common action to perform common tasks and the creation of the ECSC was firmly based upon the belief that it was essential to find solutions to common problems. This approach, so different from classical diplomacy, formed the basis of what was to become known as the Community method.[5] Although operative only in a limited field, its approach concerning the means of promoting the integration of Western Europe found favour as a model in the ensuing years, more especially because the ECSC was rapidly launched and initially worked relatively smoothly. Its early success established the credentials of this method of working to unify Western Europe and it was not long, therefore, before a new project was launched.

On this occasion the immediate problem was the outbreak of the Korean War, together with increased fears that Russia might attack in Western Europe. The question of a military contribution from West Germany was thus inevitably raised and pressed by the USA, on whom the main defence of the West now rested. Since the situation bore at least superficial resemblance to that which had made possible the launching of the ECSC, a similar attempt was made to handle this new problem. A proposal was launched for a European Defence Community (EDC) and the six members of the ECSC initialled a treaty in 1952. As before, the EDC was intended 'to kill several birds with one stone'. Since it required the military rearmament of West Germany, a number of conditions were necessary in order to make this acceptable to her western neighbours. An organisation promoting Western European unity would be a further move to attach Germany and the Germans to the West, both in a political and a psychological sense. Thus institutional arrangements of control were thought to be equally as necessary as the really novel feature of a European army in which small national units would be merged into an integrated force which would in turn be subordinate to the NATO command.[6] The parallel with the method of achieving control of the coal and steel industries is striking.

The new proposal, however, did not stand alone and for good reasons. The idea of a unified army, whilst member states still went their own ways in defining foreign policy objectives which such an army might be required to support, or continued to control their own economies including their general defence efforts, was hardly practical. Neither was the notion of an army unanswerable to democratic procedures and control compatible with ascendant Western European thinking. Almost inevitably, therefore, the project had to be enlarged with the proposal for a parallel European Political Authority whose institutions would ultimately absorb those of the ECSC and EDC and which would push forward with more general economic integration.

The total project was, therefore, very much larger and more sensitive than the launching of the ECSC and in the event it failed because of the refusal of the French Assembly to ratify the treaty creating the EDC. Other people, too, had seen a number of practical difficulties in the polyglot army. Mr Winston Churchill, we are told, drew Mr Dean Acheson a picture of a 'bewildered French drill sergeant sweating over a platoon made up of a few Greeks, Italians, Germans, Turks and Dutchmen, all in utter confusion over the simplest orders'. Each time the subject came up, said Acheson 'we went back to the baffled drill sergeant'.[7]

A solution to the immediate problem of West German rearmament was found in a different way and for this, the British can claim part of the credit. The Brussels Treaty Organisation was merged into a new body, the Western European Union, in which West Germany could make her defence contribution and Italy, too, became a member. At the same time it was agreed that West Germany should enter NATO, that the occupation of West Germany should finally be ended, that British forces should remain on the Continent as a counterbalance to rearmament and that West Germany should accept certain restrictions on her military production. A Franco–German agreement foreshadowed a solution to the question of the status of the Saar. Thus although formally the integration of Western Europe had received a set-back, the main steps had been taken towards what was an essential ingredient, that of establishing a base upon which West Germany could become a full member of the Western European community of states. Although the 'German question' was not dead, the states of Western Europe were increasingly able to put the past behind them and concentrate upon solving immediate concerns.

A new attempt at integration was soon made and in June 1955,

the Foreign Ministers of the six ECSC countries met at Messina to
discuss the possibility of general economic integration and the peaceful development of atomic energy. The former was, of course, a bigger
task than a further sectoral approach and would take longer to achieve.
Whilst it was conceived, for example by M Beyen the joint Foreign
Minister of the Netherlands who took the initiative on this occasion,
as the means towards political unity, it was not thought necessary to
stress unduly this further goal which in any case belonged to a somewhat hazy future and whose discussion at that time might well have
meant retracing the old arguments for and against political union.
The conference established an inter-governmental committee under
the chairmanship of M Paul-Henri Spaak, then Foreign Minister of
Belgium and who had already resigned from the Presidency of the
Consultative Assembly of the Council of Europe in protest at its lack
of progress towards unification. The task of the committee was to
examine the projects for both a common market and an atomic
energy organisation and to prepare the ground for further action. It
is in the report of this committee that one finds most clearly stated
the ideas which lay behind the Treaty of Rome.

The vision of the Spaak Report[8] is of a Western Europe which can
win for herself a place in the world comparable with that of the
super-powers and which, once again, has the capacity to influence
world events. It was thus searching for a way to liberate the abilities
of the European people and to improve the economic foundation of
European society. The chosen method was to be the creation of a
common market to provide the necessary productive base and which
would require certain collective measures, the establishment of a
broadly common economic policy to ensure economic expansion and
higher living standards and measures to develop and utilise European
resources including her labour reserves. Thus the Treaty of Rome,
which resulted in 1957 to give expression to the ideas of the Spaak
Report, contained the detailed means of working towards this more
general picture, with a heavy concentration upon the measures
immediately necessary to create the common market. In many respects
the report was content to ensure that the new organisation would be
able to take powers by giving it a general capacity to act and, indeed,
treaty provisions which tried to lay down specific policies for an
unknown future ten or twenty years ahead would have appeared
impractical, if not absurd. The treaty also established the institutions
necessary for action, but it is noticeable that these were cautious in
political tone. Far from developing beyond the institutions of the
ECSC towards political unification, they are generally held to be less
supra-national in character, reflecting a change of mood in Western
Europe and an unwillingness to plunge yet again into the political

debate about European unification. It must be remembered, too, that an organisation charged to integrate the whole of the economy and not a sector was clearly to be faced with larger, more difficult and often unknown, tasks so that states were likely to be more diffident about joining. The price paid for the new venture was thus caution in the political sphere and the institutions of the European Economic Community (EEC) left a great deal of power in the hands of the member states. It is essential to understand these dual features of the Treaty of Rome, namely the lack of policy guidance beyond a transitional period and the conservative nature of the institutions, in order to appreciate the present condition of the Community, for it has both to formulate current objectives and consider what institutions are necessary for their achievement.

The past not only explains one aspect of the Community's present situation, but also makes it plain that it does not exist in a vacuum. The major elements in its immediate environment at the time of creation are worth noting, for they provide the Community with some of its enduring policy issues. The states which came to form the Community were part of a wider grouping, anxious to ensure economic recovery after depression and war and committed to the recreation of a liberal, trading world economy. The efforts of the six countries to go further along the road to economic integration were potentially discriminatory with regard to other trading states such as the UK, the USA, the Scandinavian states and other European nations with whom the six had close trading ties. Thus the pursuit of the economic goal of the Treaty of Rome has always to be balanced against the need to consider relations with outside states, with whose well-being the Community's welfare is inter-dependent. Closely related is the interest of the Community, as a major trading unit, in a peaceful world, including a peaceful Europe, but members have relied primarily on their own foreign policies, defence efforts and American defence protection in this regard. There have been many conflicting views in Western Europe about defence issues, but whilst often resenting the reliance upon America in this area of policy, it has also been found extremely convenient to be relieved of much defence expenditure. This is a field which is riddled with anomalies. It contributes to a close, but often abrasive, relationship with the USA which the Community, as a unit, is ill-equipped to handle since it has no competence in defence matters.

Finally, the members of the Community have been part of a broader European movement which has recognised the need to identify the political and cultural values which are important to the area and to work in common for their pursuit. This aim is expressed through the Council of Europe. In sum, the Community can be seen as a specialised unit which forms part of several wider groupings. These constrain its overall freedom of action, but at the same time their existence and success have left the different groups free to pursue their own more specific interests. This wider context not only affects the evolution of internal Community policy because of the impact of economic affairs on the outside world, but suggests one of the major institutional weaknesses of the present day Community, namely its lack of an effective responsibility for handling external relations. Until it achieves responsibility for foreign policy and defence, it will continue to lack two basic attributes of a state as we understand that concept, whilst these omissions also inhibit its effectiveness in handling policies in the economic sphere. Despite this enormous gap in competence, and thus in effectiveness, the European Community's great weight makes it highly significant in world economics and thus in world politics, although one of the curiosities of the situation is that it is often considered by the outside world to be more of a unit than it actually is. Its attraction is demonstrated by the first round of enlargement led by the UK and by the second round, currently in the negotiating stage.

Community Institutions

The European Community (EC) in reality consists of three separate entities, each one created by its own treaty: the European Coal and Steel Community (ECSC) set up by the Treaty of Paris in 1951, valid for 50 years; the European Economic Community (EEC) by the Treaty of Rome in 1957, of unlimited duration; and the European Atomic Energy Community (Euratom) by a second, unlimited Treaty of Rome signed in 1957. Subsequently, other texts have added to, or have amended, these basic documents and the more important changes are incorporated in treaties which must be ratified by each member in accordance with its own legal processes. Thus changes in the budget procedures and the agreement to admit the UK, Ireland and Denmark to the Community form the subject of special treaty instruments and the totality of these documents, together with the legislative acts to which they give rise and the case law of the Court of Justice, can be considered as the constitution of the Community. Strange as it still appears to British doctrine, the Community constitution and its legis-lation take precedence over national decisions and a moment's reflec-tion will show that this is a necessary pre-condition for the Community to work at all, for it would be impossible otherwise to create the single economic unit, to establish the necessary confidence between the members about the environment in which they operate, or to handle external economic relations. The EC can be considered as a special form of international organisation, given the importance, complexity and far-reaching nature of the matters with which it deals, the integrative elements in its objectives and the close, intensive nature of its working methods. The fact that it does not always demonstrate a capacity to work well as a unit, together with the difficulty which arises because it is not fully competent in all attributes of the modern state, suggest that it is still in a transitional stage.

With the setting up of the EC and Euratom by the same six countries that were already operating the ECSC, there was clearly a problem in the duplication of institutions. Thus, from the start, all three had a single Assembly and Court of Justice and the two later Communities were provided with the same Economic and Social Committee. In 1965, in a document usually referred to as the Merger Treaty, a single Council and a single Commission were established to replace bodies pertaining to the individual organisations and from that time on, it has seemed more logical to refer to the whole structure as the European Community. However, the functions of the institutions still derive from the original treaties and are thus not the same in all circumstances. Important differences relate to the functions of the Council which is responsible for harmonising the work of the Commission with that of governments in the coal and steel sectors, whereas in the overall economic field it must ensure co-ordination of the general economic policies of members and is also given power to take Community decisions. Even more significant are the differences in the responsibilities of the Commission which are more direct and decisive in relation to coal and steel than in relation to the economy as a whole. If the executive (then called the High Authority) was the centre of activity for the regulation of the coal and steel industries, the focal point for the EEC was rather the dual responsibility of the Council and Commission. The following discussion relates to the powers deriving from the Treaty of Rome setting up the EEC, unless otherwise stated, and the emphasis is upon the role of the institutions in the making of policy and the taking of decisions.

Although the treaties provide the basic foundation of the Community and the formal rules whereby it operates, a knowledge of the treaties is not sufficient by itself to understand present policies. This is because there are many issues which were not originally covered and because the treaties did not attempt to write a total blue-print for the future. This is particularly important in the case of the Treaty of Rome which provided reasonably detailed rules for the initial period of creating the common market, but left subsequent problems and the formulation of many positive policies to be decided later. As the Treaty fades further into the distance therefore, it is increasingly less useful as a guide to policy which has to be made through political processes involving on occasion both Community institutions and national political structures. This introduces an air of uncertainty and fluidity into the functions and relationships of Community institutions, both with each other and with national political machinery.

All formal institutions, created by the treaties, have their part to play in the functioning of the Community. It is the totality of these activities which constitutes the Community method in decision taking which thus depends upon a *modus vivendi* existing between the units to allow the processes to operate. In practice, tensions exist between them and a traditional struggle for power is exhibited internally within the Community, as well as between the Community and the member states. The most critical struggle to date is probably still that between the Council and the Commission which formed an element in the political stagnation affecting the Community during 1965 and 1966 from which the Commission emerged chastened, but the budget debates of 1978 and 1979 demonstrate the reality of a power struggle between Parliament and Council.

A Community decision normally arises as a result of a formal proposal from the Commission to the Council, which must itself take the decision whether to accept or reject the proposal in accordance with the agreed procedure. The Council cannot amend a proposal except by a unanimous vote in order to prevent the emasculation of a general proposition in the interest of certain members. If action is subsequently required, the proposal will take one of two forms. It may become a *regulation* which is directly applicable in its precise form to all members. Alternatively, it may issue as a *directive* which is binding in its objective but allows states to achieve this in their own way. It is also possible to take a *decision* which is binding on those, such as firms, to whom it is addressed, whilst *recommendations* and *opinions*, which can also be made, have no binding force.[9] These formal acts, more particularly the regulations and directives, are constantly adding to Community law.

Behind this legal structure lies a very complex process which involves a great many people and much political machinery. However, there is little doubt that, in relation to the formulation of policy and its translation into the necessary decisions, the two key units are the Council and the Commission. It is convenient, therefore, to begin with them.

The Council consists of representatives of member governments and meetings are therefore attended by governmental ministers. Its decisions are taken by unanimous, simple, or qualified, majority voting and when the last method is used, the system is weighted both in favour of the larger members and of the necessity to carry at least one of the smaller ones along with the decision. In this way it was originally hoped to arrive at a method which would ensure that decisions were supported by a wide spectrum of opinion, neither allowing the bigger to ignore the smaller, nor the smaller members to hold the whole Community up. Originally it was intended that, as the Community became established and confidence in it grew, so the Council should increasingly move towards the use of the majority voting techniques, but states have proved extremely reluctant to allow this to happen. In 1965, an agreement was reached recognising that unanimity would continue to be used whenever a member considered the matter under discussion to be of vital national importance and subsequently the Council has used unanimous voting as its general rule with the normal understanding that a member may abstain from voting on a matter which is not of vital interest to it, but which it would rather not support, without preventing the other eight from agreeing the policy. Swifter methods of decision, particularly when no national interest is seriously at stake, are urgently necessary and will become even more essential if the Council is enlarged to accommodate twelve members rather than nine. The issue of the use of majority voting as a normal method must remain a live one and was discussed in the recent report on European Union by M Tindemans.[10]

Representatives of the Commission also attend Council meetings and play an active part in helping to reach a decision, although the Commission has no voting rights. It is here, however, that it can perform an important mediatory function between national viewpoints, allowing a position which is acceptable to members, and to the Commission as the representatives of the Community interest, to emerge.

The Presidency of the Council is held by each member state in turn for a six-monthly period and the chairmanship of many Community committees alters correspondingly. It has become the practice for each member to try to establish a particular style of working and to single out certain matters, for example speeding-up business, to which it wishes to give priority. Given that the chairman of any meeting can often influence business significantly, it can be seen that the President may occupy an important, albeit temporary, role. The President of the Council will also fulfil certain representational functions both towards other Community institutions, notably the European Parliament, and in external negotiations where he may act in association with the President of the Commission.

Although there is still some belief that the Council of Foreign Ministers is the most senior, membership depends upon the subject matter before the Council and as Community affairs have developed, so an increasingly wide range of national ministers has attended to Council business. It is not difficult to see that this growth has brought its own problems for national governments, for if Community issues are handled by various ministers briefed by their own departments, it becomes less likely that any government can see its European policy as a coherent whole. Also, the greater is the possibility that any minister can draw support from Community policy to push his own policy within his government, perhaps distancing himself from his national colleagues in so doing and the greater the problems of co-ordination for the central administrative departments which are involved in problems now surfacing in Brussels. For the Community, too, the greater specialisation of the Council creates difficulties. The ensuing compartmentalisation of business means it is more difficult to negotiate Community policy. One issue can no longer be so readily considered in relation to others, so that the once famous 'package deals' which enabled the Community to arrive at new positions are harder to achieve. The Council of Agricultural Ministers, in particular, appears to have developed a life and status of its own.[11]

The Council is served by its own secretariat which is separate from the Commission and is supported by a most important body, the *Committee of Permanent Representatives* (Coreper). It was in 1965 that the members gave formal recognition to this group, but the need for an organisation of senior officials to prepare meetings and to handle business between Council meetings had long been felt. Members of this committee are officials of ambassadorial rank, strengthened nowadays by a web of specialist and subordinate committees, often including members of home departments who travel to Brussels when they are required.

This committee is responsible for preparing the work of the Council which may also assign tasks to it and in 1966 it was agreed that it was desirable for the Commission, working through the committee, to make contact with national governments before deciding on the form of any intended proposal. It will be appreciated that a particular difficulty arises for the Community in that there is no hierarchy of relationships between the Commission and national bureaucracies both of whom will have their own responsibilities in substantive matters. As a result of its links with Commission and Council, Coreper is involved in all major stages of Community policy-making, ranging from early discussions to final Council decision taking and it forms an essential link between the Community and national governments. Many matters of policy are in fact today agreed by Coreper and only reach the Council in a formal sense.

Whilst this is one way of attempting to keep Community business, which is growing rapidly, under control, by implication it means that the Council itself is concerned only with important matters or those which, of no great substance in themselves, are yet highly political in nature. When it is remembered that domestic interests are increasingly affected by Community decisions and that such groups will wish to exert what pressure they can on their relevant home minister to act as they wish in Council, it can be seen that Council meetings have a tendency to become increasingly politicised and to be used as a way of promoting a sectional, not necessarily a total national, interest. This process has been increased by the greater skill now shown in the use of publicity to support a negotiating position. Meetings of the Council are often portrayed by the national press, radio and television networks in terms of victory and defeat for national interests. Although Council meetings are technically secret, ministers themselves will frequently provide press information, often whilst meetings are still in progress, in order to acquire political advantage. This situation is the opposite of what was originally intended when it was thought that the experience of working together would make it progressively easier to reach agreement expressive of the general good for which majority voting would be a suitable method of work.

Practical problems are also encountered by the Council. The great press of business, the fact that ministers can attend only part-time to Council affairs and the highly sensitive nature of their activities all contribute to a grave time-lag in reaching a policy decision. The Council has become a major bottleneck preventing the Community working efficiently and with any enlargement these problems become greater.[12] Suggested reforms, such as the more general use of majority voting, the creation of an inner group to handle bigger decisions, holding Cabinet meetings in all national capitals on the same day of the week in order to release ministers for EC business are resisted by states and it is clear that changes necessary for functional effectiveness in fact challenge national autonomy. Looked at from the point of view of European integration, the remaining Community institutions need to wrest power from the Council in order to restore a more balanced position. During the next few years the European Parliament is likely to be the forerunner in any possible attack.

The second essential element in the making of Community policy is the *Commission*. This now consists of thirteen members, all nationals of the nine member states and chosen on grounds of competence and capacity to act independently in the interest of the Community itself. They are thus charged not to take instructions from governments and accept the responsibility and limitations on action involved in this position. At present, France, Italy, the UK and West Germany have two members each and Belgium, Denmark, Ireland, Luxembourg, and the Netherlands have one apiece. Commissioners are chosen by common agreement of governments for a period of four years with renewable appointments. Both the President and five Vice-Presidents are chosen from the thirteen by governments for a two year renewable period. In practice, an individual can expect two terms of Presidential office, although not all Presidents have remained for so long. Many of them, however, have been men significant in national politics, thus able to meet ministers of the Council on equal terms and familiar with the type of political pressures with which the Community must grapple. This experience should enable the Commission to retain both the political stature and sense of touch which are essential attributes for its effective functioning.

Each Commissioner has responsibility for one or more major Community policies and although in form the Commission is still a collegiate body accepting responsibility for action as a group, in practice policy rests largely with the appropriate Commissioner, often in association with two or three colleagues. Adoption by the Commission is thus often formal but, unlike the Council, it has always used majority voting procedures. No other arrangements would permit the Commission to deal with the large volume of work now involved.

The Commissioners are supported in two ways. The Continental practice of a private office has been followed and each Commissioner has his own *chef de cabinet*, normally of the same nationality as himself, who is not a career bureaucrat. These assistants take many decisions on behalf of their chiefs. Secondly, there is the Commission staff itself. This is organised into General Directorates corresponding to the main areas of Community policy. In total there are only about ten thousand civil servants, including a large number of translators and interpreters. Thus, if the charges of 'bureaucracy' and slowness made about the Commission have substance, they do not arise because of the large number of people employed and another explanation must be sought. A more likely source of difficulty lies in the complexity involved in the integration of the detail of national economies and the problems of using six official languages.

The *General Directorates* are composed of a staff of various nationalities and it is normal to find that care has been taken to prevent any national viewpoint becoming predominant by ensuring that the holders of the higher posts are drawn from several member states and, in particular, that the Directors themselves are of a different nationality from the Commissioner in charge.[13] Over time, certain directorates have won a higher prestige than others, whilst the development of Community policies brings the possibility of conflict and rivalry between one directorate and another. Thus, for example, the development of a stronger regional policy might well conflict with certain tenets of competition in the common market,[14] or the desire to use the social fund to contribute to regional policy cut across other social objectives such as improving the employment position of women workers. In the resolution of policy conflicts the relative strength and competence of the directorates is likely to be one factor if not, as yet, the major one.

The General Directorates are not only responsible for the initiation of proposals which will become the basis of a Commission proposal and, ultimately, if accepted, a Community decision, but are also involved in the administration of previously agreed policies. The extent of their involvement varies and it must be remembered that a great deal of Community policy is not executed by the Commission at all, but by national administrations. One area in which the Commission is closely involved is agriculture because of the daily management of markets which the Common Agricultural Policy (CAP) involves, where a structure of management committees brings both the Commission and the national administrations into a system of joint administration. Even so, the day to day execution of the CAP, as well as the application and collection of the important levies on goods from outside, is handled by national ministers for agriculture and for customs collection on behalf of the Community. A second area of work in which the Commission is administratively concerned is competition policy, which requires the Commission to register and investigate certain agreements between firms to ensure that they conform to Community rules. Here it is in direct contact with individual firms and this is also the case in the execution of certain functions relating to the coal and steel industries.

Of rather different character is the work of the Commission in administering the various funds that the Community now possesses. Although the rules governing the operation of such funds reflect general Community policy, there may well be a degree of discretion in the allocation of monies to particular national schemes and it is usual for the Commission to be assisted by an advisory committee in the administration of monies from the social, regional and agricultural guidance funds. Since the monies themselves are disbursed to projects by national administrations, there is again close contact between home civil services and the Commission.

An important function of the Commission is to ensure that the members abide by their obligations or, as it is normally described, to act as the guardian of the treaties. It is essential that the rules of the various treaties are actively applied in each member, otherwise the operation of the common market is defeated. If members were to become cynical and lose confidence in the arrangements and in each other, the whole system would soon spiral downwards. In many cases, keeping states and firms up to the mark results simply from day to day business and through the normal liaison between them and the Commission, but in more important cases, or if there should be a deliberate evasion of the rules, other steps become necessary. The Commission can investigate circumstances where a breach of obligation is suspected and issue a *reasoned opinion*. If matters are not set right within a stated period, the Commission is entitled to refer the matter to the Court of Justice. Although the Community has few direct sanctions with which to enforce its rules, the main one being the possibility of fining firms which breach certain operational rules, states have so far accepted their obligations to abide by Community decisions. An interesting recent example of this was the British government's willingness to conform to the ruling of the Court of Justice in 1979 that it must apply EEC Regulation 1463/70 concerning the installation of a tachograph in certain road vehicles, despite the domestic difficulties involved in so doing.[15]

Most interest, however, attaches to the function of the Commission both as an initiator of policy and the exponent of the Community interest.[16] This arises in a formal sense from the fact that the Council waits upon the Commission to send it proposals upon which it must decide. Thus the Community is dependent upon the activity of the Commission and upon the quality of its work in order to function. Nowadays, since the Treaty of Rome is no longer adequate as a guide to future policy, this procedure places great power in the hands of the Commission to shape developments, even though the regular meetings of the European Council (see below) are now providing broad guidelines within which the Commission acts. In order to formulate a policy proposal, the appropriate directorate will find it necessary to undertake extensive discussions with both governmental departments and representatives of interested firms and groups and this knowledge will subsequently contribute to a Commission proposal. Once a matter has reached this stage it can then be discussed with Coreper and by Parliament and the Economic and Social Committee before finally reaching the Council itself. At each stage, extensive and lengthy discussions may be undertaken in which the Commission will almost certainly be active in order to obtain an agreed position acceptable to the member states and at the same time to enhance the process of European integration along the lines indicated by the Treaty of Rome.

The responsibilities of the Commission can be classified in several ways. Some are executive in nature, but its functions extend to the initiation of policy, the protection of the Community interest, the mediation between national interests and the protection of the treaty structure and subsequent rules. Thus the Commission is a very original body, not paralleled by any national equivalent and this remains true despite the growing importance to decision making of the Council which might have suggested that the Commission would become a neutral body for the implementation of Council decisions. This is prevented by the structure of the treaties alone and it must be remembered that the collective responsibility of the Commission is not to the Council but to Parliament which alone possesses the power to dismiss it. It is Parliament, too, which debates the annual report which the Commission is obliged to issue and which receives a verbal statement of the Commission's intentions for the year ahead. Thus the treaty prevents the Commission from becoming a creature of the Council. Both Council and Commission have a position safe-guarded by the treaty, although the balance between them has tipped in favour of the Council. Since the crisis of the mid-1960s, the Commission has been more subdued and cautious in its functioning and less aggressive in its approach to integration. It may prove to be the case that the integrative function has come to be shared with other institutions, notably through the attempts to build up political co-operation in foreign policy matters (see below). This development has to some extent by-passed the Commission.

The Court of Justice is an integral part of the institutional structure. The Community is a highly complex body, created by treaties which not only cover the responsibilities of its varied institutions and the basic rules of economic integration but which constantly give rise to new legal obligations in the form of regulations and directives. A Court is necessary for several reasons. It must ensure that the institutions act in a constitutional manner fulfilling the obligations laid on them by the treaties, but it must also ensure the observance of an ever growing volume of Community rules by states, firms and individuals. This is not just a question of pronouncing upon any possible infringe-ments of the Community legal system which may be referred to it, although these may include such wide-ranging matters as a refusal to implement a Community rule or slow application due to lax national administration, but also includes the need to guide national courts in their interpretation of Community law. It is obvious that the uniform application of Community law, although an integral part of the Community structure, is likely to be a slow business and to be difficult of achievement since it must be incorporated into nine different legal systems with their own norms and methods of work. The difficulty is compounded since in many areas Community rules continue to operate alongside national ones since the treaty does not fully cover all economic matters and the integration of two sets of law where they overlap is hardly straightforward. It is not surprising that three of the main fields which cause most work for the Court are agriculture, competition policy and social security for migrants where states have pre-existing policies of their own, where both national and Community rules are complex and where overlapping interests occur.

The Court consists of nine judges and four advocates-general, the latter being responsible for preliminary investigation of a matter and

for submitting a reasoned opinion to the judges to help them come
to a decision. In its method of working the Court is heavily influenced
by the legal systems of the members, particularly of the original six
states who created the Community in the first instance. It will hear
cases brought by the Commission against member states or against
the Council, cases brought by member states against each other or
against the Council or Commission or by a natural or legal person
against a Community decision which affects him. The Court enforces
penalties for the infringement of regulations. It is also responsible
for the interpretation of the treaty and subsequent texts if necessary
at the request of a national court or tribunal which is trying to apply
the treaty. States agreed in the Treaty of Rome to comply with the
judgement of the Court and the fact that, in practice, they do so
has been an important factor in strengthening the validity of the
Community system.

A much younger institution is the *Court of Auditors* which began
work in 1977 in response to growing demands, especially from
Parliament, for a closer audit and clarification of the Community
budget. This is now a complicated affair, made up in a tortuous way
and, since it grows by accretion, is likely to become more, rather
than less, difficult to understand. It is intended that the Court of
Auditors should monitor expenditure much more thoroughly than in
the past, by checking on the use made of Community monies by
members and on their procedures for the collection of duties and
levies.

It is time now to turn to the place of the *European Parliament* in the
institutional structure. This depends not just upon treaty provisions,
but upon the capacity that Parliament finds within itself to exploit
its position. In recent years it has become more skilful in this activity.
Its major formal control mechanism is the ability to dismiss the
Commission. This is usually considered to be a power of little value
for it cannot be exercised without bringing the Community to a halt
and Parliament has no responsibility for the appointment of a new
Commission. However, there seems no reason why it should not
continue to dismiss the Commission until it obtains satisfaction. A
vote of censure which stops before the brink can also be a way of
expressing a strongly held view on Community policy, carrying the
possibility of forcing a change of heart by the Commission or,
indirectly, by the Council and Parliament which has experimented
with this procedure. A censure vote may, therefore, be developed as
a means of preserving the general European interest, despite its use
against the Commission, from elimination by the Council where
national interests predominate. The importance of this power depends
less on the legal form than on the political weight represented by

Parliament, for if this is considerable, both the Commission, and the member governments which appoint it, are unlikely to consider it wise to flout Parliament's views.

Parliament has also become more effective in the use of its power to ask questions, both verbally and in writing, as a means of keeping both Commission and Council up to the mark whilst it receives and comments on reports from these two bodies. The process of political co-operation has been added to the subject matter which Parliament can scrutinise. Since 1974 the Foreign Ministers have been meeting four times a year with the Political Committee of the European Parliament for discussions on foreign policy issues, whilst in 1976 their work became subject to the question time procedure.

The powers of the European Parliament are not as negligible as is often supposed. The treaties lay down occasions on which Parliament must be consulted before a final decision is taken by the Council and in practice it is normally consulted on all significant issues. This is done by the formulation of opinions on Commission proposals which are studied and reported upon by the appropriate Parliamentary committee. The main Parliamentary committee session will thus debate the report from the committee on a particular proposition. The committees meet between Parliamentary sessions and are normally in close contact with the Commission whilst considering their reports and committee members may develop considerable expertise in particular problems.

The inherent weakness of the present arrangement for Parliament is that its views may be legally disregarded. It is possible that the Council would be foolish to ignore the opinion of Parliament on an important matter, for it may indicate the practicability and acceptability of a line of action in the eyes of informed opinion in the member states. In this sense, and since the Council receives the views whilst policy is still indecisive, Parliament often has an influence disproportionate to its formal powers. To increase these might not do much immediately to enhance the significance of Parliament. The real problem in achieving more power for Parliament is not that of gradually increasing its powers, but of wresting agreement from the Council that it should begin to share decision making responsibility. Suggestions have been made whereby joint responsibility could be exercised in certain matters and progressively extended to all.[17]

An important development of Parliament's powers came with the receipt of greater budgetary control. This followed the Council agreement of 1970 that the Community should become autonomous in financial matters over a phased period through allowing the proceeds of the agricultural levies and customs duties to accrue to the Community as a unit. Since it was recognised that these monies would not provide enough finance for the Community's activities, it was agreed that temporarily members would make up the necessary total by direct contributions broadly related to their relative GNPs, but that this in turn would give way to a situation in which the Community acquired a proportion of VAT levied in all member countries (see Chapter 12). There have been, and remain, grave problems in the setting up and administration of this system. Nevertheless, once the principle that the Community should become responsible for its own monies had been accepted, it was generally agreed that the normal democratic principle of Parliamentary control over public monies must be established and a treaty to give effect to these strengthened powers was signed in 1970 with amendments in 1971 and 1975. The actual stages for the establishment and adoption of the Community's budget have become extremely complex and are unlikely to have reached their final form, not least because Parliament will be anxious to make an extension of financial power a major part of its struggle to obtain a more important position in the Community structure. The logic of this is that it is the means to obtain control over policies and their relative priority.

A draft budget is made up by the Commission, normally by September, for expenditure for the following year which is then adopted by the Council acting on a qualified majority vote. This draft budget is then sent to Parliament for discussion. The key to understanding Parliament's budgetary control lies in the distinction between compulsory and non-compulsory expenditure, the former deriving from the treaty and largely consisting of the costs of the CAP. Compulsory expenditure forms about 70% of the total budget and may be modified in the first instance by a majority of Parliamentary votes cast, but these changes must subsequently be agreed, or rejected, by the Council. Non-compulsory expenditure can be modified by a Parliamentary majority of all members, but there is a given limit beyond which Parliament cannot make increases in non-compulsory expenditure. Although the Council may subsequently amend the decision, Parliament must receive the total draft budget back for a second reading and at this point it may reject the Council's changes in the non-compulsory category. Finally, Parliament is entitled to reject the draft budget entirely and demand a new one, or alternatively, it must formally approve the final form.

Once both Council and Parliament had been given budgetary powers, it was necessary to strengthen procedures for consultation between them by the 'concertation procedure'. This allows for disagreements between them to be resolved by a compromise in which mutual concessions are made and for early discussion of proposals likely to give rise to future expenditure.[18]

A major uncertainty still relates to the definition of compulsory and non-compulsory expenditure. It is in the interest of Parliament to ensure an ever-widening definition of the latter and it appears to have been successful in its aim of ensuring that Regional Fund expenditure is so classified. If it can continue to enlarge this category then, together with the possibility of an early discussion of new claims on expenditure, Parliament is well set to encroach upon effective control of new policies. The main stumbling block is the CAP which is firmly established as compulsory expenditure and as long as it absorbs a major share of total financial expenditure, it will prevent not only the development of other policies but also the growth of Parliamentary powers in the policy-making field.

The European Parliament is remarkable for having achieved the first international election. Voting took place in June 1979 and the first sitting of the new Parliament was held in July. At the time of writing, the new Parliament consists of 112 Socialists (including 18 from the British Labour Party), 108 Christian Democrats, 64 European Democrats (including 61 British Conservatives), 40 Liberals, 44 Communists and allies (19 from France and 24 from Italy), 22 European Progressive Democrats and 22 non-attached members, making 410 in all.[19] France, Italy, the United Kingdom and West Germany have 81 seats each, the Netherlands 25, Belgium 24, Denmark 16, Ireland 15 and Luxembourg 6. Whilst no immediate increase in formal powers is planned, it is likely that Parliament now possesses greater moral authority than hitherto and will seek to exploit this strength. Its capacity to do so will be enhanced if party groupings become more effective, for this will allow distinctive and more coherent views on desirable Community policy to develop. Both possibilities suggest that Parliament will seek to become more closely involved in policy matters than hitherto.

In addition, Parliament has several practical problems of great difficulty before it. There are a number of unresolved issues relating to future elections, since the ultimate goal is that of a single voting system throughout the Community whilst the dual mandate, which allows a member to retain a seat in a national Parliament, is believed by most people who have experienced it to impose intolerable strains. A major question relates to the site of Parliament. At present it has a peripatetic life with sittings held in both Luxembourg and Strasbourg whilst most committee work is carried out in Brussels. Yet so far it has been impossible to agree on the way to achieve a more viable plan. None of these matters is entirely within the competence of Parliament to solve, but the first elected Parliament is likely to spend a great deal of time on such issues which concern it closely.

Parliament is still in an evolutionary stage and a belief that it will develop into an institution akin to a national Parliament is not necessarily correct. Apart from the fact that it now has nine national models to follow, it operates in a different environment from them. The fears that it will become locked in a struggle with national Parliaments, attempting to wrest power from them, may well prove exaggerated, for the European Parliament has to concentrate primarily on its relations with Council and Commission and to formulate its views on matters which are now European rather than simply national in character.

Apart from its specific functions, Parliament plays an important role of a general consultative and informative nature, for it is a major forum within which general views can be expressed. Opinions are thus readily available to the Council and Commission and at the same time Parliament is important as a channel through which information and knowledge about the Community are transmitted back to the national environments. These functions are, however, by no means exclusive to Parliament and a vast battery of machinery exists which acts as another link in the communications chain and which plays its part in the shaping of Community decisions. One of the more formal mechanisms is the *Economic and Social Committee* which was created by the Treaty of Rome with advisory status and designed to represent the various categories of economic and social activity such as employers, unions, farmers and the self-employed, as well as the general public. It has 144 members, appointed by the Council on the basis of national lists, each member being appointed for four years and acting in a personal capacity. For practical purposes the members are considered as coming from three main groups, namely employers, union members and those representing the general interest, each national delegation reflecting this tripartite composition. It is usual to seek the opinion of the committee on all major acts of policy and today the committee is also entitled to formulate views on subjects which it itself thinks are important. The committee has found it extremely difficult to establish an effective voice in Community affairs and for this there are several reasons. Not only did the treaty give it a purely consultative role, but its heterogeneous composition suggests that it is unlikely to be able to produce a single point of view except of a very general nature. Thus the choice before the committee is either to produce an agreed, but bland, report, or to recognise the diverse interests of its members by producing a set of reports on each significant issue. Either way, the committee findings are likely to be of limited effectiveness and the search for agreement which it often undertakes means that the reports frequently appear too late to be useful. Thus the utility of the committee lies elsewhere. It is helpful to the Council and, more especially, the Commission that the views of these groups throughout the Community should be readily available before policy has hardened and the discussions in the committee provide this information, whilst meetings are one means whereby like-minded people from various countries can meet and discuss and the membership gain knowledge of Community affairs.

The committee, which is paralleled by a *Consultative Committee* confined to the coal and steel industry, by no means exhausts the Community committee structure. It is usual for the Commission to be supported by an advisory committee in the fund-giving operations and by a complex of working parties and committees for particular industries and problems. During the 1970s a *Standing Committee on Employment* was reactivated and strengthened. This is representative of national employment ministers, employers and unions as well as the Commission and is a reflection of the current concern with the state of the economy, the effect of inflation and structural change on employment levels and the particular difficulties experienced by certain groups of workers. To some extent this group overlaps with the Economic and Social Committee and there may be room for rationalisation, leaving the former to the industrial interests and the latter to develop a stronger citizen voice.

In some ways, for both interest groups and for the man in the street who wishes to make the effort, the Community, and particularly the Commission, are far more accessible than a national administration. This is in part due to the cumbersome consultative procedures, but it is also the result of a well-established Commission policy to inform and educate the public in order to mobilise opinion behind the integrative process. The Community seems to have been more successful in creating this awareness amongst opinion formers and those whose work brings them into direct contact with the EC than it has been with the general public. Thus the Community has gained an elitist air, its purpose and intentions being better understood by bankers, industrialists, union and organisational representatives than by the elusive 'man in the street'. Direct elections may start to capture his interest and attention, but it must be admitted that debates in the European Parliament have so far failed to do so.

Standing apart from these institutions is the *European Investment Bank* which was given the task of contributing to the balanced and steady development of the common market in the interest of the Community. It has three main fields of operation: to aid regional development; to help with projects made necessary by the establishment of the common market for which normal financial means are lacking; and to assist projects of common interest to members where other financial means are lacking. The Bank is thus an additional source of finance in many different circumstances, designed to assist in the development of the EC. It is in no sense, however, a grant-aiding fund but a bank operating normal banking criteria whose capital is contributed by members and by its own ability to raise money on normal markets.

It can therefore be seen that the formal structure of the institutions presents a deceptively simple picture of the working of the Community, perhaps particularly in relation to the process of decision making. There is a constant hum of discussion and negotiation in progress with both formal and informal institutions as well as with interested individuals and this is often duplicated nine times. The problem is not so much one of lack of consultation as of the lack of decisiveness which results from the accommodation of many interests and alignment of national policies in which agreement on something may have to take precedence over the soundness of policy. To this we may add the lack of consideration to points of view which cannot speak loudly enough to be heard above the hubbub and the slowness of action to which these procedures contribute. It is not surprising that the reform of the institutions has become an issue considered as one of the most urgent by several observers and a number of ideas have been put forward ranging from the use of majority voting in the Council to the setting up of a Directorate, or inner circle of states, to take decisions on behalf of the Community as a whole. In December 1978 the European Council appointed three wise men, M Biesheuvel, M Marjolin and Mr Dell, to investigate the working of the institutions and to recommend improved procedures and it is clear that, as the Community further enlarges, existing institutions will steadily become more difficult to operate.

Institutional Changes

Two major institutional innovations occurred during the 1970s reflecting the political evolution of the Community. A new stage had arrived in which major internal objectives had to be formulated and a way found of responding more effectively as a single unit on the world stage. Although these issues were seen separately, and to some extent gave rise to different institutional responses, they are in practice closely linked. The first step was the introduction of summit meetings by the heads of government which were formalised in 1974 under the name of the European Council. These now occur four times a year and are becoming more formally organised than hitherto. Occasional summit meetings had been held in the past, but with the ending of the transitional period, the need for re-commitment to the Community and for the setting of new goals was felt. The first major summit of this period was that held in The Hague in December

1969, at which the six members effectively recognised that they were so closely interdependent that they had no choice other than to continue with the Community and were thus compelled to settle matters such as the agricultural policy and budgetary changes. A vital point was the recognition that the Community possessed the political will to work for enlargement and thus to stabilise the vexing question of relations with the United Kingdom.

The Hague summit also recognised that the international stature of the Community required further consideration, since its formal responsibilities neither matched its economic weight, nor allowed effective consideration of the political aspects of its external economic relations. Individual members were at the same time continuing to handle external affairs themselves, often less effectively than had they been working together and not necessarily in ways which were readily compatible with Community policies. Such issues raised larger ones of great sensitivity including the question of the relations of the Community and individual members to the USA, to the defence of Western Europe and to the Soviet Union. In fact, from a somewhat different route and with a different emphasis, the question of the future political objectives of the Community had again been reached. It is not, however, simply the anomalies that arise because of the Community's limited ability to act as a unit externally, but the underlying problem that any attempt to rectify this situation implies the passing of responsibilities to the EC in the fields of foreign policy and defence which members are still reluctant to accept. A tentative step was taken at The Hague through a request to the Foreign Ministers to study the best way of achieving further political integration on the assumption of enlargement and to present a report. The subsequent moves to achieve political co-operation, a concept which still has an emphasis upon foreign affairs, have been important in helping the EC to identify its common aims and thus to articulate the nature of the group.

Political co-operation constitutes the second major innovation in the institutions of the Community. In 1972 an important summit meeting was held in Paris which involved the three new members in broad policy discussion for the first time and which devoted considerable attention to the strengthening of the social and regional aims of the Community. The deterioration in the international climate and the preoccupation of member governments with economic matters at home seemed to require frequent meetings of heads of government anxious to find ways of maintaining the Community and to make a start on economic and monetary integration whilst dealing with economic difficulties. The emergence of differences of policy and priority between governments in their reactions to these difficulties have made summit meetings essential as a means of establishing the extent of common ground which, in turn, can form the basis for more precise action. Since the Community of the nine is not the same political animal as that of the original six and it operates in very different circumstances shaped by recession and the severe rise in oil prices, matters of which the Treaty of Rome was blissfully unaware, new political authority is required and at the present time this is resulting from the European Council. At first sight this seems to have strengthened the inter-governmental structure of the Community at the expense of the supra-national element, but this may prove too simple a judgement since it is also concrete recognition by the members that their fortunes, both economic and political, are now inextricably intertwined and require the formulation of joint goals and policies over a wide field indeed. The possibility of informal discussion of general issues, whether economic or political, domestic or world-wide, is a necessary preliminary to further, formal integration. Summit meetings are enlarging the scope of the subject matter in which the EC is seen to have a legitimate interest as well as limiting its formal supra-national character. This development suggests that, in the next stage of the Community, broad political initiative may rest with national political leaders rather than with the Commission, whose dynamic role as the initiator forcing the pace of European integration has been, at least temporarily, superseded. Integration may result less from the use of the Commission as a battering ram meeting national sovereignty head on and more from these new forms of particularly close national co-operation, but it is early to predict the consequences for the nature of the Community.

Meanwhile, the discussions of the Foreign Ministers led to six-monthly meetings between them, more frequent, regular meetings of senior foreign office officials and the appointment of liaison officers in the foreign ministries themselves. External problems, including disagreements with the USA, reactions to the oil crisis and, subsequently, the possibility of talks between the West and the Eastern bloc all demanded consideration in a Community, as well as in a national, context and for this the political co-operation machinery proved useful. By the time of the Paris summit meeting in 1972, member states had laid down for themselves an ambitious programme of activity designed to lead to a 'European Union', although much remained to be defined, and the conference pinpointed a number of external issues to be pursued. These included the need to maintain a constructive dialogue with the USA, Canada and Japan, to act jointly in matters of overseas trade policy and for members to make a concerted and constructive contribution to the Conference on Security and Co-operation in Europe. Foreign Ministers were to meet more frequently in order to handle this last issue.

Many of the plans for internal development were sent awry by the oil crisis of 1973 and the world economic recession, whilst considerable tension with the USA built up over policy in the Middle East. These events demonstrated the weakness of the EC which was unable to act as a single unit in the face of adverse external pressures and the Committee of Foreign Ministers reacted with an attempt to identify the constituent elements of the European Identity as understood in 1973. This reformulation of the common elements between member states is a wide-ranging document whilst its stress on the importance of the EC developing a 'single voice' for external matters, through which it might assert the influence its world strength provides, appeared particularly necessary. Foreign policy co-ordination, not unification, is the current stage[20] and since the political co-operation machinery still exists apart from the established institutions, it cannot yet be said to be fully part of the EC structure. It helps to complicate still further the working, and effectiveness, of these institutions. Yet to merge the political co-operation machinery into the existing Commission, which is now heavily concerned with technicalities and the execution of policies from the Treaty of Rome, might in practice lead to the former losing its freshness and drive. At the same time, the distinction between political co-operation and Community affairs has become less obvious and the machinery more closely linked partly because of the overlap of subject matter with which they both deal. This became clear at the time of the Conference on Security and Co-operation in Europe and continues to show itself over the Middle East and the problem of oil supplies. Thus the summit conference of Paris 1974 formally agreed that the distinction between EC affairs and political co-operation was untenable. It is only possible on occasion to separate foreign policy from the external responsibilities deriving from the treaty and ultimately the machinery will have to respond to this fact.

Despite these developments, the uncertainty about Community objectives and methods of working remained. In 1974 M Tindemans was asked by the summit meeting to tour the capitals and write a report on the concept of the European Union and this brought out into the open a long-standing question of whether the members of the Community, particularly on the economic front, did in fact constitute an effective whole and if not, whether the concept of a two tier Community would be preferable. In this, those states who felt they could progress further and faster towards economic and monetary union should form an inner circle leaving the others linked in some looser grouping. 'It is impossible at the present time to submit a credible programme of action if it is deemed necessary that in every case all stages should be reached by all the States at the same time. The divergence of their economic and financial situations is such that, were we to insist on this, progress would be impossible and Europe would continue to crumble away.'[21] This development, it was suggested, might be paralleled on the political side by steps towards a citizens' Europe to include action in matters such as consumer rights, environmental protection and the safeguarding of fundamental rights, a strengthening of a common stand in foreign policy which could then be applied by members and a tentative start on defence issues. Institutional reform would be required in order to increase the efficiency of the Council, improve the position of other institutions and to achieve a better balance between them.

An assessment of the goals and institutions of the EC as they stand today is bound to be tentative, but it seems clear that the efficiency of the latter can hardly be judged without some view of the former. There have been great institutional changes since 1957 and these reflect the changing environment within which the EC has had to operate as well as changing views about its tasks. The need to adjust to a period of economic difficulty, rather than growth, brought into the open the question of whether prosperity is in fact a pre-condition for the type of integration the EC was set up to achieve. The introduction of new members, of very different political and legal traditions and whose economies had unique features, also clouded the certainty of the past. In the immediate future, two further mouthfuls have to be digested. The first is a process of absorption of members from Southern Europe and the second the adjustment to the impact of a directly elected Parliament. Both changes must affect the institutions and may strengthen the argument that the original structure has taken the integrative process about as far as it can. If adaptation of existing mechanisms proves insufficient to overcome the practical problems associated with enlargement, internal pressure may itself generate sufficient force to release the political energy necessary for a further decisive step. Despite these problems, it is clear that the EC has established itself as a new type of international entity which is found valuable by the members and which is strong enough to exert a magnetic pull on its neighbours. Thus it should be expected to continue to exist and develop whilst its attempts to create appropriate forms will continue to attract fascinated attention.

Notes

1   The Treaty text for this chapter is taken from Sweet and Maxwell, *European Community Treaties*, 3rd edn, 1977.

2   There is a considerable literature on the post-1945 attempts to give Europe new political institutions. See e.g. Bodenheimer 1967, Camps 1964, Haas 1968, Lindberg 1963, Mayne 1970, Palmer and Lambert 1968 and Pryce 1973.

3   On OEEC and the various moves to create European organisations, see Palmer and Lambert 1968.
4   The Schuman Plan of 9th May 1950 is printed in Royal Institute of International Affairs, *Documents on International Affairs*, 1949–50, pp. 315–7.
5   This is very clearly explained by Max Kohnstamm in his essay *The European Tide*. See Graubard, S. (ed.), *A New Europe?*, 1964, especially pp. 151–2. The author was part of the Dutch delegation for the ECSC talks and subsequently has had a distinguished career in European Community institutions.
6   There were several versions of the plan during the negotiations but it is unnecessary to consider the details here.
7   Barker, E., 1971, p. 107.
8   *Comité intergouvernemental créé par la conférence de Messina. Rapport des chefs de délégation aux Ministres des Affaires Etrangères*, Bruxelles, 1956.
9   Terminology under the Treaty of Paris is confusingly different. *Decisions* are binding in entirety, *recommendations* binding as to ends, but not means, and *opinions* have no binding force.
10   Tindemans, L., *European Union*, European Commission, *Bulletin of the European Communities*, Supplement 1/76, p. 30.
11   Edwards, G. and Wallace, H., *The Council of Ministers of the European Community and the President-in-Office*, A Federal Trust Paper, 1977, p. 6.
12   *Ibid.*, p. 103.
13   Coombes, D., 1970, p. 132.
14   Buck, T., Regional policy and European integration, *Journal of Common Market Studies*, Vol. XIII, 1975, p. 375 and Chapter 11 of this book.
15   Minister of Transport, written answer 5 March 1979, *Hansard*, 23 Feb.–8 March 1979, Col. 457.
16   Noel, E., *Working Together*, Office for Official Publications of the European Communities, Brussels 1975, p. 15. Noel is the Secretary-General of the Commission.
17   Report of the Working Party examining the problem of the enlargement of the powers of the European Parliament, (Vedel Report), European Commission, *Bulletin of the European Communities*, Supplement 4/72.
18   *Powers of the European Parliament*, London Office of the European Parliament, Sept. 1978, p. 21.
19   There is still some fluidity in the groupings. Turnout ranged from 32% of the electorate in the UK, to 99% in Belgium.
20   For a recent assessment, see Hill, C. and Wallace, W., Diplomatice trends in the European community, *International Affairs*, Jan. 1979.
21   Tindemans, L., *op. cit.*, p. 20.

References

Barker, E., *Britain in a Divided Europe 1945–70*, Weidenfeld & Nicolson 1971.
Bodenheimer, S., *Political Union, a Microcosm of European Politics*, Sijthoff 1967.
Camps, M., *Britain and the European Community, 1955–63*, Oxford University Press 1967.
Coombes, D., *Politics and Bureaucracy in the European Community*, Allen & Unwin 1970.

Graubard, S. (ed.), *A New Europe?*, Oldbourne Press 1964.
Haas, E.B., *The Unity of Europe*, Oxford University Press 1968.
Lindberg, L., *The Political Dynamics of European Economic Integration*, Stanford
    University Press 1963.
Mayne, R., *The Recovery of Europe*, Weidenfeld & Nicolson 1970.
Open University, *The European Economic Community: History and Institutions.
    National and International Impact*, Open University Press 1973.
Palmer, M. and Lambert, J., *European Unity*, Allen & Unwin 1968.
Pryce, R., *The Politics of the European Community*, Butterworths 1973.

3

The Basic Statistics
of the EEC

A M EL-AGRAA[1]

The purpose of this chapter is to provide the reader with a brief summary of the basic economic statistics of the EEC which are used in the analytical chapters. For comparative purposes and in order to preserve a general sense of perspective, similar information is given for Canada, Japan, the USA, the USSR (where available), and for the three potential EEC member nations — Greece, Portugal and Spain.

The major preoccupation of this chapter is with description; the analysis of most of these statistics and the economic forces that determine them is one of the main tasks of the rest of this book. For example, the analysis of the composition and pattern of trade prior to the inception of the EEC and subsequent to its formation is the basic aim of the theoretical and empirical section of the book. Moreover, the policy chapters are concerned with the analysis of particular areas of interest: the CAP, the role of the Community budget, competition and industrial policies, the regional policy, etc., and these specialist chapters contain further relevant and more detailed information.

The statistical data used in this chapter are not intended to provide a comprehensive coverage of all the comparative information needed for a proper understanding of each nation's economic situation in isolation, nor in relation to the EEC as a whole, but rather to give some notion of the general economic structure of the individual countries. Hence the choice of the years 1975 and 1977 as the reference years is, for the purposes of this chapter, somewhat arbitrary. 1977 is the latest year for which data are available at the time of writing.

The Basic Statistics

1. Table 3.1[2] gives information about agricultural area, tillage, population and its annual average increase, population density, and the crude

41

birthrate. The data are more or less self-explanatory but a few points warrant particular attention.

The Community of the Nine has a larger population (259 millions) than any country in the advanced Western world. This population exceeds that of the USSR (about 250 millions) and is considerably more than twice that of Japan. The population of the Nine plus that of the three potential EEC member nations (about 315 millions) exceeds that of the USSR and Japan taken together.

The annual average rate of increase in population between 1964 and 1974 was similar for all members of the EEC (about 0.7%), except for Belgium and the UK (0.4%) and the Netherlands (1.1%). Greece showed a rate similar to that of the UK (0.5%), Spain a rate similar to that of the Netherlands (1.0%), while Portugal had a negative rate (−0.2%). Canada, Japan and the USA had high rates (1.5, 1.2 and 1.0% respectively).

The crude birthrate for Ireland is distinctly different from that of the remaining members of the EEC. Also, the rates for the potential member nations, particularly those for Portugal and Spain, are in excess of the average for the EEC as a whole. There is no contradiction between these figures and those for the annual average rates of growth of population since differences in the infant mortality rates, death rates, population composition, migration, etc., would readily explain any apparent discrepancies between the two sets. The figures of particular importance are the annual average rates of growth.

However, one should be careful not to read too much into such comparisons — there is always the danger that they distract the reader from some obvious and basic realities of life: the cultural diversity of the member nations of the EEC as opposed to the common historical evolution and economic development of the USA, the contrasting political systems of the countries compared, etc.

The present member nations of the EEC and their potential partners have higher population densities than Canada and the USA. However, the population densities within the EEC exhibit great diversity, with Belgium and the Netherlands at the top of the league, France and Ireland at the bottom, and Germany, the UK, Italy, Luxembourg and Denmark (in descending order) occupying the middle. The potential partners also belong to the bottom of this league. It should be stressed that these considerations have important implications for potential growth rates and for future social policies.

Apart from Denmark and Ireland, tillage as a percentage of total agricultural area for the member countries of the EEC is about fifty; in Denmark tillage is in excess of 90%, while in Ireland the rate is about one quarter. Although Greece falls into the general pattern for the EEC as a whole, Portugal and Spain exhibit a pattern similar to that of Denmark.

2. Table 3.2 provides data on total civilian employment and gives the percentage sectoral distribution of civilian employment in terms of the broad categories of Agriculture, Forestry and Fishing, Industry, and 'Other'. The table also gives information about unemployment as a percentage of the *total* labour force.

It is interesting to note that, with the exception of Ireland and Luxembourg, the members of the EEC have similar unemployment rates. Ireland has the highest rate, while Luxembourg has virtually no unemployment. Note also that Canada and the USA show very high unemployment rates, while Japan comes at the bottom of the table.

Of particular interest is the relative size of the 'Other' sector. This is mainly the tertiary (this comprises such divergent items as banking, distribution, insurance, transport, catering and hotels, laundries and hairdressers, the professional services of the most varied kind, publicly and privately provided, etc.), or Services, sector and is, for most of the countries under consideration, the largest. For instance, the size of this sector in the UK was 57.3% in 1977 and the equivalent figures for France, Germany and the USA were 53%, 50% and 67% respectively. This is a significant point, particularly since it has frequently been alleged in the recent past that the size of this sector is the cause of the slow rate of growth of the UK economy; there is nothing in the data to suggest that the UK is unique in this respect.

As one would expect, all the countries considered show a decline in the percentage of the labour force engaged in agriculture. However, the three potential EEC members show a higher percentage of the labour force engaged in agriculture than all the present EEC excluding Ireland. This point is of particular significance in discussing the implications for the Common Agricultural Policy when the potential membership actually materialises, and is considered in some detail in the chapter on the CAP.

Since this book does not contain a chapter specifically devoted to the employment problems and policies of the EEC, this may be the appropriate point to consider briefly certain aspects of this topic. Employment is a political and socio-economic issue which needs to be tackled in all its elements. It is quite obvious that the solution of the unemployment problem necessitates a close integration of economic policies and social and manpower policies. The unemployment problem has two basic features. First, there is the transitional problem: given existing levels of unemployment and possible rates of growth of population, the achievement of acceptable levels of manpower utilisation will inevitably be slow, and in some countries may take many years. In addition, there is the longer-term problem: the effect of evolving structures of the labour force, attitudes to work and changing social objectives which may affect employment in a fundamental sense.

3. Table 3.3 gives a longer-term perspective for manpower utilisation and unemployment rates. One should note that between 1973 and 1975 unemployment either grew more slowly than in the boom years of the 1960s or fell and that the maximum declines in the 1973–75 recession were much greater than any that had occurred in the 1960s (the reader should note that the absolute levels of unemployment of these countries are not strictly comparable due to differences in measurement techniques).

A great deal of the slack in manpower utilisation which developed during the years 1973–1975 was absorbed by various measures which diverted the growth of overt unemployment. Working hours fell in a number of countries, jobs were preserved by subsidies to employers, by restrictions on dismissals or deterrents such as redundancy payments which make employers reluctant to dismiss labour. As a result, output per employee fell in many cases.

The table also gives some indication of the change in working hours in the major countries. Many of the figures refer only to manufacturing and may therefore be more sensitive to a recession than those for the economy as a whole, but they do indicate that working hours dropped more than the 1960–70 trend would have suggested. The biggest fall was in Japan. This explains some of the fall in output per employee, but the fall in working hours does not by any means explain the whole of this decline.

4. Table 3.4(a) gives total GDP and per capita GDP for 1975 and 1977, together with the rates of growth of GDP between 1958 and 1964 and between 1965 and 1975. Where available, similar growth rates of GDP per capita are also given. Table 3.4(b) gives indices of production.

One of the salient features of Table 3.4(a) is the disparity between the member nations of the EEC in terms of the per capita GDP: Ireland, Italy and the UK are far behind the rest of the EEC. Apart from these three countries there is some similarity between the rest of the EEC, Canada and the USA. The per capita GDP of Denmark for 1977 exceeds that of the USA.

Another significant point is that of the three potential partners,

Greece and Spain are very similar to Ireland and Italy respectively in terms of per capita GDP, while Portugal is in a league of its own.

The reader should also note that the 'net national product' of the USSR for 1971 was 288 thousand million US dollars and the per capita 'income' for the same year was 1,175 US dollars (Cairncross 1974, p. 20), which is equivalent to 1,645 due to differences in definition. In 1974 the per capita income (using GDP equivalent terminology) was 2964 according to the *National Economy of the USSR, 1974*.

For the period 1958—64, the UK showed the slowest rate of growth of GDP of all the countries. Indeed, if a longer period is considered (1953—64), the average exponential growth rate of the UK is only 2.7%, with the USA next in the league with 3.1% (Kaldor 1966, p. 5). On the other hand, Japan shows exceptionally high growth rates — for the period 1953—64, the average exponential growth rate is 9.6%.

A word of caution is necessary here. One should not be tempted to conclude from these data that the performance of the UK can be attributed to its failure to join the EEC at an earlier date. There are more fundamental causes than that. For instance, Kaldor (1966, p. 3) suggests that the basic problem with the UK economy is that it suffers from 'premature maturity':

> ...fast rates of economic growth are associated with the fast rate of growth of the 'secondary' sector of the economy — mainly the manufacturing sector — and this is an attribute of an intermediate stage of economic development: it is the characteristic of the transition from 'immaturity' to 'maturity'; and . . . the trouble with the British economy is that it has reached a high stage of 'maturity' *earlier* than others, with the result that it had exhausted the potential for fast growth before it had attained particularly high levels of productivity or real income per head.

Brown (1977, p. 30) suggests:

> There certainly remains strong evidence that the inferior rate of growth of our capital stock is the biggest factor in our slow growth of output, though the other factors I have mentioned — notably the much slower 'moving-up' of labour from low-productivity to higher-productivity employments, and what we may politely call our 'more sensible' working pace — no doubt assist it.

5. Table 3.5 gives information about the percentage use of GDP in terms of private consumption, collective consumption of the general government, gross fixed capital formation (particularly expenditure on machinery and equipment), changes in stocks, and the balance of exports and imports of goods and services.

With minor variations, members of the EEC show similar structures in their use of GDP, with about 60% private consumption expenditure,

20% gross fixed capital formation and 8% expenditure on machinery and equipment. The potential partners are similar to the EEC in terms of expenditure on gross fixed capital formation, but they spend more on private consumption, particularly Portugal (75%).

The reader might be tempted to conclude that there is a similarity between the UK and the USA. However, longer-term trends for the years 1953—76 suggest that the UK spends a smaller proportion of its GDP on investment (17.26%) than any of its competitors except for the USA (14.50%, see Kern 1978). Note the exceptionally high percentage spent by Japan on machinery and equipment — is this the cause of, or is it due to, its high rate of growth?

6. Table 3.6 provides data on various aspects of what can loosely be referred to as the 'government sector'. It gives information about current government revenue and expenditure as a percentage of GDP, net official development assistance to developing countries and multi-lateral agents, and expenditure on R & D in natural sciences and engineering. The table also provides data on total official reserves.

There is a fair similarity between the member nations of the EEC with respect to their current government expenditure (40% of GDP), except for the Netherlands (50%). In terms of government revenue, Belgium, France, Germany and the UK are similar (40% of GDP), while Luxembourg and the Netherlands have higher shares (50%), and Ireland and Italy have slightly lower shares (35%).

The three potential partners are similar to each other in terms of both government revenue and expenditure. However, the government sector in these countries seems to play a less significant role when compared with the EEC — amounting to only about a quarter of GDP. The same remarks apply to Japan, but Canada and the USA (which are fairly similar in structure) occupy a middle ground.

A particularly interesting feature of the table is the information on the percentage of GDP spent on net official development assistance to developing countries and multilateral agents. The Netherlands is at the top of this league, while Japan, the USA and Italy (in that order) occupy the bottom. One does not want to dwell too much on this matter, but the information suggests that the advanced Western world and Japan, in resisting the demands made by the developing world, are more interested in the absolute figures than in percentages. The percentages clearly indicate the significant implications for development assistance of the developing countries' plea (through UNCTAD) that this figure should be raised to one per cent of donor countries' GDP, particularly since such a request weighs heavily against Germany, Japan and the USA.

For a proper and detailed discussion of the role played by the governments' budgets, the reader is advised to turn to Professor Brown's chapter on the role of the Community budget.

7. Table 3.7 gives more detailed information on exports and imports of goods, and about receipts from, and expenditure on, tourism.

Belgium and Luxembourg (BLEU), Ireland and the Netherlands show a very high figure for imports as a percentage of GDP (between 40–50%), and an almost equally high figure for exports as a percentage of GDP (40–46%). France and Germany have very low equivalent percentages for export (about 18%) and France has equally low figures for imports. The rest of the EEC have percentages in the 25% region.

An interesting point to note is the unique position of Germany in comparison with the rest of the EEC. For the two years considered, Germany shows higher percentages for exports than for imports, but the opposite is true of the rest of the EEC.

Of the three potential partners, the figures for imports as a percentage of GDP for Greece and Portugal are similar to those of Denmark and the UK (25–30%), but Spain has percentages equivalent to those of France. However, all three potential partners show very low values for exports as a percentage of GDP. Indeed, even though Greece relies heavily on remittances from Greek citizens living abroad and on income from tourism, its balance of payments shows chronic deficits.

Canada is very similar in this respect to the UK, while Japan and the USA (with very low percentage figures for both exports and imports) are in a different category altogether.

8. (i) Tables 3.8 and 3.9 should be considered together: they give respectively the percentage figures for the share of total imports of the importing country coming from the EEC and the share of total exports of the exporting country to the EEC. The reader should be warned that these figures are not strictly comparable, because for the years 1957–64 the EEC refers to the original Six, while for the years 1974–76 the EEC refers to the Nine. For an analysis of the proper trends, the reader should consult Chapter 5.

BLEU, Ireland and the Netherlands conduct a very high percentage of their trade within the EEC (55–70%). In spite of the fact that the UK is at the bottom of this league, it now conducts one third of its total trade within the EEC. Note, however, that until 1969 the original Six were rather 'open' economies and that they conducted the majority of their international trade among themselves; the UK is of course even more 'open' in worldwide terms, but not in intra-EEC terms.

The three potential partners send a very high percentage of their exports to the EEC (46–50%), and in terms of imports, Greece and

Portugal depend fairly heavily on the EEC (40%), while Spain shows a less heavy dependence (33%).

(ii) Tables 3.10 and 3.11 give information about the total extra-area imports of the EEC by major commodity groups and by source of supply. The data relate to the period 1953–59 which is used to represent the trend of extra-area imports prior to the formation of the EEC and to the period 1959–70 which represents a period after its creation. Hence the 1953–59 data are actual, while the 1959–70 are hypothetical and are calculated on the assumption that the 1953–59 trend would have continued in the absence of the formation of the EEC. The tables also give the actual 1970 data.

The differences between the actual 1970 data and the hypothetical data are given in column (6). These differences are attributed by Balassa (1975) to the impact of the formation of the EEC. As stated earlier, a proper analysis of these trends is given in Chapter 5 of this book. In the present Chapter it is sufficient to state that in the period 1959–70 the UK, continental EFTA and other less-developed countries experienced a decline in their exports to the EEC in comparison with the period 1953–59. In terms of commodity groups, given the same assumptions, Food, Beverages (particularly Tropical Beverages), Tobacco, Chemicals and Other Manufactures were adversely affected.

9. Finally, Table 3.12 gives the average tariff rates for the major groups of commodities (specified in terms of SITC classification) in 1958. These tariff rates are discussed in Chapter 5 and, in Chapter 17, there is a discussion of what changes were effected on them as a result of the international tariff negotiations conducted since 1958.

Notes

1   I am grateful to my colleague Mr J.K. Bowers for valuable comments on an earlier draft of this chapter.
2   All tables for this chapter may be found at the end of the chapter.

References

Balassa, B. (ed.), *European Economic Integration*, North-Holland Publishing Co. 1975.

Brown, A.J., What is wrong with the British Economy?, *The University of Leeds Review*, Vol. 20, 1977.

Brown, A.J., Inflation and the British sickness, *The Economic Journal*, Vol. 89, March 1979.

Cairncross, Sir Alec, *et al.*, *Economic Policy for the European Community*, Macmillan 1974.

Clark, C., *British Trade in the Common Market*, Stevens and Sons 1962.

Kaldor, N. Lord, *Causes of the Slow Rate of Economic Growth of the United Kingdom*, Inaugural Lecture, Cambridge University Press 1966.

Kern, D., An international comparison of major economic trends, 1953—76, *National Westminster Bank Quarterly Review*, May 1978.

Economist Intelligence Unit, *Britain and Europe*, London, 1957.

Eurostat, *Basic Statistics of The Community*, for various years.

OECD, *The OECD Observer*, for various years.

OECD, various publications including country surveys, economic indicators, etc.

Table 3.1 Area and Population

	Area ('000 sq. km)	Year	Agricultural Area ('000 sq. km)	Tillage ('000 sq. km)	Population ('000)	Population Density (inhabitants per sq. km)	Crude Birth Rate (per '000)
Belgium	30.5	1975	15.3	8.1	9801 (0.4)[+]	321	12.1
		1977	15.2	8.1	9830	322	12.4
Denmark	43.1	1975	29.4	26.6	5060 (0.7)	117	14.2
		1977	29.3	26.5	5089	118	12.2
France	549.1	1975	324.2	189.2	52,743 (0.8)	96	14.1
		1977	322.3	190.9	53,084	97	14.0
West Germany	248.6	1975	133.0	80.6	61,829 (0.7)	249	9.7
		1977	132.3	80.1	61,400	247	9.5
Ireland	70.3	1973	48.4	12.4	3,127 (0.7)	44	21.6
		1977	48.5	12.5	3,180	45	21.4
Italy	301.2	1974	175.0	122.9	55,812 (0.7)	185	15.1
		1977	175.3	123.2	56,446	187	13.4
Luxembourg	2.6	1975	1.3	0.6	359 (0.8)	138	11.1
		1977	1.3	0.6	355	137	11.4
Netherlands	40.8	1975	20.9	8.5	13,654 (1.1)	335	13.0
		1977	20.8	8.5	13,853	340	12.5
United Kingdom	244.0	1975	185.8	69.6	56,042 (0.4)	230	12.5
		1977	185.7	69.8	55,919	229	11.7

Greece	132.0	1974	88.2*	38.9	9,046 (0.5)	69	15.7a
		1977	88.2	39.0	9,268	70	15.5
Portugal	92.0	1975	42.0	36.7*	9,449 (−0.2)	103	19.3
		1977	41.3	36.0	9,773	106	18.6
Spain	504.8	1975	280.6	208.3	35,219 (1.0)	70	18.8
		1977	275.8	206.6	36,672	73	18.0
Canada	9,976.1	1975	635.6	392.6	22,831 (1.5)	2	15.7
		1977	640.6	401.6	23,316	2	15.5
Japan	372.3	1974	58.6	56.2	110,990 (1.2)	298	17.2
		1977	57.8	55.4	113,860	306	15.5
USA	9,363.4	1974	4301.6	1882.2	213,540 (1.0)	23	14.7
		1977			216,817	23	15.3

Sources for all the tables: Eurostat, *Basic Statistics for The Community, The OECD Observer* and OECD various statistical publications.

a = 1974

* = estimate

+ The figures in brackets show the total increase in population given in annual average for 1964—74.

Table 3.2 *Employment*

	Year	Total civilian employment ('000)	% of which in: Agriculture, forestry and fishing	Industry	Other	Unemployment rate as % of total labour force
Belgium	1975	3,748	3.6	39.9	56.5	4.2
	1977	3,711	3.3	37.9	58.8	6.3
Denmark	1975	2,332	9.8	31.5	58.7	4.9
	1977	2,414	9.1	30.4	60.5	5.1
France	1975	20,764	11.3	38.5	50.1	4.1
	1977	20,962	9.6	37.7	52.7	4.9
West Germany	1975	24,828	7.3	46.0	46.7	4.1
	1977	24,511	6.8	45.3	47.9	4.0
Ireland	1975	1,030	24.5	29.8	45.7	8.0
	1977	1,022	23.1	30.3	46.6	9.4
Italy	1975	18,818	15.8	44.1	40.1	3.3
	1977	19,847	15.9	38.6	45.5	7.1
Luxembourg	1975	150	6.2	47.3	46.5	0.1
	1977	147	5.9	45.1	49.0	0.5
Netherlands	1975	4,535	6.6	34.8	58.6	4.3
	1977	4,555	6.3	33.2	60.5	4.5
United Kingdom	1975	24,632	2.7	40.9	56.4	3.4
	1977	24,550	2.7	40.0	57.3	5.5
Greece	1975	3,190*	35.4*	28.2*	36.4*	3.0
	1977	3,167*	28.4*	30.3*	41.3*	1.1
Portugal	1975	3,081	28.2	33.6	38.2	5.3
	1977	3,781	32.5	33.1	34.4	7.8
Spain	1975	12,576	21.9	38.5	39.6	4.7
	1977	12,462	20.7	37.4	41.9	6.3
Canada	1975	9,363	6.1	29.3	64.6	6.9
	1977	9,754	5.7	28.9	65.4	8.1
Japan	1975	52,230	12.7	35.8	51.5	1.9
	1977	53,420	11.9	35.4	52.7	2.0
USA	1975	84,783	4.0	29.0*	67.0*	8.3
	1977	90,546	3.6	28.9*	67.5*	6.9

* = estimate.

N.B. The unemployment data are not strictly comparable.

Table 3.3 *Manpower Utilisation and Unemployment Rates (changes in percentage terms)*

	Employment		Hours worked per person		Output per man hour		Unemployment % of labour force	
	1960 −1973	1973 −1975	1960 −1973	1973 −1975	1960 −1973	1973 −1975	1960 −1973	1974
Belgium) Luxembourg)	0.7	—[+]	−1.2	—	5.4	—	2.2	2.6
Denmark	1.3	—	−1.5	—	5.0	—	1.1	2.1
France	0.7	−0.5	−0.5	−2.1	5.5	3.6	1.6	2.3
West Germany	0.1	−2.8	−0.9	−2.7	5.5	4.0	0.8	2.2
Italy	−0.7	1.2	1.9	—	7.8	—	3.3	2.9
Netherlands	0.9	—	—	—	—	—	1.3	3.0
United Kingdom	0.1	0.0	−0.5	−0.8	3.4	0.1	1.9	2.1
Canada	2.9	3.1	−0.3	−1.4	2.8	−0.8	5.3	5.4
Japan	1.2	−0.8	−1.0	−5.3	10.1	6.2	1.3	1.4
USA	1.9	0.1	0.1	−0.2	2.3	−2.4	4.8	5.4

*Ireland is omitted due to lack of data.
+Dashes in tables indicate figures not available.

Table 3.4(a) *Gross Domestic Product*

	Year	GDP (in million US $)	GDP per capita	Years	Annual rate of growth of GDP	per capita GDP
Belgium	1975	62245	6352	1958—64	4.7	4.0
	1977	79210	8060	1965—75	3.8	—
Denmark	1975	35451	7006	1958—64	5.9	5.1
	1977	46020	9040	1965—75	2.7	—
France	1975	335744	6360	1958—64	5.3	4.0
	1977	380660	7170	1965—75	4.0	—
West Germany	1975	424835	6871	1958—64	5.8	4.0
	1977	516200	8410	1965—75	3.8	—
Ireland	1975	7800	2492	1958—64	—	—
	1977	9380	2940	1965—75	4.0	—
Italy	1975	172104	3084	1958—64	6.1	5.4
	1977	196050	3470	1965—75	4.0	—
Luxembourg	1975	2197	6102	1958—64	—	—
	1977	2750	7700	1965—75	1.3	—
Netherlands	1975	81202	5949	1958—64	5.4	4.0
	1977	106390	7680	1965—75	4.1	—
United Kingdom	1975	228820	4089	1958—64	3.9	3.1
	1977	244340	4370	1965—75	2.3	—
Greece	1975	20980	2320	1958—64	5.0*	—
	1977	26210	2830	1965—75	5.25	—
Portugal	1975	14620	1550	1958—64	4.7*	—
	1977	16300	1670	1965—75	—	—
Spain	1975	101040	2870	1958—64	5.5*	—
	1977	115590	3150	1965—75	2.0	—
Canada	1975	159707	6995	1958—64	4.3	2.3
	1977	200250	8590	1965—75	1.6	—
Japan	1975	490634	4437	1958—64	—	—
	1977	694360	6100	1965—75	7.3	—
USA	1975	1513828	7087	1958—64	4.3	2.7
	1977	1878840	8670	1965—75	0.9	—

* = estimate.

Table 3.4(b) *General Indices of Industrial Production (excluding construction)*

	1958 = 100										1975 = 100					
	'54	'55	'56	'57	'59	'60	'61	'62	'63	'64	'72	'73	'74	'76	'77	'78
Belgium	92	99	105	105	104	112	119	125	135	145	100	109	111	108	108	111
Denmark	87	89	90	96	112	121	128	139	—	—	104	107	106	109	110	113
France	—	82	89	96	101	110	116	122	128	138	99	105	108	109	110	112
West Germany	75	86	93	97	107	120	127	133	137	150	101	108	107	107	110	113
Ireland	—	—	—	—	—	—	—	—	—	—	94	103	107	109	118	129
Italy	77	84	90	96	111	128	142	156	169	170	96	106	110	112	112	114
Luxembourg	85	96	103	104	104	114	117	112	113	124	111	124	128	106	107	108
Netherlands	—	—	—	—	109	122	126	133	139	151	93	100	105	106	107	108
UK	—	—	—	—	105	113	113	114	119	127	100	108	105	103	107	111
Greece	—	—	—	—	—	—	—	128	137	152	84	97	96	111	113	—
Portugal	76	81	88	94	106	116	127	134	146	—	91	103	108	—	—	—
Spain	—	—	—	—	—	—	—	—	—	—	85	98	107	106	119	—
Canada	83	92	100	101	108	108	112	120	127	138	93	102	107	105	109	—
Japan	—	—	—	—	—	—	—	—	—	—	101	116	112	111	116	—
USA	92	103	107	107	113	116	117	126	133	141	102	110	110	110	116	123

Source: *Eurostat*

Table 3.5 *Use of Gross Domestic Product*

	Year	Use of GDP in %				
		Private consumption	Collective consumption of general government	Gross fixed capital formation	Change in stocks	Balance of exports and imports of goods and services
Belgium	1975	60.5	16.8	22.3 (7.8)	− 0.6	+ 1.0
	1977	62.0	−	21.2 (6.4)	−	−
Denmark	1975	58.1	24.7	19.9 (8.0)	− 1.7	− 1.0
	1977	56.2	−	23.3 (7.4)	−	−
France	1975	62.3	14.5	23.4 (9.2)	− 1.1	+ 0.9
	1977	62.0	−	22.6 (9.3)	−	−
West Germany	1975	60.9	14.7	21.5 (9.9)	− 0.4	+ 3.3
	1977	58.8	−	20.9 (8.6)	−	−
Ireland	1975	67.7	20.6	22.3 (9.9)	− 4.3	− 6.3
	1977	64.7	−	24.7 (−)	−	−
Italy	1975	67.8	13.6	21.1 (8.8)	− 1.2	− 1.3
	1977	63.9	−	19.8 (8.5)	−	−
Luxembourg	1975	59.9	15.0	29.2 (8.6)	+ 2.8	− 6.9
	1977	61.8	−	25.8 (−)	−	−
Netherlands	1975	57.8	18.0	21.2 (9.3)	− 0.7	+ 3.7
	1977	58.3	−	21.1 (8.6)	−	−
United Kingdom	1975	61.4	22.2	19.9 (8.8)	− 1.3	− 2.2
	1977	59.2	−	18.1 (9.0)	−	−

Greece	1975	71.6	—	21.0 (8.4)	— —
	1977	66.7	—	23.0 (8.4)	— —
Portugal	1975	84.6	—	13.6 (7.7)	— —
	1977	75.5	—	20.4 (—)	— —
Spain	1975	69.3	—	23.2 (9.2)	— —
	1977	69.0	—	21.5 (—)	— —
Canada	1975	57.4	20.1	24.1 (8.4)	− 0.2 − 1.4
	1977	56.7	—	22.7 (—)	— —
Japan	1975	56.6	11.1	30.9 (14.2)	+ 1.3 + 0.1
	1977	58.0	—	30.0 (10.5)	— —
USA	1975	64.3	19.4	16.2 (6.9)	− 1.0 + 1.1
	1977	64.6	—	17.5 (7.5)	— —

*The figures in brackets show the percentage spent on machinery and equipment.

Table 3.6 *The Government Sector*

	Year	Current government expenditure and revenue as % of GDP		Net official development assistance to less developed countries and multilateral agents (% of GDP)	Gross domestic expenditure on R & D in natural sciences and engineering	Total official reserves (US $million)
		Expenditure	Revenue			
Belgium	1975	41.6	40.7	0.59	1.2	5206
	1977	43.5	41.8	0.46	—	4535
Denmark	1975	43.0	45.0	0.58	1.1	915
	1976	42.8	46.5	0.60	—	2471
France	1975	38.9	40.6	0.62	1.8	9728
	1977	40.4	42.2	0.60	—	10692
West Germany	1975	41.7	40.9	0.4	2.1	34798
	1977	41.3	43.5	0.27	—	41353
Ireland	1973	34.8	35.0	—	0.7	1837
	1975	43.3	36.8	—	0.8	2064
Italy	1975	39.8	34.7	0.11	0.8 (b)	6654
	1977	42.5	37.4	0.10	0.9 (a)	11380
Luxembourg	1975	42.1	50.6	—	—	5206
	1976	44.4	52.8	—	—	4535
Netherlands	1975	50.5	53.6	0.75	1.9	7387
	1977	52.3	54.0	0.85	1.9	5822
United Kingdom	1974	39.5	40.0	0.37	2.1	4230
	1976	41.5	40.6	0.37	—	13100

Greece	1974	24.6	26.7	—	—	925
	1977	29.0	29.4	—	—	914
Portugal	1974	22.6	23.0	—	—	1302
	1976	31.1	28.3	—	0.2	1507
Spain	1974	22.0	23.1	—	—	5284
	1977	23.4	26.7	—	0.3	7963
Canada	1975	37.1	37.4	0.58	1.0 (a)	5843
	1977	37.0	36.4	0.51	1.0 (a)	3507
Japan	1975	20.8	23.5	0.24	1.8 (a)	16604
	1977	22.3	24.5	0.21	1.7 (a)	25714
USA	1975	33.9	30.7	0.26	2.3 (b,c)	18319
	1977	32.6	32.0	0.22	2.3 (a)	15032

a = 1976.
b = includes some or all expenditure on the social sciences and/or humanities.
c = excludes all capital expenditures.

Table 3.7 *Foreign Trade Sector*

	Year	Total imports as % of GDP	Total exports as % of GDP	Foreign tourism (US $million)	
				Receipts	Expenditures
Belgium*	1975	49.3	46.3	864	1410
	1977	49.1	45.7	993	1635
Denmark	1975	29.1	24.6	746	642
	1977	28.8	21.9	940	942
France	1975	16.2	15.6	3470	3064
	1977	18.5	16.7	4377	3920
West Germany	1975	17.5	21.2	2848	8502
	1977	19.5	22.8	3804	10805
Ireland	1975	49.1	41.4	265	153
	1977	57.4	46.8	323	237
Italy	1975	22.3	20.2	2582	1051
	1977	24.3	23.0	4762	894
Luxembourg*	1975	49.3	46.3	864	1410
	1977	49.1	45.7	993	1635
Netherlands	1975	43.3	42.4	1106	1657
	1977	42.9	41.1	1110	2454
United Kingdom	1975	23.4	19.2	2442	1921
	1977	26.1	23.5	3805	1921
Greece	1975	25.3	10.9	644	92
	1977	25.9	10.4	981	89
Portugal	1975	26.2	13.3	242	200
	1977	30.4	12.4	404	135
Spain	1975	16.1	7.6	3404	385
	1977	15.4	8.8	4003	533
Canada	1975	21.3	20.2	1525	2065
	1977	19.7	20.8	1616	2829
Japan	1975	11.8	11.4	252	1367
	1977	10.2	11.6	424	2151
USA	1975	6.4	7.1	4876	6417
	1977	7.9	6.4	6164	7451

*Belgium and Luxembourg are counted together as BLEU.

Table 3.8 *Imports from EEC Countries (Percentage Share of Total Imports of Importing Country)*

	1957	1958	1959	1960	1961	1962	1963	1964	1974	1975	1976
Belgium) Luxembourg)	43.5	46.6	47.1	47.9	50.6	51.0	52.5	53.3	66.1	67.2	67.5
Denmark	31.2	35.6	36.7	38.5	39.4	37.8	35.9	35.4	45.5	45.8	47.2
France	21.4	21.9	26.8	29.4	31.5	33.6	35.8	37.4	47.6	48.8	50.0
West Germany	23.5	25.8	29.0	29.9	31.3	32.5	33.4	34.9	48.1	49.5	48.2
Ireland	—	—	—	—	—	—	15.4	15.6	68.3	69.2	69.4
Italy	21.4	21.4	26.7	27.7	29.5	31.2	33.0	32.7	42.4	43.0	43.6
Netherlands	41.1	41.9	44.4	45.8	49.2	50.2	51.6	52.0	57.4	56.9	55.2
United Kingdom	12.1	14.2	14.0	14.6	15.4	15.8	16.0	16.6	30.0	32.4	32.2
Greece	40.8	42.7	37.9	33.6	38.1	43.4	39.8	42.3	43.3	42.5	39.7
Portugal	37.1	39.2	39.0	38.2	38.1	36.6	34.7	33.1	43.5	40.2	41.7
Spain	21.3	23.8	22.3	25.2	26.1	29.7	33.6	35.9	35.8	33.6	33.1
Canada	4.2	4.7	5.3	5.3	5.5	5.5	5.2	5.4	9.6	9.8	8.5
Japan	—	4.9	5.0	4.7	5.4	6.1	5.9	5.6	6.4	5.8	5.6
USA	11.7	12.5	15.6	15.0	15.2	15.0	14.8	15.2	19.0	17.3	14.8

Table 3.9 *Exports to EEC Countries (Percentage Share of Total Exports of Exporting Country)*

	1957	1958	1959	1960	1961	1962	1963	1964	1974	1975	1976
Belgium) Luxembourg)	46.1	45.1	46.3	50.5	53.2	56.8	60.8	62.6	69.9	70.6	73.7
Denmark	31.2	31.2	31.7	29.5	29.1	28.4	28.8	28.1	43.1	45.0	45.7
France	25.1	22.2	27.2	29.8	33.5	36.8	38.2	38.8	53.2	49.2	50.6
West Germany	29.2	27.3	27.8	29.5	31.7	34.0	37.3	36.5	53.2	43.6	45.7
Ireland	—	—	—	—	—	—	7.5	11.5	74.1	79.4	75.8
Italy	24.9	23.6	27.2	29.6	31.3	34.8	35.5	38.0	45.4	45.1	47.8
Netherlands	41.6	41.6	44.3	45.9	47.6	49.2	53.3	55.7	70.8	71.1	72.1
United Kingdom	14.6	13.9	14.8	15.3	17.4	19.3	21.1	20.6	33.4	32.3	35.6
Greece	52.5	47.9	44.1	33.0	30.5	35.7	32.8	37.5	50.1	49.7	50.0
Portugal	22.2	24.6	22.8	21.8	21.8	23.2	21.8	20.7	48.2	50.3	51.5
Spain	29.8	28.2	27.8	38.5	37.7	38.0	37.9	38.9	47.4	44.7	46.4
Canada	8.3	8.6	6.2	8.3	8.4	7.3	7.0	6.8	12.6	12.5	11.9
Japan	—	4.3	3.9	4.3	5.0	5.6	6.1	5.5	10.7	10.2	10.8
USA	15.3	13.6	13.6	16.8	17.0	16.8	17.0	17.2	21.9	21.3	22.1

Table 3.10 *EEC Extra-Area Total Imports (US $million)*

	Actual imports 1959	Hypothetical imports in 1970 calculated at growth rates of extra-area imports for the period		Actual imports 1970		Differences between actual and hypothetical imports 1970 i.e. (5) − (2)
		In 1959 prices		In 1959 prices	In 1970 prices	
		1953—59	1959—70			
	(1)	(2)	(3)	(4)	(5)	(6)
Extra-area imports, total						
0 + 1 − 07 Food, beverages, tobacco	3193	7219	5876	5876	6172	−1047
2 + 4 Raw materials	4729	8347	8123	8123	9001	+654
3 Fuels	2460	6950	8343	8343	7766	+816
5 Chemicals	682	3490	2982	2982	2532	−958
71 + 72 Machinery	1031	1849	4147	4147	5716	+3867
73 Transport equipment	319	1121	1341	1341	1644	+523
6 + 8 Other manufactures	2873	11794	9691	9691	10878	−916
0 to 8 − All of above	15337	40770	40503	40503	43709	+2939
07 Tropical beverages	779	1479	1163	1163	1315	−164
0 − 8 All commodities	16116	42249	41666	41666	45024	+2775

Source: Balassa, B., *European Economic Integration*, North-Holland Publishing Co. 1975, p. 399.

Table 3.11 *EEC Extra-Area Imports (US $million)*

	Actual imports 1959	Hypothetical imports in 1970 calculated at growth rates of extra-area imports for the period (in 1959 prices)		Actual imports 1970		Differences between actual and hypothetical imports 1970 i.e. (5) − (2)
		1953–59	1959–70	In 1959 prices	In 1970 prices	
	(1)	(2)	(3)	(4)	(5)	(6)
USA	2448 100.0	6625 270.6	7024 286.9	7791 318.3	8718 356.1	+2093
UK	1298 100.0	4100 315.9	4389 338.1	3442 265.2	3944 303.9	−156
Continental EFTA	2448 100.0	6887 281.3	6794 277.5	5805 237.1	6565 268.2	−322
Other developed countries*	1866 100.0	4284 229.6	3844 206.0	5502 294.9	6100 326.9	+1816
Centrally planned economies	942 100.0	2538 269.4	2422 257.1	2851 302.7	3016 320.2	+478
Associated developing countries	1344 100.0	3155 234.7	2729 203.1	3330 247.8	3521 262.0	+366
Other less-developed countries	5770 100.0	14660 254.1	14464 250.7	12945 224.4	13160 228.1	−1500
Extra-area imports, total	16166 100.0	42249 262.2	41666 258.5	41666 258.5	45024 279.4	+2775

Source: Balassa, B., *European Economic Integration*, p. 88.
*Australia, Canada, Japan, New Zealand, South Africa and those European countries that were not members of either the EEC or EFTA during the period under consideration (Finland, Greece, Iceland, Ireland, Spain and Turkey).

Table 3.12 *Average Tariffs (%) 1958*

	Chemicals (5)	Leather, etc. (61)	Rubber manufacturers (62)	Wood mfrs. etc. except furniture (63)	Paper, paperboard etc. (64)	Textiles etc. except clothing (65)	Non-metallic mineral manufrs. (66)	Silver, platinum, gems, jewellery (67)
Benelux	7	11	17	11	14	14	12	5
France	16	11	17	19	16	19	16	13
West Germany	8	12	10	7	8	11	6	3
Italy	17	18	19	22	18	20	21	7
EEC (Six)	12	12	18	16	15	16	13	6
Denmark	4	11	8	4	6	9	5	5
United Kingdom	15	16	21	15	13	23	17	11
Canada	11	17	18	12	17	21	21	13
USA	24	17	18	18	10½	26	13	29

Source: PEP, *Atlantic Tariffs and Trade*, Allen and Unwin 1962.
The figures are subject to the reservations stated in the source.
The figures in brackets refer to SITC classifications.

Iron and steel (681)	Ordnance (691)	Manufacturers of metal (n.e.s. 699)	Machinery other than electric (71)	Electric machinery etc. (72)	Transport equipment (73)	Building parts and fittings (81)	Furniture (821)	Clothing (84)	Footwear (851)	Instruments (86)
5	9	11	8	11	17	15	13	20	20	13
13	14	20	18	19	29	19	23	26	21	22
7	7	10	5	6	12	8	8	13	10	8
17	17	23	20	21	34	25	21	25	21	17
10	11	16	13	15	22	17	17	21	19	16
1	1	6	6	8	8	8	11	19	19	3
14	22	21	17	23	25	15	20	26	25	27
12	13	18	9	18	17	16	25	25	24	19
13	26	23	12	20	13	20	24	32½	19	29

Part II

Theory and Measurement

This section of the book is devoted to the discussion of the theoretical aspects of the EEC and to the measurement of the impact of the formation of the EEC on trade and production.

The whole section is basically concerned with two concepts: 'trade creation' and 'trade diversion'. These can be illustrated rather simplistically as follows:

In table 1 the cost of beef per lb. is given in new pence for the UK, France and New Zealand. With a 50% non-discriminatory tariff rate the cheapest source of supply of beef for the UK is the home producer. When the UK and France form a customs union, the cheapest source of supply becomes France. Hence the UK saves 10p. per lb. of beef making a total saving of £1m. for ten million lbs. This is **'trade creation'**: **the replacement of expensive domestic production by cheaper imports from the partner.**

In table 2 the situation is different due to a lower initial non-discriminatory tariff rate (25%) by the UK. Before the customs union, New Zealand is the cheapest source of supply. After the customs union, France becomes the cheapest source. There is a total loss to the UK of £1m. since the tax revenue is claimed by the government. This is **'trade diversion': the replacement of cheaper initial imports from the outside world by expensive imports from the partner.**

In tables 3(a) and 3(b) there are two commodities: beef and butter. The cost of beef per lb. is the same as in the previous examples and so is the cost of butter per lb. Note that table 3(a) starts from the same position as table 1 and table 3(b) from the same position as table 2. Here the UK does not form a customs union with France, rather it reduces its tariff rate by 80% on a non-discriminatory basis. This gives a saving of £2m. in comparison with the customs union situation. Therefore, **a non-discriminatory tariff reduction is superior to customs union formation.**

Table 1 *Beef*

	UK	France	New Zealand
The cost per unit	90p	80p	70p
UK domestic price with a 50% tariff rate	90p	120p	105p
UK domestic price when the UK and France form a customs union	90p	80p	105p

Total cost before the customs union = 90p × 10m. lbs. = £9m.
Total cost after the customs union = 80p × 10m. lbs. = £8m.
Total savings for the UK consumer = £1m.

Table 2 *Beef*

	UK	France	New Zealand
The cost per unit	90p	80p	70p
UK domestic price with a 25% tariff rate	90p	100p	87½p
UK domestic price when the UK and France form a customs union	90p	80p	87½p

Total cost to the UK government before the customs union
  = 70p × 10m. lbs. = £7m.
Total cost to the UK after the customs union = 80p × 10m. lbs. = £8m.
Total loss to the UK government = £1m.

Table 3(a) *Beef*

	UK	France	New Zealand
The cost per unit	90p	80p	70p
UK domestic price with a 50% tariff rate	90p	120p	105p
UK domestic price with a non-discriminatory tariff reduction of 80% (i.e. tariff rate becomes 10%)	90p	88p	77p

Total cost to the UK before the tariff reduction = 90p × 10m. lbs. = £9m.
Total cost to the UK after the tariff reduction = 70p × 10m. lbs. = £7m.
Total savings for the UK = £2m.

Table 3(b) *Butter*

	UK	France	New Zealand
The cost per unit	90p	80p	70p
UK domestic price with a 25% tariff rate	90p	100p	87½p
UK domestic price with a non-discriminatory tariff reduction of 80% (i.e. tariff rate becomes 5%)	90p	84p	73½p

Total cost to the UK before the tariff reduction = 70p × 10m. lbs. = £7m.
Total cost to the UK after the tariff reduction = 70p × 10m. lbs. = £7m.
Total savings for the UK = nil

Now consider tables 3(a) + 3(b) in comparison with tables 1 and 2. The total cost for tables 1 + 2 + 3 before the customs union = £9m. + £7m. = £16m.
The total cost for tables 1 and 2 after the customs union = £8m. + £8m. = £16m.
The total cost for table 3 after the customs union = £7m. + £7m. = £14m.
Hence, a non discriminatory tariff reduction is more economical for the UK than the formation of a customs union with France.

This dangerously (?) simple analysis has been the inspiration of a massive literature on customs union theory. Admittedly, some of the contributions were misguided in that they concentrated on a non-problem.

Chapter 4 tackles the basic concept of 'trade creation' and 'trade diversion' considers the implications of domestic distortions and scale economies of the basic analysis and discusses the terms of trade effects. Chapter 5 discusses the measurement of the theoretical con-cepts discussed in the preceding chapters. The section concludes with a note on the state of the customs union.

4

The Theory of
Economic Integration

A J JONES*

The purpose of this chapter is to present a unified view of the different and often apparently conflicting strands of the most rigorously developed branch of the theory of economic integration, customs union theory. By doing this it is hoped to suggest some pitfalls to be avoided as well as a few insights which might usefully be applied to other branches of the subject.

The analytical framework adopted here will be confined to the standard model of customs union theory derived from the modern theory of tariffs. Thus throughout the argument it will be assumed that the world can be split into three separate economies: the home country, the (potential) partner and the rest of the world. It will also be assumed that all goods produced and consumed in the world can be aggregated into the two composite commodities, the 'importables' (x) and the 'exportables' (y) of the home country.

This simplifying assumption enables the use of various geometrical tools of analysis, but the range of choice between them has been a persistent source of confusion in the development of the analysis. Most of the more rigorous formulations have employed the geometrical techniques of two-commodity space: indifference curves, production and consumption possibility frontiers and offer curves. Such tools do have many advantages. They help to clarify the basic assumptions of the model, welfare conclusions can be shown by direct reference to the properties of indifference curves or consumption possibility frontiers, and the general equilibrium nature of the analysis is evident at all times. On the other hand, they have proved to be rather complex

* This chapter is based on my essay of the same title in Bowers, J.K. (ed.), *Inflation, Development and Integration: Essays in Honour of A.J. Brown*, Leeds University Press 1979. I am grateful to the editor for his permission to draw heavily on that essay.

to handle, especially when the economic relationships of all three economies need to be examined and, even in the simplest formulation of the problem, they have been the source of at least one notable 'red-herring': concern to demonstrate the possible gains that might arise even for so-called 'trade-diverting' customs unions (in particular see Lipsey 1960, Bhagwati 1971 and Johnson 1974). This problem, however, has been avoided by the use of the demand and supply curve techniques which have provided the other main line of development and which have almost always been the initial source of insights into the subject. Unfortunately, the proponents of the two-commodity techniques have derided these simple methods as representing an inferior, partial equilibrium approach. Indeed, in the presentation of customs union theory using only demand and supply curves, this limitation has often been apologetically admitted, but the impression that the two-commodity general equilibrium model and the demand and supply curve analysis of customs unions necessarily represent different theories is mistaken.

In figure 4.1, the home country's (general equilibrium) demand curve for importables (dd_x) can be regarded as being derived directly from the assumptions of the two-commodity model without significant modification.[1] The curve ss_x is similarly derived directly from the production possibility frontier without modification of any assumptions and is the marginal opportunity cost curve of the home country's production of importables. Given the standard assumption (in both approaches) that there is perfect competition in the commodity market, it follows that ss_x can also be regarded as the domestic supply curve of importables. Although the diagram focuses on the market for a single commodity, it nonetheless remains a two-commodity model in which there is only one commodity price variable (the terms of trade, p) and in which information about the second commodity is provided by the fact that all areas in figure 4.1 are measured in units of y.

This property of the diagram raises a problem which has long been a matter of dispute in economic theory. It will be argued here that any area bounded by dd_x, ss_x, and appropriate terms of trade lines is a measure (in units of exportables) of the change in the gains from trade caused by changes in the international terms of trade or by changes in the policies being pursued by the home country. Thus, in figure 4.1, suppose that the international terms of trade are fixed at p^w and that a tariff on imports leaves the effective foreign supply curve of importables to the home market at $p^t d^t$. The effects of the removal of the tariff on both the domestic terms of trade (the fall from p^t to p^w) and the change in the volume of imports (the increase from $x_s^t x_d^t$ to $x_s^w x_d^w$) are readily identified (and have identical

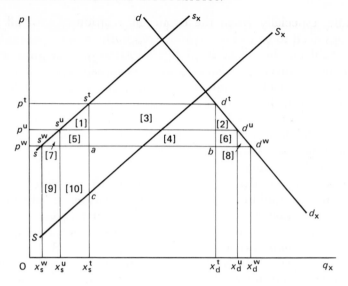

Figure 4.1 *The Small Country Model of the Formation of a Customs Union*

counterparts in two-commodity space). The welfare effects are identified as the gross gains from increased trade $(s^w s^t d^t d^w)$ less the loss of tariff revenue $(as^t d^t b)$. The net gains from trade of this policy change can thus be split into the gains from increased specialisation (the production effect $s^w s^t a$) and the gains from increased exchange (the consumption effect $b d^t d^w$). Like the change in tariff revenue (and its offset due to the change in the domestic terms of trade on the initial volume of imports), the gains from specialisation are identified in terms of a commodity measure which has an exact counterpart (which is used in the same way) in two-commodity space. Following Hicks, it is also accepted that the compensating variation provides a commodity measure of the welfare consequences of the consumption effect of a price change. When compensation is actually paid or received, this measure is entirely appropriate and dd_x can be interpreted as a compensated demand curve, so that the familiar triangle under the demand curve is the exact counterpart of the compensating variation shown in two-commodity space. When tariff changes are being considered, however, it is generally assumed that compensation is not paid, with the result that the simple Hicksian measure (whether in two-commodity space or in diagrams such as figure 4.1) can at best be considered an approximation of the appropriate welfare change. In two-commodity barter models (and in n-commodity general equilibrium models in which homothetic preference functions are assumed), however, a precise measure of the consumption effect can be defined. This is provided by the limit of the sum of Hicksian compensating variations obtained when the price change is regarded as a set of small, successive steps with no compensation being paid. Within the limited framework of this model such a measure is well-defined and, although it cannot readily be depicted in two-commodity space, it corresponds exactly to the measure of the consumption effect identified above.

The 'Small Country' Model

With these tools of analysis, the presentation of the basic and most widely influential form of customs union theory is straightforward. This model abstracts from the problems of evaluating welfare change in the other economies by assuming that the home economy is 'small' relative to the two foreign economies, which are regarded as offering fixed, but different, terms of trade. As the formation of a customs union with the lower cost source of imports would be identical in its effects to the adoption of a policy of free trade, the analysis focuses on the effects of forming a customs union with the higher cost foreign source of supply. In figure 4.1, this information is shown by the fixed terms of trade p^w offered by the rest of the world and p^u offered by the potential partner.

The traditional formulation of this model proceeds by identifying an initial non-discriminatory tariff policy in the home country. In terms of figure 4.1, this results in the tariff-inclusive export supply curve of the rest of the world becoming the effective foreign supply curve of importables ($p^t d^t$) for the home market. The formation of the customs union is accomplished by the removal of the tariff on imports from the partner and the adoption of a common external tariff at least as high as the prohibitive tariff which the partner is implicitly levying initially on imports of commodity x from the rest of the world. As a result of these tariff changes, the tariff-free export supply curve of the partner ($p^u d^u$) becomes the effective foreign supply curve to the home economy. Consequently, there is both an increase in the volume of trade (from $x_s^t x_d^t$ to $x_s^u x_d^u$) and the diversion of all trade from being with the rest of the world to being with the partner. The net welfare effects of this change, *compared with the initial policy*, consist of the gains from increased specialisation (the production effect, area [1]) the gains from increased exchange (the consumption effect, area [2]) and the uncompensated loss in tariff revenue, area [4]. Despite much pedantic confusion over terminology, the first two effects can be combined into the gains from increased trade (i.e. the 'trade creation' effect), whilst the loss associated with diverting trade to a higher cost source of supply is identified as the 'trade diversion' effect.

Since, in this formulation, both the initial tariff policy and the difference between the two foreign terms of trade are purely arbitrary, it follows that no *a priori* conclusions can be generated about the relative sizes of the trade creation and trade diversion effects. A welcome consequence of this has been the stimulus given to empirical studies of actual proposals for customs unions and free trade areas. Despite this gain, however, this formulation of the issue of customs union formation must be recognised as containing two crucial flaws.

Constraints on Policy Choice

The first of these is the failure of the approach to give explicit consideration to the basis of the determination of government policy and in particular to the existence of constraints on policy choice. It is perhaps a fair criticism of much economic analysis of government policy that inadequate attention has been paid to these issues but, at present, the most helpful approach seems to be based on the assumption that governments seek to maximise a social welfare function given the constraints that might affect policy choice. If all policy instruments are regarded as costlessly and freely variable, it would follow that governments would always employ a policy of optimal intervention, the basic principles of which are (a) that only 'first-best' policy instruments should be used to intervene at the exact points in the economy at which the problems exist which are preventing the market mechanism from producing the socially optimal result and (b) that such policy instruments should be set at the optimal rate in order to offset the problem exactly and so produce the desired result.

Since the basic models of customs union theory abstract from problems of time, uncertainty and money, the analysis here need identify only five policy instruments. Lump-sum income transfers are the first-best method for redistributing income and the assumption that these are being optimally used provides the basis for the derivation of the social indifference curves on which both demand functions and welfare judgements are based. Similarly, taxes (and subsidies) directed at factor use, at production and at consumption provide the first-best means of offsetting the externalities and market imperfections which arise, respectively, in the factor market, in production and in consumption. It is the (implicit) assumption of the previous analysis that these are also being optimally employed which enables the demand and supply curves of figure 4.1 to be used to convey information about the social as well as the private valuation of the costs and benefits of domestic production and consumption. As with the domestic policy instruments, it then follows that taxes (and subsidies) directed at international trade are also first-best policy instruments whose optimal use arises when (and only when) they are used to offset externalities (such as 'public good' arguments for greater national self-sufficiency) and market imperfections (such as monopoly power) which occur in international trade.

Given this picture of unconstrained optimal policy choice, it is a simple conclusion that, as no such foreign distortions are postulated in the standard model, the optimal tariff policy is one of free trade. Both the initial tariff and the policy of forming a customs union with the partner country are therefore not rational policy choices and the inconclusive result of the attempt to rank them should occasion little surprise.

This result, however, rests upon the assumption that all first-best policy instruments are freely and costlessly variable. If this assumption is abandoned, it is helpful to distinguish between constraints on domestic policies and constraints on trade policies. The latter will be considered subsequently but, initially, the argument will follow the attempts to rationalise customs union formation by the assumption of constraints on the use of domestic policies. These will be exemplified throughout this chapter by the assumption that the use of production taxes and subsidies is constrained though, by analogy, the resulting analysis could be applied to the loss of any other domestic first-best instrument.

The effect of this assumption is to introduce the possibility that the social and private valuation of costs of domestic production may differ. This is illustrated in figure 4.1 by the introduction of SS_x as the socially valued marginal cost curve of the domestic production of importables, whilst ss_x retains its earlier interpretation as the privately valued marginal cost or supply curve. With no constraints on policy choice, optimal intervention would involve the use of a production subsidy which would shift ss_x to coincide with SS_x. Given the assumed constraint, however, the optimal use of tariff policy changes. Imposing a tariff still brings about consumption effect losses and privately valued production effect losses, but it is now also necessary to take into account the difference between the social and the private valuation of marginal opportunity costs of production. Thus, in the case of the non-discriminatory tariff policy which raises the effective foreign supply curve of importables to the home market to $p^t d^t$, the consumption and privately valued production effects are measured as $bd^t d^w$ and $s^w s^t a$ respectively, as above. The socially valued production effect, however, is the net gain shown by area [9 and 10]. In the case illustrated, this gain exceeds the consumption loss and, indeed, the diagram has been drawn so that this non-discriminatory tariff represents the (second-best) optimal rate, such that the marginal consumption loss $(d^t b)$ is just equal to the marginal production gain (ac).

As I have pointed out elsewhere, however, the introduction of constraints on domestic policy choice in the home country is insufficient to enable the small country model to provide a rational justification for the formation of a customs union (Jones 1980). A full consideration of this problem involves distinguishing between the optimal effective preferential tariff policy and the formation of a customs union. By introducing two foreign economies into the theory of tariffs, customs union theory identified two policy instruments for optimal intervention in international trade — taxes (and subsidies) on trade with the partner and taxes (and subsidies) on trade with the rest of the world. Given the 'small country' assumption of fixed foreign terms of trade, the effect of any non-discriminatory policy is for all trade to be with the lower cost source of supply – the rest of the world. To have any effect on the source of trade it is necessary for the home country to adopt an effective preferential policy, such that the rate of duty on imports from the partner is lower than on those from the rest of the world by at least the difference in the terms of trade of the two foreign sources of supply (i.e. by at least $p^w p^u$). If there are no constraints on policy choice, this preferential policy need not involve the formation of a customs union (or a free trade area). Thus consider first the adoption of the minimal effective tariff preference to alter the pattern of trade. With a (specific) tariff duty of $p^w p^t$ on imports from the rest of the world, an effective preferential policy is achieved by imposing the (lower) tariff rate $p^u p^t$ on imports from the partner. The result of this is to leave the effective foreign supply curve of importables as $p^t d^t$ with domestic consumption and production the same as with the optimal non-discriminatory tariff. Given the preference, however, $p^t d^t$ is no longer solely the (tariff-inclusive) export supply curve of the rest of the world, but is also the (tariff-inclusive) export supply curve of the partner. Domestic consumers may therefore buy from either source and, to the extent that imports are diverted from the lower cost source of supply, the sole result of this for the home country is a reduction in tariff revenue. In the limit, if the tariff preference is just sufficient to divert all trade to the partner, the home country's tariff revenue loss is shown by area [4], i.e. it is equal to the Vinerian trade diversion effect. Compared to the optimal non-discriminatory policy, the granting of such a preference is thus an unambiguous source of loss to the home country. It is, however, superior to the form of preferential policy implied by membership of a customs union.

This can be seen by following the procedure first suggested by Cooper and Massell (1965) of introducing the alternative policy choice of the non-discriminatory reduction in the import tariff to the level (which will here be identified as the 'A' rate) at which the domestic terms of trade would be identical to those which would result from membership of the customs union. This 'A' tariff is shown in figure 4.1 as the specific rate $p^w p^u$. Comparison of this policy with joining the customs union again shows identical effects for the internal terms of trade, production, consumption, the volume of trade, and economic surplus. The sole difference between the two policies is that, with the non-preferential tariff policy, imports from the rest of the world yield tariff revenue measured by area [4 + 5 + 6] whereas, with the customs union, these imports are diverted to the tariff-free source, the partner.

Further, the net welfare effect of moving from the initial tariff to the 'A' rate is inevitably one of loss, since the initial tariff is here assumed to be the (second-best) optimal non-discriminatory tariff. Thus, compared to this optimal initial policy, the following welfare losses associated with different policy choices can be noted:

(a) the preferential lowering of the tariff on imports from the partner to the level $p^u p^t$, whilst retaining the tariff rate $p^w p^t$ on imports from the rest of the world, causes a maximum loss of tariff revenue equal to the Vinerian measure of trade diversion i.e. area [4] ;

(b) the unilateral non-discriminatory tariff reduction from the optimal rate, $p^u p^t$, to the 'A' rate, $p^w p^u$, results in a consumption effect gain, area [2 + 6], which is outweighed by the (socially valued) production effect loss, area [10] ; and

(c) membership of the customs union (or free trade area) with the initial tariff retained on imports from the rest of the world, whilst the tariff on imports from the partner is completely removed, involves the Cooper and Massell measure of trade diversion loss i.e. area [4 + 5 + 6], in addition to the loss identified in (b).

Thus membership of the customs union appears unambiguously worse than either (a) or (b), with these also being inferior to the initial position (which itself remains only a second-best choice depending for its validity on the existence of constraints on the use of domestic policy instruments).

Within this model, however, two routes do exist by which membership of a customs union may be justified. Both routes require the recognition of the existence of 'external' constraints on the choice of tariff policies, in addition to the constraints on domestic policies so far considered. These 'external' constraints reflect the provisions of international agreements and treaties which limit the choice of tariff policies and which are reinforced by the fear of international retaliation. In particular, signatories of GATT (General Agreement on Tariffs and Trade, a multilateral international treaty signed in 1947) agree to refrain from the discriminatory use of tariffs except in the case of membership of a customs union (or free trade area). Thus the optimal preferential policy may not be regarded as a realistic option for many countries and, with the distinction between customs unions and free trade areas being unimportant from the standpoint of the present argument, the only relevant comparison is that involving the formation of a customs union with the maintenance or reduction of the level of the existing non-discriminatory tariff. Given the assumptions so far made, this still leaves membership of a customs union as an inferior policy option, but this conclusion can now be reversed by introducing the further assumption that there are externalities in the form of public good benefits associated with trade with the partner (and/or public good losses associated with trade with the rest of the world). Such public good arguments make preferential trade taxes and subsidies a first-best policy choice and, whilst the external constraints on tariff policies rule out the use of such instruments, it is possible that the discrimination arising out of membership of a customs union may be a superior second-best alternative to any non-discriminatory tariff. Indeed, the original formation of the EEC may be partly explained in these terms, with the public good benefits of greater intra-European trade being viewed as a step towards the political goal of greater European unity and possibly also with public good losses being associated with at least marginal imports from the then dominant USA.

As an alternative to this essentially political justification for membership of a customs union, the recognition of 'domestic' constraints on tariff choice suggests a further possible explanation. The inertia and partial ignorance which pervades policy-making means that the initial non-discriminatory tariff may indeed be sufficiently above the optimal level for it to be inferior to membership of a customs union. In such a case, given the assumptions of the model so far employed, a policy of non-discriminatory tariff reduction is clearly superior to membership of a customs union. It is easy, however, to identify many domestic political forces which are resistant to the policy of unilateral tariff reduction and a modification of the assumptions so far employed can both suggest why this is so and why membership of a customs union may be acceptable.

The model illustrated in figure 4.1 is based on assumptions of perfect and costless mobility of factors between sectors so that, for example, as the domestic terms of trade fall from p^t to p^u and domestic supply of commodity x decreases, there is an immediate and costless reallocation of factors to the y-industry and an expansion of output in that industry equal to $x_s^u s^u s^t x_s^t$. Recognition of the delays and social costs involved in such reallocation, however, means that this increased production of y may not be immediately forthcoming and that there may be short-run unemployment and balance of payments difficulties as factors which have been shed from the x-industry fail to find immediate employment to increase production and exports of the y-industry. The existence of such real, even though short-run, adjustment costs is a powerful source of resistance to unilateral tariff cuts. Of course, similar adjustment costs may also be associated with the policy of joining a customs union and, if comparison is restricted to that between membership of a customs union and unilateral reduction of the tariff to the 'A' rate, it may appear that, as both involve exactly the same change in the domestic terms of trade, membership of a customs union would mean exactly the same adjustment costs and would remain an inferior choice because of the tariff revenue foregone. This follows, however, only because of the assumption that resource reallocation stems solely from actual changes in the domestic terms of trade facing producers. In a world without perfect knowledge, however, investment decisions are based on uncertainly held expectations of the future and it is arguable that the prospects of membership of a cutsoms union may provide earlier and clearer signals of the possibilities of expanding production and exports of the y-industry (for which the partner will be removing the tariff on imports from the home country whilst retaining it against possible imports from the rest of the world) than would the unilateral reduction of the home country's tariff. In turn, this may mean that the resultant saving in adjustment costs may outweigh the loss of tariff revenue when membership of the union is compared with the non-discriminatory 'A' tariff.

It is noticeable, however, that both these justifications for membership of a customs union go considerably beyond the normal confines of the 'small country' model and that, in particular, they give some emphasis to the role of the partner economy, either as a political friend or as a provider of preferential treatment in favour of the home country's exports. This points to the second crucial flaw in the standard model. In addition to paying no attention to the role of contraints on policy choice, it concentrates its attention so much on the consequences for the home country that it effectively excludes consideration of the effects that the home country's policy decisions may have on the partner and the rest of the world.

The 'Small Union' Model

To rectify this weakness, it is helpful to proceed initially by retaining the assumption that the terms of trade of the rest of the world are fixed, whilst recognising the existence of the partner as another small country which can be modelled in the same way as the home economy.

The resulting model is depicted in figure 4.2 with $e^*e^*_x$ in part (a) of the diagram being drawn as the partner's (tariff-free) export supply curve of x, derived from its domestic demand $(d^*d^*_x)$ and supply $(s^*s^*_x)$ curves drawn in part (b). If it is initially assumed that both countries are following first-best domestic policies, then the optimal tariff policy for both economies is free trade. Equally, acceptance of constraints on the use of first best domestic policies results in the second-best argument for non-discriminatory use of trade taxes. If both countries can in fact unilaterally adopt the second best optimal (non-discriminatory) level of trade taxes, any preferential tariff arrangement remains inferior. Thus, in the special case illustrated in figure 4.2, the optimal non-discriminatory tariff for both the home and the partner economy would be to raise their internal terms of trade to p^t. For the home country, an import tariff of the specific rate $p^w p^t$ would accomplish this, but the partner would require combining this import tariff with the same rate of export subsidy to be able to export $x^*_d x^*_s$ of x at the terms of trade offered by the rest of the world. The requirement, however, points to a further possible constraint on the use of trade taxes, since the use of export subsidies runs counter to the provisions of GATT and their use may well be constrained by the fear of international retaliation. In such circumstances, even if the partner sets its non-discriminatory tariff at the optimum level, without export subsidies the net outcome would be the inferior self-sufficiency position, p^*.

Compared with this situation the effect of the home country granting a preference to the partner may bring net benefits. This arises because, although the home country necessarily still loses through at least the trade diversion effect, the granting of the preference to the partner has significant welfare effects in the partner economy which may be larger than the net losses for the home economy. In order to simplify the illustration as far as possible, figure 4.2 has been constructed so that the optimal preferential policy consists of forming a customs union which has a common external tariff of the same height as the optimal non-discriminatory tariffs in both countries. A consequence of this is that the sole effect for the home country is the trade diversion loss of tariff revenue shown by area [4] .[2] The partner, on the other hand, obtains the privately valued gains in specialisation and exchange shown by area [1* + 2*] stemming from its exports of x to the

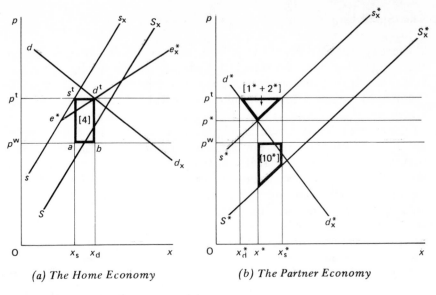

(a) The Home Economy   (b) The Partner Economy

Figure 4.2 *The 'Small Union' Model*

home country, plus the socially valued gain shown by area [10*] arising from increased production of that commodity. Since the partner's gains exceed the losses of the home country, the formation of the customs union is justified from the viewpoint of the combined membership of the union. The attractiveness of such a policy to the home country, however, would clearly depend on arrangements for a satisfactory *quid pro quo* to offset the inevitable loss that it suffers. (For similar conclusions see El-Agraa in Bowers 1979 and in El-Agraa and Jones 1980.) Again it is tempting to apply the analysis to the development of economic integration in Western Europe and, in particular, to the case of the UK application for membership with commodity *x* being regarded as agricultural products. The model in figure 4.2 then points to the unambiguous trade diversion loss to the UK associated with acceptance of the CAP[3] and thus to the need to identify a substantial gain arising from another aspect of UK membership of the EEC in order to justify UK entry.

One of the most widely canvassed sources of such gains rests upon the existence of economies of scale, rather than the constant or increasing costs postulated so far. Surprisingly little rigorous attention has been given to the problem but, following the analysis of Corden 1972, it is possible to examine the case for the formation of a customs union in the presence of economies of scale with the aid of figure 4.3.

Instead of the (privately valued) marginal cost curves of earlier

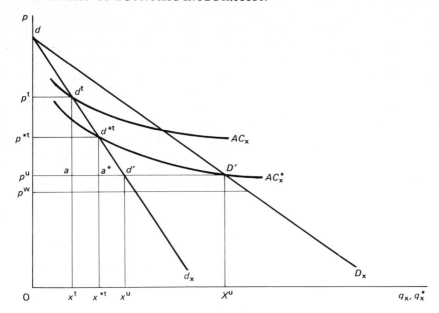

Figure 4.3 *Economies of Scale in the Small Union Model*

diagrams, it is helpful to represent the cost relationships in terms of the average (opportunity) cost of producing commodity x – shown by AC_x for the home country and AC_x^* for the partner. Again for the purposes of illustration, figure 4.3 represents a particularly simple case in which the internal demand curves of both the home country and the partner are identical, as shown by dd_x, with dD_x representing the combined demand curve after the union is formed. The given terms of trade of the rest of the world are again shown by p^w and it is assumed that, whatever the scale of production, neither the home nor the partner industry can produce with (privately valued) average costs at or below this level.[4] As with the previous models, unless the presence of an uncorrected distortion between privately and socially valued costs of production is introduced, the optimal policy for both countries is free trade, with no internal production of commodity x. The introduction of uncorrected distortions between social and private valuations of domestic production with the assumed unavailability of first-best domestic policy means for dealing with this can again produce a second-best justification for the use of a non-discriminatory tariff. In the case of falling costs, however, there is only one possible value for the second-best tariff — the 'made-to-measure' tariff. This is defined as the tariff which just enables domestic production to supply the domestic market without the opportunity to obtain monopoly profits and is thus shown as the tariff rate required to raise the foreign supply price to the point at which domestic average costs equal average revenue (given by the demand curve). Any higher tariff must be inferior since the loss of consumers' surplus and a reduced (socially valued) production effect gain must exceed any monopoly profit. Equally, any lower tariff would be unable to support domestic production and would therefore be inevitably inferior to a policy of free trade. Thus the justification of the made-to-measure tariff as the second-best optimal rate requires only that the socially valued production effect associated with its imposition outweighs the consumption effect loss compared with free trade.

In order to simplify figure 4.3, the socially valued average cost curves are not shown but, on the assumption that they are low enough in both economies to justify unilateral tariff intervention the second-best (made-to-measure) tariff rates are shown as $p^w p^t$ and $p^w p^{*t}$ for the home and partner countries respectively. Such tariffs, however, are not optimal from the viewpoint of the combined membership of the union. From the union viewpoint the optimal tariff policy is for the home and partner countries to form a customs union with a common external tariff set at the made-to-measure rate. In figure 4.3 this is shown as $p^w p^u$, with the result that the consumption effect in both economies must be one of gain.[5] Since in the diagram it is the partner's industry which is regarded as having lower costs, it also follows that the partner's industry takes over the whole union market and thus benefits from a socially valued production effect gain. On the other hand, with the usual assumptions about the nature of the distinction between social and private valuations of costs and about the location of national enterprises, it can be shown that, for the home country, the socially valued production effect loss will outweigh the consumption effect gain. Thus again therefore, the possibility of the formation of the customs union being formed depends not only on the net gain to the union as a whole, but on an adequate *quid pro quo* for the home country. The possibility of similar results can also be shown where initial production of x is in either one or neither of the member countries.

On the other hand, if the economies of scale are interpreted as economies accruing to an integrated industry, rather than from plant economies of scale or economies of scale internal to a national industry, the possibility exists that although the partner industry may gain control of the whole market, the location of some of its producing units may move to the home country. Thus, unless the socially valued production effects are necessarily linked with domestic ownership of the industry, it may be that the socially valued production effects might not be so adverse for the home economy and that the net outcome may even be net gain in the home as well as the partner economy, even without the arrangement of a *quid pro quo*. Nonetheless in the context of UK membership of the EEC, a Briton is left with the hope that it is the UK which most closely approximates the role of the more competitive partner economy, though the empirical support for such a hope seems sadly lacking.

Of course, it might appear even more relevant to point out that the only basis for these gains is the assumed constraint on domestic policies (as well as on trade taxes) and that it would be much better for all economies if sufficient political will was applied to the problem of removing the constraints on domestic policy choice. The economies of scale argument, however, does suggest a potentially more powerful case for economic integration. In the argument up to this point, externalities and market imperfections other than those which arise directly in international trade, have been regarded as being confined within each country. If this assumption is relaxed, the possibility exists of private decisions taken in one country having external effects not only within that economy but for other countries as well. From a wider, international viewpoint, even the optimal *national* use of first-best policies may then be sub-optimal. In such a case the first-best solution requires the establishment of international authorities with the power to use appropriate first-best policies. The optimal limits of the jurisdiction of such international authorities are determined in principle by the equality of the marginal benefits from 'internalising' such externalities and the marginal costs associated with setting up (and controlling) such international authorities. Of course, in many cases such costs may be very high, especially in a changing world in which optimal policy intervention will require the capacity for flexible response, and the scope for the delegation of first-best domestic policies to such international authorities has so far proved to be very limited. With international constraints on the use of tariff policies being more readily accepted, however, with the imperfect use of national policies to offset externalities and market imperfections which overflow national boundaries, and with such externalities being more significant among countries with close economic ties, it follows that a second-best case may exist for the formation of a customs union between closely linked economies. Such a case is analogous to the second-best case for the national use of tariffs in the presence of domestic distortions. Given the inability of the partners to adopt appropriate first-best policies to offset distortions which are internal to the union, the optimal use of a second-best instrument, such as the common external tariff, is justified.

The 'Large Union' Model

The final step in the development of customs union theory (discussed for example, by Arndt 1968) comes with the relaxation of the assumption of constant terms of trade in the rest of the world, with the resulting implication of the price-making powers of each separate economy. The immediate result of this is to place the argument in the context of oligopolistic interdependence, therefore introducing the possibility of exploring the problem of tariff-making within the format of whatever theory of oligopoly seems most appropriate. Although the few analyses which have extended the analysis of customs union theory to this (large union) case have not tackled this problem explicitly, the most useful assumption seems to be to treat the rest of the world as being unable to pursue a unified tariff policy in reaction to the decisions of the home and partner countries (thereby reflecting the diverse nature suggested by the naming of the third economy).[6]

Two main versions of the large union model can then be identified. The first of these is illustrated in figure 4.4 and extends the earlier arguments, in all of which the partner is treated as an actual or potential exporter of the home country's importables. This places the home country in the position of a monopsonist and, if it were not for the threat of retaliation, the optimal unilateral tariff policy would involve the imposition of different tariff rates on imports from the two sources so that the home country would, in effect be acting as a profit-maximising discriminating monopsonist. With this possibility eliminated by assumption, however, the optimal unilateral policy involves the imposition of a non-discriminatory tariff on imports set at the optimal rate, such that the marginal cost of obtaining imports is equated with their marginal value.

In figure 4.4 the home country's marginal valuation of imports is shown by the import demand curve, mm_x, whilst the average cost of obtaining imports is provided by the kinked (tariff-free) total foreign supply curve EE_x, which is obtained as the summation of the export supply curves of the partner $(e^* e_x^*)$ and the rest of the world $(e^w e_x^w)$. The marginal cost of obtaining imports is thus shown by $E'E_x'$ and the optimal non-discriminatory tariff (shown here for simplicity as a specific duty) is the non-discriminatory rate which raises the tariff-inclusive foreign supply to $E^t E_x^t$, i.e. to intersect mm_x at the same point as $E'E_x'$.[7] It follows from this that the tariff-inclusive export supply curves of the partner and the rest of the world are given by $e^{*t} e_x^{*t}$ and $p_1^w e_x^{wt}$ respectively, with the internal terms of trade being identified as p_0^t in the home country, p_0^* in the partner and p_0^w in the rest of the world.

As with the earlier illustrations, figure 4.4 has been drawn to

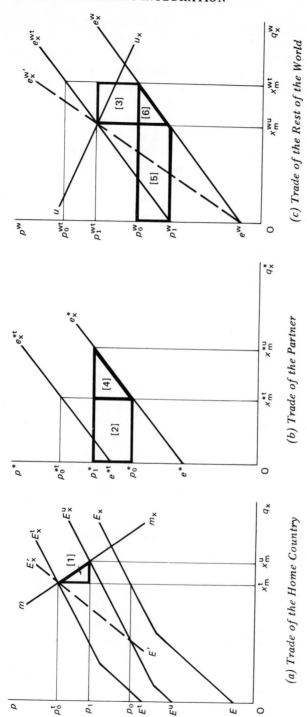

(a) Trade of the Home Country

(b) Trade of the Partner

(c) Trade of the Rest of the World

Figure 4.4 The 'Large Union' Model

represent a special case which simplifies the comparison of the optimal non-discriminatory policy with membership of a customs union. From the viewpoint of the union as a whole, it is the export supply curve $(e^w e_x^w)$ of the rest of the world which represents the average cost of obtaining imports of x, and it is the combination of the home country's import demand curve (mm_x) and the partner's export supply curve $(e^* e_x^*)$ which yields the union demand (and marginal valuation) curve (uu_x) for imports from the rest of the world. By analogy with the optimum tariff argument for the home country alone, it therefore follows that the optimal common external tariff from the viewpoint of the whole union is that which raises the tariff-inclusive export supply curve $(p_1^w e_x^{wt})$ to intersect the import demand curve (uu_x) at the same point as the marginal cost of imports curve $(e^w e_x^{w'})$. It follows, further, that the initial (optimal) tariff of the home country from its purely national viewpoint is equal (but only in the special case shown) to the optimal external tariff for the customs union judged from the combined viewpoint of the union as a whole. The effects of forming an optimal customs union can thus be compared with the optimal unilateral policy for the home country in this special case, simply by identifying the results which flow from the complete removal of the home country's initial tariff on imports from the partner, whilst retaining it on imports from the rest of the world. In terms of the positive effects, this policy change can be seen to shift the (policy-inclusive) total foreign supply of importables to the home market to the kinked curve $E^u E_x^u$, which is constructed as the summation of the tariff-free export supply curve of the partner $(e^* e_x^*)$ and the tariff-inclusive export supply curve of the rest of the world $(p_1^w e_x^{wt})$. The internal terms of trade of the partner rise to p_1^*. The change in trade for each country can be identified as corresponding to the volume of trade creation for the home country $(x_m^t x_m^u)$, the volume of trade creation for the partner economy $(x_m^{*t} x_m^{*u})$ and the volume of trade diverted $(x_m^{wu} x_m^{wt})$.

The welfare effects are identified by the numbered areas shown in the diagram and they can be named as follows:

[1] is the trade creation effect gain for the home country;
[2] is the terms of trade effect gain for the partner which is exactly equal to a loss (in tariff revenue) suffered by the home country;
[3] is the trade diversion effect loss for the home country and like (2), corresponds to a loss of tariff revenue on imports;
[4] is the trade creation effect gain for the partner;
[5] is the terms of trade effect loss for the rest of the world which corresponds exactly to a gain (in tariff revenue) for the home country; and

[6] is the trade diversion effect loss for the rest of the world.

Combining these effects produces several different viewpoints, the most obvious of which are those of the rest of the world which unambiguously loses, and the partner, which unambiguously gains. Less obviously, the union as a whole will also gain (providing that the common external tariff is optimal), but the net effects for both the home country and the whole world are uncertain. In the example shown, the home country is in fact a net loser, and this is probably the more likely outcome since a necessary (but not sufficient) condition for the home country to gain is that the elasticity of the partner's export supply curve should be lower than that of the export supply curve of the rest of the world. Indeed, as the controversy over the UK contribution to the EEC budget indicates, the home country's welfare will also be affected by what happens to the tariff revenue on the imports which it continues to obtain from the rest of the world If the revenue is not retained by the home country but is, at least in part, redistributed via a central budget to the partner, the balance of gain and loss shifts even further in favour of the partner and against the home country.

This may suggest again that the successful formation of the customs union will depend on appropriate arrangements for international compensating transfers being made but, whilst not wishing to reduce the significance of such issues, it should be recalled that the comparison is made with the situation in which the home country has adopted an optimal unilateral policy with no retaliation from the partner. If the partner, however, is also prepared to pursue an active tariff policy, it may be able to pose the threat of causing a greater loss to the home country than that arising from membership of the customs union, by itself pursuing a unilateral policy of imposing nationally optimal taxes on international trade without regard to the effect on other economies. As El-Agraa (1979) has pointed out, co-operation in tariff policies can be more attractive than retaliation. In the case of the formation of customs unions, the potential gains for members from co-operation stem not only from the benefits of free trade among members, but also from the gains of being able to exploit their joint power in the face of a passive tariff policy in the rest of the world.

From the global viewpoint, both the unilateral tariff policies of individual countries and the formation of customs unions are inevitably sub-optimal. Whilst the rest of the world is unable to react and to co-operate with the home and partner countries to arrive at a globally optimal solution based on full international co-operation, the possibility exists for groups of countries to obtain aggregate benefit for themselves by pursuing co-operation on a more limited scale. From the global viewpoint, therefore, developments such as the formation of the customs union of the EEC and the hesitant steps towards regional monetary integration must be judged as desirable or not to the extent to which they either facilitate or prevent co-operation on a wider international scale.

The 'large union' model has so far been exemplified by a very special case. It is easy to see, however, that the probability that the optimal common external tariff will be different from the optimal non-discriminatory tariff of the home country could be handled by an analysis which split the formation of the customs union into the two steps: (i) the adoption of the initial (optimal) tariff of the home country as the common external tariff and (ii) the change in the common external tariff to the rate which is optimal from the viewpoint of the union as a whole. Step (i) would then involve the same kind of effects as shown in figure 4.4, but would not necessarily bring net gain to the union, whilst step (ii) would bring net gains which would modify the effects identified in step (i) without introducing any different sources of welfare change. The only interesting possibility suggested by the extension of the simple case already analysed is that ignorance or external constraints may prevent step (ii). In this case the common external tariff would not be optimal, so that the justification for the formation of the union would then depend on the empirical evaluation of trade creation, trade diversion and terms of trade effects. Equally, it can be acknowledged that the initial national tariff may not be optimal and this possibility could also be taken into account by introducing the further step of considering the effects of the move from the initial tariff to the optimal non-discriminatory level. As in the 'small country' model, however, the gains accruing from such a step should not be attributed to economic integration, unless there were effective constraints preventing such unilateral action.

The alternative version of the large union case adds little new to the argument. In such a case, the optimal solution from the joint viewpoint of both economies again involves the co-operation required for the establishment of the optimal common tariff on imports – a policy outcome which corresponds to the joint monopoly profit-maximising solution of oligopoly theory. This can again provide a rationale for membership of a customs union and its application may also be relevant to the EEC, especially in the light of the evidence from Petith (1977) that terms of trade gains may have been a significant consequence of integration in Western Europe.

Summary

This survey of customs union theory suggests four principal conclusions. The first is that the rationale for regional economic integration rests upon the existence of constraints on the use of first-best policy instruments. Thus, in the case of the 'large union' model, the optimality of regional economic integration depends upon the inability or unwillingness of the rest of the world to co-operate successfully with member countries in obtaining globally optimal solutions. In the 'small union' and 'small country' models, further constraints must be recognised — on the domestic use of first-best policy instruments and on the unilateral use of export subsidies and preferential trade taxes. Economic analysis has had little to say about the nature of such constraints and presumably the evaluation of any regional scheme of economic integration should incorporate a consideration of the validity of the view that such constraints do exist to justify the pursuit of second- rather than first-best solutions.

Secondly, even when the existence of constraints on superior policy instruments is acknowledged, it is misleading to identify the results of regional economic integration by comparing an arbitrarily chosen common policy with an arbitrarily chosen national policy. Of course, ignorance and inertia provide sufficient reasons why existing policies may be non-optimal, but it is clearly wrong to attribute gains which would have been achieved by appropriate unilateral action to a policy of regional integration. Equally, although it is appropriate to use the optimal common policy as a point of reference, it has to be recognised that this may overstate the gains to be achieved if, as seems highly likely, constraints and inefficiencies in the political processes by which policies are agreed prove to be greater among a group of countries than within any individual country.

Although the first two conclusions raise doubts about the case for regional economic integration, in principle at least, a strong general case for economic integration does exist. As with the 'large union' model or the 'small union' model, in which economies of scale may be in part external to national industries, this case rests essentially upon the recognition of the externalities and market imperfections which extend beyond the boundaries of national states. In such circumstances, unilateral national action will not be optimal whilst integrated action offers the scope for potential gain.

As with the solution to most problems of externalities and market imperfections, however, customs union theory frequently illustrates that a major stumbling block to obtaining the gains from joint optimal action lies in agreeing an acceptable distribution of such gains. Thus the fourth conclusion is that the achievement of the potential gains from economic integration will be limited to countries able and willing to co-operate to distribute the gains from integration so that all partners may benefit compared to the results achieved by independent action. It is easy to argue from this that regional economic integration may be more easily achieved than global solutions but, as the debate about monetary integration in the EEC illustrates, the difficulties of obtaining potential mutual gain may well founder in the presence of disparate views about the distribution of such gains and weak arrangements for redistribution.

Notes

1　The only difference arises over the normal treatment of the expenditure of tariff revenue. Most of the formulations using the two-commodity techniques employ the assumption that this is redistributed to consumers who spend it, in the same manner as factor income, on both commodities. When demand and supply analysis is used, however, it is simpler to regard the tariff revenue as being returned solely in the form of the numeraire commodity (exportables).

2　It can be noticed that, in general, the optimal preferential policy from the joint viewpoint of both members is determined where the marginal net gains to the partner just equal the marginal net losses to the home country. Only in special cases will this involve the formation of a customs union but, given the assumed constraints on other forms of preferential policy, the argument here identifies the crucial comparison between optimal non-discriminatory policies and the optimal available preferential policy — formation of a customs union. It should also be noticed that the general comparison made here is not crucially dependent on the simplification that $e^*e^*_x$ intersects p^td^t at d^t. If the intersection had been to the left of d^t, the sole effect for the home currency would have been a diminished trade diversion loss, as some trade would have been retained with the rest of the world. On the other hand, if $e^*e^*_x$ had intersected dd_x below d^t, membership of the customs union would have also involved the further net losses associated with the move away from the terms of trade given by the optimum second-best tariff level — as analysed above in the small country model of customs union formation.

3　The actual loss may well be higher than this, both because the UK domestic agricultural policy had proved more able to use first-best policy instruments and because the actual CAP is far from being optimal, even on second best grounds. (For further discussion of the CAP see Chapter 7.)

4　If average costs of production do fall to the level given by the terms of trade of the rest of the world, domestic production (and exports) of commodity x can be achieved without protection.

5 Total consumption (equal to total production) in the union after it is formed is shown as X^u, with x^u being national consumption in both member countries. Accordingly, the consumption effect gain for the home country is $p^u p^t d^t d^u$ and for the partner is $p^u p^t d^{*t} d^u$. Of these gains, $p^u p^t d^t a$, and $p^u p^{*t} d^{*t} a^*$ are 'cost reduction' effects and, in general, may be significantly larger than the triangle-like areas of gain under demand curves which are the sole components of the consumption effect in the increasing opportunity cost models and which are also present in this case, as shown by areas $a d^t d^u$ (for the home country) and $a^* d^{*t} d^u$ (for the partner). To simplify the diagram, the socially valued production effects are not identified but they pose no difficulties being given, in principle, by comparison of the volume of production multiplied by the amount by which socially valued average costs fall below the world price level before and after the formation of the union.

6 It will continue to be assumed however, that fear of retaliation will restrain both the home and partner from any other policy choices than those of non-discriminatory tariffs and full membership of a customs union.

7 It can be noted that, in *ad valorem* terms, this optimal rate can be expressed as $(M - A)/A$, where M and A represent the marginal and average cost of obtaining imports respectively. Since it is a well known result that $(M - A)/A = 1/\eta$ where η is the elasticity of the A curve, it follows that this optimal rate is identified as equal to the reciprocal of the elasticity of the foreign supply curve — a familiar result which has surely attracted more attention than it deserves as its practical significance is at best limited to the case of log-linear functions.

References

Arndt, S.W., On discriminatory versus non-preferential tariff policies, *The Economic Journal*, vol. 78, 1968.

Balassa, B., Trade creation and trade diversion in the European common market, *The Economic Journal*, vol. 77, 1967.

Bhagwati, J., Customs unions and welfare improvement, *The Economic Journal*, vol. 81, 1971.

Bowers, J.K. (ed.), *Inflation, Development and Integration: Essays in Honour of A.J. Brown*, Leeds University Press, 1979.

Cooper, C.A. and Massell, B.F., A new look at customs union theory, *The Economic Journal*, vol. 75, 1965.

Corden, W.M., Economies of scale and customs union theory, *Journal of Political Economy*, vol. 80, 1972.

El-Agraa, A.M., On optimum tariffs, retaliation and international co-operation, *The Bulletin of Economic Research*, May 1979.

El-Agraa, A.M. and Jones, A.J., *The Theory of Customs Unions*, Philip Allan 1980.

Johnson, H.G., Trade-diverting customs unions: a comment, *The Economic Journal*, vol. 84, 1974.

Jones, A.J., Domestic distortions and customs union theory, *The Bulletin of Economic Research*, May 1980.

Lipsey, R.G., The theory of customs unions: a general survey, *The Economic Journal*, vol. 70, 1960.

Petith, H.C., European integration and the terms of trade, *The Economic Journal*, vol. 81, 1971.

5

Measuring the Impact of Economic Integration

A M EL-AGRAA

A growing area of research in the field of international economic integration is concerned with the measurement of the impact of the formation of the EEC and EFTA on the economies of member states and on the outside world. The purpose of this chapter is to explain the nature of the problem, to evaluate the attempts at measurement that have so far been made and to suggest an alternative approach.

Nature of the Problem

It is extremely important to comprehend the nature of the methodology of measuring the impact of international economic integration in order to appreciate the difficulties associated with such measurements.

Assume that the world is constituted of three mutually exclusive and collectively exhaustive areas: the EEC, EFTA and the rest of the world (W). The object of the exercise is to contrast the world trade matrix[1] Y as it appears in year t (indicated by a subscript), with the situation that would have materialised in year t if the EEC and EFTA had not been formed. The latter is referred to as the 'anti-monde' — alternative world in which all events except one are identical — or non-integration position. The differences between this hypothetical position and the actual position can then be attributed to:

(a) trade creation: the substitution of cheaper imports from the partner country for expensive domestic production;

(b) trade diversion: the replacement of cheap *initial* imports from non-partners by expensive imports from a partner country;

(c) external trade creation: the replacement of expensive domestic production by cheaper imports from a non-partner country due to a reduction in the common external tariff rate which is necessary in a customs union but not in a free trade area;

(d) 'supply-side diversion; i.e. the replacement of exports to non-partners by exports to partners'[2]; and

(e) balance of payments induced adjustments due to (a)–(d) which are made necessary for equilibrating purposes.

Let us adopt the notation used by Williamson and Bottrill where:

c_{ii} = intra-ith area trade creation;

d_{ij} = diversion of the ith area's imports from area j;

d_{ii} = $\sum_{j \neq i} d_{ij}$ = diversion of ith area's imports (to area i);

e_{ij} = increase in i's imports from j caused by external trade creation;

e_i = $\sum_{j} e_{ij}$ = total external trade creation of area i;

r_{ij} = increase in i's imports from j caused by balance of payments reactions;

s_{ij} = reduction in j's exports to i caused by supply-side constraints;

x_{ij} = (hypothetical) imports of area i from area j in the non-integration position;

x_i = $\sum_{j} x_{ij}$ = (hypothetical) imports of area i in the non-integration position;

y_{ij} = actual imports of area i from area j;

y_i = $\sum_{j} y_{ij}$ = actual imports of area i.

The world trade matrix Y is:

	Exports by			
	EEC	EFTA	W	Total
EEC	y_{11}	y_{12}	y_{13}	y_1
Imports of EFTA	y_{21}	y_{22}	y_{23}	y_2
W	y_{31}	y_{32}	y_{33}	y_3

The world trade matrix can be disaggregated to show the various effects that followed the formation of the EEC and EFTA. Both these areas could have led to internal trade creation and/or could have diverted imports from W. Also, the EEC may have been responsible for external trade creation (in the partner-countries that levelled down their external tariff rates) and external trade destruction (in the low-tariff partner-countries who raised their external tariff rates to the level of the common external tariff rates). 'The attractions of partners' markets may have directed some EEC and EFTA exports away from non-partners' markets, but this effect may have been partially, wholly, or more than fully offset by the greater competitiveness of exports from those blocs resulting from the advantages of a larger "home" market.' (Williamson and Bottrill 1971, pp. 324–325.) Also, every trade flow in the matrix may have been affected by reactions made necessary in order to re-equilibrate payments positions.

The Y matrix can be disaggregated to show all these changes:

$$
\begin{bmatrix} y_{11} & y_{12} & y_{13} \\ y_{21} & y_{22} & y_{23} \\ y_{31} & y_{32} & y_{33} \end{bmatrix} =
$$

$$
\begin{bmatrix} x_{11} + c_{11} + d_{11} + r_{11} & x_{12} - d_{12} + e_{12} - s_{12} + r_{12} & x_{13} - d_{13} + e_{13} + r_{13} \\ x_{21} - d_{21} - s_{21} + r_{21} & x_{22} + c_{22} + d_{22} + r_{22} & x_{23} - d_{23} + r_{23} \\ x_{31} - s_{31} + r_{31} & x_{32} - s_{32} + r_{32} & x_{33} + r_{33} \end{bmatrix} \quad (1)
$$

Most of the studies in this field have disregarded some of these effects, particularly the supply-side constraints and the balance of payments re-equilibrating reactions. This amounts to assuming that s_{ij} and v_{ij} are equal to zero. This leads to the much simpler framework:

$$
\begin{bmatrix} y_{11} & y_{12} & y_{13} \\ y_{21} & y_{22} & y_{23} \\ y_{31} & y_{32} & y_{33} \end{bmatrix} = \begin{bmatrix} x_{11} + c_{11} + d_{11} & x_{12} - d_{12} + e_{12} & x_{13} - d_{13} + e_{13} \\ x_{21} - d_{21} & x_{22} + c_{22} + d_{22} & x_{23} - d_{23} \\ x_{31} & x_{32} & x_{33} \end{bmatrix} \quad (2)
$$

This implies that:

$$
y_i = x_i + c_{ii} + e_i
$$

Even though this methodology is very useful for analysing the overall effects of the formation of the EEC and EFTA, it is inadequate for analysing the effects on particular countries. For example, the method cannot provide information about the consequences for the UK of membership of the EEC. In order to deal with this problem, it is necessary to alter the matrix so as to allow for at least two areas for each of the EEC and EFTA. This would provide the freedom to investigate the impact of the formation of EFTA and the EEC on one member of the EEC (UK), on that country's relationship with EFTA, with a particular member of EFTA (Norway) and with the rest of the world. Hence, the matrix should look like this:

		Exports by					
		EEC		EFTA		W	Total
		(1)	(2)	(3)	(4)		
		UK	Rest of EEC	Norway	Rest of EFTA		
Imports of	EEC	(1) y_{11}	y_{12}	y_{13}	y_{14}	y_{15}	y_1
		(2) y_{21}	y_{22}	y_{23}	y_{24}	y_{25}	y_2
	EFTA	(3) y_{31}	y_{32}	y_{33}	y_{34}	y_{35}	y_3
		(4) y_{41}	y_{42}	y_{43}	y_{44}	y_{45}	y_4
	W	(5) y_{51}	y_{52}	y_{53}	y_{54}	y_{55}	y_5

Disaggregating in terms of trade creation, trade diversion and external trade creation (assuming $s_{ij} = 0$ and $r_{ij} = 0$) gives:

$$\begin{bmatrix} y_{11} & y_{12} & y_{13} & y_{14} & y_{15} \\ y_{21} & y_{22} & y_{23} & y_{24} & y_{25} \\ y_{31} & y_{32} & y_{33} & y_{34} & y_{35} \\ y_{41} & y_{42} & y_{43} & y_{44} & y_{45} \\ y_{51} & y_{52} & y_{53} & y_{54} & y_{55} \end{bmatrix} =$$

$$\begin{bmatrix} \underline{\quad\quad} & x_{12} + c_{12} + d_{12} & x_{13} - d_{13} + e_{13} & x_{14} - d_{14} + e_{14} & x_{15} - d_{15} + e_{15} \\ x_{21} + c_{21} + d_{21} & \underline{\quad\quad} & x_{23} - d_{23} + e_{23} & x_{24} - d_{24} + e_{24} & x_{25} - d_{25} + e_{25} \\ x_{31} - d_{31} & x_{32} - d_{32} & \underline{\quad\quad} & x_{34} + c_{34} + d_{34} & x_{35} - d_{35} \\ x_{41} - d_{41} & x_{42} - d_{42} & x_{43} + c_{43} + d_{43} & \underline{\quad\quad} & x_{45} - d_{45} \\ x_{51} & x_{52} & x_{53} & x_{54} & x_{55} \end{bmatrix}$$

$$(4)$$

The matrix could of course be made more suitable for studying the impact of the formation of the EEC and EFTA on particular areas of the rest of the world, e.g. the impact of UK membership of the EEC on imports from New Zealand. This can easily be done by an appropriate breakdown of W. The most significant consideration that remains is the effect of the formation of the EEC and EFTA on their economies and on the outside world.

Thus the problem of measuring the impact of economic integration relates to the empirical calculation of the indicated changes in the world trade matrix. However, it seems evident that any sensible approach to the analysis of these changes should have the following characteristics:

(a) it should be capable of being carried out at the appropriate level of disaggregation;
(b) it should be able to distinguish between trade creation, trade diversion and external trade creation;

(c) it should be capable of discerning the effects of economic growth on trade that would have taken place in the absence of economic integration;

(d) it should be 'analytic': it should be capable of providing an economic explanation of the actual post-integration situation;

(e) it should be a general equilibrium approach capable of allowing for the effects of economic integration on an interdependent world.

Previous Studies

A truly comprehensive survey of previous studies is not available in any single source, but the works of Louvain University (1963), Balassa (1975), Sellekaerts (1973), Aitken (1973), the Dayals (1977), Waelbroeck (1977), and Mayes (1978) between them come very close to it. There is therefore no need to add to these existing sources. However, a few general comments may be in order.

Most of the measurements can be broadly classified as *ex ante* or *ex post*. The *ex ante* estimates are based on *a priori* knowledge of the pre-integration period (i.e. structural models) while the *ex post* studies are based on assumptions about the actual experience of economic integration (i.e. residual-imputation models).

There are two types of *ex ante* studies: those undertaken before the EEC and EFTA were actually operative and those undertaken after they became operative.[3] The most influential studies to use this approach are those of Krause (1968) who predicted the trade diversion that would be brought about by the EEC and EFTA on the basis of assumptions about demand elasticities, and Han and Leisner (1970) who predicted the effect on the UK by identifying those industries that had a comparative cost advantage/disadvantage *vis-à-vis* the EEC and finding out how they were likely to be affected by membership, on the assumption that the pattern of trade prior to UK membership provided an indication of the underlying cost conditions and that this would be one of the determinants of the pattern of trade and domestic production after membership. This approach is of very limited advantage, however, for the simple reason that 'it does not provide a method of enabling one to improve previous estimates on the basis of new historical experience' (Williamson and Bottrill 1971, p.326).

The most significant studies to use the *ex post* approach are those of Lamfalussy, Verdoorn and Meyer zu Schlochtern (1964), who all use a relative shares method; Balassa (1967 and 1975), who uses an income-elasticity of import demand method;[4] the EFTA Secretariat, who use a share of imports in apparent consumption method;[5]

Williamson and Bottrill, who use a more sophisticated share analysis;[6] Prewo, who uses an input-output method;[7] and Barten *et al.*, who use a medium-term macroeconomic method.[8] The advantage of the *ex post* method is that it can be constructed in such a way as to benefit from historical experience and hence to provide a basis for continuous research. However, the major obstacle in this approach concerns the difficulty regarding the construction of an adequate hypothetical post-integration picture of the economies concerned.

A Critique of Previous Studies

There are some general and some specific points of criticism to be made of these studies. Let me start with the general points.

(a) All the studies, excepting the Truman (1975) and the Williamson and Bottrill (1971) studies and to a certain extent the Aitken (1973) and Mayes (1978) studies, assume that the formation of the EEC (or EFTA) has been the sole factor to influence the pattern of trade. Since the EEC and EFTA were established more or less simultaneously (there is a year's difference between them), it is unjustifiable to attribute changes in the pattern of trade to either alone. After all, EFTA was established in order to counteract the possible damaging effects of the EEC!

(b) Most of the recent studies ignore the fact that Britain used to be a member of EFTA before joining the EEC. Since the UK is a substantial force as a member of either area, it seems misleading to attempt estimates which do not take into consideration this switch by the UK. This point of course adds force to the previous one.

(c) In the period prior to the formation of the EEC and EFTA, certain significant changes were happening on the international scene. The most significant of these is that the discrimination against the US dollar was greatly reduced. Is it at all possible that such developments had no effect whatsoever on the trade patterns of the EEC and EFTA? It seems unrealistic to assume that this should have been the case.

(d) All the studies, except for Truman (1975), deal with trade data and this is in spite of the fact that a proper evaluation of the effects of economic integration requires analysis of both trade and production data. Trade creation indicates a reduction in domestic production combined with new imports of the same quantity from the partner, while trade diversion indicates new imports from the partner combined with less imports from the outside world *and* a reduction in the rest of the world's production.

(e) Tariffs are universally recognised as only one of many trade impediments, yet all the studies, except Prewo (1974), are based on the assumption that the only effect of economic integration in Western Europe is on discriminatory tariff removal. This is a very unsatisfactory premise, particularly if one recalls that the EEC had to resort to explicit legislation against cheap imports from India, Japan and Pakistan! Moreover:

> As has long been known, the level of tariffs is more difficult to measure than it would seem at first sight. Tariff schedules are public, but their interpretation is often made difficult by peculiar institutional clauses. Furthermore, it is difficult to obtain a good measure of the restrictive impact of tariffs. Average tariff rates will not do, for, if the rate is zero on one good and prohibitive on another, the average tariff is zero. It is necessary to use *a priori* weights, which inevitably is arbitrary ... [Others] raised a more subtle issue by proposing to use input-output analysis to measure the effective *rates of protection* achieved by tariffs on value added. This approach raises a host of problems. The assumptions of fixed technical coefficients and of perfectly competitive price adjustments are both debatable. It is clear that the concept of effective protection ... relies on oversimplified assumptions.
>
> (Waelbroeck 1977, p. 89)

(f) The Dillon and the Kennedy rounds of tariff negotiations resulted in a global tariff reduction which coincided with the first stage of the removal of tariffs. This point lends support to the previous one.

More specifically, however:

(a) In all these studies, the integration effect, whether trade creation or trade diversion, is estimated by the difference between actual imports and extrapolated imports for a post-integration year. The extrapolation of imports is done by a time trend of imports or by relating imports with income or consumption in the importing country. The difference between the actual and estimated imports would be due to (i) autonomous changes in prices in the supplying and importing countries, (ii) changes in income, consumption or some other variable representing macroeconomic activity, (iii) changes in variables other than income/consumption and autonomous price movements, (iv) revision of tariffs and/or other barriers as a result of integration, and (v) residual errors due to the random error term in the estimating equation, misspecification of the form of the equation, errors in data, omission or misrepresentation of certain variables etc. The studies ... try to segregate the effect of (ii) only. The remaining difference between the actual and estimated imports would be due to (i), (iii), (iv) and (v), but it is ascribed only to (iv), i.e., the effect of revision of tariff and/or other barriers to trade as a result of integration. Clearly, it is a totally unreliable way of estimating the integration effect on trade creation or trade diversion. Even if prices are included as an additional variable in the estimating equation, it would amount to segregating the effect of (i) and (ii), so that the difference between the actual and estimated imports would be due to (iii), (iv) and (v). It would still be wrong to ascribe it to (iv) only. The error term at (v) is often responsible for a divergence of ± 10% between the actual and estimated imports, which might often over-shadow the effect of integration. For this reason, the 'residual method' used by Balassa, the EFTA Secretariat and many others, is highly unreliable for estimating the trade creation and trade diversion effects of integration.

(Dayal, R. & N. 1977, pp. 136–7)

(b) The integration effect, whether trade creation or trade diversion, takes place in two stages: the effect of tariff changes on prices and the effect of price changes on trade. These two effects need to be separately estimated, before the trade creation and trade diversion effects of integration can be arrived at.

(Dayal, R. & N. 1977, p. 137)

(c) The accuracy of the *ex ante* forecasts of trade effects depends on the reliability of the price elasticities that are used. In addition to this general problem, a key issue is whether the effect of a tariff is the same as that of an equivalent price change . . . Tariff elasticities substantially exceed the usual import-demand elasticities. The elimination of a tariff is perceived by business as irreversible . . .

(Waelbroeck 1977, p. 90)

It therefore seems inevitable to conclude that:

All estimates of trade creation and diversion by the EEC which have been presented in the empirical literature are so much affected by *ceteris paribus* assumptions, by the choice of the length of the pre- and post- integration periods, by the choice of benchmark year (or years), by the methods to compute income elasticities, changes in trade matrices and in relative shares and by structural changes not attributable to the EEC but which occurred during the pre- and post-integration periods (such as the trade liberalization amongst industrial countries and autonomous changes in relative prices that the magnitude of no . . . estimate should be taken too seriously.

(Sellekaerts 1973, p. 548)

Moreover, given the validity of my criticisms, one should not take seriously such statements as:

There are a number of studies that have reported on attempts to construct such estimates. Individually the various methods must be judged unreliable, and the same is true of a new method developed in the present paper. But collectively the available evidence is capable of indicating conclusions of about the same degree of reliability as is customary in applied economics. That is to say, there is a wide margin of uncertainty about the correct figure, but the order of magnitude can be established with reasonable confidence.

(Williamson and Bottrill 1971, p. 323)

It is difficult to see the collective virtue in individual misgivings!

The Alternative

It seems evident that there is nothing wrong with the methodology, but that the problems of actual measurement are insurmountable. However, I do believe that these difficulties are due to some basic misconceptions regarding the welfare implications of trade creation and trade diversion: trade creation is good and trade diversion is bad — using the Johnson (1974) definition.

In an interdependent macroeconomic world, trade creation is inferior to trade diversion for the country concerned (see El-Agraa 1978) and both are certainly detrimental to the outside world. This conclusion is also substantiated by Johnson's work which incorporates the collective consumption of a public good — Johnson (1965). It therefore seems rather futile to attach too much significance to the welfare implications of the trade creation/diversion dichotomy. Moreover:

> ... trade creation and trade diversion ... are static concepts. Their effects are once-for-all changes in the allocation of resources. At any date in the future their effects must be measured against what *would otherwise have been*, not by what is happening to trade at that time. In the economic theorist's model without adjustment lags, the introduction of a scheme for regional integration causes a once-for-all shift to more intra-integrated area trade and less trade with the outside world, and the forces that *subsequently* influence the allocation of resources become once again cost changes due to technological advance, and demand changes due to differing income elasticities of demand as real income rises as a result of growth [,] ... call the first set of forces affecting the allocation of resources *integration induced* and the second set *growth induced* ... The two sets of forces ... are intermixed (the problem becomes even more complex conceptually if integration itself affects the growth rate). The more sudden the integration, the more likely it is that integration induced effects will dominate, at least for the first few years; but the longer the time lapse the more would normal growth-induced effects dominate. The morals are: (1) the longer the time since a relatively sudden move towards integration, the harder it is to discern the effects by studying changes in the patterns of trade; and (2) the more gradually the integration measures are introduced, the more will the effects be mixed up, even in the short term, with growth induced effects.
>
> (Lipsey 1977, pp. 37—38)

For all these reasons I suggest that the measurement of the impact of economic integration should be confined to estimating its effect on intra-union trade and, if possible, to finding out whether or not any changes have been at the expense of the outside world. The statistical procedure for such estimates should be straightforward if one uses my interdependent global macro model and incorporates into it the import demand functions suggested by the Dayals (1977). One can then utilise the concepts of income and substitution effects (suggested by the Dayals) without some of the unnecessary detail created by using simple marginal utility functions. (The model and the estimates should be ready in the near future.)

For what it is worth, it can be stated that (according to Balassa, Williamson and Bottrill) intra-EEC trade in 1969 was about 50% more than it would have been had the EEC not been formed, and that this increase was partly due to trade creation and partly to trade diversion. Moreover, even though the outside world suffered from EEC trade diversion, it gained from external trade creation, but not to the same extent.

Notes

1 An equivalent world production matrix is also necessary, see (a)–(e).
2 'It is possible that the fast growth of EEC and EFTA intra-trade in the years immediately following their formation (and also of EEC intra-trade in 1969) was particularly at the expense of slower growth in exports to . . . [W]. There is no conclusive evidence as to whether this was an important factor. In the long run, however, one would expect supply bottlenecks to be overcome, and one might also expect their effect to be counteracted by the greater competitive strength resulting from a larger 'home market'. We therefore follow a well-established precedent in assuming $s_{ij} = 0$ (no supply-side diversion exists).' (Williamson and Bottrill 1971, p. 325)
3 See for instance, Verdoorn 1954, Janssen 1961, and Krause and Salant 1973.
4 'Ex-post income elasticities of import demand were defined as the ratio of the average annual rate of change of imports to that of GNP, both expressed in constant prices. Under the assumption that income elasticities of import demand would have remained unchanged in the absence of integration, a rise in the income elasticity of demand for intra-area imports would indicate gross trade creation – increases in intra-area trade – irrespective of whether this resulted from substitution for domestic or for foreign sources of supply. In turn, a rise in the income elasticity of demand for imports from all sources taken together would give expression of trade creation proper, i.e. a shift from domestic to partner-country sources. Finally, trade diversion, a shift from foreign to partner-country producers, would be indicated by a decline in the income elasticity of demand for extra-area imports'. (Balassa 1975, p. 80)
5 The EFTA Secretariat's study is based on the assumption that had EFTA not been established, the import shares in the apparent consumption of a particular commodity in any of the EFTA countries would have developed in the post-integration period in precisely the same fashion as they had during the pre-integration period 1954–9. (See EFTA Secretariat 1969 and 1972.)

6 'We believe that the most promising hypothesis is that originally introduced
by Lamfalussy. According to this, the share performance of the jth supplier
in markets where he neither gains nor loses preferential advantages gives a
good indication of his hypothetical performance in markets which were in
fact being affected by integration. In terms of the present analysis, the rest
of the world provides a control which indicates what share performance
would have been in EEC and EFTA markets if these two organizations had
not been formed.' (Williamson and Bottrill 1971, p. 333) The methods
selected are: (a) using an *a priori* formula which ensures that the predicted
gain in market shares will be small if the previous market share was either
very small or very large; (b) extrapolating from a regression of data on
relative export shares; and (c) assuming that market shares would have
remained constant in the absence of economic integration.

7 Prewo (1974) uses a gravitational model which links the national input-
output tables of the EEC countries by a system of trade equations. In
this model, trade between members of the EEC is assumed to be proportional to demand in the importing, and supply in the exporting, country
and inversely proportional to trade impediments, whereas extra-area
imports are assumed to be related to demand in the EEC countries. In this
model, changes in final demand have a direct effect on imports of final
goods, as well as an indirect effect through their impact on the imports
of inputs for domestic production.

　　The basis of the analysis is that the 'difference between the actual trade
flows of the customs union and the hypothetical trade flows of the customs
union's anti-monde is taken to be indicative of the integration effects.'
(Prewo 1974, p. 380)

8 'It basically consists of eight similarly specified country models which are
linked by *bilateral trade equations* and equations specifying the formation
of import and export prices.' (Barten *et al.* 1976, p. 63)

References

Aitken, N. D., The effects of the EEC and EFTA on European trade: a temporal
cross-section analysis, *American Economic Review*, vol. 68, 1973.

Balassa, B., Trade creation and trade diversion in the European Common Market,
The Economic Journal, March 1967.

Balassa, B., *European Economic Integration*, North-Holland Publishing Co. 1975.

Barten, A. P. *et al.*, COMET: a medium-term macroeconomic model for the
European Economic Community, *European Economic Review*, vol. 7, 1976.

Clavaux, F. J., The import elasticity as a yardstick for measuring trade creation,
Economia Internazionale, November 1969.

Dayal, R. and N., Trade creation and trade diversion: new concepts, new methods
of measurement, *Weltwirtschaftliches Archiv*, vol. 113, 1977.

El-Agraa, A. M., On trade diversion, *Leeds Discussion Paper*, No. 66, 1978.

El-Agraa, A. M., On trade creation, *Leeds Discussion Paper*, No. 67, 1978.

El-Agraa, A. M., Can economists provide a rationale for customs union formation?, *Leeds Discussion Paper*, No. 68, 1978.

Han, S. S. and Leisner, H. H., *Britain and the Common Market*, University of
Cambridge, Department of Applied Economics, Occasional Paper No. 27,
1970.

Janssen, L. H., *Free Trade, Protection and Customs Union*, Economisch Sociologisch Instituut, Leiden, 1961.

Johnson, H. G., Trade-diverting customs unions: a comment, *The Economic Journal*, Sept. 1974.

Johnson, H.G., An economic theory of protectionism, tariff bargaining and the formation of customs unions, *The Journal of Political Economy*, vol. 73, 1965

Krause, L.B., *European Economic Integration and the United States*, The Brookings Institution, Washington DC, 1968.

Krause, L.B. and Salant, W.S. (eds), *European Economic Integration and the United States*, vol. 53, The Brookings Institution, Washington DC, 1973.

Kreinin, M. E., On the dynamic effects of a customs union, *The Journal of Political Economy*, vol. 72, 1964.

Kreinin, M. E., Trade creation and diversion by the EEC and EFTA, *Economica Internazionale*, May 1969.

Kreinin, M. E., Effects of the EEC on imports of manufactures, *The Economic Journal*, vol. 82, 1972.

Lamfalussy, A., Intra-European trade and the competitive position of the EEC. *Manchester Statistical Society Transactions*, March 1963.

Lipsey, R.G., Comments, in Machlup, 1977, pp. 37—40.

Machlup, F., *Economic Integration, Worldwide, Regional, Sectoral*, Macmillan 1977.

Major, R. L., The Common Market: production and trade, *National Institute Economic Review*, August 1962.

Major, R.L., World trade in manufactures, *National Institute Economic Review*, July 1960.

Major, R.L. and Hays, S., Another look at the Common Market, in University of Louvain, *The Market Economy in Western European Integration*, 1963.

Mayes, David G., The effects of economic integration on trade, *Journal of Common Market Studies*, vol. XVII, No 1, Sept. 1978.

Prewo, W. E., Integration effects in the EEC, *European Economic Review*, vol. 5, 1974.

Sellekaerts, W., How meaningful are empirical studies on trade creation and diversion?, *Weltwirtschaftfliches Archiv*, vol. 109, 1973.

Truman, E.M., The European Economic Community: trade creation and trade diversion, *Yale Economic Essays*, Spring 1969.

Truman, E.M., The effects of European economic integration on the production and trade of manufactured products, in Balassa 1975.

University of Louvain, *The Market Economy in Western European Integration*, Louvain, 1963.

Uribe, P., Theil, H. and De Leeuw, C. G., The information approach to the prediction of interregional trade flows, *The Review of Economic Studies*, July 1966.

Verdoorn, P. J., A customs union for western Europe: advantages and feasibility, *World Politics*, vol. 6, 1954.

Verdoorn, P.J., and Meyer zu Schlochtern, F.J.M., Trade creation and trade diversion in the Common Market, in Collège d'Europe, *Intégration européenne et réalité économique*, Bruges, 1974.

Waelbroeck, J., Measuring the degree or progress of economic integration, in Machlup 1977.

Walter, I., *The European Common Market,* Praeger 1967.
Williamson, J. and Bottrill, A., The impact of customs unions on trade in manufactures, *Oxford Economic Papers,* vol. 25, No. 3, July 1971.

EFTA Secretariat, *The Effects of the EFTA on the Economies of Member States,* Geneva, 1969.
EFTA Secretariat, *The Trade Effects of the EFTA and the EEC 1959–1967,* Geneva, 1972.

Part II Appendix:
The State of
the Customs Union

A M EL-AGRAA

Since this section of the book is concerned with the customs union aspects of the EEC (the elimination of intra-EEC trade impediments and the establishment of the CET i.e. Common External Tariff), it seems appropriate to conclude it with a short account of their achievement by the EEC.

The Treaty of Rome called for the abolition during the period of transition (Article 13) of customs duties on members' imports in force at the time of signing. According to the Treaty (Article 8), the arrangements specified were to be accomplished within twelve years starting from 1 January 1958, i.e. by 31 December 1969. The period of transition (which was itself a subject of great discussion, particularly since France was very anxious to secure its accomplishment within the specified period) was divided into three stages of four years each. Each stage was to include progressive reductions of intra-EEC tariffs, as well as bring national tariffs closer to the CET level.

The Treaty also called for the abolition of intra-EEC import quotas. This had in fact been partially attained before the Treaty came into effect through the measures of trade liberalisation achieved earlier by the IMF, GATT and the OEEC.

In addition, the Treaty called for the establishment of the CET and specified that it should be set at the level of the arithmetical average of the tariffs in force on imports from the outside world (Article 19). The tariffs taken as the basis for calculating the arithmetical average were those operated by the EEC partners on 1 January 1957.

Table A.1 (a) details the elimination of intra-EEC tariffs on industrial products and table A.1 (b) the adoption of the CET for both industrial and agricultural products. The point to emphasise is that both elements were accomplished simultaneously and a year and a half ahead of schedule.

Table A.1 (a) *EEC Intra-Area Tariff Reductions (%)*

	Acceleration of									
	1/1/59		1/1/61		1/7/62		1/1/65		1/7/67	
		1/7/60		1/1/62		1/6/63		1/1/66		1/7/68
Individual reductions made on 1/1/57 level	10	10	10	10	10	10	10	10	5	15
Cumulative reduction	10	20	30	40	50	60	70	80	85	100

Table A.1 (b) *The Establishment of the CET (%)*

	Acceleration of				
	1/1/61	1/1/62	1/7/63	1/1/66	1/7/68
Industrial products adjustment	30		30		40
Cumulative adjustment	30		60		100
Agricultural products adjustment		30		30	40
Cumulative adjustment		30		60	100

Source: European Commission, *First General Report on the Activities of the Communities,* Brussels, p.34.

It should be noted, however, that progress was not as smooth as the figures might suggest. For example, the exports of Italian kitchen equipment adversely affected the equivalent French industry and led at one stage to the imposition of a temporary tariff on French imports of Italian refrigerators. Also, in the case of the CET, some special provisions were made for Italy — see the Treaty.

In 1973, Treaties of Accession were signed with Denmark, Ireland and the UK. Therefore, these new members had to eliminate tariffs and quantitative restrictions on imports from the EEC with reciprocal arrangements by the Six. They also had to adjust their external tariffs to the EEC CET level. The required reductions in tariffs and adjustments to the CET level are given in table A.2(a) and A.2(b). These, however, do not cover all groups of commodities; for example, customs duties on coal imports were to be abolished from the date of accession, those on certain groups of commodities given in Annex III of the Treaty of Accession were abolished on 1 January 1974, etc. In the case of the CET, those tariffs which differed by less than 15% were to be adjusted on 1 January 1974.

As for quantitative restrictions, these were abolished from the date of accession. Measures having equivalent effect were to be eliminated by 1 January 1975 at the very latest.

All three new members of the EEC experienced no great difficulties in accommodating these changes.

Table A.2(a) *New Members Intra-Tariff Reductions (%)*

	1/4/73	1/1/74	1/1/75	1/1/76	1/7/77
Individual reductions made on 1/1/72 level	20	20	20	20	20
Cumulative reduction	20	40	60	80	100

Table A.2 (b) *Approaching the CET (%)**

	1/1/74	1/1/75	1/1/76	1/7/77
Individual adjustment made on 1/1/72 level	40	20	20	20
Cumulative adjustment	40	60	80	100

* For products which differ by more than 15% from CET
Source: European Commission, *Bulletin of the European Communities*, no. 8, 1978.

Part III

Policy

The previous section of the book was devoted to the customs union aspects of the EEC but, as indicated in Chapter 1, the EEC is more than a customs union. This final section of the book provides more or less a full discussion of the EEC policies: the competition and industrial policies, the Common Agricultural Policy, the transport policy, the regional policy, the fiscal policy, the social policy, the energy policy, the factor mobility, external trade policy and the vital question of monetary integration. The Section is not fully comprehensive since it lacks a specific chapter on employment policies, but achievements in these areas are considered in the social policy chapter and in the concluding chapter.

6
Competition and Industrial Policy

B T BAYLISS

Industrial policy embraces all acts and policies of the state in relation to industry. Such policy can be either positive or negative, i.e. positive in relation to the State's participation in, or control of, industry; or negative, to the extent that it might be the industrial policy of the State to minimise intervention in industry.

The increasing influence of the state in industry has been a feature of post-war European development. This 'positive' industrial policy covers such areas as: the distribution of resources between industries (including such areas as energy, pricing, monopolies and restrictive practices); the structure of industry (including such areas as the degree of concentration, its location, state aid towards declining and expanding industries, the public sector); industry and the environment; conditions of employment; and fiscal and monetary policy. In other words, industrial policy embraces all aspects of State attitudes towards industry in its economic, social and environmental setting.

The Treaty of Rome covers certain aspects of industrial policy. In particular these deal with such factors as state aid, dominant firms, cartels, the right of establishment, the free movement of capital and labour, dumping, and the creation of the common market itself. The Treaty is, however, not comprehensive in the areas covered, nor does it specify the interrelationship between areas of policy where they are covered by the Treaty.

It appears that the Founding Fathers of the Treaty of Rome considered that once a common market was established, this would of its own volition result in industrial policies and change related to a new situation, i.e. the birth of a common market.

The Commission in its first major statement on industrial policy also stressed the 'Community aspects' of such a policy. 'The new framework for industrial activity is that of the Community: it is therefore for the Community to review its industrial structures and

113

to co-ordinate the operations of member states or even to adopt the measures required itself'.[1]

During the 1960s the Commission saw the creation of a single market and moves to achieve 'European firms' through legal and fiscal harmonisation as the major emphasis of its policy; industrial structure as such received minor consideration. By the end of the decade, however, two aspects of industrial policy became very marked.

Firstly, not only was there no spontaneous move towards the creation of an industrial policy catalysed through the creation of a common market, but a real indifference to its existence. Secondly, the decline of industries in prosperous areas (as opposed to development areas) highlighted the structural aspects of industry alongside the regional aspects.

Thus in March 1970 the Commission presented a *Memorandum on Industrial Policy in the Community* in an attempt both to galvanise action in this area and to argue the importance of the structural aspects of industrial policy.

The 1970 Memorandum developed six principal themes:

1 The removal of remaining barriers to the creation of a single market.
2 The harmonisation of company law and taxation, and the creation of a Community capital market.
3 The reorganisation of industry to adapt it to the needs of the Common Market.
4 The promotion of technology.
5 The social and regional aspects of industrial development.
6 Relations with third countries.

Following lack of progress in relation to this Memorandum the Commission attempted three years later to focus attention on a particular aspect of industrial policy, rather than remaining with a broad strategy, in an attempt to instigate some activity in this policy area. In May 1973 following a request from the Paris Summit the previous year, the Commission submitted to Council an *Action Programme in the Field of Technological and Industrial Policy*.

The Programme centred on nine areas of action:[2]

1 Abolition of technical barriers to trade.
2 Liberalisation of public contracts.
3 Abolition of fiscal barriers to co-operation between firms.
4 Abolition of legal barriers to co-operation between firms.
5 Community promotion of advanced technology undertakings.
6 Restructuring and modernisation of certain industrial sectors.
7 Concentration and competition.

8 Exports and credit insurance.
9 Raw-material supplies — particularly non-ferrous.

But like the Memorandum three years earlier, little ensued from it.

Essentially a broad strategy of industrial policy had failed on account of both lack of interested parties in the member states and differences in the economic philosophies of member governments. In other words, neither inside nor outside Government is there any strong body of feeling that such a policy would bring benefits which would otherwise not be forthcoming. An analysis of the reasons for the failure of a broad based industrial policy is the domain of the political commentator,[3] but in one wide area of industrial policy, namely competition, there have been some notable achievements, and the remainder of this chapter is devoted to that aspect of industrial policy.

Competition policy with the EEC covers a wide range of industrial activities including, alongside the more conventional aspects of price-setting and monopoly control, such activities as public sector industries, state aid, multinationals and restrictions on imports and exports.

In a resolution of 7th June 1971 the European Parliament requested the Commission to prepare an annual report on the development of competition policy. In its first such report,[4] the Commission spelt out its philosophy of competition:

> Competition is the best stimulant of economic activity since it guarantees the widest possible freedom of action to all. An active competition policy pursued in accordance with the provisions of the Treaties establishing the Communities makes it easier for the supply and demand structures continually to adjust to technological development. Through the interplay of decentralised decision-making machinery, competition enables enterprises continuously to improve their efficiency, which is the *sine qua non* for a steady improvement in living standards and employment prospects within the countries of the Community. From this point of view, competition policy is an essential means for satisfying to a great extent the individual and collective needs of our society.

With respect to the rules of competition applicable to enterprises the Commission has commented:[5]

> The Community's policy must, in the first place, prevent governmental restrictions and barriers — which have been abolished — from being replaced by similar measures of a private nature. Agreements on quotas as well as agreements for the purpose of dividing the Common Market into regions, or of dividing up or fragmenting markets by other means are in flagrant contradiction to the provisions of the Treaties.

The basic market economic argument relates to the role of competition, in the absence of externalities, in the optimum allocation of resources. But neither this nor indeed the dynamic and pragmatic arguments espoused by the Commission provides an adequate explanation of the competition rules contained in the Treaties of Paris and Rome.

The driving force behind the European Coal and Steel Community was political. In the Schumann communiqué of 9th May 1950 which formalised the original idea of the ECSC, the view was expressed that 'the solidarity in production thus established will make it plain that any war between France and Germany is not merely unthinkable but materially impossible'. The Allied Powers in Germany under the leadership of the United States had split up the major industrial and commercial concerns into separate organisations with operations regionally constrained, and France was keen to exercise a continuing control over a re-emerging German industry.

The French were thus prepared to surrender some control over their own industry in order to exercise some control over the future form of German industry. The Germans for their part were keen to participate in a European Community as this proffered a far preferable situation to one where their coal and steel industries were under the control of the Allies.

Although the wishes of the United States had to be taken into account in the formulation of the Paris Treaty, it was the hand of the French which was overriding, a fact clearly underlined by the appearance of a Treaty in which the only official and authentic text was in the French language, and where the single original was deposited in the archives of the French Government.

The desire of the French to prevent a renewed concentration of the German coal and steel industries found expression in Articles 65 and 66 of Chapter VI of the Treaty of Paris. Basically, under Article 65, 'all agreements . . . tending directly or indirectly, to prevent, restrict or distort the normal operation of competition within the common market are forbidden', and under Article 66, 'any course of action shall require the prior authorisation of the High Authority . . . if it has in itself the direct or indirect effect of bringing about . . . a concentration between undertakings'.

In the six years (1951–57) between the signing of the Paris and Rome Treaties, substantial changes took place in the relative political and negotiating strengths of the member countries of the European Coal and Steel Community. The Rome Treaty was drawn up, signed and ratified in four official languages (Dutch, French, German and Italian) instead of solely in French, and this time it was the Germans who were to both determine and dictate the pertinent competition clauses in the Treaty.

The change of emphasis between the two Treaties is nowhere more marked than in the preamble. Of the five points covered by the preamble to the Paris Treaty, four are devoted to 'peace' and 'bloody conflict', whereas in the Rome Treaty only one of eight preamble points is so devoted.

A substantial change in the powers of the two executives (the High Authority of the ECSC and the Commission of the EEC) accompanied the change in political emphasis and the inclusion of all sectors rather than just two. Under the Paris Treaty, 'it shall be the duty of the High Authority to ensure the attainment of the objects set out in the Treaty',[6] whereas under the Rome Treaty, 'with a view to ensuring the achievement of the objectives laid down in this Treaty, and under the conditions provided for therein, the Council shall ensure the co-ordination of the general economic policies of the Member States; and dispose of a power of decision'.[7]

Thus, in general, power for ensuring compliance with the objectives of the Treaties was removed from the Executive and given to the Council, with the resulting increased opportunity for individual countries to determine the course of policies.

This change in emphasis in the two Treaties in so far as the political aspects are concerned can be summarised as follows: the force behind the Coal and Steel Community was the desire to so integrate the member countries' economies that war was 'materially impossible', and simultaneously to control the reformation of German industry. The corollary of this was a powerful executive able to both determine and enforce policy — with this intention the High Authority was given power to raise its own budget (up to 1% of the Coal and Steel production of the member states — Article 50 of the Treaty of Paris), and the power to impose fines (in the case of prices, fines could be twice the value of the offending sales and double that in the case of repetition — Article 64 of the Treaty of Paris).

By contrast, by the time of the Treaty of Rome negotiations, Europe had recovered from the worst of the war devastation and was beginning to enjoy what was to be an unparalleled growth in production and standards of living. There was much greater emphasis in the Rome Treaty on social questions, and politicians no longer saw the need to hand over large responsibilities to a powerful executive in order to ensure a speedy implementation of Treaty provisions. The Council — a body which did not even appear in the original Schumann proposals — thus assumed much more real power under the Rome Treaty.

The extension of the Common Market to include all sectors also necessitated a weakening of the power of the executive. The Paris Treaty dealt with two sectors and their specific problems, thus solutions to those problems were sought within the Treaty articles themselves. In the Rome Treaty only broad outlines of policy could be included, detailed policies for individual sectors being impossible within the framework of a Treaty. The development of such policies *ex post* the Treaty could not be left entirely to the Commission, hence the need to give the Council a much more prominent role. In summary, the articles of the Paris Treaty are much more akin to Resolutions in the EEC than the articles of the Rome Treaty.

An exception to this change in the relative powers of the Executives under the Paris and Rome Treaties is witnessed in relation to Competition Policy. It is thus of interest to consider the pre-Treaty negotiations and the determination of the competition clauses in the Treaty of Rome.

It has frequently been argued that the hopes and demands of German industrialists and French agriculturalists during the negotiations were the overriding factors in determining the competition and agricultural policies, i.e. the competition policy which the Germans wanted was the *quid pro quo* for the agricultural policy which the French wanted. Although there is some truth in this supposition, it is not a fair reflection of the trade-offs made during the negotiations.

Agriculture, like transport, has a separate chapter in the Rome Treaty, and although the outlines of a common agricultural policy are defined in the Treaty, the policy itself was only established in negotiations between the Six following the signing of the Treaty. It was in these post-Treaty negotiations that the Germans found themselves in strongest opposition to the French proposals. In the pre-Treaty negotiations the Germans insisted on a rigorous competition policy as the *quid pro quo* for agreeing to the French demands in relation to Euratom and the association of overseas territories (mainly the French West African territories).

It is of interest to reflect upon the overseas territories question briefly. At the time of Treaty negotiations the African countries were seeking independence and the French saw their inclusion in the Rome Treaty as a means of retaining their own influence in these countries, whilst at the same time sharing the cost of maintaining such influence, in terms of aid, with the other five and Germany in particular. The French were very concerned about the ability of their industry to stand up to competition, but they needed German aid for their former colonies and were thus prepared to concede to German demands in relation to competition.

Thus in the few years between the signing of the Paris and Rome Treaties it was German industry that had not only become the most competitive industrial force in Europe but which was also required to finance the French ambitions in relation to its African territories.

The basic German philosophy towards the economy is that of the free market and there has been little change in the Federal Government's attitudes during the last quarter of a century: total state expenditure as a percentage of National Product, for example, has hardly changed, with such expenditure equivalent to an average of 30% of National Product in the 1970s and 1960s and 29% in the 1950s.

In order to safeguard this basic philosophy and to ensure that new restrictive practices did not handicap German industrial exports to other EEC countries, the Germans insisted in the post-Treaty negotiations on the implementation of competition policy that the Commission be given strong Executive powers in relation to competition. It was during this post-Treaty phase that the Germans found themselves in strongest conflict with the French in relation to agriculture, and the Community agreement to the control of competition policy demanded by the Federal Republic in this post-Treaty phase was the *quid pro quo* for the French demands in relation to agriculture.[8]

The German competition views towards control found expression in Regulation No. 17 of the Council of February 1962 relating to the Competition Articles 85 and 86 of the Treaty of Rome which deal with Restrictive Practices and Dominant Positions. Under Article 9 of that Regulation the Commission was granted powers to apply Articles 85 and 86 of the Treaty, and in the exercise of such powers was accorded both substantial investigatory rights (Article 14) and extensive pecuniary enforcement rights (Article 15).

The Commission is empowered to:

(a) examine the books and other business records;
(b) take copies of extracts from the books and business records;
(c) ask for oral explanations on the spot;
(d) enter any premises, land and means of transport of undertakings.

If the Commission is supplied with incorrect or misleading information it may levy substantial fines, and in the case of infringement the Regulation allowed fines up to one million Units of Account, or in excess of this if they did not exceed 10% of the previous year's turnover of an undertaking.

Decisions of the Commission can all be the subject of appeal to the Court of Justice. These extensive powers of the Executive, which far exceed anything, for instance, in the United Kingdom, with appeal only to the Court of Justice, have taken the development of this part of competition policy out of the political arena.

Similar powers of jurisdiction and enforcement of penalties were granted to the High Authority under the Treaty of Paris,[9] but, as is discussed below, the terms of reference of the High Authority were much narrower than those granted to the Commission under the Treaty of Rome.

Scope of Competition Policy

The Treaty of Rome encompasses many aspects of competition, which include:

(a) Patents, Licensing Agreements and Trade Marks
(b) Price Discrimination and Fixing
(c) Resale Price Maintenance
(d) State Aid
(e) Abuse of Dominant Market Positions
(f) Dumping
(g) Quantitative Restrictions on Imports and Exports
(h) Mergers and Concentrations
(i) State Undertakings.

Its range is thus much wider than the competition policy envisaged by the Treaty of Paris, and indeed the main emphasis of the Paris Treaty (Mergers and Concentrations) is not specifically covered by the Rome Treaty. Merger policy has, in fact, to be dealt with under the Dominant Position clauses (Article 86) or under the 'catch-all' article, Article 235.[10]

Many of the Communities' policies have their origins both in national policies of member states and compromise. The Competition Policy is an exception to this in that the policy has developed as a result of case law promulgated by the Commission and the Court of Justice. It has thus been specifically developed for a specific purpose and it is to be assumed that it should be free of many of the problems that have arisen through attempting to modify national policies to deal with Community problems. Such modification has often had to be achieved through substantial compromise, as for instance is witnessed in the Common Agricultural and Transport Policies.

The law embodied in the Treaties of Paris and Rome and the clarification of that law by Community institutions constitutes a body of law which is quite separate from both the municipal law of member states and international law. Not only is this body of law separate from the national laws of member states, it is also independent of them in that it can be enforced upon Government, institutions and individuals of member states without reference to or action on the part of such a state.

The independence of Community law is made quite explicit in

section 2(1) of the European Communities Act which requires that the Act's provisions 'are without further enactment to be given legal effect or used in the United Kingdom'.

Not only is Community law both separate and independent of national law, it takes precedence over it in cases of conflict between the two. Mr Rippon, the chief UK negotiator for entry of the United Kingdom into the European Communities, speaking in the House of Commons in February 1972 with respect to the European Communities Bill, commented:

> Clause 3 subsection (1) provides for the acceptance of the jurisprudence of the European Court. As the 1967 White Paper (Cmnd. 3301) recognises, the directly applicable provisions of the Community are designed to take precedence over the domestic law of member states, in the sense that they prevail in the case of a conflict. By accepting the directly applicable law in clause 2(1) and accepting the jurisprudence of the European Court in clause 3(1), the Bill provides the necessary precedence. In relation to statute law, this means that the directly applicable provisions ought to prevail over future Acts of Parliament in so far as they might be inconsistent with them. In practice this means that it would be implicit in our acceptance of the Treaties that the United Kingdom would, in future, refrain from enacting legislation inconsistent with Community law.
>
> (Hansard, 15 February 1972, vol. 831, col. 278)[11]

Although the Community institutions have the power to impose pecuniary obligations on institutions and individuals of member states they do not have power of enforcement. Under Article 192 of the Treaty of Rome, member states are required to enforce any pecuniary obligations on persons other than states under their jurisdiction. To refuse to do so would place them in breach of their Treaty obligations.[12]

Competition policy is restricted to inter-member state trade and relations. Thus, for example, Article 85 on Restrictive Practices refers to 'practices which are likely to affect trade between member states', and Article 92 on state aid which refers to aid which 'adversely affects trade between member states'.

Such a constraint covers both direct and indirect effects. If, for example, aid is granted to a non-exporting UK firm, the activities of that firm may reduce exports of other EEC firms to the UK, or they may influence the operating base of a competing UK firm to the extent that its exports are affected. Thus although the influence on trade may be indirect, as opposed to direct, this would still be covered by the Treaty obligations and the competition regulations ensuing from them.

Moreover, the competition policy encompasses firms in third countries and legally independent firms in member states in a manner which is not found in the national legislation of any member state and which has important implications in international law.

As has been pointed out above, EEC competition regulations only apply to those situations where trade *between* Community countries is affected. Thus actions having a purely domestic effect in a member state or having an effect outside the EEC are excluded. On the other hand, actions occurring outside the EEC, but having effects within it, are included. This latter interpretation has consequently had important implications for multinational companies.

Companies incorporated outside the Community but having trading relations with it can, for the purposes of competition law, be grouped into three categories. Firstly, those who have a corporate presence in the Community through, for example, a branch; secondly, those who have a subsidiary in the Community; and thirdly, those with no presence of any type in the Community.

The case of the formal corporate presence falls quite clearly under the Treaty provisions. In the case of subsidiaries (even not entirely owned) of firms incorporated outside the Community, the Commission and the Court of Justice have ruled that in the case of 'restrictive practices' parent companies are responsible for the actions of their legal independent subsidiaries, and that in the case of 'dominant market positions' the world position of the parent company is to be taken into account.

Both the Commission and the Court of Justice have relied upon an analysis of economic cause and effect to interpret the legal implications of the Rome Treaty. Thus it is not a case of legal nicety, but of economic fact, which has determined decisions. In law, parent and subsidiary are separate legal entities, but the European Court of Justice has ruled:

> The fact that the subsidiary has its own legal personality does not serve to rule out the possibility that its conduct is attributable to the parent company. This could be the case where the subsidiary, even though it has its own legal personality, does not independently determine its own market behaviour but essentially follows the instructions given to it by the parent company.
>
> (The Dyestuffs Case, 1972)

Thus where, for example, two parent companies outside the EEC agree to fix prices and their subsidiaries pursue such a policy, an offence has been committed even though the subsidiaries have not individually come to any price fixing agreement with each other.

In relation to the 'abuse of a dominant position', the Court has held that the position of a non-EEC parent in the world market and not just in the EEC market is relevant (Commercial Solvents Case 1974). Also, if an external parent acquires control of a number of companies in the EEC, with each of the acquired companies having legally independent subsidiary status, all the companies including parent and subsidiaries can be treated as one company for the purposes of deciding whether such mergers are desirable in the public interest (Continental Can Case 1971).

It follows, therefore, that if companies wholly outside the EEC and without affiliates, branches or subsidiaries there pursued a common policy which had detrimental effects upon the EEC, action could theoretically be taken against them under the Community competition law. Such action might imply the use of commercial power, e.g. the banning or limiting of imports into the EEC from those companies.

Development of Competition Policy

Three distinct elements can be isolated in the development of competition policy. Initially, as already noted, the principal aim of policy was to prevent private barriers to trade building up in place of governmental ones which were being dismantled between member states of the Community. With the end of the transitional period, another aspect of policy became increasingly important, namely the desire to foster competition as an allocations and efficiency stimulating instrument. In this respect, account had to be taken of the changing structure of industry and particularly the cross-frontier developments within the Community. In the two decades since the establishment of the European Economic Community, industry has changed its structure and practices in order to take advantage of the enlarged markets. Competition policy has thus increasingly had to take account of those changes, structures and practices where they result in constraints on competition. Finally, states have increasingly sought to aid certain depressed sectors and regions since the establishment of the EEC and this has been particularly noticeable since the world depresssion which has existed since 1974. As a result, a policy towards state aid has had to be developed within the framework of competition policy in order to prevent state practices militating against the twin aims of competition policy — namely, the development of a single market and the propagation of efficiency.

Reference has already been made to the wide scope of competition policy, and coverage of these must of necessity be restricted. In the following paragraphs, some of the more important aspects of that policy are dealt with under three headings: Restrictive Practices; Dominant Positions; and State Aid and State-Owned Undertakings. Policies relating specifically to the European Coal and Steel Community have had to be excluded.

Restrictive Practices

Under Article 85 of the Rome Treaty any agreements, decisions or concerted practices between enterprises which affect intra-Community trade and where competition is prevented, restricted, or distorted, are as a general rule prohibited. An exception to this general rule is made where such practices 'contribute to the improvement of the production or distribution of goods or to the promotion of technical or economic progress while reserving to users an equitable share in the profit resulting therefrom', providing that the restrictions are indispensable to the objects quoted above and competition is not eliminated in respect of a substantial proportion of the goods involved.

The Article is of great interest in that at the time of the signing of the Rome Treaty only Germany had legislated to any general degree in relation to restrictive practices; and even in the case of that country the legislation had only been passed in July 1957. Since then, with the exception of Belgium,[13] all the original six member states have introduced legislation curbing restrictive practices.

During the 1970s the twin pressures of inflation and consumer protection have left their mark on restrictive practice legislation, and it is interesting to note that it was only in the last few years that France and Italy introduced comprehensive legislation in this area. Previously, a very limited constraint existed under the provision of Article 1379 of the Civil Code in Italy, and under an Ordinance 45–1483 of June 1945 in France certain controls over prices could be exercised.

Common pressures have led to similarities in national legislation in Europe, but both Community and national policies differ markedly from legislation in the United States in that, in contrast to US anti-trust legislation, they differentiate between 'good' and 'bad' cartels. Thus under Article 85, if benefits accrue from the restrictive practices, then it is not contrary to the Treaty, whereas cartels in the US are held to be detrimental and *per se* illegal.

Reference has already been made to the powers accorded the Commission under Regulation 17 and two procedural points should be mentioned here. Firstly, under Articles 4 and 5 of that Regulation, both existing (i.e. at the time of entry into force of the Regulation) and new agreements had to be ratified, and under Article 2 the Commission was empowered to grant 'Negative Clearance' i.e. to rule that there were no grounds for action on its part under Article 85.

The inapplicability of the prohibition of restrictive practices provided for under paragraph 3 of Article 85 (see above) can apply to specific agreements or to groups of agreements. In relation to group Negative Clearance, the Council adopted a regulation in 1965 empowering the Commission to exclude by regulation from the prohibition certain agreements relating to:

(a) only two undertakings;
(b) industrial property rights — in particular of patents, utility models, designs or trade marks;
(c) rights to use a method of manufacture or knowledge relating to the use, or to the application, of industrial processes.

The Commission was empowered under this Council regulation to specify the exact details of the exemptions, and this it did in a regulation in 1967. Under this regulation the prohibition of Article 85 was declared not to apply to agreements to which only two undertakings are party and whereby:

(a) one party agrees with the other to supply only to that other certain goods for resale within a defined area of the common market; or
(b) one party agrees with the other to purchase only from that other certain goods for resale; or
(c) the two undertakings have entered into obligations as in (a) or (b) above, with each other in respect of exclusive supply and purchase for resale.

A second regulation made by Council in 1971 empowered the Commission to declare the following categories of agreements free of the Article 85 prohibition:

(a) the application of standards or types;
(b) the research and development of products or processes up to the stage of industrial application, and exploitation of the results, including provisions regarding industrial property rights and confidential technical knowledge;
(c) specialisation, including agreements necessary for achieving it.

In relation to points raised in this Council regulation and also in the Council regulation of 1965 (in so far as they were not covered by the Commission's regulation of 1967), as well as to some additional specific points, the Commission has issued four notes. These notes deal with: exclusive dealing contracts with commercial agents (1962); patent licensing agreements (1962); co-operation between enterprises (1968); and agreements of minor importance (1970).

Generally, the Commission gave its considered view that agency agreements and a wide range of patent licensing agreements did not fall under the prohibition. Under its notice on co-operation between enterprises, the Commission listed a range of co-operative activities which it considered to be beneficial and consequently not subject to prohibition. These include co-operation in market research, in accounting, research and development, joint use of production facilities, execution of orders, selling agreements, advertising and labelling.

In its note on co-operation, the Commission went as far as to say that not only did it recognise that co-operation among large enterprises can be economically desirable without presenting difficulties from the angle of competition policy, but that it considered that it had a *duty* to facilitate co-operation among small and medium-sized companies.

The Commission's fourth note dealt specifically with its concern for small and medium-sized firms in that it declared its view that the prohibition did not apply if the agreement did not cover more than 5% of the turnover in identical products and where the aggregate turnover of the parties did not exceed 15 million Units of Account or, in the case of the distributive trades, 20 million Units of Account.

Where restrictive practices emerge which neither fall into the exemption categories, nor are clearly covered under the four notes, a body of case law has been developed.

In the development of case law dealing with patent licensing agreements, it has been held that even where these comprise a restraint on trade, exemption can be granted if the restriction is not appreciable due to the small share of the market held by the licensee.[14] Exemption may, however, also be granted even where a major share of the market is concerned. Thus even where the licensing arrangements covered the whole of the Community, and one licensee held 20% of its national market and another 40% with its licences, exemption was granted (Davidson Rubber Co. 1972). In this instance it was held that the patent promoted economic progress through allowing mass-production at low cost. Thus the advantages were held to outweigh the dis-advantages in that the consumers derived a fair share of the increased profit resulting from the lower production costs.

By contrast, industrial property rights (trade marks) have been suppressed in relation to intra-Community trade. Industrial property rights are national rights and confined to a national territory, and in cases where a manufacturer desires rights in several countries, application must be made in each individual country, and rights granted are specific to that country and the regulations in it.

In cases where such agreements have led to territorial constraints of trade, such as when the import of goods by a trader in member state A from member state B constitutes a trade mark infringement of another firm in A, such infringement is not upheld under Com-munity competition law, as it comprises a restrictive practice under the terms of Article 85.[15]

In cases where Article 85 cannot be applied to prevent territorial restraints to trade through industrial property rights, because no 'agreement' in the terms of Article 85 exists, the Court has acted through Article 36 of Chapter 1 on the Elimination of Quantitative Restrictions. Thus, for example, where entirely independent firms have the same trade mark in different countries, the Court has ruled that no trade-mark infringement exists where the owner of the trade-mark in one member state exports to the other member state ('Hag' Case 1974). Also, where trade-marks are owned by parent and subsidiary in different countries ('Negram' Case 1974), imports between these two countries, by other firms, of goods covered by the trade-mark, cannot be prevented on account of any trade-mark infringement.

Exclusive territorial rights will, however, be allowed where the consumer is seen to benefit from them. In the Omega Case (1970), for example, which dealt with the question of exclusive retail outlets, the Commission ruled that Omega watches were highly technical and relatively expensive and 'any approval as authorised Omega dealers of all the retailers in the Common Market who have the necessary professional qualifications . . . would reduce the sales possibilities of each to a few units each year. The result would be a deterioration rather than an improvement of the services expected of them by the manufacturer as well as by the consumers'.

An extremely firm position has been taken by the Commission and the Court in relation to price-fixing cartels as evidenced in the Dyestuffs case quoted above, where substantial fines were levied.

Dominant Positions

Under the terms of Article 86 of the Treaty of Rome, any actions which 'take improper advantage of a dominant position' and which affect trade between member states is prohibited.

Some of the most important (and controversial in terms of international law) developments in Community law have taken place with respect to Article 86. Of primary importance has been the development of the concept that it is economic control and not legal control that is of relevance here. Thus a parent company can be held responsible for the actions of a legally independent subsidiary, and the combined trade of parent and subsidiary is the relevant measure in assessing whether a dominant position exists.[16] These principles apply even in those cases where the parent is incorporated outside the Community.

Recently the definition of dominance has been extended to apply to situations other than those where the undertaking dominates through sheer size (United Brands Case 1978). Dominance can derive from a combination of several factors which taken separately would not necessarily be determinate. Thus dominance occurs where an undertaking has 'the power to behave to an appreciable extent independently of its competitors, customers and alternatively of its consumers' (judgement in United Brands Case 1978).

The Court has also ruled (ABG Case 1977) that a dominant position can arise in a situation of shortage (such as the recent oil crisis) where all customers become dependent upon their suppliers and competition between suppliers no longer exists. In such a case, any discrimination between customers in the allocation of the available supplies would constitute an abuse of a dominant position.

However, despite the legal history created in the area of dominant positions, it is also in this area where the Community has been least successful in the formulation of policy — namely in relation to mergers. Mergers can only be dealt with under Article 86 if an abuse of the dominant positions results from the act of merger itself. It is highly unlikely that the mere act of merging can of itself result in an abuse, and any subsequent abuse is irrelevant to the merger *per se* as the Community certainly has no powers to order a company to divest itself of any part of its assets.

At the Paris Summit of October 1972 it was held that merger regulation was required and that the use of all dispositions of the Treaty including the 'catch-all' Article 235 should be made.[17] Following this declaration, the Commission prepared a proposal for a regulation on the Control of Mergers. Basically the proposal was aimed at those mergers 'whereby the undertakings involved acquire the power or enhance their power to hinder effective competition'.[18] It proposed excluding from the regulation mergers where the turnover involved was low or where the share of the total market involved was small. The 'regulation' has, however, still failed to pass the proposal stage.

Interestingly, recent research co-ordinated by the Berlin based International Institute for Management, covering a period of ten years and 765 merger cases in Belgium, France, the Netherlands, the UK, Germany, Sweden and the US has suggested that mergers do not result in improved efficiency, lower prices, expanded sales and increased benefits for the consumer. It is suggested that current mergers often seem akin to empire-building with no demonstrable social benefit to compensate for the inherent reduction in competition.

Such findings underline the importance of making progress in this area of competition policy.

State Aid and State-Owned Undertakings

As a general rule state aid which favours certain enterprises or products[19] and which distorts trade between member states is, under the terms of Article 92, 'incompatible with the Common Market'. However, as with Article 85, this incompatibility is not absolute. Thus three types of aid are specifically deemed to be compatible and other types of aid *may* be deemed to be compatible.

The three *de jure* exceptions relate to:

(i) aid of a social character to individuals where no discrimination on basis of origin exists;
(ii) aid related to national calamities;
(iii) aid to assist regions of the Federal Republic affected by the division of Germany.

Over and above these three categories, aid may be deemed compatible if it is intended to aid:

(i) development of underdeveloped regions;
(ii) promotion of important projects with a European interest;
(iii) development of certain activities or certain economic regions;
(iv) any situation specified by the Council.

As a rule, it is for the Commission to decide whether aid is compatible with the aims of the Common Market, with leave for appeal to the Court, but in 'exceptional circumstances' any type of aid may be approved by the Council.

No aid may be modified or introduced without the member state in question informing the Commission in due time in order to enable it to submit its comments. If states act precipitately, any interested party can have the aid declared illegal (e.g. Lorenz *versus* Federal Republic of Germany 1973), and if the Commission subsequently deems the aid incompatible, it can order repayment of the aid (e.g. Commission *versus* Federal Republic of Germany 1973).

Of prime importance in the development of competition policy have been exceptions (i) and (iii) in the second group of exceptions mentioned above, namely, aid to underdeveloped regions and aid to certain activities or economic regions.

In the early stages of the Community, the main emphasis was on aid to underdeveloped regions. It was a basic aim of the Treaty to help regions of 'serious' unemployment and 'abnormally low' living standards, and there was thus both a common interest and obligation upon signatories of the Rome Treaty towards aiding these areas.

As this was a Community obligation, 'serious' and 'abnormally low' must be interpreted in relation to the Community as a whole and not in relation to an individual country. There have thus been differences of opinion between individual states, who have viewed the situation from a national viewpoint, and the Commission who has viewed the situation from a Community viewpoint.

By the mid-1960s, however, the problems of declining regions and declining industries became increasingly more important, and took precedence over the development of underdeveloped regions. Unlike aid to underdeveloped regions which is, as an aim of the Community, by definition of common interest — the only question open to debate is what constitutes an underdeveloped region; sectoral or regional aid for declining industries and areas is only compatible within the Treaty in so far as it 'does not change trading conditions to such a degree as would be contrary to the common interest'.

Massive aid has been granted by states to these declining industries and regions, and the Commission, both on account of the level of aid and the difficulty of assessing its effect on the Community, found itself unable to keep abreast of the problem. A major problem faced by the Commission in this connection was the competition between member states to woo foreign investors to these areas by all manner of incentives. It was thus a major achievement of the Commission in 1973 to instigate a Resolution in the Council detailing eight principles for such sectoral and regional aid. These principles aimed both at regulating competition between states for foreign investment and at assisting the Commission in its task of evaluation.

In relation to state enterprises, a differentiation must be made between state monopolies and public sector companies.

Chapter 2 of Title I of the Rome Treaty deals with the Elimination of Quantitative Restrictions as between member states, and basically the Treaty requires that all quantitative restrictions on imports and all measures with equivalent effect shall be terminated in trade between member states. Article 37 of that chapter relates to state monopolies of a commercial character including any body 'by means of which a member state shall *de jure* or *de facto* either directly or indirectly control', and requires that policies of such monopolies or bodies be adjusted so as to ensure the exclusion 'of all discrimination between the nationals of member states in regard to conditions of supply or marketing of goods'.

In interpreting this article, the Commission has maintained that its objective is the same as that for other products as covered by Articles 30–34 of Chapter 2. That is, the free movement of goods must not be hindered.

In order to ensure this free movement the Commission has argued that not only is the removal of discrimination required, but that Article 37 also aims at excluding the 'possibility' of discrimination — such a possibility resulting from powers concerning import, export, or distribution of products. The Commission thus concluded that the most effective course of action was the elimination of the exclusive rights of the state monopolies, and it has been successful in a number of areas in obtaining agreement to such a policy from member states.

Public sector companies are required to observe the rules of the Treaty in exactly the same manner as private enterprises. It seems clear that they are only specifically picked out in the Treaty on account of the ability of member states to use such enterprises to influence trade between member states, a classic example being the manipulation of railway tariffs so as to assist exports and handicap imports.[20]

The only difference between private and state owned or controlled companies[21] is in relation to the enforcement of the Treaty provisions. Private undertakings can be fined, but in the case of public sector companies the Commission has only the options of issuing directives or decisions to the member states (Article 90.3) or commencing proceedings in accordance with Article 169.

Conclusion

In conclusion, it can be stated that the development of industrial policy has been severely handicapped by the lack of interest outside government and divergences of opinions as between governments, but in the area of Competition Policy it has achieved some notable successes. In particular, success has been achieved in relation to restrictive practices, but mergers and state aid continue to present major problems.

Notes

1 European Commission, *Tenth General Report on the Activities of the Community*, 1967, p.34.

2 For a summary of each of these nine action areas see J-C. Eeckhout, Towards a common European industrial policy, *The Irish Banking Review*, Dec. 1975.

3 For an interesting analysis of the reasons for failure see M. Hodges, Industrial policy: a directorate general in search of a role, in Wallace, H. and W. and Webb, C., *Policy Making in the European Communities*, John Wiley 1977.

4 European Commission, *First Report on Competition Policy*, Brussels, 1972, p.11.

5 European Commission, *First Report on Competition Policy*, Brussels, 1972, p.13.

6 Article 8 of the Treaty setting up the European Coal and Steel Community.

7 Article 145 of the Treaty establishing the European Economic Community.

8 In the event, the Germans were to do extremely well out of the Common Agricultural Policy, but no one seemed aware of that possibility at this early stage.

9 Articles 65 and 66 of the Treaty setting up the European Coal and Steel Community.

10 Article 235 of the Treaty of Rome reads: 'If any action by the Community appears necessary to achieve, in the functioning of the Common Market,

one of the aims of the Community in cases where this Treaty has not provided for the requisite powers of action, the Council, acting by means of a unanimous vote on a proposal of the Commission and after the Assembly has been consulted, shall enact the appropriate provision'.

11   Quoted by P.S.R.F. Mathijsen in *A Guide to European Community Law*, (Sweet & Maxwell/Mathew Bender, 1975), where a full discussion of the position in individual member states can be found.

12   Paragraphs 1 and 2 of Article 192 read:
'Decisions of the Council or of the Commission which contain a pecuniary obligation on persons other than States shall be enforceable.
Forced execution shall be governed by the rules of civil procedure in force in the State in whose territory it takes place. The writ of execution shall be served, without other formality than the verification of the authenticity of the written act, by the domestic authority which the Government of each Member State shall designate for this purpose and of which it shall give notice to the Commission and to the Court of Justice.'

13   The only restriction in Belgium appears under Article 1, paragraph 2 of the legislative decree of January 22, 1945, relating to national supplies and charging prices higher than normal.

14   Burroughs-Delplanque (1971) and Burroughs/Geha-Werke (1971).

15   In the classic Grundig/Consten (1966) case, for example, Grundig authorised its sole distributors, including the French firm Consten, to register in their own names its trade-mark 'Gint'. When other French firms imported Grundig equipment directly from German wholesalers, they were sued by Consten for trade-mark infringement. Such infringement was not recognised under Community competition law.

16   *Op. cit.* Continental Can and Commercial Solvents.

17   'The Heads of State or of Government consider it necessary to seek to establish a single industrial base for the Community as a whole. This involves ... the formulation of measures to ensure that mergers affecting firms established in the Community are in harmony with the economic and social aims of the Community, and the maintenance of fair competition as much within the Common Market as in external markets in conformity with the rules laid down by the Treaties'. Final Declaration of the Heads of State or of Government, Paris, October 1972.

18   European Commission, *Third Report on Competition Policy*, Brussels, 1974, p. 33.

19   As the Treaty refers to aid to certain enterprises and certain products, general economic measures relating to such things as tax and interest rates do not constitute 'aid' in ther terms of the Treaty.

20   For a fuller discussion see Bayliss, B.T., Transport in the European Communities, *Journal of Transport Economics and Policy*, Vol. XIII, No. 1, January 1979.

21   Enterprises which are accorded 'special or exclusive rights' by the state are included alongside public sector companies even if not wholly owned by the state.

References

Bellis, J.-F., Potential competition and concentration policy: relevance to EEC antitrust, *Journal of World Trade Law*, vol. 10, no. 1, Jan/Feb 1976.

Cananbley, C., Price discrimination and EEC cartel law: a review of the Kodak decision of the Commission of the European Communities, *The Antitrust Bulletin*, vol. 17, no. 1, Spring 1972.

Chard, J.S. & Macmillen, M.J., Sectoral aids and community competition policy: the case of textiles, *Journal of World Trade Law*, vol. 13, No. 2, March/April 1979.

Eeckhout, J-C., Towards a common European industrial policy, *The Irish Banking Review*, December 1975.

George, K.D. & Joll, C. (eds), *Competition Policy in the United Kingdom and European Economic Community*, Cambridge University Press, 1975.

Hodges M., 'Industrial policy: a directorate general in search of a role' in Wallace, H., Wallace, W. and Webb, C., *Policy Making in the European Communities*, John Wiley 1977.

Jacquemin, A.P., Application to foreign firms of European rules on competition, *The Antitrust Bulletin*, vol. 19, No. 1, Spring 1974.

Joliet, R., Resale price maintenance under EEC antitrust law, *The Antitrust Bulletin*, vol.16, no. 3, Fall 1971.

Jones, R.T., Relevance for the EEC of American experience with industrial property rights, *Journal of World Trade Law*, vol. 10, no. 6, 1976.

Loewenheim, U., Trademarks and free competition within the European Community, *The Antitrust Bulletin*, vol. 21, no. 4, Winter 1976.

McLachlan, D.L. & Swann, D., *Competition Policy in the European Community*, Oxford University Press, 1967.

Mathijsen, P.S.R.F., State aids, state monopolies, and public enterprises in the Common Market, *Law and Contemporary Problems*, vol. 37, No. 2 Spring 1972.

Mathijsen, P.S.R.F., *A Guide to European Community Law*, Sweet & Maxwell/Matthew Bender, 1975.

Ritter L., & Overbury, C., An attempt at a practical approach to joint ventures under the EEC rules on competition, *Common Market Law Review*, vol.14, no. 4, November 1977.

Swann, D., *The Economics of the Common Market*, Penguin Books, 1972.

Timberg, S., Antitrust in the Common Market: innovation and surprise, *Law and Contemporary Problems*, vol. 37, no. 2, Spring 1972.

Waelbroeck, M., The effect of the Rome Treaty on the exercise of national industrial property rights, *The Antitrust Bulletin*, vol. 21, no. 1, Spring 1976.

European Commission, *Tenth Annual Report on the Activities of the Community*, Brussels, 1967.

European Commission, *Competition Law in the European Economic Community and in the European Coal and Steel Community*, Brussels, 1972

European Commission, *Annual Competition Reports*.

Hansard, vol. 831, 15 February 1972.

7

The Common Agricultural Policy

A M EL-AGRAA[1]

The EEC, unlike EFTA, extends its free trade arrangements between member states to agriculture and agricultural products. The term agricultural products is defined as 'the products of the soil, of stock-farming and of fisheries and products of first-stage processing directly related to the foregoing' (Article 38). Moreover, the EEC dictates that the operation and development of the common market for agricultural products must be accompanied by the establishment of a 'common agricultural policy' among member states (Article 38).

One could ask: why should the common market arrangements extend to agriculture? Such a question is to some extent irrelevant. According to GATT 'a customs union shall be understood to mean the substitution of a single customs union territory for two or more customs territories, so that . . . duties and other restrictive regulations of commerce are eliminated with respect to *substantially all* the trade between the constituent territories of the union' (GATT 1952). It is quite obvious that excluding agriculture from the EEC arrangements would be in direct contradiction with this requirement (see next section). In any case:

> a programme of economic integration which excluded agriculture stood no chance of success. It is important to appreciate that the Rome Treaty was a delicate balance of national interests of the contracting parties. Let us consider West Germany and France in terms of trade outlets. In the case of West Germany the prospect of free trade in industrial goods, and free access to the French market in particular, was extremely inviting. In the case of France the relative efficiency of her agriculture . . . as compared with Wes. Germany held out the prospect that in a free Community agricultural market she would make substantial inroads into the West German market . . . Agriculture had therefore to be included.
>
> (Swann 1973, p. 82)

The purpose of this chapter is: to discuss the need for singling out agriculture as one of the earliest targets for a common policy; to specify the objectives of the common agricultural policy (CAP); to explain the mechanisms of the CAP; to make an economic evaluation of its implications and to assess the performance of the policy in terms of its practical achievements (or lack of achievements) and in terms of its theoretical viability.

Before tackling these points, it is necessary to give some general background information about agriculture in the EEC at the time of its formation and at a more recent date.

General Background

The economic significance of agriculture in the economies of member states can be demonstrated in terms of its share in the total labour force and in GNP. Table 7.1 gives this information. The most significant observations that can be made regarding this information are:

(i) at the time of the signing of the treaty many people in the original Six were dependent on farming as their main source of income; indeed, 25% of the total labour force was employed in agriculture — the equivalent percentage for the UK was less than five;

(ii) the agricultural labour force was worse off than most people in the rest of the EEC;[2]

(iii) a rapid fall in both the agricultural labour force and in the share of agriculture in GNP[3] occurred between 1955 and 1970 and between 1970 and 1975.

It is also important to have some information about the area and size distribution of agricultural holdings. This is given in table 7.2 where the figures in brackets refer to 1974/5.

The most significant factor to note is that in the original Six, around 1966, approximately two thirds of farm holdings were between 1 and 10 hectares in size. At about the same time, the equivalent figure for the UK was about one third.

A final piece of important background information that one needs to bear in mind is that, except for Italy and the UK, the EEC farming system is an owner-occupier system rather than one of tenant farming.

Table 7.1 *The Share of Agriculture in the Total Labour Force and in National Output (%)*

Country		Belgium	France	West Germany	Italy	Luxembourg	Netherlands	Denmark	Ireland	UK
Labour force	1955	9.3	25.9	18.9	39.5	25.0	13.7	25.4	38.8	4.8
	1970	4.1	12.7	5.6	13.1	11.0	5.8	9.0	25.7	2.7
	1975	3.4	10.9	7.1	15.5	6.1	6.5	9.3	23.8	2.7
National output (a)	1955	8.1	12.3	8.5	21.6	9.0	12.0	19.2	29.6	5.0
	1970	4.2	6.6	3.3	9.8	3.3	6.1	6.4	16.9	2.7
	1975	3.2	5.6	2.9	8.7	3.5	4.7(b)	7.4(c)	18.1(c)	1.9

Sources: Ritson (1973), EEC, *The Common Agricultural Policy* (1973) and *Eurostat.*
(a) Gross Value added at market prices.
(b) At factor cost.
(c) 1974.

Table 7.2 *Area and Size Distribution of Agricultural Holdings*

	Belgium	France	W.Germany	Italy	Luxembourg	Netherlands	THE SIX	Denmark	Ireland	UK
Area 1968 (in millions of hectares)										
Total	3.05[3]	55.14	24.75	30.13	0.26	3.66	116.99	4.31	...	24.40
Agricultural land	1.61	33.52	13.87	21.37	0.136	2.23	72.74	2.98	...	13.02[1]
Forests	0.60[3]	12.78	7.18	6.15	0.08	0.30	27.09	0.47[2]	...	1.85
	1967	1967	1968	1967	1968	1966	—	1967	...	1968
Size of agricultural holdings (holdings of one hectare or more)										
Number (thousands)	147 (106)	1,577 (1,225)	1,186 (905)	2,649 (2,173)	7.6 (6.0)	203 (144)		152 (130)	... (267)	358[3] (273)
Distribution in percentages										
1–5 hectares	36 (29.8)	24 (20)	40 (34.4)	65 (68.4)	23 (19.2)	35 (24.9)	47	12 (11.9)	... (20.4)	22 (14.5)
5–10 hectares	27 (22.1)	19 (15.3)	23 (19.8)	19 (17.8)	15 (12.2)	24 (21.3)	20	22 (19.3)	... (21.1)	12 (12.5)
10–20 hectares	24 (26.9)	26 (23.3)	24 (23.4)	10 (8.4)	24 (18.4)	27 (30.6)	18	19 (28.2)	... (30.5)	24 (15.8)
20–50 hectares	11 (17.7)	24 (29.8)	12 (19.5)	4 (3.7)	34 (40.9)	13 (20.6)	12	32 (32.6)	... (22.2)	21 (26.8)
50 hectares and over	2 (3.2)	7 (11.7)	1 (2.9)	2 (1.7)	4 (9.3)	1 (2.2)	3	15 (7.8)	... (5.6)	21 (30.5)
Average area per holding (ha):										
about 1967	10.5	19.0	10.7	8.5	17.8	10.7	11.9	18.8	...	30.0
about 1960	8.2	16.7	10.1	6.8	13.4	9.9	10.6	16.0	...	26.0

Sources: Eurostat and Marsh and Ritson (1971).
1. Adjusted area
2. 1965
3. 1959
* Figures in brackets relate to 1974/5.

The Problems of Agriculture

The agricultural sector has been declining in relative importance and those who have remained on the land have continued to receive incomes well below the national average. Governments of most developed countries have, therefore, always found it necessary to practise some sort of control over the market for agricultural commodities through price supports, subsidies to farmers, import levies, import quotas, etc. In this section I shall analyse the background to such practices.

It should be plain to all that the production of many agricultural commodities is subject to forces that lie beyond the direct control of the farmers concerned. Drought, floods, earthquakes, and to some extent invasions of pests, for instance, would lead to an actual level of agricultural production far short of that *planned* by the farmers. On the other hand, exceptionally favourable conditions could result in *actual* production being far in excess of that *planned* by farmers. It is therefore necessary to have some theoretical notions about the effects of such deviations between planned and actual agricultural produce on farmers' prices and received incomes.

The predictions of economic theory can be illustrated by reference to a simple diagram. In figure 7.1, SS represents the range of quantities that farmers plan to supply to the market at various prices in a particular period of time given a certain set of 'market circumstances', for example, agricultural input prices, farmers' objectives for produc-

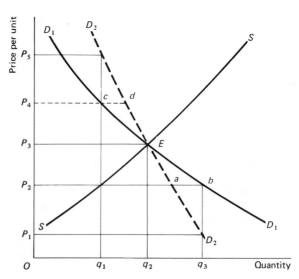

Figure 7.1

tion, agricultural technology, etc. DD represents the various quantities that consumers of agricultural products plan to purchase at alternative prices in a specific period of time given a certain set of 'market circumstances', for example, consumers' tastes for agricultural products, their incomes, population size and composition, etc. D_1D_1 and D_2D_2 represent two such demand curves, with D_2D_2 being less elastic than D_1D_1.

If consumers' plans and producers' plans actually materialise, P_3 will be the equilibrium price which will clear the equilibrium output Oq_2 off the market. Moreover, as long as this situation is maintained, agricultural prices (representd by P_3) will remain stable and agricultural incomes (represented by the area OP_3Eq_2) will also remain stable. However, *actual* agricultural production may fall short of, or exceed, the equilibrium planned production Oq_2 for any of the above-mentioned reasons. If a shortage occurs such that actual output is Oq_1, the price will rise above the equilibrium level to P_5 (for D_2D_2) or P_4 (for D_1D_1). In the case of an actual supply of Oq_3, the price will fall to P_1 or P_2 respectively. Therefore, when the actual agricultural produce deviates from the planned output, fluctuations in agricultural prices will result such that an excess actual output reduces prices and a shortage in output increases prices. The extent of these price fluctuations is determined by the price elasticity of demand: the more (less) price inelastic the demand curve, the wider (narrower) the margin of price fluctuations.

Moreover, as long as the demand curve does not have a price elasticity of unity, agricultural incomes will fluctuate from the planned level OP_3Eq_2: with a price elastic (inelastic) demand curve, an actual shortage will result in a lower (higher) income for the farmers and an actual excess supply will lead to higher (lower) incomes.

At this point it is appropriate to mention two further characteristics of agriculture in advanced economies. Firstly, as people's incomes rise they tend to spend a smaller proportion of it on agricultural products: the income elasticity of demand is low. (People spend relatively less on food as their incomes rise, therefore they spend even less on agricultural products because a higher proportion of the expenditure on food goes on processing, packaging and presentation.) Hence poor (rich) nations tend to spend a large (small) proportion of their income on agricultural products. The data given in table 7.3 give an approximate representation of this point for food (as a representative of agricultural products).

Secondly, because of advances in technology and growth of factors of production, average incomes have been rising in developed economies. Agricultural economists would argue that for the same

Table 7.3 *Relationship Between the Proportion of Income Spent on Food in a Household and the Income Group to which the Household belongs in the UK (1971)*

Income group (Given by gross weekly earnings of the head of the household only)	*Expenditure of the household on food as a percentage of the gross earnings of the head of the household*
Over £69 per week	Less than 13
£45–£69 per week	12–18
£27–£45 per week	18–29
£14–£27 per week	27–52
Under £14·per week (non OAP)	More than 37
Under £14 per week (OAP)	More than 20

Source: Ritson (1973), p. 97.

reason, agricultural outputs tend to rise at at least the same rate as those of the non-agricultural sector. Once it is realised that consumers would want to spend relatively more on non-agricultural products as their living standards rise (the income elasticity of demand is high for these products), it is inevitable to conclude that there would be a relative tendency for a fall in the demand for farm products. Hence farm incomes would tend to lag behind the incomes of those engaged in the non-farm sector.

Furthermore, once one appreciates that the demand for most agricultural (non-agricultural) products has a low (high) price and income elasticity and that agriculture as an industry is becoming at least as efficient as the national average (due to technological progress in the agricultural sector, the supply curve is moving to the right all the time), then it is easy to understand that the agricultural (non-agricultural) price levels and incomes have a tendency to relative decline (rise) with economic growth. This adds a new dimension to the problem in that an 'agricultural stabilisation policy' must be introduced with the aim not simply of stabilising agricultural prices and incomes, but also of raising agricultural incomes to the national average – if only for equity reasons.

However, the assumption that agricultural outputs tend to rise at at least the same rate as those of the non-agricultural sector does not stand up to close scrutiny. In the UK, according to the Cambridge Department of Applied Economics Programme for Growth 12, agricultural productivity grew at a rate of 1.6% per annum compound during the period 1948–68, as against 1.8 for manufacturing. In the UK, manufacturing productivity growth has been low and agricultural productivity growth, because of the form of policy, high. In the rest of Europe the disparity will be much greater. Since agriculture started as a low productivity industry, the disparity has indeed worsened — the impact of science and technology on farming is less than on manufacturing for two reasons: firstly, agriculture is characterised by decreasing returns to scale while manufacturing is characterised at least by constant returns to scale; secondly, there are severe institutional constraints on increasing the size of farms, therefore technology can only make its impact from specialisation within the existing farm structure. Economies of specialisation are limited within this constraint and furthermore there are offsetting losses of economies of joint production (from rotations, etc.) which are more pronounced in agriculture than elsewhere and are virtually lost from specialisation. Hence the problem of agricultural incomes stems from declining agricultural productivity (in comparison with manufacturing productivity) rather than from inelastic demand for agricultural products. In any case, the elasticity has not been so low once population growth is taken into account. (For a forceful and detailed explanation of these points, see Bowers 1972.)

This is a more convincing argument in that it suggests that the setting of reasonable agricultural prices, given the declining relative efficiency of agriculture, ensures declining agricultural incomes. Hence, the way to increasing agricultural productivity is to encourage the marginal agricultural labour to seek alternative employment. This view is consistent with the structural problem of the EEC, where declining farm incomes are attributed to the fact that labour does not flow out of agriculture quickly enough (trapped resources with low salvage values).

The above suggests why most advanced mixed economies have been adopting some kind of agricultural support policies. Other arguably more important considerations include historical factors, strategic considerations and the strength of the agricultural lobby.

Agricultural Support Policies

From the foregoing analysis and observations, one is in a position to attempt a specification of the necessary elements in an agricultural policy and to point out the difficulties associated with such a policy.

In most advanced mixed economies where living standards have been rising, an agricultural policy must:

(i) as a minimum requirement, avoid impeding the *natural* process of transferring resources from the agricultural sector to the

non-agricultural sector of the economy, and if necessary
promote this process;

(ii) aim at protecting the incomes of those who are occupied in the
agricultural sector. The definition of the farm sector raises a
number of problems, for instance:

should one's policy be devised to guarantee prosperity to any who might
wish at some future date to enter agriculture — and moreover to assure a
reasonable rate of return for any amount of capital that they may wish to
invest in farming? Or should one's policy be geared to those already in the
industry who have made resource allocation decisions based on expectations
of the future which governments then feel under an obligation to realise?

(Josling 1969, p. 176.)

(iii) aim at some kind of price stability, since agriculture forms the
basis of living costs and wages and is therefore the basis of
industrial costs;

(iv) make provision for an adequate agricultural sector since security
of food supplies is essential for a nation[4];

(v) ensure the maintenance of agriculture as a family business, and
the maintenance of some population in rural villages.

Unfortunately these objectives are, to a large extent, mutually
contradictory. Any policy which aims at providing adequate environmental conditions, secure food supplies and agricultural incomes
equal to the national average interferes with the economy's natural
development. However, the provision of stable farm incomes, let alone
rising farm incomes, is not compatible with the provision of stable
agricultural prices. This point can be illustrated by reference to figure
7.1.

Suppose that $D_1 D_1$ is a demand curve which has unit price elasticity
along its entire range. In order to keep farmers' incomes constant it
would be necessary to operate along this curve, keeping farmers'
incomes equal to $OP_3 Eq_2$. If agricultural production deviates from
Oq_2, the following will ensue:

(i) when output is equal to Oq_3, the authority in charge of the
policy must purchase ab in order to make certain that the price
level falls only to P_2 rather than P_1, therefore ensuring that
farmers' incomes remain at the pre-determined level,

(ii) when output is equal to Oq_1 the authority must sell cd in order
to achieve the price level P_4 rather than P_5.

Hence a policy of income stability can be achieved only if the price
level is allowed to fluctuate, even though the required level of
fluctuation in this case is less than that dictated by the operation of
the free market forces.

On the other hand, a policy of maintaining constant price levels (constant P_3) will give farmers higher incomes when output is Oq_3 (by $q_2q_3 \times OP_3$) since the authority will have to purchase the excess supply at the guaranteed price, and lower incomes when output is Oq_1 (by $q_1q_2 \times OP_3$). Therefore, a policy of price stability will guarantee income fluctuations in such a manner that higher (lower) agricultural outputs will result in higher (lower) farmers' incomes.

This throws light on another aspect of agricultural policies: if the average farm prices are set at too high a level this will encourage farmers to increase production, since at the guaranteed price they can sell as much as they can produce. This, in effect, results in a perfectly elastic supply curve at price level P_3. In such circumstances, an excess supply of these commodities could result. This is a point that has to be borne in mind when assessing the CAP.

EEC Member Policies

Prior to the formation of the EEC, member countries (except for Holland) had adopted different practices in their agricultural stabilisation policies. This is an appropriate point to turn to a discussion of these policies.

Agricultural policies in Western Europe as a whole since the Second World War have been rather complicated, but a substantial element of these policies has been the support of prices received by farmers for their produce. In this respect, a variety of methods has been practised:

(i) *Deficiency Payments Schemes* (supplements to market determined prices). These refer to policies of guaranteed farm prices which the government ensures by means of deficiency payments. These prices become the farmers' planning prices. This system was used in the UK before it joined the EEC.

(ii) *Variable Levies or Import Quota Systems*. These systems are concerned with policies which impose threshold prices and charge levies on imports equal to the difference between world prices and the threshold prices.

(iii) *Market Control Systems*. These aim at limiting the quantities of agricultural produce that actually reach the market. This can be achieved by ensuring that the produce is marketed by single private authorities (agencies) or by certain government departments. The quantity that is not allowed to reach the market can 'either be destroyed, stored (to be released when prices rise), exported, donated to low income countries or needy groups within the home economy, or converted into another product which does not compete directly with the original one. Examples of this last course of action are "breaking" of eggs for use as egg powder and rendering some cereals and vegetables unfit for human consumption (usually by adding a dye or fish oil) but suitable for animal feed' (Ritson 1973, p. 99). This system was widely used in the original Six.

(iv) *Direct Income Payments*. This term describes schemes whereby incomes are transferred to the farmers without these bearing any relationship to the level of output. The nearest to this system is the Swedish system.

Let us now turn to an analytical consideration of these schemes. The analysis of (i), (ii) and (iv) is slightly different from that illustrated by figure 7.1 in that one needs to deal with products which compete with imports. This is because most Western European countries were net importers of most agricultural products at the time of the inception of the EEC.

Assume (unrealistically in the context of the EEC since Western Europe is a large consumer) that the level of imports does not influence the world prices of agricultural commodities and that, allowing for transport costs and quality differentials, the import price level is equal to the domestic price. Then consider the different support systems with reference to figure 7.2.

In figure 7.2, P_w is the world price, Oq_1 is the domestic production level and q_1q_4 is the free trade level of imports. When a deficiency payment scheme is in operation, P_d becomes the guaranteed farmer price. This leads to an increase in domestic production (from Oq_1 to Oq_2) which guarantees the farmer a deficiency payment of P_wP_dbc [equal to $(P_d-P_w) \times q_1q_2$] and which results in foreign exchange savings of q_1acq_2. On the assumption that the supply curve is a reflection of the marginal social opportunity cost of resources used in production (for a detailed discussion of this see El-Agraa 1978a and El-Agraa and Jones 1980) it is possible to make some significant remarks regarding this new farm revenue.

The area q_1abq_2, in an extremely simple analysis, approximates the value of the extra inputs attracted into agriculture by the deficiency payment policy. The area P_wP_dba represents the additional producer's surplus, or economic rent.[5] This can be thought of as an income transfer in favour of the farming sector.[6] Area abc represents the net loss to the society for adopting this policy; this is because the price for the consumer remains at P_w and therefore the level of imports is equal to cf.

When a variable levy scheme is in operation, the relevant farmer

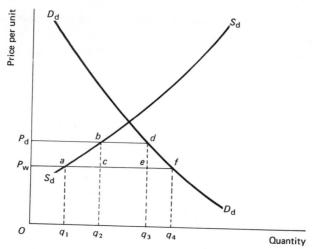

Figure 7.2

price equals the threshold price so that P_d becomes the price facing both farmers and consumers. Hence, the effects on the agricultural producing sector are exactly the same as in the previous case. However, the foreign exchange savings would now be equal to $q_1 a c q_2$ plus $q_3 e f q_4$ due to the fall in consumption by $q_1 q_2$ (from $O q_4$ to $O q_3$) – imports fall to bd. The loss of the policy is therefore equal to the areas abc and def. Area $bced$ represents a transfer from the consumers to the government.

Under extremely restrictive assumptions, it can be demonstrated that the operation of a quota system equal to $q_2 q_3$ produces the same result as a variable levy of the same equivalence.[7] There is another problem here relating to who gains the area $bced$, which in the variable levy system represents government revenue: if the government assumes responsibility or if the importers are well organised there is no problem, but if the foreign exporters are well organised they can absorb this area in the form of economic rent or excess profit.

In a purely static analysis, direct income subsidies have no economic costs (see Johnson 1966) particularly since they do not harm the consumer or the foreign supplier. However, for these subsidies to be strictly neutral in their economic impact, they should be paid in such a manner as to 'allow the recipients to leave farming without prejudice to their income from the payment scheme'.[8]

From the foregoing analysis it is evident that the income transfer system is the most efficient mechanism for farm support and that the variable levy or import quota system is the least efficient in this respect.[9] This is because the income subsidies and deficiency payment schemes allow the consumer to decide according to the cheapest international prices available, while the variable levy and import quota systems interfere with both producers and consumers. This comparison should be borne in mind when reading the conclusions of this chapter.

Objectives of the CAP

Due to the variety of agricultural support policies that existed in Western Europe at the time of the formation of the EEC, it was necessary to subject agriculture to equal treatment in all member states. Equal treatment of coal and steel (both necessary inputs for industry and' therefore of the same significance as agriculture) was already under way through the ECSC and the importance of agriculture meant that equal treatment here was vital.

The objectives of the CAP are clearly defined in Article 39 of the Treaty. They are:

   (i) 'to increase agricultural productivity by promoting technical progress and by ensuring the rational development of agricultural production and the optimum utilisation of all factors of production, in particular labour';
  (ii) to ensure thereby 'a fair standard of living for the agricultural community, in particular by increasing the individual earnings of persons engaged in agriculture';
 (iii) 'to stabilise markets';
 (iv) 'to provide certainty of supplies';
  (v) 'to ensure supplies to consumers at reasonable prices'.

  The Treaty also specifies that in:

working out the Common Agricultural Policy, and any special methods which this may involve, account shall be taken of:
  (i) the particular nature of agricultural activity, which results from agriculture's social structure and from structural and natural disparities between the various agricultural regions;
 (ii) the need to effect the appropriate adjustments by degrees;
(iii) the fact that, in the member states, agriculture constitutes a sector closely linked with the economy as a whole.

The Treaty further specifies that in order to attain the objectives set out above a common organisation of agricultural markets shall be formed:

This organisation shall take one of the following forms depending on the product concerned:
  (a) common rules as regards competition;
  (b) compulsory co-ordination of the various national marketing organisations; or
  (c) a European organisation of the market.

Moreover, the common organisation so established:

> may include all measures required to achieve the objectives set out . . ., in particular price controls, subsidies for the production and distribution of the various products, stock-piling and carry-over systems and common arrangements for stabilisation of imports and exports.
>
> The common organisation shall confine itself to pursuing the objectives set out . . . and shall exclude any discrimination between producers and consumers within the Community.
>
> Any common policy shall be based on common criteria and uniform methods of calculation.

Finally, in order to enable the common organisation to achieve its objectives, 'one or more agricultural orientation and guarantee funds may be set up'.

The remaining Articles (41– 47) deal with some detailed considerations relating to the objectives and the common organisation.

The true objectives of the CAP were established after the Stresa conference in 1958 which was convened in accordance with the Treaty. The objectives were in the spirit of the Treaty:

(i) to increase farm incomes not only by a system of transfers from the non-farm population through a price support policy, but also by the encouragement of rural industrialisation to give alternative opportunities to farm labour;

(ii) to contribute to overall economic growth by allowing specialisation within the Community and eliminating artificial market distortions;

(iii) preserving the family farm and . . . ensuring that structural and price policies go hand in hand.

It can be seen, therefore, that the CAP was not preoccupied simply with the implementation of common prices and market supports; it also included a commitment to encourage the structural improvement of farming, particularly when the former measures did not show much success (see the later section on assessment). Regarding the latter point, the main driving force has been the Mansholt Plan[10] of 1968. Dr Sicco Mansholt, who was the Agricultural Commissioner at the time, emphasised that market supports by themselves would not solve the agricultural problem. The Plan, which basically relates to the guidance aspects of the CAP, proposed the following principal measures:

(a) A first set of measures concerns the structure of agricultural production, and contains two main elements:

   (i) One group of measures, varying widely in character, must be taken to bring about an appreciable reduction in the number of persons employed in agriculture. Older people will have to be offered a supplementary annual income allowance if they agree to retire and thereby release land; younger farmers should be enabled to change over to non-farming activities; the children of farmers, finally, should be given an education which enables them to choose an occupation other than farming, if they so desire. For the two latter categories, new jobs will have to be created in many regions. These efforts at reducing manpower should be brought to bear with particular force on one group of persons within agriculture, namely, those who own their farm businesses, inasmuch as the structural reform of farms themselves . . . largely depends upon the withdrawal of a large number of these people from agriculture.

(ii) Secondly, far-reaching and co-ordinated measures should be taken with a view to the creation of agricultural (farming) enterprises of adequate economic dimensions.[11] If such enterprises are to be set up and kept running, the land they need will have to be made available to them on acceptable terms; this will require an active and appropriate agrarian policy.

(b) A second group of measures concerns markets, with the double purpose of improving the way they work and of adjusting supply more closely to demand:

(i) Here a major factor will be a cautious price policy, and this will be all the more effective as the enterprises react more sensitively to the points offered by the market.

(ii) A considerable reduction of the area of cultivated land will work in the same direction.

(iii) Better information will have to be made available to all market parties (producers, manufacturers and dealers), producers will have to accept stricter discipline and there will have to be some concentration of supply. Product councils and groupings of product councils will have to be set up at European level to take over certain responsibilities in this field.

(c) In the case of farmers who are unable to benefit from the measures described, it may prove necessary to provide personal assistance not tied either to the volume of output or to the employment of factors of production. This assistance should be payable within specified limits defined in the light of regional factors and the age of the persons concerned.

After a lengthy discussion the Council issued three Directives (72/159–161) in April 1972. These related to proposals similar to those suggested in the Mansholt Plan. However, although the precise method of implementation of these proposals was left to the discretion of national governments, about a quarter of the necessary outlay would be borne by the CAP guidance section.

The CAP Price Support Mechanism

Although the CAP machinery varies from one product to another, the basic features are more or less similar. The farmers' income support is guaranteed by regulating the market so as to reach a price high enough to achieve this objective. The domestic price is partly maintained by various protective devices. These prevent cheaper world imports from influencing the EEC domestic price level. But in addition, certain steps are taken for official support buying within the EEC, so as to eliminate from the market any actual excess supply that might be stimulated by the guaranteed price level. These surpluses may be disposed of in the manner described in the section on the policies of the EEC member nations.

More specifically, the basic features of the system can be represented by that originally devised for cereals, the first agricultural product for which a common policy was established.

A 'target price' is set on an annual basis and is maintained at a level which the product is expected to achieve on the market in the area where cereal is in shortest supply — Duisburg in the Ruhr Valley.

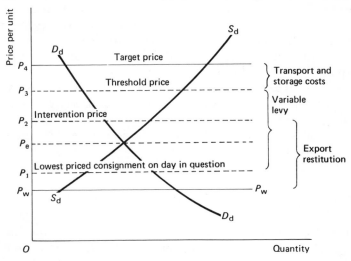

Figure 7.3

The target price is not a producer price since it includes the costs of transport to dealers and storers. The target price is variable, in that it is allowed to increase on a monthly basis from August to July in order to allow for storage costs throughout the year.

The 'threshold price' is calculated in such a way that when transport costs incurred within the EEC are added, cereals collected at Rotterdam should sell at Duisburg at a price equal to or slightly higher than the target price. An import levy is imposed to prevent import prices falling short of the threshold price. The import levy is calculated on a daily basis and is equal to the margin between the lowest priced consignment entering the EEC on the day — allowing for transport costs to one major port (Rotterdam) - and the threshold price. This levy is then charged on all imports allowed into the EEC on that day. All this information is illustrated in figure 7.3.

It is quite obvious that as long as the EEC is experiencing excess demand for this product, the market price is held above the target price by the imposition of import levies. Moreover, import levies would be unnecessary if world prices happened to be above the threshold price since in this case the market price might exceed the target price.

If target prices result in an excess supply of the product in the EEC (see figure 7.3), the threshold price becomes ineffective in terms of the objective of a constant annual target price and support buying becomes necessary. A 'basic intervention price' is then introduced for this purpose. This is fixed for Duisburg at about 7 or 8% below the target price. Similar prices are then calculated for several locations within the EEC on the basis of costs of transport to Duisburg. National intervention agencies are then compelled to buy whatever is offered to them (provided it conforms to standard) of the 'proper' product at the relevant intervention price. The intervention price is therefore a minimum guaranteed price.

Moreover, an export subsidy or *restitution* is paid to EEC exporters. This is determined by the officials and is influenced by several factors (world prices, amount of excess supply, expected trends) and is generally calculated as the difference between the EEC intervention price (P_2) and the world price (P_w).

The Green Money

The various agricultural support prices are fixed by the Council in Units of Account. For each member country there is a 'Green Rate' at which the support prices are translated into national prices. The Unit of Account had originally a gold content equal to a US dollar, but in 1973 was linked to the 'joint float'. This implies that if a member country devalues (revalues) its currency, its farm prices expressed in terms of the national currency rise (fall). It should also be noted that the scope for changing Green currency rates gives the member countries scope for altering internal farm prices *independently* of price changes determined at the annual reviews for the EEC as a whole. In August 1969 the French franc was devalued by 11.11% which obviously disturbed the common farm price arrangements in favour of the French farmers, and the rise in their price level would obviously have stimulated their farm production and aggravated the excess supply problem (see next section). Moreover, the devaluation of the Unit of Account would not have improved matters in such a situation, since it would have depressed the price level for the farmer in the rest of the EEC, even though it would have nullified the effects of the devaluation of the French franc. Therefore, a more complicated policy was adopted: the French intervention price was reduced by the full amount of the devaluation so as to eliminate the unfair benefit to the French farmer; French imports from and exports to the rest of the EEC were to be restored by asking France to give import subsidies and levy duties on her exports to compensate for the effects of the devaluation. The term 'Monetary Compensatory Amounts' (MCAs) was coined to describe this system of border taxes and subsidies. Since then, the MCA system has become general in application and more complicated with the changes in the rates of exchange of the currencies of other EEC members.

Even though the EEC has recently announced its intention to discontinue the MCA system, it seems that it will be with us for some time yet. The system therefore warrants some further explanation. It should be remembered that one of the basic aims of the CAP is to establish a uniform set of agricultural prices for all the participating nations. Since these prices are expressed in Units of Account, when a member country decides to devalue its currency (i.e. its official rate), the prices of agricultural products will rise in terms of the domestic currency by the full percentage of devaluation (given a simple analysis). This increase in the domestic prices will distort trade between the member nations and its effect on intra-EEC trade can be fully eliminated (again in a simple analysis) by imposing equivalent taxes on the export of these products and by granting equivalent subsidies to the imports of the products. This in effect amounts to operating a system of multiple exchange rates. On the other hand, when a member of the EEC decides to revalue its currency, it will have to tax intra-EEC imports and subsidise intra-EEC exports to eliminate a fall in agricultural prices. Hence, since the 'green rates' of exchange — known as 'representative rates' — are officially used for converting prices expressed in Units of Account into national currencies — official rates — it follows that when the 'green rate' deviates from the official rate, these taxes on, and subsidies to, intra-EEC traded agricultural products are used to maintain uniform agricultural prices. This is the MCA system which, once adopted by a member of the EEC, will remain until that country is able to restore its 'green rate' to that on the foreign exchange market.

The MCA system is therefore basically simple; it became complicated because of several factors. First, the French devaluation of 1969 was followed almost immediately by the German revaluation and the French and the Germans asked for the adoption of MCAs which were to be eliminated within periods of two and three years respectively. Secondly, the EEC agreed to these arrangements and met part of the cost, hence increasing the financial burden of the CAP. Thirdly, the later weakness of the US dollar was used as a reason by the EEC to introduce MCAs in order to protect its farmers from 'worldwide unfair competition' — the EEC claimed this was because the US, being a net exporter of agricultural products, was able to determine the world price level for agricultural products and this was in spite of the fact that the Unit of Account was fixed in terms of dollars! Finally, the floating of the pound sterling in 1972 and the Italian lira in 1973, which led to the sinking of both, encouraged the use of MCAs to protect the stronger EEC currencies from agricultural price increases.

The reader who is particularly interested in this area of the CAP is advised to read Irving and Fearn (1975), Josling and Harris (1976), Mackel (1978), and Hu (1979). Hu demonstrates that Germany has recently been the main beneficiary of this system!

Financing the CAP

Intervention, export restitution and the MCA system need to be financed. The finance is supplied by the EEC central fund called FEOGA (Fonds Européen d'Orientation et de Garantie Agricole), the European Guidance and Guarantee Fund, so named to incorporate the two basic elements of the CAP: support and guidance. At the time of inception of the CAP it was expected that the revenues collected from the imposition of extra area import levies would be sufficient to finance FEOGA. Since then, the rapid rise in agricultural outputs has led to a reduction in EEC imports and therefore to a reduction in receipts from levies. Also, the cost of the support system has increased beyond expectation (see the McDougall Report 1977 and Chapter 12). It has therefore become necessary to make provision for direct budgetary contributions from national governments on the basis of a formula which is discussed in some detail in the McDougall Report.

In order to put the expenditures in their proper perspective, it should be noted that the general budget of the EEC makes provision for the administrative expenses of the European Parliament, the Council of Ministers, the Court of Justice, the ECSC, and the European Development Fund, and for the administrative costs and the other operational expenditures of the Commission, which include the Agricultural Guarantee and Guidance Funds, the Social Fund, and the Regional Development Fund. For the financial year 1978 it amounts to some 12,300 million European Units of Account (EUA) or, roughly, £7,000 million, of which agricultural expenditure accounts for about three-quarters. The revenue from agricultural levies is estimated at about 1180 million EUA, approximately 10% of the total budget.

Assessment

Judged in terms of its own objectives, the CAP would seem to have had several successes. Firstly, the various agricultural support systems that existed prior to the formation of the EEC have been liquidated and a common, yet highly complicated, system has been achieved. Secondly, to a qualified extent, intra-EEC free trade in agricultural products has been accomplished through the removal of all intra-EEC trade impediments. Thirdly, the EEC as a whole has become more or less self-sufficient in farm products going to the final consumer even though the Community still depends a great deal on imported agricultural raw materials, for example, fertilisers and animal feed. Fourthly, Directive 75/268 which deals with mountain and hill farming in certain disadvantaged areas was adopted in 1975 and this amounted to a recognition of the fact that special provision would have to be made for these areas. Finally, it could be claimed that the CAP has achieved *some* progress in increasing the size of farm holdings — see the figures in brackets in table 7.2.

On the debit side, the CAP has failed to achieve any progress on the structural aspect of encouraging farmers to seek alternative occupations (even though the drift from land to industry is a natural process), etc. — hence the Mansholt Plan. Moreover, the CAP has been the cause of embarrassing surpluses: the butter and beef mountains; the wine lakes; earlier on, the grain and sugar surpluses; and more recently the milk lake. Also, the CAP has had the effect of making the prosperous farmers richer, but has not helped the poorer farmers as it has retained them in the industry through high intervention price levels. Finally, the CAP has failed to provide reasonable and stable prices for the consumer; indeed, the initial prices were set at the high German level.

These successes and failures have to be examined more carefully. Firstly, most economists would agree that the embarrassing surpluses are caused by the high level of intervention prices. This of course has serious consequences for the financing of the policy (see the MacDougall Report, the section on financing the CAP and Chapter 12). Secondly:

> ...low earnings in agriculture are the consequence of low alternative earnings arising from disparities in education levels in rural areas. But in these circumstances any price policy based on some concept of giving to farm resources the ability to achieve parity incomes with the non-farm population is doomed to failure. Higher prices are largely translated into the purchase of more inputs from the non-farm sector (fertilisers and machinery) and into the values of assets the supply of which are fixed (mainly land). Input suppliers and landlords gain, but the new entrants get no benefit. This accounts for the seemingly insatiable appetite of farm programmes for public money and the desire to hide the appropriations

in the form of higher food costs even if the same transfer could be made more efficiently by direct payments. Agriculture adjusts in size to the level of support it is given; price support policies have never influenced long-run resources returns appreciably. The implication of this is that the only way to raise farm incomes is to control the inflow of resources into agriculture, or to increase the level of education in rural areas.

(Josling 1969, pp. 268–9)

Thirdly, the MCA system which most observers had thought was a temporary phenomenon has become very well established in the mechanism of the CAP without member states fully adjusting to it. The MCA system seems a positive deterrent to intra-EEC trade — traders have great difficulty in predicting MCAs and would presumably offset this by adding them to their margins. This has created unequal prices and has justifiably led to the use of the term 'the uncommon market'.

In global terms, the CAP has been seen as undermining the interests of the Third World. This point has two elements to it: firstly, by disposing of surpluses at subsidised prices to countries like the USSR, the EEC is depriving the Developing World of potential export earnings; secondly, and most importantly, the EEC, in protecting its own agriculture, is competing unfairly against imports from these same countries. Indeed, some economists would argue that under free international trade conditions, Western Europe would have no comparative advantage in agriculture, hence the industry would disappear altogether under such circumstances.

A possible response to these claims is that 'it would be churlish to question such a goal of a prosperous agriculture contributing to economic growth in the community,' (Josling 1969, p. 268) particularly in a world where agriculture is a highly protected industry, as is the case in the EEC's most eminent competitors like the US and Japan. Moreover, agriculture should be seen as an industry for which the EEC has a socio-political preference (secure food supplies and pleasant environmental conditions?) in terms of output and employment; this is the case of a preference for a collective good discussed in detail elsewhere (see, for example, El-Agraa 1978a and El-Agraa and Jones 1980). Also, absolutely free trade in agriculture would be detrimental to the interests of countries like France and Italy, unless the argument for free trade is applied simultaneously to *all* industries. Finally, the EEC does not produce the same range of agricultural products as does the Developing World.

However, these responses have no solid foundation. It is difficult to see why it is churlish to question the goal of a prosperous agriculture particularly when this goal can only be achieved, if at all, at the expense of alternative goals — it is a question of priorities. Moreover, the EEC *does* compete with countries like Argentina, Australia, Canada, New Zealand, USA, etc. in terms of sugar, cereals, vegetables and beef; the self-sufficiency figures published by the Commission do not reflect this because they are a manifestation only of the protectionist nature of the CAP. Also, it is nonsensical to compare the EEC with the USA when the USA is a net exporter and the EEC is basically (under free trade conditions) a net importer of agricultural products. Finally the argument for a social preference for employment in agriculture is not very appealing in the context of the EEC, particularly since the world supplies are cheaper and the movement away from agricultural employment, which is what the CAP structural policies are trying to promote, is a 'natural' phenomenon.

The gist of this argument is that agricultural economists seem preoccupied with the 'trade creation' elements of the CAP and seem to ignore completely the 'trade diversion' aspects of it. (For a detailed discussion of these concepts see El-Agraa 1978b and c, El-Agraa and Jones 1980 and Chapter 4.) Because trade diversion has been ignored, the successes (!) have been exaggerated and the failures have been underestimated.[12]

Conclusions

Having explained the CAP, its mechanisms, financing, successes and failures, it is now possible to attempt some final conclusions.

Firstly, the structural problems and the embarrassing surpluses still remain, partly because the intervention prices are set at too high a level. The only justification for such high prices is that the authorities are not in a position to know the shapes of the relevant supply and demand curves for agricultural products, but when the authorities err consistently, it must be because they wish to do so.[13] A lower level of intervention prices should dispose of the surpluses problem and should encourage people who are inefficiently engaged in the farm sector to seek alternative employment (see, for example, Marsh and Ritson 1971).

Secondly, the CAP has failed to adopt the most efficient method of implementing its own objectives. It was clearly demonstrated that direct subsidies and deficiency payments are, in that order, economically superior to the variable levy system. Presumably the reason for not using subsidies in the first place was the problem of finding sources of finance. But with the surpluses and the substantial requirements for supporting artificially high prices draining the finances of FEOGA, a central budget finance system (more on this in the MacDougall Report) which would make subsidies possible is inevitable, particularly when the potential membership of Greece, Portugal and Spain (all with large agricultural sectors – see table 2.2) materialises.

Thirdly, the CAP has been a success for the EEC in that one system has been adopted to replace the elaborate support systems that had existed before. (Some commentators have gone to the extent of stating that the only success of the CAP is that it exists!) However, it can be argued that the common system contains the worst features of all the others. It is arguably also more protective than any member state on its own would contemplate being.

It is time that the CAP system was reformed with the object of adopting the most efficient support system and incorporating into it elements for the removal of any possible damage to the Developing World. An income subsidy system accompanied by the appropriate intervention price levels should produce the desired effect: no single policy measure can be expected to tackle the sort of problems facing the agricultural industry.

Notes

1   I wish to express my thanks to Messrs C.J. Black, J.K. Bowers and I.G. Simpson and to Professor A.J. Brown for helpful comments on an earlier draft of this chapter. They are, of course, not to be held responsible for any shortcomings that remain in my argument.

2   'A rough indication of average levels of income of people working in agriculture, relative to incomes of people in other occupations, can be obtained by comparing agriculture's share of the total workforce with its share of national output. Such a comparison suggests that, when the EEC was formed, average agricultural incomes in the three largest countries, France, Germany and Italy, were only about half those of other occupations.' (Ritson 1973, p. 96)

3   'Agricultural incomes have risen, but in France, Germany and Italy there is little evidence that the gap in incomes between agriculture and other occupations has diminished.' (Ritson 1973, p. 69)

4   It is argued by some that the provision of an adequate agricultural sector incidentally helps to ensure a pleasant environment for the nation's inhabitants. However, there is considerable argument that intensive agriculture is detrimental to the environment, e.g. removal of hedges, odours from intensive livestock, etc. (see Bowers 1972).

5   'This does not, however, accrue to farmers alone; in fact it represents increased return to fixed factors in both farming and in the purchased input industries.' (Josling 1969, p. 296)

6   'It is possible to derive expressions for the *average* cost (in terms of extra resources or budget payments) of achieving a unit of objective, in this case income transfer. Such calculations are meaningful if comparing the policy with a free market. More relevant in the case of a policy where the level of guaranteed price can be changed from year to year is the *marginal* cost of gaining an additional unit of objective.' (Josling 1969, p. 272)

7   Bhagwati (1965) demonstrates that tariffs and quotas can be equivalent in their effects only if it is assumed that free competition exists in both the importing countries and in the industry under consideration.

8   Josling 1969, p. 277. For a more detailed discussion of distortions, the reader should consult Johnson 1966 and Chapter 4.

9   For an estimate of the average and marginal costs of some of these policies the reader should consult Josling 1969, pp. 278–280.

10   This refers to a series of six documents which were submitted to the Council in December 1968. The first of these was called *Memorandum on the Reform of Agriculture in the European Economic Community*, in *Bulletin of the European Community*, 1969, Supplement. The series is available in one volume as *Le Plan Mansholt*, Brussels, July 1969.

11   The average size of holding in the UK in 1970–1971 was in excess of three times that in the original Six – if one were to include farms of less than one hectare, the difference would be more extreme.

12   Using 1953–69 annual observations, Thorbecke and Pagoulatos 1975 (p. 322) reached the conclusions: (a) 'the formation of the CAP has affected the pattern of international trade flows by inducing a shift from extra-EEC producers to partner countries or domestic sources of supply for nine out of ... fourteen individual commodity groups ...' and (b) 'agricultural protectionism in the Community has slowed down the rate of labour out-migration ...'.

13   Mr Roy Jenkins is unable to clarify this position. 'I mentioned a minute ago the question of surpluses. They are not always a bad thing. *It is better for the consumer to have a small surplus than a small shortage.* But that is not the same with European milk production. One-sixth of milk output is already surplus to requirements, while total consumption of milk products is declining. We shall not be able to persuade Europe's taxpayers and consumers to support that indefinitely. We cannot expect importers and other exporters of milk outside Europe to relieve us of that burden, even though we can dispose of some part outside the Community.' In *European Community*, Sept. 1978, p. 9. The emphasis is not in the original text.

References

Allen, G.H. (ed.), *British Agriculture in the Common Market*, School of Agriculture, Aberdeen, 1972.

Bergman, D. *et al.*, *A Future for European Agriculture*, Atlantic Institute, Paris, 1970.

Bhagwati, J., On the equivalence of tariffs and quotas, in Baldwin, R.E. *et al.*, *Trade, Growth and the Balance of Payments*, North-Holland Publishing Co., 1965.

Bowers, J.K., Economic efficiency in agriculture, in *Decision Making in Britain III*, Parts 1–6, Agriculture, Open University 1972.

El-Agraa, A.M., Can economists provide a rationale for customs union formation?, *Leeds Discussion Paper*, no. 68, 1978a.

El-Agraa, A.M., On trade diversion, *Leeds Discussion Paper*, no. 66, 1978b.

El-Agraa, A.M. On trade creation, *Leeds Discussion Paper*, no. 67, 1978c.

El-Agraa, A.M. and Jones, A.J., *The Theory of Customs Unions*, Philip Allan, 1980.

Ellis, F., Marsh, J. and Ritson, C., *Farmers and Foreigners — The Impact of the Common Agricultural Policy on the Associates and Associables*, Overseas Development Institute, London, 1973.

Heidhues, T. *et al.*, *Common Prices and Europe's Farm Policy*, Trade Pol cy Research Centre, Thames Essay, no. 14, 1978.

Hu, Yao-Su, German agricultural power: the impact on France and Britain, *The World Today*, Nov. 1979.

Irving, R.W. and Fearne, H.A., *Green Money and the Common Agricultural Policy*, Centre for European Agricultural Studies, Wye College, Ashford Kent, 1975.

Johnson, H.G., Optimum trade interventions in the presence of domestic distortions, in Baldwin, R.E. *et al.*, *Trade Growth and the Balance of Payments*, North-Holland Publishing Co. 1965.

Josling, T., The Common Agricultural Policy of the European Economic Community, *Journal of Agricultural Economics*, May 1969.

Josling, T. *et al.*, *Burdens and Benefits of Farm-Support Policies*, Trade Policy Research Centre, London, 1972.

Josling, T. and Harris, S., Europe's green money, *The Three Banks Review*, March 1976.

Knox, F., *The Common Market and World Agriculture*, Praeger 1972.

Lipsey, R.G., *An Introduction to Positive Economics*, Weidenfeld and Nicolson 1975.

Mackel, C., Green money and the Common Agricultural Policy, *National Westminster Bank Review*, February 1978.

Marsh, J. and Ritson, C., *Agricultural Policy and the Common Market*, Chatham House PEP, European Series, no. 16, 1971.

Ritson, C., The Common Agricultural Policy, in *The European Economic Community: Economics and Agriculture*, Open University 1973.

Rogers, S.T. and Davey, B.H. (eds), *The Common Agricultural Policy and Britain*, Saxon House 1973.

Swann, D., *The Economics of the Common Market*, Penguin Modern Economics Texts 1972.

Thorbecke, E. and Pagoulatos, E., The effects of European economic integration on agriculture, in Balassa B. (ed.), *European Economic Integration*, North-Holland Publishing Co. 1975.

European Commission, Memorandum on the reform of agriculture in the European Economic Community, *Bulletin of the European Communities*, Supplement, Jan. 1969.

European Commission, *Report of the Study Group on the Role of Public Finance in European Integration*, Brussels, 1977 (The MacDougall Report).

8

The Transport Policy

K M GWILLIAM

Introduction

The two main impediments to free international trade in goods are tariffs (tariffs are taken to represent all trade impediments other than transport costs) and transport costs. Both have the effect of protecting the producer in his own local markets, from the competition of producers in other localities. A global reduction in transport costs has the same effect as a bilateral tariff reduction in increasing the market area for efficient producers. Like tariff reductions, transport cost reductions may increase total welfare without necessarily increasing the welfare of all parties concerned. Also, like tariff structures, transport cost structures, if consciously managed, can have the effect of protecting selected groups.

The importance of a transport policy in a common market is thus obvious. Without it, any 'benefits' of multilateral tariff reductions might be vitiated by compensatory transport rate controls. The member states of the EEC are well aware of this, and of their long history of management of the transport system as a conscious instrument of national economic policy. Thus, in the earlier development of the European Coal and Steel Community, where the commodities concerned had a high transport cost component, measures to avoid conscious national discrimination being reintroduced through the transport back door were absolutely crucial. Article 70 of the Treaty of Paris firmly excluded such a possibility.

This basic similarity between tariffs and transport costs explains not only the need for a transport policy, but also to some extent the forms which that policy has taken and the difficulties which its formulation has faced. Whilst the economic objectives spelt out in Article 2 of the Treaty of Rome are of a kind and at a level of generality which would be acceptable to all member states, transport policy is seen itself as merely instrumental in achieving these objectives. In Articles 74–84, which deal specifically with the transport sector, transport policy objectives are set out in much more structural terms. Primarily, transport policy is to be so arranged as to contribute in the best possible way to the development of a freer, competitive, market in goods and services. Secondly, insofar as it is compatible with the primary objective, it should aim to achieve a free market in transport itself. The Treaty contains a number of specific prohibitions on discrimination and permissive powers for a wider ranging policy to be developed subsequently. In the event, the subsequent attempts by the Commission to create a policy have been largely devoted to such measures as controls on entry, price controls and harmonisation of conditions of operation, which have immediately been of a restrictive rather than liberalising nature. The reason for this direction being adopted is the obsession of the Commission with eliminating distortions of competition between modes or states, for which a transparent uniformity has been considered necessary.

It is plain that the achievement of a common policy on this basis has been very difficult. In this chapter we attempt to explain why this has been so, and to examine the nature of the common policy that has emerged. There appear to be two characteristics of transport policy which contribute significantly to these difficulties. Firstly, there is the very complex and delicate balance of the existing national transport policies, which we exemplify in the next section by reference to UK policy. Secondly, there are differing traditions within the EEC concerning the role of transport policy within the broader sphere of economic policy, which we discuss in the following section. The common policy is then described and discussed, and in the concluding section we speculate on the extent to which the development of a satisfactory common transport policy depends on the emergence of a more realistic assessment of the relationship between national and community policies.

The Constitution of a National Transport Policy – The Case of the UK

Although the member states in some respects have similar histories and problems, one of the most striking features about national transport policy is the delicate balance that appears to exist within a disparate package of policy instruments. Subtle variations, both between countries and over time, in the emphasis placed on particular policy objectives may stimulate quite different, but equally appropriate, responses according to the precise composition of the initial policy package. A forced uniformity in one instrument may upset the balance in quite different ways.

At a very general level one can discern three principal objectives in transport policy. First, to contribute to economic growth and to higher national prosperity, particularly through providing an efficient service to industry, commerce and agriculture. Second, to meet social needs by securing a reasonable level of personal mobility, in particular by maintaining public transport for the many people who do not have the effective choice of travelling by car. Third, to minimise the harmful effects of transport, such as loss of life and damage to the environment.

At this level of generality there is little political dispute in the UK about objectives. Moreover, even in seeking policy instruments to achieve these objectives, there is no fundamental difference between the mainstream thought of the leading political parties. In 1968 it was a Labour government which liberalised entry to the road haulage industry. In a policy review of 1976 and 1977, the Labour government explicitly rejected an approach based on centralised national demand forecasting and planning. Equally significantly, however, Conservative administrations have retained restrictions on entry to the bus industry and have tolerated substantial subsidies to both bus and rail modes of public transport. What both parties claim to seek is a balanced transport policy, drawing on the best elements both of private enterprise and the profit motive and of planning and control. It is only at a finer level of prescription that significant political differences begin to emerge.

Thus, governments of different persuasions in the UK have used the same three main sets of powers: those of organisation, of regulation, and of taxation (including subsidisation). The direct powers of organisation are mainly exercised in determining the scope, administrative structure and objectives of the nationalised industries. The powers of regulation include the regulation of entry to the sector or to parts of the sector; control of the physical and commercial conditions of operation in the sector; and general and specific price controls. The financial powers consist mainly of control over the level and structure of taxation of road users on the one hand, and the level and structure of subsidies to public transport agencies, whether nationally, locally or privately owned, on the other. All the EEC members use this same range of instruments.

What is of major concern, in the context of appraising a common EEC transport policy, is the way in which the instruments have been combined in pursuit of the fundamental objectives.

Efficiency

There are a number of levels at which efficiency needs to be ensured:

(i) At the sectoral level, the total amount of transport provided should be adequate but not excessive. (In theoretical terms the marginal productivity of factor inputs in the transport sector should be equal to those in other sectors).

(ii) Within the transport sector we need an efficient allocation of resources and traffics between modes. This we shall call the intermodal resource allocation dimension.

(iii) The structure of each mode of transport should be that which allows the demand for that mode to be met at least cost. (In theoretical terms this would be achieved if, for every output, the short-run and long-run marginal cost had been equated through the adaptation of plant or system size).

(iv) Each individual operator must also be operating in such a way as to make efficient use of the assets at his disposal in the short run. This we shall call the X-efficiency dimension.

In transport, as in other sectors, the existence of indivisibilities, of uncertainty, of finite gestation periods for investment, of externalities, and of varying incidences of economies of scale makes the simultaneous achievement of all these levels of efficiency extremely difficult to attain.

In *urban passenger transport* the main concern has been with the intersectoral and intermodal resource allocation dimensions.

The prevalent view is that better and more coherent planning is needed at the local level, which should be part of the wider planning for the areas concerned and should be under local democratic control. This implies that local authorities should have comprehensive transport planning responsibilities and powers and should have the widest range of possible instruments of planning at their disposal. Much of recent institutional change in the UK has been devoted to this end.

Despite this apparent trend to decentralise, central government retains substantial influence. As an important source of funding of local authorities, it is able to affect the spatial distribution of expenditure on urban transport. Moreover, it has in fact used the leverage that this allocation function gives it to mould the composition of local policies. In particular it has militated against uncontrolled extension of general fares subsidy for urban public transport.

Nevertheless, it is clear that, in the long run, widely differing local transport plans may emerge. In particular, local variations may affect the balance between traffic restraint, public transport subsidy, road pricing and road investment policies as means of countering traffic congestion. As far as regulation is concerned there has been little dispute, over a period of nearly 50 years, that a very high degree of administrative co-ordination is desirable. Since 1930 this has been exercised through the quasi-independent Traffic Commissioner vested with powers to control both the level of public transport service provided and the fares charged. More recently, however, there has been concern both regarding the possibility that this system may have suppressed desirable innovation and regarding the apparent conflict between the responsibilities of the Traffic Commissioner and the elected local representatives.

Similarly, the question of internal efficiency of public transport operation has received relatively little attention. But, as public transport is increasingly viewed as a component part of a comprehensive local strategy for transport, reflecting local objectives and priorities, there has been a growing concern to ensure that appropriate management objectives are set for public transport operators, also reflecting these general transport policy objectives. Reliance on 'budgetary equilibrium' (enshrined in EEC policy statements) may not fit well into this framework.

For *inter-urban passenger transport* an efficient allocation of resources and traffic between modes is sought through the market mechanism. Each mode is expected to meet the costs properly attributable to it. This implies that both public and private road passenger transport are expected to meet the attributable costs of infrastructure use through taxation and that the public transport modes should be set broadly commercial objectives. Structurally the inter-urban bus sector is subject to control of service level and price through a licensing system. National ownership of a large proportion of the industry is accompanied by effective decentralisation of management to regional operating companies. Competition between bus, rail and the private car thus involves some freedom to use discriminatory pricing schemes (particularly for rail transport). Further competition from domestic air transport is controlled by the Civil Aviation Authority which, nevertheless, allows considerable freedom to operators (mostly the nationalised British Airways) to offer promotional fares so long as the general obligation to cover costs is met.

There are a number of problems associated with this attempt to seek efficient co-ordination through a competitive market. The theoretical basis for the allocation of road track costs is widely thought to be weak; the definition of the 'proper contribution' which inter-city rail services should make to the joint costs of system operation is essentially arbitrary; and the possibility of competitive over-investment in capacity between the modes is a source of concern for the government. But, subject to these limitations, a structure does exist within which the modes are expected, through the pursuit of traditional commercial objectives, to secure an efficient service. The real problems arise in the non-urban transport demands which do not fall on the major inter-city corridors. Here the problem is that demand is often so sparse that certain rail transport services cannot be viably maintained, and in some circumstances no public transport service at all would be provided if the market mechanism were relied upon. The difficulty is to provide a mechanism to secure the continuation of socially desirable, but unremunerative, public transport services in specific localities, without introducing distortions in the general competitive framework.

For *freight transport* the aim of government has similarly been to provide a basis for fair competition between modes by requiring them to meet the infrastructure costs for which they are responsible and also to operate without subsidy. For rail transport this is interpreted as a requirement to meet simply the avoidable costs of provision where track is shared with passenger services. The seeds of controversy in this solution are obvious. It is claimed that, in most instances, the arrangement results in rail freight obtaining free use of track. On the other hand, whilst for road-haulage vehicles as a whole, attributable track costs are fully covered, it is argued that this is not the case for the largest and highest mileage lorries which are the really important source of distortion.

Structurally, the road-haulage sector has been uncontrolled since the abandonment of the restrictive licensing system in 1968. Whilst the Foster Committee, which reported in 1978, recommended tighter enforcement of the controls on the *quality* of road-haulage operators, it did not propose any return to *quantity* controls.

Social Objectives

In Britain the pursuit of social objectives in transport policy is restricted almost exclusively to the passenger sector. At a general level the objective may be seen as that of maintaining an adequate level of personal mobility for those people who do not have the choice of travel by car. Effectively, this reduces to the objective of attempting to maintain adequate public transport services in the face of increasing incomes and car ownership levels.

For the most part the responsibility for pursuing this objective devolves to local authorities who have interpreted it in very different ways. The South Yorkshire Metropolitan County have taken it to require a general low public transport fares policy, with 50% of the costs of public transport being covered by subsidy. Oxfordshire, in contrast, have taken the view that it can be adequately achieved by policies of self-help with local community bus schemes, usually entirely self-financing, meeting needs which are not met by the conventional bus operator on a commercial basis. Only in the case of certain local rail services, which central government requires British Rail to maintain as part of the public service obligation, is the responsibility exercised centrally.

Although central government does not act as the direct source of support, it does have leverage through its position as the ultimate source of a large part of the money which local government is able to disburse. It has used this power to try to ensure that subsidies are directed to specific groups (old age pensioners or school children) or to maintain services which might otherwise be withdrawn entirely (e.g. in rural areas). It has discouraged blanket subsidy to keep down general fare levels in urban areas. But, despite its efforts, that is where the bulk of bus support actually goes.

Safety and Environment

The objective of maintaining a safer and more tolerable environment is, for the most part, pursued by the designation of technical standards. Weights and dimensions of heavy vehicles are controlled, as is the condition in which they are maintained and operated; and local traffic regulation powers can be used to control the routes taken by heavy vehicles. Whilst it has been argued that heavy vehicles should be charged a special tax because of their environmental impact, the government view has been that this impact cannot be satisfactorily measured and that it would be difficult to arrange the counterpart compensation for those who suffer the impact. Hence, with the exception of a scheme of capital grant for rail sidings to secure environmental benefits from the transfer of traffic from road to rail, direct market instruments are not generally used for environmental purposes. In this respect, the British approach is very similar to that in other EEC member states.

Variety of Objectives and Instruments of Transport Policy in the EEC

Our brief examination of UK transport policy has shown how complex and delicate are the institutional and statutory mechanisms developed in pursuit of the generally unobjectionable aims of efficiency, equity and the maintenance of an acceptable environment. The ease with which six, or nine, or whatever number of such national policies can be integrated into a common EEC transport policy will clearly depend on the compatibility of the national transport objectives and the institutions generated to achieve those objectives. It is to such a comparison that we now turn.

The national transport policies of the individual member states have some common antecedents. Before the development of road transport, policy in most member countries had been directed at controlling the rates and conditions of carriage of an effective rail monopoly. From this starting point it was a relatively easy step to the subsequent position where governments manipulated rates to further their wider social and political aims.

With the advent of road haulage competition, the scope for internal cross subsidy in rail transport was diminished. It became clear that the railways were in a position to meet social obligations only if they were given financial aid or protected from this competition. Whilst governments ostensibly justified restrictions on the road goods transport industry in the 1930s, on the basis of the supposed ill effects of 'cut throat' competition in that industry, protection of the railways was in fact equally important. Hence, structural controls were introduced to buttress the continued use of railway rates policy as an instrument of social and political strategy.

Within this common broad framework there emerged some significant differences between the social and political objectives pursued through the use of transport policy. This had consequential effects on the burden of control of the road sector; on the level of the compensatory protection of the rail sector; and hence, eventually, on the roles adopted by the alternative transport modes from country to country. In Germany and France, where road legislation is the most restrictive, only about two-fifths of the total ton-kms performed by the transport industry are by road, whereas in the UK, with a more liberal system, the road share is about four-fifths.

There appear to be four policy areas within which one can discern very distinct differences in approach between the traditional policies of the member countries of the EEC, namely trade policy, regional policy, social policy and industrial policy.

Transport and International Trade

This chapter opened with the observation that transport costs could be viewed as directly equivalent to tariffs in their effect on trade patterns. The degree to which the potential of transport policy in this respect has been exploited has varied greatly.

The most systematic policies have probably been those of Germany. Whilst the programme of autobahn construction in the interwar years has frequently been attributed to economic nationalism, it was probably in the manipulation of railway rates that transport policy achieved its greatest effect on trade patterns. Immediately prior to the creation of the European Coal and Steel Community, home produced coal in Germany was being carried at rates up to 23% lower than those for imported coal. For German exports, the special seaport tariffs offered lower rates for merchandise carried to German ports, as a means of countering the competition from lower cost routes through Dutch ports. Germany was not alone in pursuing these types of policy. In France, for instance, rock sea salt intended for export was carried at rates up to 38% below those charged for internal movements.

Not all of the EEC member countries have the same history in this respect. At the other end of the spectrum, the Dutch have traditionally operated land transport essentially as a commercial sector. Their railways remained profitable for longer than those of most countries and it was not until 1954 that they introduced legislation to control entry into the road haulage sector. Whilst passenger services in the Netherlands are now very heavily subsidised for social reasons, it is still the ostensible objective of transport policy for freight transport to be provided on a purely commercial basis.

Transport and Regional Policy

The problem of regional imbalance in activity rates is common to most of the members of the EEC. Even the small, wealthy and densely populated Netherlands has, in Limburg, its problem area. In some cases (e.g. South Wales and the North East of the UK) the problem is due to the decline of traditional industries, in some (e.g. Brittany and the Italian Mezzogiorno) it is the absence of an established industrial base; in some (e.g. border areas of West Germany) it is the post war loss of the local industrial focus due to border changes.

The views that are taken of the extent to which transport policy can help to solve these problems vary greatly. In West Germany, regional development objectives appear to be given some importance in road investment planning, whereas in most of the other member countries there appears to be rather more scepticism about the effects of such an indiscriminatory aid. In a number of countries, including France, West Germany and Italy, discriminatory rail rates have traditionally been used to this end. For instance, even before the development of an EEC common transport policy which made provision for such measures only as an exception to a general policy of non-discrimination, the carriage of machinery and materials destined for Southern Italy attracted reductions of up to 50% of normal rail tariffs. In contrast to this, the historic objection to 'undue preference' in rail rates in the UK made no such policy-directed exceptions.

The member countries differ not only in policy for the regions, but also in the extent to which and the ways in which responsibility in transport policy is delegated. In West Germany, as a Federal Republic, the Länder have substantial powers in the determination of transport policy. Similarly, in the UK, in principle at least, policy on public transport within the counties is devolved to them as an essential part of a comprehensive land use and transport strategy. Problems have already arisen in reconciling local and central government objectives in the UK. The difficulties of constucting a Community policy are undoubtedly increased by the existence of multiple levels of responsibility within the member states.

Transport and Social Policy

Whilst most countries would view the provision of public transport as in some sense to be a 'public service', the precise way that implied obligation is interpreted varies. There are three different dimensions deserving comment in this context.

Firstly, it is becoming increasingly common for some level of service to be specified as a policy aim. In the Netherlands, objectives for the railway operator are specified in terms of minimum frequencies to be provided on different types of line. In Britain, the 1974 Transport Act requires British Rail to maintain services at the level prevailing at the date of the act. In most of the member states, closure of rail routes requires government permission. Faced with a secularly declining demand which is also price inelastic, this objective can only be achieved by increased subsidy or by increased prices.

The second dimension in which public service may be interpreted is thus the price dimension. Here the national objectives are much more variable. In Italy, rail fares are fixed by law and the railway company is allowed annual fare increases up to a maximum of 10% per annum. In the Netherlands, the level of fares must not rise by more than the general cost of living index. At the other extreme, in Britain, after a period of price restraint (imposed on all the nationalised industries) the objectives of different types of rail service are now specified in financial terms. Inter-city services, for example, are expected to meet fully allocated costs.

The third dimension in which public service is sometimes seen is that of employment. Whilst in most countries the employment in public transport, and particularly in rail transport, is falling, in Italy employment in rail transport has increased. This is partly due to the fact that the level of employment is set by law and that as hours of work are reduced, the establishment is correspondingly increased.

Transport and Industrial Policy

The relationship between transport policy and other dimensions of national economic policy differs greatly between member states. In Germany, at one extreme, transport policy is seen as being largely instrumental in the pursuit of more fundamental regional or industrial policy objectives. Thus road investment appraisal in Germany is based on the contribution that improvements make to these strategic objectives to a much greater extent than in other countries. Similarly, though the German railways have been losing heavily on freight transport, the pressure from industry to eliminate these deficits has been curiously muted. In the UK, in contrast, much attention is paid in infrastructure investment policy and in rail pricing policy to the need to ensure efficient allocation of resources *within the transport sector*. Such fundamental differences in viewpoint not only make relative efficiency difficult to assess, but inevitably make it difficult to arrive at an agreed common transport policy except at a very general level. It is to the search for the reconciliation of these differences in a common policy that we now turn.

The Initiation of a Common Policy

The foundation of the common transport policy lies in the Treaty of Rome. Articles 74—84 of the Treaty set out some specific injunctions on discrimination in transport and, more importantly, give powers to the Commission to make proposals for a wide-ranging common policy to achieve the general objectives of the common market.

The Commission presented its first proposals for the development of the common transport policy in April 1961, in a Memorandum commonly associated with the name of M Lambert Schaus, the first Transport Commissioner. The Schaus Memorandum attempted to provide some logical structure for a transport policy, taking as a starting point the general community objective of a freer and more competitive market. But it also identified four special characteristics of the transport sector, namely:

(i) a high degree of public intervention in provision of infrastructure;
(ii) low supply and demand elasticities leading to unstable prices;
(iii) large, traditional public service obligations;
(iv) complex relationships between transport and other sector objectives.

It was the view taken of these special characteristics that set the tone of the common transport policy developments for the next 12 years. This was very clearly spelt out by the Commission at the time:

> The key to the system is the following. Since competition is the main government principle of the European Community, and since the special aspects of transport hinder the normal play of competition, action must be based on removing the special aspects or on neutralising their effects where they continue to exist.
>
> European Commission, Memorandum on the general lines of a common transport policy, *Bulletin*, April 1961.

The important role of public authorities in the provision of infrastructure, the importance of the public service obligations, and the need to relate transport to other sector policies, remain largely undisputed. But it was the credence given to the supposed instability of the transport sector that led the Commission towards an interventionist policy both on conditions of entry (licensing) and on price controls in the road transport sector. In fact, the evidence of low supply and demand elasticities and consequent price instability tends to be anecdotal rather than statistical. For example, when the Geddes Committee examined these issues in the UK in 1964 it came to the conclusion that they yielded support for intervention.

The policy proposed in the Schaus Memorandum was to have three objectives:

(i) elimination of obstacles which transport may put in the way of the establishment of the Common Market as a whole;
(ii) integration of transport on the Community level (the free movement of transport services within the Community);
(iii) general organisation of the transport system within the Community.

Eliminating Discrimination

The first objective encompassed the elimination of such obstacles to free movement as discrimination on the grounds of nationality, unjustifiable State aids, and barriers to frontier crossing of a physical, fiscal or technical kind. Progress on this front appears to have been substantial. Although there have been difficulties such as the infamous case of the Saarland tariffs (see Gwilliam and Mackie 1975, p. 359), action under Regulation 11 of July 1961 led to the elimination of most published rates involving conscious national discrimination by the end of 1964. Where more general support tariffs were allowed to continue under the provisions of Article 80(2) of the Treaty of Rome, their breadth of application and effects were monitored and confined. These measures were accompanied by action to improve the physical facilities for frontier crossing, with the result that the achievement of this objective has effectively ceased to be a contentious issue.

An Integrated Community Network

The second objective was mainly concerned with freedom of establishment, freedom of operation and technical harmonisation as means of integrating the transport market throughout the Community. Complete freedom of establishment would be the ultimate in integration, but progress towards this aim has been very slow. A proposed regulation on common rules for access to the occupation of road haulier was submitted to the Council in June 1967. But it was not until mid-1975 that the next step was taken, with a proposed regulation for mutual recognition of certain qualifications.

It is the absence of complete freedom of establishment which makes freedom of international operation so important. For rail and waterway transport, no great problem exists because of the long standing existence of such arrangements as the Berne Conventions and the Act of Mannheim. For road passenger transport considerable progress has been made also. In 1966 a regulation was enacted which provided for the progressive liberalisation of movement for unscheduled services, whilst in 1972 provision was made for the authorisation of regular and shuttle services between member states.

The real problems have arisen in road haulage, where all of the original six member countries operated restrictive licensing systems. Clearly, any attempt to control and restrict national operators would be seen as of limited value, if foreign hauliers had freedom of operation. International operation can, therefore, usually only be carried out by hauliers in possession of the requisite licences. In the past, the number of such licences available to foreign hauliers had been fixed under bilateral agreements, but more recently multi-national agreements have been reached within the European Community and between the member states of the European Conference of Ministers of Transport (comprised of the EEC member states plus Austria, Greece, Norway, Portugal, Spain, Sweden, Switzerland, Turkey and Yugoslavia). But 95% of international freight movement by road is still arranged through bilateral agreements, which have varied according to the liberality of national legislation in negotiating countries. However, under no agreement is the right of 'cabotage' allowed, i.e. the right of a foreign haulier to undertake purely national carriage within the territory of another country.

The multilateral 'Community' quota of 1200 licences was introduced for an experimental period of three years by Regulation 1018 in July 1968. A series of regulations extended the period of application and increased the quota by 15% per annum from 1973 onwards. Although a further proposed regulation submitted as part of the 1975 measures follows the same pattern of extending the size of the quota but not completely eliminating the bilateral agreements, the magnitude of the increase proposed is of a quite different order, doubling the number of Community licences in one step. In the event, no immediate increase was agreed by the Council of Ministers. When, one year later, the Community quota scheme was finally adopted as a permanent measure, only a 20% increase in the existing number of permits was agreed.

Harmonisation of the conditions of operation in the EEC transport sector has been seen as one way of overcoming this resistance to liberalisation. Primarily, harmonisation has been considered necessary in order that there shall be fair and free competition between operators of different nationality in the liberalised market. Where the employment conditions in road transport are concerned, 'levelling-up' was also considered necessary to avoid distortion between modes resulting from more rigorous restraints existing for rail transport. Finally, there is also a social case for 'levelling-up' in the terms and conditions of employment.

Three main areas of harmonisation have been suggested — fiscal, social and technical.

Fiscal harmonisation has not been completely achieved in road transport. The Community has standardised the conditions for free admission of fuel in tanks of vehicles engaged in international transport, but has still not resolved the problem of double taxation of road vehicles, despite a Commission proposal as early as 1964 that vehicles should only be taxed in their country of registration. Moreover, the levels of fuel taxation, and their basis, still vary from country to country.

Fiscal harmonisation for rail transport occupies a crucial position in the whole strategy. The Schaus Memorandum argued for commercial freedom and financial autonomy for operators, but also recognised the conflict between this freedom and the social obligations that were required particularly of rail undertakings. The reconciliation of these apparently incompatible lines of thought was provided for in a trio of regulations adopted in 1969 and 1970. Regulation 1191 defined public service obligations and established a common procedure for granting compensation; Regulation 1192 aimed at eliminating discrepancies between the treatment of railways and other transport sectors, by 'normalising' accounts; and Regulation 1107 expanded the list of public service obligations which could be compensated, and defined other aids which could be granted, for 'co-ordination' purposes. The logic of this system requires that the impact of all the valid departures from normal commercial freedom are costed and allowed for. Thereafter any subsequent deficits would be illegitimate and the railways would be required, by whatever means necessary, to eliminate them. In the event, the system appears to have operated quite differently. Rail subsidies emerging from the varying national transport policies have been comprehensively allocated, *ex post*, to the legitimising regulations. Neither the definition of legitimate interventions nor the allocation of costs is sufficiently well developed to act as the driving force in a control mechanism. Moreover, it is doubtful whether they ever can be developed adequately for this function.

Social harmonisation has only a slightly happier history. After several years of discussion and negotiation, Regulation 543/69 controlled minimum age and composition of road transport crews as well as their working times and rest periods. Again, however, despite the introduction of an on-board monitoring device (the tachograph), by Regulation 1463/70, implementation has proved very difficult. The UK Government has only begun to take steps to enforce implementation after a ruling against it by the Court of Justice.

The problems of *technical harmonisation* have differed significantly between modes. In the case of rail transport, harmonisation through the International Railways Union was already prevalent and the only issue of significance to arise concerned the introduction of automatic coupling; even this was agreed eventually in the wider forum of the European Conference of Ministers of Transport. In waterway transport, the technical characteristics of the vehicle are very strictly constrained by the characteristics of the infrastructure and common policy took the form of an agreement of common standards for the construction of new equipment, rather than constraint on the use of existing equipment.

Again in this aspect of policy, the real problems have concerned road haulage. A first set of proposals limiting the maximum length, width, height, weight and axle weight for various categories of road vehicles was submitted to the Council early in 1963. The Council quickly reached agreement on everything except axle loadings and overhangs. Despite the advice of the Commission to proceed with a regulation covering the agreed matters, the Council decided to hold the whole matter in abeyance until a comprehensive agreement could be reached. Such an agreement finally appeared to have emerged in the spring of 1972 when the Council adopted a number of 'guidelines' reflecting unanimity on the major technical standards. Unfortunately, at this time it became clear that the three acceding countries would not be easily persuaded to accept more than 10 tonnes per single axle load. The 'more liberal' newcomers wanted freedom of entry into the road haulage industry but, for environmental reasons, wished to control vehicle weights more rigorously. A period of negotiation therefore commenced in which a compromise was sought in the trade-off between these objectives. No directive was therefore immediately adopted and some of the original Six retreated towards their own negotiating positions and widespread disagreement reappeared.

Common National Transport Regulation

The third policy area defined by the Schaus Memorandum concerned the general organisation of the transport system in the member countries of the Community. The justification for common rules relating to purely internal transport in the member countries is less evident than in matters relating to international movements and the degree of uniformity that is ultimately achieved, or even sought, may well depend on the wider philosophical question of the nature of the Community.

The Schaus Memorandum envisaged a high degree of integration involving common rules on tariffs, entry to national transport markets, relationship between operators and the state, infrastructure policy and social policy in the transport sector. The newly emerging, more liberally oriented, Commission view seems to be much more modest. While it puts even more emphasis than ever on infrastructure, the central role of common tariff rules seems to have been abandoned and it is doubtful if the search for a set of entry conditions common to all member states can survive except insofar as they provide a necessary stepping stone to a more liberal entry to the Community-wide transport market. Even in infrastructure the philosophy underpinning the increased emphasis seems more closely related to the desire to remove impediments to the establishment of the general common market conditions of free movement, than to a philosophy of unification and standardisation *per se*.

The explanation of these changes seems to lie partly in a growing sense of disillusionment about the prospects of exercising effective control of such a disaggregated and complex sector as transport operation, and partly in an unproven optimism that influence can be exercised both more easily and more effectively through infrastructure policy. Certainly, the history of the individual policies can be read in this light.

Prices

The 1961 Memorandum envisaged that rates should be both 'transparent' (i.e. published) and controlled. This was thought necessary in order to prevent monopolistic exploitation of dominant positions through high prices on the one hand, or price and service instability through excessive competition on the other. There emerged quite naturally from this rationale the concept of an upper limit and a lower limit — the bracket rate. On the basis of information about costs of transport it was presumed that it would be possible to determine a range of likely full costs of operation for each mode of transport that would exclude the possibility of either exploitation or uneconomic price cutting.

Though this philosophy was given an added academic gloss by the arguments of the Allais report in 1965, progress in implementing it has been very slow. Regulation 1174 of July 1968 introduced a system of bracket tariffs for international road haulage only, but even this regulation has had a very chequered history. Numerous problems arose concerning conditions for specific contracts and the publication of rates and in 1972 the Commission itself reported that there were very considerable divergences between member states and its manner of implementation. Although initially it had been envisaged that Regulation 1174 was merely a first step towards a wider application to domestic traffic and to all modes, the Commission now seems to have abandoned the task. Amongst the set of measures proposed in late 1975 was the replacement of the mandatory bracket tariff by a purely advisory reference tariff system. Hence, the tariff control ceases to be an instrument of organisation of the national markets and becomes merely a guideline to the Commission in assessing whether actual rates involve illegal discrimination. Whether, incidentally, it is more likely to act as a stimulus to collusion remains to be seen.

Control of Entry

The background to the development of a Community policy on *control of national transport capacity* was the pre-existence of more or less restrictive regimes in all six of the original member states. When, in June 1965, the member states reached agreement on the organisation of the transport market, this agreement included the presumption that a common domestic licensing system would be introduced which represented a compromise between the various national systems (see Bayliss 1973).

In June 1967 the Commission submitted a draft regulation to the Council on entrance to national road haulage markets, a revised version of which was explained to the Council by a Note from the Commission in late 1971. The Note referred to the necessity of creating 'a climate of healthy competition' and stated with reference to market entry:

> The Commission is of the opinion that there is still a completely valid need for common rules to be introduced to provide for a harmonisation of the conditions in which the national markets operate and to enable, on the one hand, serious disturbances of the market resulting from excess of capacity to be avoided and, on the other hand, to promote the development of capacity in step with the requirement of the economy.

The proposed regulations were not to apply to transport by firms on their own account, in light vehicles, by scheduled haulage services or for very short distance traffic.

For the rest — the bulk of long distance public haulage — the market was to be divided into a short-distance zone (Zone A) and a long-distance zone (Zone B). In order to obtain initial access to Zone A the applicant was required to provide information on the transport services (in vehicle kms) he intended to operate within the capacity requested during the first year of activities and also on the anticipated receipts. The applicant had to justify his statements through documentation which in particular was to include statements from customers. A licence was to be granted only if the anticipated costs and receipts compared favourably with 'normal costs' and 'normal receipts', as determined by the licensing authority.

Expansion of capacity in Zone A was only to be allowed if, in relation to anticipated new traffic, the same conditions as for a new-comer were fulfilled and if existing operations compared favourably with the 'norm' as determined by the licensing authority. For Zone B, applicants were expected to fulfil similar conditions to those required for Zone A, but in addition each member state was to set an overall capacity limit for the zone. This capacity limit was to be determined by reference to medium-term economic policy, forecasts of traffic demand and the development of highway infrastructure.

Clearly, in the ten years from 1961 to 1971 the basic philosophy of the Commission had not changed. Competition was to be the key to the system, but controls were necessary because of inherent disturbances in the market. The 1971 licensing proposals were a mixture of existing regulations in each of the six member states, but the Council of Ministers could not agree on the formulation of common rules.

By October 1973 the Commission had begun to modify its position. In a communication submitted to the Council in 1973 it stood firmly by its 1961 Memorandum declaration that 'transport undertakings and users should benefit from the advantages of competition', but a certain softening on its previous position on licensing control was perceptible in the statement that, 'for goods transport, the common transport market will function freely subject to essential corrective measures'.

By 1975, the Commission had reached the point where as a general rule it did not see the necessity for capacity controls, and only saw the necessity of legislation to provide for these should market conditions at a specific time warrant them. In particular, the Commission commented:

> The view may be taken, however, particularly in order to take account of features inherent to each member state, that Community regulations may do no more than lay down the general principles on which national regulations are to be based, while leaving the member states the necessary latitude to choose the means used.
>
> (ECMT 1975)

At the same time the Commission further suggested:

1. In the field of road transport, the states must seek to provide a satisfactory balance between supply and demand for transport through a system of market supervision, without recourse to quotas of authorisations, or the imposition of any quantitative restriction.
2. Existing restrictions must be removed gradually in conjunction with the progress planned for international transport operations.
3. The right will be progressively given to non-resident hauliers to conduct domestic transport operations while performing an international transport operation — for a period to be determined (e.g. one month).
4. The trade will establish, with the involvement of the users, 'recommended' tariffs differing according to the type of goods and conditions of carriage. The choice between the various techniques available for fixing tariffs will be left to the judgement of the trade.

Member states are, however, expected to keep the market continually under supervision and if a serious disturbance appears in the market, a member country may take measures affecting capacity and rates and conditions of carriage.

Infrastructure Investment Policy

In very distinct contrast to these views on management of the market, the 1973 Memorandum from the Commission to the Council of Ministers argued for increased attention to infrastructure policy as part of a process of bringing transport arrangements more closely into co-ordination with other community policies. Some kind of common infrastructure investment policy has always been intended by the Commission. But its early attempts to set out principles for the definition of a network of routes of community importance, and to indicate priorities, produced unacceptable implications for the autonomy of member states in allocating investment funds. In place of these proposals of supranational centralisation the Council of Ministers, in a decision in February 1966, adopted a much more modest consultation procedure which left the submission of projects for consultation to the discretion of the member states.

This procedure has been seen to suffer from two major defects. Firstly, the existing consultation procedure did not give any adequate indication of what information should be provided and at what stage in the development of projects. The content and style of information requirements was the subject of a report in 1973 (Gwilliam, Petriccione, Voigt and Zighera) and an attempt to strengthen the institutional arrangements is contained in the 1976 proposal to set up a standing committee on infrastructure to allow a continuing exchange of information and comment from an early stage, on programmes as well as on specific projects.

The second weakness was complementary to the first. Members were jealous of their own powers to determine priorities in national investment budgets. In a second proposed regulation in early 1976, the embryo of a common transport investment fund is provided for, in the form of Community aid for transport infrastructure investment of Community interest.

Infrastructure Pricing

The prosecution of a common policy with regard to the allocation of infrastructure costs began rather later than that concerning investment decisions, but has been pursued more rapidly and more vigorously. The stimulus for harmonising infrastructure pricing is the fear that inappropriate structures of charges for the use of infrastructure will lead to distortions in the competition between modes and might even be used as a covert way of retaining conscious national discrimination in trade.

The theoretical studies of the early Sixties led to a proposal for a common system in which infrastructure charges would both reflect marginal social costs and meet an overall budgetary equilibrium requirement. The Council having accepted this in principle in December 1967, the Commission went on to develop two proposals. The first, which was adopted by the Council in June 1970, was for a regulation setting up a common accounting system for expenditures on rail, road and inland waterway infrastructures. The initial set of accounts produced under the regulation, which included the information for the three new member countries in an appendix, was presented at the end of 1974.

The second, more substantive, proposal has proved much more difficult to progress. In July 1968 the Commission proposed a directive on the adjustment of national taxation systems on commercial vehicles to relate differences in rates of tax to differences in marginal costs of road use. It soon became clear that national governments would wish to examine the implications of this practical proposal very closely and that early adoption was unlikely. In order to attempt to maintain the impetus, the Commission therefore submitted, in June 1971, a more general proposal for a common infrastructure charging scheme which would record support for the general principles set out in the Allais and Malcor 1970 reports. A further study of Oort 1975 has examined alternative ways of reconciling the marginalist and budgetary equilibrium objectives. A draft regulation requiring the pricing strategy to be applied to heavy goods vehicles, is presumably before the Council of Ministers.

The infrastructure policies so far can be summarised thus. On investment appraisal, an initial system of consultation has proved too weak and remedies are being sought in the form of a better institutional arrangement and the creation of a Community investment budget. In pricing, proposals lie before the Council of Ministers, both on the matter of the general principle of infrastructure pricing and on the more specific matter of the adjustment of taxation systems for commercial vehicles. But, in both areas, legislation has been postponed pending the satisfactory completion of technical studies regarding the effects of the proposed measures on implementation.

The Future of a Common Transport Policy

The difficulties of achieving a common transport policy have been a mounting source of frustration. They have been accentuated by the entry of new members, peripherally located, with rather different transport structures, problems and histories. The enlargement of the European Economic Community in 1973 thus seems to have in part coincided with, and in part created, a watershed in the development of the common transport policy. Until that time, the policy aims of the Commission seemed to be dominated by the desire to introduce a common scheme of regulation of transport operation in the member states. Since 1973, however, the Commission appears to have reappraised its view that harmonisation in the transport sector was a pre-requisite for liberalisation and to have come to a radically different conclusion. Whilst the objective of harmonising conditions of operation has not been abandoned, it is now considered possible to pursue this end concurrently with liberalisation, rather than as a pre-requisite for it. Moreover, the development of a transport infrastructure policy seems to have been translated from a peripheral to a central role.

Three features appear to dominate the scene. Firstly, there is a disillusionment concerning the possibility of effectively operating a complex common system controlling transport operations, especially where the separate national governments are only half-hearted in support of the measures. Secondly, there is the liberalising influence of the new member states, which not only has the effect of blocking new measures of restriction, but also contributes to undermining the unity of the Community on matters where hard negotiated compromises seemed to have been accepted. Thirdly, the increased emphasis of the Commission on a closer relationship between sector policies and objectives makes it easier to raise objections to policies conceived in the internal context of the transport sector. Moreover, it may also be easier to argue that existing national regulations represent a delicate balance between modal and sectoral policies which will be adversely affected by tinkering in particular sub-sectors.

In total, it is difficult to escape the prognostication that the inertia which has hitherto characterised the development of the common transport policy will continue, and even be accentuated. Infrastructure appears to be the sole exceptional area where new initiatives are proposed. But even here the initiatives may turn out to be modest in content and effect, co-ordinating national investment activities and attempting to iron out the more obvious deficiencies in international infrastructure provision. The more contentious matter of common infrastructure pricing, despite all the effort devoted to it in the last eight years, still seems a long way from resolution.

Thus, in the short term, the common transport policy will have little effect on the existing national entry controls and rate controls of the individual member states. Nor does it seem likely that the fiscal system under which the transport system operates will come under any effective supranational control. Of course, that is not to say that there are no problems in transport policy, but merely that the problems that *do* exist are predominantly domestic and must be approached primarily in the context of domestic policies.

The conflicts which have occurred between member states over the common policy and between the Commission and member states, seem to have resulted from a particular institutional anomaly: member states have comprehensive national transport policies. The Treaty of Rome, and development subsequently, imply that a comprehensive common policy is also possible. So we have concurrent powers in transport policy formulation, without any convention on the division of function.

The way in which the Council of Ministers operates means that, *de facto*, member states are able to retain such powers as they choose. Unfortunately the Commission, which has the responsibility for policy formulation, has responded to this situation by what may be termed the 'foot in the door' strategy. It has remained idealistic in terms of its ultimate intention to have a comprehensive community policy, but increasingly realistic in terms of the measures proposed.

On the face of it, this seems to be very reasonable. But the effect is that the Commission has produced a succession of preparatory regulations which make sense only if the ultimate regulatory objectives for which they were preparing are likely to be acceptable. The railway accounts regulations prepare for a tight community control on rail subsidies; the HGV (Heavy Goods Vehicles) taxation proposal prepares for a common infrastructure charging scheme; even the new infrastructure committee appears to be arranged as a precursor to a common infrastructure appraisal policy. If those ultimate ends are not acceptable, the preparatory stages are at best wasteful, and at worst contrary to the objectives of the Treaty insofar as they increase effective transport costs.

The conclusion concerning the next steps in developing a common transport policy is clear. The community must fundamentally reassess the kind of common transport policy that it wants, and define some federal division of function between member states and the community. Without such a reassessment the future of the common policy is bleak indeed.

References

Allais, M., Duquesne de la Vinelle, L., Oort, C.J., Seidenfuss, H.S. and del Viscoro, M., Options in transport policy, *The EEC Studies, Transport Series*, no. 1, Brussels, 1965.

Bayliss, B.T., Licensing and entry to the market, *Journal of Transport Planning and Technology*, vol. 2, no. 1, 1973.

Gwilliam, K.M., and Mackie, P.J., *Economics of Transport Policy*, Allen and Unwin 1975.

Gwilliam, K.M., Petriccione, S., Voigt, F. and Zighera, J.A., Criteria for the co-ordination of investments in transport infrastructure, *The EEC Studies, Transport Series*, no. 3, Brussels, 1973.

Malcor, R., Problèmes posés par l'application pratique d'une tarification pour l'usage des infrastructures routières, *The EEC Studies, Transport Series*, no. 2, Brussels, 1970.

Oort, C.J., *Study of possible Solutions for allocating the Deficit which may occur in a system of charging for the use of infrastructures aiming at budgetary equilibrium*, the European Commission, Brussels, 1975.

Carrier Licensing, Report of the Geddes Committee, HMSO, London, 1965.

European Commission, *Memorandum on the General Lines of a Common Transport Policy*, Brussels, April 1961.

European Commission, *Communication from the Commission to the Council on the Development of the Common Transport Policy*, COM(73), Brussels, 24 October 1973.

9

European Monetary Integration: The Basic Analysis

A M EL-AGRAA

Although the Treaty of Rome does not specifically state that a European monetary union should be established, its architects foresaw the EEC evolving into a fully-fledged common market with complete monetary and economic integration of its members. The serious monetary upheavals of 1970, which culminated in the devaluation of the French franc and in speculation in favour of the German mark leading to its eventual revaluation, prompted the Ministers at The Hague to agree in principle to the establishment of an economic and monetary union. The Community later agreed to introduce a complete monetary union by 1980, in stages, with the first phase to begin on January 1st, 1971. Later when the Six became nine and the world monetary system was in complete disarray, it was inevitable that the 1980 date should be waived. In 1978, the Bremen Conference affirmed its commitment to achieving the objective in the near future by adopting the European Monetary System (EMS).

In spite of this progress, some influential economists have expressed great doubts as to whether there will be any gains from monetary integration and have emphasised the (so-called) costs to members of such a union. The purpose of this chapter is to reappraise the whole issue with the object of finding out whether or not there is a case against complete monetary integration.

What is Monetary Integration?

Monetary integration has two essential components: an exchange rate union and capital market integration. An exchange rate union is established when member countries have what is, in effect, one currency. The actual existence of one currency is not necessary, however, (one could of course argue that the adoption of a single currency would guarantee the irreversibility of undertaking membership of a monetary union, which would have vast repercussions for the discussion in terms of actual unions, a point which I shall discuss later because if member countries have *permanently* fixed exchange rates amongst themselves, the result is effectively the same even though the member currencies may vary in unison relative to non-member currencies.

Convertibility refers to the *permanent* absence of all exchange controls for both current and capital transactions, including interest and dividend payments (and the harmonisation of relevant taxes and measures affecting the capital market) within the union. It is of course absolutely necessary to have complete convertibility for trade transactions, otherwise an important requirement of customs union formation is threatened, namely the promotion of free trade between members of the union. Convertibility for capital transactions is related to free factor mobility and is therefore an important aspect of *capital market integration* which is necessary in common markets, not in customs unions or free trade areas.

Monetary integration takes place when an exchange rate union is accompanied by capital market integration. (In spite of the fact that these two components are essential elements in the definition, Corden (1972) contends that both in theory and in practice a distinction can be made between them. For example, it is possible to have fixed exchange rates without private capital movements (allegedly the case in Europe) or fluctuating exchange rates with complete freedom of movement for private capital (the US–Canada relationship). Whether or not such a distinction can be made in the case of the envisaged European Monetary Union is a point that I shall discuss shortly.)

In practice, this definition of monetary integration should specifically include:

(a) an explicit harmonisation of monetary policies;
(b) a common pool of foreign exchange reserves;
(c) a single central bank.

There are important reasons for including these specifications. Suppose union members decide either that one of their currencies will be a reference currency, or that a new unit of account, say the *Europa*, will be established. Also assume that each member country has its own foreign exchange reserves and conducts its own monetary and fiscal policies. If a member finds itself running out of reserves, it will have to engage in a monetary and fiscal contraction sufficient to restore the reserve position. This will necessitate the fairly frequent meeting of the finance ministers or central bank governors, to consider whether or not to change the parity of the reference currency.

If they do decide to change it, then all the member currencies will have to move with it. Such a situation could create several difficulties:

(a) Each finance minister might fight for the rate of exchange that is most suitable for his own country. This might make bargaining hard; agreement might become difficult to reach and the whole system might be subject to continuous strain.

(b) Each meeting might be accompanied by speculation about its outcome. This might result in undesirable speculative private capital movements into or out of the union.

(c) The difficulties that might be created by (a) and (b) may result in the reference currency being permanently fixed relative to outside currencies, e.g. the US dollar.

(d) However, the system does allow for the possibility of the reference currency floating relative to non-member currencies, or floating within a band. If the reference currency does float, it might do so in response to conditions in its own market. This will be the case, however, only if the union requires the monetary authorities in the partner countries to vary their exchange rates so as to maintain constant parities relative to the reference currency. They will then have to buy and sell the reserve currency so as to maintain or bring about the necessary exchange rate alteration. Therefore, the monetary authorities of the reference currency will, in fact, be able to determine the exchange rate for the whole union.

(e) Such a system does not guarantee the permanence of the parities between the union currencies that is required by the definition of monetary integration. There is the possibility that the delegates will not reach agreement, that one of the partners might finally choose not to deflate to the extent necessary to maintain its rate at the required parity, in that a surplus partner might choose neither to build up its reserves, nor to inflate as required and so might allow its rate to rise above the agreed level.

These problematical possibilities make it necessary to include in the definition of monetary integration the harmonisation of monetary policies and the common pool of foreign exchange reserves under the authority of a single central bank. The bank would operate in the market so as permanently to maintain the exchange parities among the union currencies and, at the same time, it would allow the rate of the reference currency to fluctuate, or alter intermittently, relative to the outside reserve currency. For instance, if the foreign exchange reserves in the common pool were running down, the bank would allow the reference currency, and with it all the partner currencies, to depreciate. This would have the advantage of economising on the use of foreign exchange reserves, since all partners would not tend to be in deficit or surplus at the same time. Also surplus countries would automatically be helping deficit countries.

However, without explicit policy co-ordination, a monetary union would not be effective. If each country conducted its own monetary policy, and hence could engage in as much domestic credit creation as it wished, surplus countries would be financing deficit countries without any incentives for the deficit countries to restore equilibrium. If one country ran a large deficit, the union exchange rate would depreciate, but this might put some partner countries into surplus. If wage rates were rising in the member countries at different rates, while productivity growth did not differ in such a way as to offset the effects on relative prices, those partners with the smaller inflation of wage rates would be permanently financing other partners.

Therefore, monetary integration which explicitly includes the three requirements specified will do away with all these problems. Incidentally, this also suggests the advantages of having a single currency! .

European Monetary Integration

For the purposes of this chapter, it is of the utmost importance to establish the nature of the envisaged European economic and monetary union in the light of the agreed definition of monetary integration.

According to the EEC 1972 document on 'Economic and Monetary Union', usually referred to as the Werner Report:

> ... The Community would, according to the Council resolution:
> 1. Constitute a zone where persons, goods, services and capital would move freely - but without distorting competition, or creating structural and regional imbalances — and where economic under-takings could develop their activities on a Community scale;
> 2. Form a single monetary entity within the international monetary system, characterised by the total and irreversible convertibility of currencies; the elimination of fluctuation margins of exchange rates between the [members]; the irrevocable fixing of their parity relationships. These steps would be essential for the creation of a single currency, and they would involve a Community-level organisation of central banks;
> 3. Hold the powers and responsibilities in the economic and monetary field that would enable its institutions to ensure the administration of the economic union. To this end, the necessary economic policy decisions would be taken at Community level and the necessary powers would be attributed to Community institutions.

The Community organisation of central banks would assist, in the framework of its own responsibilities, in achieving the objectives of stability and growth in the Community.

These three principles would apply to:

(a) The internal monetary and credit policies of the union;
(b) Monetary policy *vis-à-vis* the rest of the world;
(c) Policy on a unified capital market and capital movements to and from non-member countries;
(d) Budgetary and taxation policies, as related to the policy for stability and growth . . .
(e) Structural and regional action needed to contribute to the balanced development of the Community.

As progress was made in moving closer to the final objectives, Community instruments would be created whenever they seemed necessary to replace or complement the action of national instruments. All actions would be interdependent; in particular, the development of monetary unification would be backed by parallel progress in the convergence, and then the unification of economic policies.

Hence, it is clear that the envisaged economic and monetary union in the EEC is consistent with, and satisfies all the requirements of, the accepted definition of monetary integration.

The Gains and Losses

It is important to ask the question: are there any gains and losses for countries from membership of a monetary union?

The gains and losses due to membership of a monetary union could be both economic and non-economic, i.e. political, sociological, etc. Some of the non-economic effects are too obvious to discuss and, in any case, should be left to experts in their respective fields. In the economic field, the gains could be briefly summarised:

(a) The common pool of foreign exchange reserves already discussed has the incidental advantage of economising in the use of foreign exchange reserves – see Section 1. In the context of the EEC this will reduce the role of the US dollar or 'reduce Europe's dependence on the dollar.' (Corden 1972, p. 5).

(b) If the EEC adopted a common unit of account (the *Europa*), it would be inevitable for it to become a major world currency able to compete with the dollar on equal terms. The advantages of such a currency for the EEC are too well established to discuss here. However, the use of an area's currency as a major reserve currency doubtless imposes certain burdens on the area, but in this particular case, it would create an oligopolistic international monetary situation which could either lead to collusion, resulting in a permanent sensible reform of the international monetary situation, or intensify the situation and lead to a complete collapse of the international monetary order. The latter possibility is of course extremely likely to result in the former outcome!

(c) There also exist the classical advantages of having permanently fixed exchange rates (or one currency) among members of a monetary union for free trade and factor movements. Stability of rates enhances trade, encourages capital to move to where it is most productively rewarded and ensures that labour will move to where the highest rewards prevail. It seems unnecessary to emphasise that this does not mean that *all* labour and *all* capital should be mobile, but simply enough of each to generate the necessary adjustment for any situation.

(d) The integration of the capital market has a further advantage. If a member country is in deficit (assuming that countries can be recognised within such a union!), it can borrow directly on the Community Market, or raise its rate of interest to attract capital inflow and therefore ease the situation. However, the integration of economic policies within the union ensures that this help will occur automatically under the auspices of the common central bank. Since no single area is likely to be in deficit permanently, such help can be envisaged for all the members. (Hence, there is no basis for Corden's 1972 assertion: 'No region . . . can borrow indefinitely to sustain real-wages and consumption levels that are out of line with the region's productivity and the demand for its products', p. 169.)

(e) When a monetary union establishes a central fiscal authority with its own budget, then the larger the size of this budget, the higher the degree of fiscal harmonisation (the McDougall Report 1977). This has some advantages:

  (i) Regional deviations from internal balance can be financed from the centre.

  (ii) The centralisation of social security payments financed by contributions or taxes on a progressive basis 'would have some stabilising and compensating effects and so would modify . . . adverse effects of monetary integration'. (Corden 1972, p. 171. This is a point much emphasised in the McDougall Report — see Chapter 11).

(f) There are negative advantages in the sense that a monetary union is necessary for maintaining the EEC as it exists; for example, the CAP would be undermined if exchanges were to be flexible (see Ingram's excellent 1973 exposition of this and other themes and Chapter 8 of this book).

The losses from membership of a monetary union are emphasised by Corden. Assume that the world is constituted of at least three countries and that, in order to maintain both internal and external equilibrium, one country (A) needs to devalue its currency relative to the outside world (C), while another country (B) needs to revalue *vis-à-vis* C. Assume also that countries A and B use fiscal and monetary policies for achieving internal equilibrium. If A and B were partners in an exchange-rate union, they would devalue together — which is consistent with A's policy requirements in isolation — or revalue together — which is consistent with B's requirements in isolation — but they would not be able to alter the rate of exchange in a way that was consistent for both. In such circumstances, the alteration in the rate of exchange could leave A with an external deficit, hence forcing it to deflate its economy and create unemployment, or it could leave it with a surplus, hence forcing it into accumulating foreign reserves or allowing its prices and wages to rise. Hence if countries deprive themselves of rates of exchange (or trade impediments) as policy instruments, they 'impose on themselves losses that are essentially *the losses* resulting from enforced departure from internal balance.' (Corden 1972, p. 8. The emphasis is not in the original text.)

It is important to follow Corden's explanation (Corden 1972, p.10) of the enforced departure from internal equilibrium. Suppose a country is initially in internal equilibrium but has a deficit in its external account. If the country were free to vary its rate of exchange, the appropriate policy for it to adopt to achieve overall balance would be a combination of devaluation and expenditure reduction. When the rate of exchange is not available as a policy instrument, it is necessary to reduce expenditure by more than is required in the optimal situation with the result of extra unemployment. The excess unemployment, which can be valued in terms of output or whatever, is the cost to that country of depriving itself of the exchange rate as a policy instrument. The extent of this loss is determined, *ceteris paribus*, by the marginal propensity to import and to consume exportables, or, more generally, by the marginal propensity to consume tradables relative to non-tradables.

The expenditure reduction which is required for eliminating the initial external account deficit will be smaller the higher the marginal propensity to import. Moreover, the higher the marginal propensity to import, the less the effect of that reduction in expenditure on demand for domestically produced commodities. For both reasons, therefore, the higher the marginal propensity to import, the less domestic unemployment will result from abandoning the devaluation of the rate of exchange as a policy instrument. If the logic of this explanation is correct, it follows that as long as the marginal propensity to consume domestic goods is greater than zero, there will be some cost due to fixing the rate of exchange. A similar argument applies to a country which cannot use the exchange rate instrument when it has a surplus in its external account and internal equilibrium: the required excess expenditure will have little effect on demand for domestically produced goods and will therefore exert little inflationary pressure if the country's marginal propensity to import is high.

This analysis is based on the assumption that there exists a trade-off between rates of change in costs and levels of unemployment – the much criticised Phillips curve. Corden contends that if one assumes that money wages are not adjusted in response to changes in the cost of living (and hence in the exchange rates) to the extent of maintaining a given, or pre-existing, level of *real* wages, then (Corden 1972, p. 10) it is possible to argue that at any moment in time there will exist a particular level of money wages and labour productivity in each country and, therefore, there will be a particular set of rates of exchange which, when combined with the appropriate monetary and fiscal policies in different countries, will achieve both internal and external equilibrium in these countries simultaneously. As money wages and labour productivities change over time, a new set of rates of exchange will be needed to maintain overall equilibrium. Here, as in the previous explanation, the extent of the losses from abandoning the rate of exchange as a policy instrument to rely exclusively on expenditure-changing policies will depend, *ceteris paribus*, on the marginal propensity to consume tradables.

Corden concedes that the mention of different countries within a monetary union is misleading. He maintains that in such circumstances the question of internal equilibrium should be considered in terms of regions in a country. However, he insists that, generally speaking, 'one particular level of aggregate demand associated with the appropriate exchange rate for the country (union) as a whole can maintain full employment in one region, but it may lead to inflation in another. If inflation in most regions is to be avoided, excessive unemployment in some regions may have to be tolerated' (Corden 1972, p. 163).

I have quoted freely and extensively from Corden simply because his work is recognised as classic in this context. The reader needs to digest his argument as explained by him before considering its limitations, as I see them. These are:

(a) It is clearly stated in the definition of monetary integration that the fixity of exchange rate parities within the union (or the adoption of one currency) does not mean that the different member currencies cannot vary in unison relative to extra-union currencies, i.e. devalue/revalue the *Europa* relative to the US dollar. Hence the union is not foregoing the availability of exchange rate variations *vis-à-vis* the outside world. This limitation applies to regions only.

(b) In a proper monetary union, an extra deficit for one region can come about only as a result of a revaluation of the union currency – the union as a whole has an external surplus *vis-à-vis* the outside world. Such an act would increase the foreign exchange earnings of the surplus region, and hence of the union as a whole, provided the conditions for a successful revaluation exist. The common central bank and the integration of monetary policies will ensure that the extra burden on the first region is alleviated: the overall extra earnings will be used to help the region with the extra deficit. Needless to say, such a situation does not lead to surplus regions financing deficit regions indefinitely because no single region is likely to be in deficit or surplus permanently and because the policy co-ordination will not allow one region to behave in such a manner unless there are reasons of a *different* nature.

(c) Even if one were to accept Corden's argument at its face value, his assumptions are extremely controversial. For instance, devaluation can work effectively only when there is 'money illusion', otherwise it would be pointless and would not work. Is it really permissible to assume that trade unionists in the EEC suffer from money illusion? Johnson, Ingram and others (in Krause and Salant 1973, pp. 184–202) have all pointed to the fallacious nature of such an assumption in the context of the EEC. Corden's response has been to suggest that exchange rate alterations may work if money wages are forced up because the catching-up process is never complete. Such an argument is far from convincing simply because the catching-up process has no validity as a true adjustment: it cannot be maintained indefinitely because, sooner or later, trade unionists will allow for it when negotiating money wage increases.

(d) One must remember that in practice there would never be a separation between the exchange rate union and capital market integration. Once one allows for the role of convertibility for capital transactions, capital will always come to the rescue. Corden has reservations about this too (Corden 1972, p. 168):

> ... in the short run capital integration can help, but in the long run, while having its own advantages, it cannot really solve the problem ... No country or region can borrow indefinitely on a private market, however open and efficient the market is, to sustain levels of real wages, and hence real consumption levels which are too high, bearing in mind the productivity of the country or region.

Corden is switching grounds here: devaluation is nothing but a temporary adjustment device as the discussion of the monetary approach to the balance of payments has shown. Why then should devaluation be more desirable than short-term capital adjustment? Moreover, for a region that is permanently in deficit, all economists would agree that devaluation is no panacea.

(e) The EEC allows for free labour mobility and this will also help in the adjustment process. Even though Corden (1972, p. 168) does concede this point, he believes that labour mobility may:

> ... marginally reduce problems of internal balance caused by integration, but it would take prolonged unemployment generating a spirit of hopelessness to lead to substantial emigration out of some of the Community countries into others. Furthermore, if monetary integration gets too far ahead of psychological integration — the suppression of existing nationalisms and sense of attachment to place, in favour of a European nationalism and an American-style geographic rootness — then it is not hard to imagine the intensity of nationalistic reaction to any country's depopulation.

This is yet another unreasonable argument which presupposes that the problem region is a *permanently* depressed area. Since no region in the union is ever likely to experience chronic maladjustments, labour mobility needs only to be marginal and nationalistic depopulation is far from the truth (see chapter 12).

(f) Finally, and more fundamentally as far as Corden's own argument is concerned, a very crucial element is missing. Corden's analysis relates to a country in internal equilibrium (the combination of unemployment and inflation that a country prefers from an internal viewpoint) and external deficit. If this country were outside a monetary union, it could devalue its currency. Assuming that the necessary conditions for effective devaluation prevailed, then devaluation would increase the national income of the country, would increase its price level, or result in some combination of the two. Hence a deflationary policy would be required to restore the internal balance.

However, if the country were to lose its freedom to alter its exchange rate, it would have to deflate in order to depress its imports and restore external balance. Corden claims that this alternative would entail unemployment in excess of that prevailing at the initial situation.

The missing element in this argument can be found by specifying how devaluation actually works. Devaluation of a country's currency results in changes in relative price levels and is price-inflationary for, at least, both exportables and importables. These relative price changes, given the necessary stability conditions, will depress imports and (maybe) increase exports.

Hence, the deflationary policy which is required (to accompany devaluation) in order to restore internal balance should eliminate the *newly injected 'inflation'* as well as the extra national income.

By disregarding the 'inflationary' implications of devaluation, Corden reaches the unjustifiable *a priori* conclusion that membership of a monetary union would necessitate extra sacrifice of employment in order to achieve the same objective. Any serious comparison of the two situations would indicate that no such *a priori* conclusion can be reached — Corden is not comparing like with like. It is, therefore, inevitable to conclude that, at the worst, the economic advantages of monetary integration far outweigh any possible (if any) disadvantages.

The Transition to Monetary Integration

It was pointed out in the previous section that the most pessimistic conclusion that an economist can reach is that the gains from European monetary integration must exceed any possible losses from its formation. If that is the case, why is it that Corden's argument has been so dominant in this field?

The answer is twofold. Firstly, it is because economists have failed to point out the fallacy in Corden's argument. Secondly, it is due to his distinction between a *complete* and a *pseudo* exchange rate union and to his equating the latter with the envisaged monetary union in the EEC. The latter point should be discussed in some detail.

The *pseudo* union, unlike the *complete* union, does not allow for economic policy co-ordination, a pool of foreign exchange reserves and a common central bank. It therefore creates the problems discussed in the definitional section. This raises the practical question: is the envisaged European monetary union equivalent to a *pseudo* union?

The Werner Report (which was endorsed by the Community Council of Ministers in February 1971, but the implementation of which was later temporarily halted for reasons discussed in the Marjolin Report 1975) recommended the following (the emphasis is not in the original text):

(a) An economic and monetary union could be attained during this decade, if the plan had the permanent political support of the member governments;
(b) The first phase should begin on January 1, 1971, and could technically be completed within three years. This phase would be used to make the Community instruments more operational and to mark the beginnings of the Community's individuality within the international monetary system;
(c) *The first phase should not be considered as an objective in itself; it should*

be associated with the complete process of economic and monetary integration. It should therefore be launched with the determination to arrive at the final goal;

(d) *In the first phase consultation procedures should be strengthened; the budgetary policies of the member states should accord with Community objectives; some taxes should be harmonised; monetary and credit policies should be co-ordinated; and integration of financial markets should be intensified.*

There are therefore two points to emphasise about the first stage of the envisaged European monetary union. Firstly, it is more than a pseudo exchange rate union — the underlined points, particularly (d), clearly indicate this. Secondly, it is only the *first stage* in a *process* leading to complete monetary integration. Even Corden admits that this first stage, even though it might take a long time to achieve, cannot be the permanent reality.

The confusion between the ultimate objective (complete monetary integration) and the first stage as a step in that direction is clearly demonstrated by the discussion relating to whether or not the EEC (or some members of it) is a feasible or optimum currency area. Such a discussion, useful as it may be, has no relevance here: the fact that the nine members of the Community *are committed* to monetary integration has been substantiated by the declaration of the summit meeting of July 1978. (One way of exposing the fallacious nature of this argument is: if it can be conclusively proved that the US is more than a feasible currency area, should economists advise its disintegration?) There are, of course, great *difficulties* in the *transition* to complete monetary integration, but no economist is able, or should even attempt, to predict that these difficulties would be permanent ones. In the words of Ingram:

> . . . Perhaps the modes of thought used by economists cause them to neglect important economic aspects of the changing institutional structure of Europe. We should not forget that economists were also skeptical about the European Common Market . . .
>
> (Ingram 1973)

(Readers interested in a critical evaluation of the approach to the theory of economic integration are advised to consult El-Agraa 1978, or refer to El-Agraa and Jones 1980.)

Conclusion

The conclusion of this chapter is that the alleged disadvantages of monetary integration apply only to the so-called *pseudo* exchange rate union. Such a union is neither consistent with the first stage of

European monetary integration, nor with its nature as a *process* leading to complete union. All economists would concede the difficulties associated with a transitional phase, but none of them, in their strict area of competence, should pass political judgements regarding the reality of attaining the ultimate objective. The EEC is here to stay and, as the 1978 Bremen Declaration stated, monetary union is to remain a very clear objective. (See the text of the Jenkins 1977 speech which was delivered in Florence.) Moreover, as far as overcoming the difficulties of achieving monetary union are concerned, a number of proposals have been made (see Chapter 10).

In his latest book, Corden (1977) finally concedes the point that there is no long-term case against European monetary integration. This, however, does not now transform him into a firm believer in it, particularly since he still emphasises that the events of 1973–75 vindicated the short-term case against it. So presumably he will not object to being described now as a mild supporter of European monetary union.

Finally, the EMS, which is designed to eliminate violent currency fluctuations (by establishing a currency zone in which the management of exchange rates is subject to very strict control by means of a new European Currency or Unit of Account) and to promote closer economic and monetary integration (by establishing a European Monetary Fund with an exchange stabilisation pool of fifty billion US dollars initially), could be a step in the right direction (see Chapter 10).

References

Corden, W.M., Monetary integration, *Essays in International Finance*, Princeton University, no. 93, April 1972.

Corden, W.M., The adjustment problem, in Krause, L.B. and Salant, W.S. (eds), *European Monetary Unification and Its Meaning for the United States*, The Brookings Institution, Washington DC, 1973.

Corden, W.M., *Inflation, Exchange Rates and the World Economy*, Oxford University Press 1977.

El-Agraa, A.M., Can economists provide a rationale for customs union formation?, *Leeds Discussion Paper*, no. 68, 1978.

El-Agraa, A.M., Common markets in developing countries, in Bowers, J.K. (ed.), *Inflation, Development and Integration: Essays in Honour of A.J. Brown*, University of Leeds Press, 1979.

El-Agraa, A.M. and Jones, A.J., *The Theory of Customs Unions*, Philip Allan 1980.

Ingram, J.C., State and regional payments mechanisms, *Quarterly Journal of Economics*, 73, 1959.

Ingram, J.C., A proposal for financial integration in the Atlantic Community, in *Factors Affecting the US Balance of Payments*, Joint Economic Committee Print, 87th Cong., 2nd session, Washington DC, 1962.

Ingram, J.C., The case for European monetary integration, *Essays in International Finance*, no. 98, April 1973.

Johnson, H.G., Problems of European monetary union, in Krauss, M.B. (ed.), *The Economics of Integration*, Allen and Unwin, 1973.

Jenkins, R., Europe's present challenge and future opportunity, *Bulletin of the European Communities*, 10, 1977.

Krause, L.B. and Salant, W.S. (eds), *European Monetary Unification and Its Meaning for the United States*, The Brookings Institution, Washington DC, 1973.

Krauss, M.B. (ed.), *The Economics of Integration*, Allen and Unwin 1973.

McKinnon, R.I., Optimum currency areas, *American Economic Review*, 53, September 1963.

Mundell, R.A., A theory of optimum currency areas, *American Economic Review*, 51, September 1961.

European Commission, *Action Programme of the Community for the Second Stage*, Brussels, October 1962.

European Commission, Report to the Council and the Commission on the realisation by stages of economic and monetary union in the Community, *Bulletin of the European Communities*, Supplement No. 11, 1970, (The Werner Report).

European Commission, *Report of the Study Group 'Economic and Monetary Union 1980'*, Brussels, March 1975 (The Marjolin Report).

European Commission, *Report of the Study Group on the Role of Public Finance in European Integration*, 2 vol., Brussels, April 1977, (The MacDougall Report).

10

European Monetary Integration: The Transition

A M EL-AGRAA

The preceding chapter was devoted to a discussion of the theoretical arguments for and against European monetary integration and to an examination of the proposals of the Werner Report in the light of that discussion. The aim of the present chapter is to supplement that discussion by considering the practical problems inherent in a situation of transition, to explain briefly the plans put forward regarding possible ways of achieving monetary union, to specify the proposals of the Bremen Declaration for a European Monetary System (EMS) and to evaluate these considerations in the context of the conclusions of the previous chapter.

At this point it should be remembered that complete monetary integration means the permanent and irrevocable fixing of members' exchange rates, the complete convertibility of capital, and the establishment of an EEC central bank to be vested with the powers of controlling a pool of members' foreign exchange reserves and of coordinating the economic and monetary policies of the whole Community.

The General Background

It is necessary for the purposes of this chapter to recall the brief reference made in Chapter 1 of this book to the positions of the 'monetarists' and the 'economists' regarding European monetary integration. The 'monetarists', whose leading protagonist is France, insist on the immediate implementation of *irrevocably fixed rates of exchange* within the EEC, accompanied by the imposition of very strict controls over capital mobility; the coordination and harmonisation of economic policies should be introduced at a later date. The 'economists', on the other hand, whose main leader is West

Germany, propose the more or less immediate introduction of the coordination and harmonisation of economic policies, to be followed almost immediately by complete freedom of capital mobility; only then should the irrevocable fixing of exchange rates be implemented. The 'monetarists' are mainly influenced by their interest in achieving a successful Common Agricultural Policy; the adoption of permanently fixed rates of exchange would, for example, eliminate the problems which led to the MCA system of border taxes and subsidies discussed in Chapter 7. The 'economists' are influenced by the fact that the members of the EEC are at different stages in their economic development and they are particularly worried that the permanent fixing of exchange rates would force the 'weaker' members to manage their economies by interest rate policies with the result of increasing their unemployment levels. However, the point is a general one in that the fixing of exchange rates could lead to heavy inflation in West Germany, resulting in an underpricing of her industrial commodities. For France, who needs to restructure her agricultural sector, and the UK, who needs to restructure her industrial sector, the fixing of exchange rates could result in balance of payments deficits which would force them to adopt deflationary policies with resulting high levels of unemployment.

The Werner Report is essentially a compromise between the positions of the 'monetarists' and the 'economists'. The Report, however, has remained essentially a background document in that it has become a blueprint for European monetary integration, without ever becoming embodied in a Council Resolution (Robson 1974).

The Transition to Monetary Integration

The Werner Report recommended the establishment of the EMU by *stages,* with the achievement of complete monetary integration by 1980. The monetary upheavals of the 1970s, the oil crisis and the entry negotiations of the new members made that target impossible; hence the Marjolin Report recommended the postponement of that date. It is therefore necessary to reflect on the nature of the transition to monetary integration.

In the previous chapter the conclusion was reached that the recommendations of the Werner Report are consistent with *complete* monetary integration, in that the stages *taken together* do lead to the attainment of the ultimate goal. Hence the problems associated with Corden's pseudo-exchange-rate union cannot be envisaged in the context of the Werner Report, unless one is convinced that the EEC is never likely to proceed beyond the first stage, i.e. the first stage will become the permanent reality. I shall return to this point shortly, but it ought to be mentioned that the Werner Report was not the only set of recommendations available to the EEC; a number of proposals were made and are still being made regarding the minimisation of the costs of transition — see Meade (1973), Johnson (1973a & b), Coffey and Presley (1971), Magnifico and Williamson (1972), Cairncross *et al.* (1974), Giersch *et al.* (1975) and Tindemans (1976). Since the literature on this subject is extensive, brief reference to it would not do it justice. I shall therefore give only a summary of the main categories of ideas. For a more detailed discussion, the reader is advised to consult Coffey and Presley (1971), Cairncross *et al.* (1974), Coffey (1977) and Corden (1977).

There are four basic groups of recommendations on ways of tackling the problems of the transition to European monetary integration.

Monetary Integration All at Once

This amounts to introducing *all* the necessary ingredients of complete monetary integration *together* as soon as a commitment has been made to launch the EMU. An EEC central bank is created and is vested with the powers of controlling the pool of all members' foreign exchange reserves, of conducting the Community monetary and economic policies and of producing the legal tender and therefore the money base. Such a step has to be a decisive, definitive and irrevocable one, so that all possible expectations are immediately adjusted once and for all. Hence this proposal gives all the advantages and none of the disadvantages of complete monetary integration. The essence of this proposal is to tackle the problems of transition through the simple act of eliminating the process of transition itself.

Since this is the best method, why has it not been adopted by the EEC? According to Cairncross *et al.* (1974, p. 31):

> to abandon exchange-rate changes completely and finally without indicating how imbalances will be dealt with in future . . . would be to run serious risks in relation to both economic stability and to that political will without which economic union will not hold.

However, if these serious risks are to disappear, the EEC central bank has to be responsible for tackling the regional problems that are likely to arise as a result of the EMU — those problems that worry the 'economists'. Hence, the regional problem has to become part and parcel of the management of the EEC economic and monetary policies conducted by the central bank. It is therefore evident that an 'all at once' implementation of the EMU cannot be envisaged without a properly functioning EEC central bank; hence the prior commitment of the member countries to a political union (see the previous chapter) becomes an absolute necessity.

The Step-by-Step Approach

This approach is in effect that of a considerable number of the proposals and certainly forms the essence of the Werner Report. There are two sets of recommendations within this approach broadly consistent with the two sides of the 'monetarists' and 'economists' dichotomy, but they can be treated together — for a detailed description the reader should consult Cairncross et al. (1974).

The step-by-step approach means that exchange rate margins are narrowed over a period of time and that the narrowing of the margins is very gradual. Some collaboration between the members is envisaged, such that those with balance of payments surpluses come to the rescue of those with deficits. At a later stage, the pooling of all foreign exchange reserves is introduced and then follows the complete and irrevocable elimination of all exchange rate margins. Finally, when the member nations declare their solemn commitment to monetary integration, an EEC central bank with the necessary powers is created.

It should be emphasised that this approach is, strictly speaking, not very different from the 'all at once' approach, provided those participating make the political commitment that is necessary for the effective support of *all the stages* leading to the implementation of complete monetary integration, i.e. members must not only declare themselves to act, but must also be seen to act in the spirit of the final goal. Otherwise, the national versus Community interests discussed in the previous chapter become the order of the day and therefore reduce the whole exercise to a pseudo-exchange-rate union. Hence this approach cannot be envisaged without the political commitment of the participants *from the start*.

Approaching the EMU via the 'Snake'

In this set of proposals, members of the EEC approach monetary integration via the 'snake'; they join the 'snake' when they feel ready to do so. Hence those who are either ready for or keen on achieving monetary integration go ahead, while those who are either not yet ready or not so eager join when they are. From there on the process is similar to the step-by-step approach. Hence, the most vital moment

comes when those members who are in the 'snake' take a solemn vow
to go the whole way to monetary integration. Such a step, as already
indicated, is not feasible without the prior political commitment of
the members.

This approach is similar to that advocated by the Tindemans Report
(1976) and is different from the Werner Report in that the various
stages do not have to be coordinated. It could be argued, however,
that a lack of coordination is necessary if member countries are to be
free to join if and when they are ready or feel so inclined. As Corden
(1977) has pointed out, this amounts to there being a 'two-tier EEC',
consisting of those moving towards monetary integration via the
'snake', and the others. For a general background discussion, the
reader should consult Cairncross *et al.* (1974), Coffey (1977) and
Chapter 4.

Parallel-Currency Proposals

The fourth set of proposals is for achieving monetary integration
through the creation of a parallel currency called the Europa. One
version of this proposal calls for the creation of a Europa supported
by US dollars, gold and SDRs, as well as by the domestic currencies
of members of the EEC. The Europa is held by the EEC central
banks alone, or by them and by members of the general public. The
implication of this is that countries of the EEC have the freedom of
altering their own rates of exchange relative to the Europa and that
the Europa itself can be devalued or revalued relative to the US
dollar. The object of the exercise is for member nations to narrow
the margins between their domestic currencies and the Europa with
the eventual permanent and irrevocable fixing of their parities.

The second version of this approach was suggested by Giersch
et al. (1976). This is different from the first in that the Europa has a
constant purchasing power and is therefore 'inflation proof'. The
Europa is held simultaneously with local currencies and it is hoped
that the competition between the Europa and the local currencies
proves favourable to the former. When the Europa becomes dominant,
it establishes itself as the EEC currency.

It is obvious that if such a parallel currency is introduced and
proves to be more attractive than local currencies, a mechanism of
controlling its supply must be created. This must be an EEC central
bank which must have the power to conduct its financial operations
anywhere within the EEC. Hence such an EEC central bank cannot
be established and cannot function properly without the necessary
backing of the EEC nations. There is therefore a need for the prior
political commitment to support it and to guide it in the direction of
the ultimate objective of monetary integration.

It is therefore evident that none of these four sets of proposals can be achieved without a firm commitment by the participating nations to a United States of the EEC countries. I shall return to this point shortly.

The Bremen Declaration

At this juncture it is appropriate to ask: how do the Bremen Declaration (6 and 7 July 1978), its Bonn affirmation (16 and 17 July 1978) and its adoption by the Council in the form of a Resolution 'on the establishment of the European Monetary System (EMS) and related matters' on 5 December of the same year fare in the context of the proposals considered in the previous section? To answer this question meaningfully, it is necessary to explain the aims of the EMS.

The EMS was introduced with the immediate support of six of the EEC nations. Ireland, Italy and the UK adopted a wait-and-see attitude; 'time for reflection' was needed by Ireland and Italy and a definite reservation was expressed by the UK. Later, Ireland and Italy joined the system, while the UK expressed a 'spirit of sympathetic cooperation'. The EMS was to start operating on 1 January 1979, but France, who wanted assurances regarding the MCA system (see chapter 7), delayed that start.

The main features of the EMS are given in the annex to the conclusions of the EEC Presidency (*Bulletin of the European Communities*, No. 6, 1978, pp. 20–21):

1 In terms of exchange rate management, the European Monetary System (EMS) will be at least as strict as the 'snake'. In the initial stages of its operation and for a limited period of time, member countries currently not participating in the 'snake' may opt for somewhat wider margins around central rates. In principle, intervention will be in the currencies of participating countries. Changes in central rates will be subject to mutual consent. Non-member countries with particularly strong economic and financial ties with the Community may become associate members of the system. The European Currency Unit (ECU) will be at the centre of the system; in particular, it will be used as a means of settlement between EEC monetary authorities.

2 An initial supply of ECUs (for use among Community central banks) will be created against deposit of US dollars and gold on the one hand (e.g. 20% of the stock currently held by member central banks) and member currencies on the other hand in an amount of a comparable order of magnitude.

   The use of ECUs created against member currencies will be subject to conditions varying with the amount and the maturity; due account will be given to the need for substantial short-term facilities (up to 1 year).

3 Participating countries will coordinate their exchange rate policies *vis-à-vis* third countries. To this end, they will intensify the consultations in the appropriate bodies and between central banks participating in the scheme.

Ways to coordinate dollar interventions should be sought which avoid simultaneous reserve interventions. Central banks buying dollars will deposit a fraction (say 20%) and receive ECUs in return; likewise, central banks selling dollars will receive a fraction (say 20%) against ECUs.

4   Not later than two years after the start of the scheme, the existing arrangements and institutions will be consolidated in a European Monetary Fund.

5   A system of closer monetary cooperation will only be successful if participating countries pursue policies conducive to greater stability at home and abroad; this applies to deficit and surplus countries alike.

Thus, in essence, the EMS envisages the creation of an EEC currency zone within which there is discipline for managing exchange rates. This discipline is similar to that practised within the 'snake' arrangements. This however does not apply to all the Nine, since wider margins of fluctuation for those not participating in the 'snake' are allowed for. The ECU, which is similar to the European Unit of Account in that it is a basket of all EEC currencies, will be at the heart of the system; it will be the means of settlement between the EEC central banks. The EMS will be supported by a European Monetary Fund (EMF) which, within two years, will absorb the short-term financing arrangement operating within the 'snake', the short-term monetary support agreement which is managed by the European Monetary Cooperation Fund and the medium-term loan facilities for balance of payments assistance (*Bulletin of the European Communities*, No. 12, 1978). The EMF will be backed by approximately 20% of national gold and US dollar reserves and by a similar percentage in national currencies. The EMF will issue ECUs which will be used as new reserve assets. Hence, an Exchange-Stabilisation Fund (which is scarcely different from the Cairncross *et al.* (1974) proposal for an Exchange-Equalisation Account) able to issue about 50 billion US dollars will be created (*Bulletin of the European Communities*, No. 12, 1978).

Since the ECU is only an official EEC reserve asset, necessary interventions in the markets for foreign exchange will be conducted with national currencies and for this purpose only EEC currencies are allowed. It is also envisaged that the use of ECUs credited against reserves will be unconditional, but the use of ECUs credited against national currencies will be subject to provisos more or less equivalent to those in the 'conditional drawings' from the IMF — see De Grauwe and Peeters (1978). There will be provision for substantial short-term borrowing for day-to-day intervention. The repayment period will be 45 days with the possibility of a further three months for specified amounts. It is intended that adjustments in rates of exchange will be based on mutual consent.

Section 4 of the annex stresses the point that the status of associate membership will be conferred on those countries with close economic and financial ties with the EEC, for example, Austria, Norway, etc. As far as other currencies are concerned, and particularly against the US dollar, there will be close coordination of exchange rate policies.

Finally, and more importantly, the annex stresses the point that the success of closer monetary cooperation will depend largely on closer policy coordination in both the domestic and international fields.

As De Grauwe and Peeters (1978) have indicated, the EMS differs from previous attempts in at least two important respects. The first difference is that an exchange rate management mechanism will be introduced and that the ECU will play a central role in it. The second difference is that the EEC currency zone will be backed by a considerable pool of foreign exchange reserves which could provide confidence in the system and therefore enhance its stability.

However, apart from the technical problems regarding its actual operation (these are rigorously and excellently analysed by De Grauwe and Peeters 1978), the EMS cannot work without the coordination of monetary policies (De Grauwe and Peeters 1978, p. 22) and cannot cope with the problems of the weaker areas without a deliberate policy regarding the redistribution of the gains and losses. Finally, the EMS does not envisage a *particular* future date for fixing exchange rates completely — 'margins should be gradually reduced as soon as economic conditions permit to do so' (*Bulletin of the European Communities*, No. 12, 1978, pp. 10–11).

In spite of its superiority over previous proposals, the EMS *is not complete monetary integration*. It lacks the EEC central bank (vested with the appropriate powers) which is necessary for coordinating monetary and economic policies.

Conclusion

Before the conclusion of this chapter is stated, the reader should be reminded that European monetary integration, even though it is not specifically mentioned in the Treaty of Rome, has become a significant topic for discussion as a result of the international monetary upheavals of the late 1960s and early 1970s. Fluctuations in rates of exchange, their unfavourable implications for the CAP and the growing need, at least in some quarters, for a 'monetary counterweight' to the US dollar, and for a proper reform of the international monetary system, were major factors which together have promoted interest in closer European monetary integration. That is not the whole story, however, particularly since in some European quarters monetary integration is being seen as the vehicle for promoting

the political unity of the EEC nations — see Denton (1974). Therefore, the discussion of European monetary unification should be
seen in the wider context of both international monetary policy and
EEC economic policy: the tackling of exchange rate instability and
its adverse effects on inflation, economic growth and the progress
towards European economic unity.

As far as this chapter is concerned, it is evident from the discussion of the transition to monetary integration that no set of proposals
can work without the prior political commitment of the EEC to a
United States of its member nations. Hence transition is a problem
only if that political commitment is not forthcoming.

This seemingly obvious conclusion is of great significance when
considered in the context of West European unification. The achievement of a United States of Western Europe was initially sought in
terms of political unification (see Denton 1974 and Chapter 2) but
this proved rather ambitious, particularly when World War II wounds
were still fresh in people's minds. Hence further developments were
introduced by the back door. The idea of economically beneficial
customs unions was well advertised (remember the UK referendum!)
and it was hoped that this would encourage membership. The grand
design was that once member economies had become highly interdependent and consolidated into an economic union, political unity
would be easy to achieve. That approach was misguided, particularly
since the theory of customs unions pointed out the costs involved
(see Chapter 4 and El-Agraa and Jones 1980). However, this lesson
was either quickly forgotten or completely ignored, because new
attempts were made to seek political unification via monetary integration. As it turned out, the 'sensitive issue of political sovereignty'
could not be by-passed in this way and this is in spite of the fact that
'nations in the European Community do not now have a great deal of
monetary autonomy. With monetary union, they would not be sacrific-
ing very much on that score, and they might even be acquiring some
policy weapons that they do not have at the present' (Ingram 1973,
p. 187).

The discussion in this chapter has hopefully demonstrated that
there is no possibile means of achieving complete monetary integration without the prior declaration of irrevocable commitment to
political unification. Indeed, attempts at achieving monetary unification without its political prerequisite might result in crises that could
set back or altogether destroy any prospect of political unity. The
conclusion of this chapter is, therefore, that there is no hope for
achieving West European politican unification via roundabout routes.
Even though political sovereignty is a very sensitive issue, it will
have to be confronted directly.

References

Burrows, B., Denton, G.R. and Edwards, G. (eds), *Federal Solutions to European Issues*, Macmillan Press 1977.

Cairncross, Sir Alec *et al.*, *Economic Policy for the European Community: the Way Forward*, Macmillan Press 1974.

Coffey, P. and Presley, J., *European Monetary Integration*, Macmillan Press 1971.

Coffey, P., *Europe and Money*, Macmillan Press 1977.

Corden, W.M., *Inflation, Exchange Rates and the World Economy*, Oxford University Press 1977.

De Grauwe, P. and Peeters, T., *The European Monetary System after Bremen: Technical and Conceptual Problems.* Paper delivered for the *International Study Group*, London School of Economics, 1978.

Denton, G.R. (ed.), *Economic Integration in Europe*, Weidenfeld and Nicolson 1969.

Denton, G.R. (ed.), *Economic and Monetary Union in Europe*, Croom Helm 1974.

El-Agraa, A.M. and Jones, A.J., *The Theory of Customs Unions*, Philip Allan 1980.

Giersch, H. *et al.*, A currency for Europe, *The Economist*, 1 November, 1975.

Ingram, J.C. Comments, in Krause, L.B. and Salant, W.S. (eds), *European Monetary Unification and Its Meaning for the United States*, The Brookings Institution, Washington DC, 1973.

Johnson, H.G., Problems of European monetary union, in Krauss, M.B. (ed.), *The Economics of Integration*, Allen & Unwin 1973a.

Johnson, H.G., Summary of conference and various discussions, in Krause, L.B. and Salant, W.S. (eds), 1973b.

Magnifico, G. and Williamson, J., *European Monetary Integration*, Federal Trust, London, 1972.

Meade, J.E., The balance-of-payments problems of a European free-trade area, in Krauss, M.B. (ed.), 1973.

Robson, S., Economic management in a monetary union, in Denton, G.R. (ed.), 1974.

Tindemans, L., European union, *Bulletin of the European Communities, Supplement*, 1976.

European Commission, *Report of the Study Group 'Economic and Monetary Union 1980'*, Brussels, March 1975 (The Marjolin Report).

European Commission, *Bulletin of the European Communities*, 1977 onwards.

11
Fiscal Policy I: Tax Harmonisation

A M EL-AGRAA

The Meaning of Fiscal Policy

Very widely interpreted, fiscal policy comprises a whole corpus of 'public finance' issues: the relative size of the public sector, taxation and expenditure, and the allocation of public sector responsibilities between different tiers of government (Prest 1979). Hence fiscal policy is concerned with a far wider area than that commonly associated with it, namely, the aggregate management of the economy in terms of controlling inflation and employment levels.

Experts in the field of public finance (Musgrave and Musgrave (1976) rightly stress that 'public finance' is a misleading term, since the subject also deals with 'real' problems) have identified a number of problems associated with these fiscal policy issues. For instance, the *relative size of the public sector* raises questions regarding the definition and measurement of government revenue and expenditure (Prest 1972), and the attempts at understanding and explaining revenue and expenditure have produced more than one theoretical model (Musgrave and Musgrave 1976 and Peacock and Wiseman 1967). *The division of public sector responsibilities* raises the delicate question of which fiscal aspects should be dealt with at the central government level and which aspects should be tackled at the local level. Finally, the area of *taxation and expenditure criteria* has resulted in general agreement about the basic criteria of *allocation* (the process by which the utilisation of resources is split between private and social goods and by which the 'basket' of social goods is chosen), *equity* (the use of the budget for achieving a fair distribution), *stabilisation* (the use of the budget as an instrument for achieving and maintaining a 'reasonable' level of employment, prices and economic growth and for achieving equilibrium and stability in the balance of payments), and *administration* (the practical possibilities of implementing a particular tax system and the cost to the society of operating such a system). However, a number of very tricky problems are involved in a consideration of these criteria. In discussing the efficiency of resource allocation, the choice between e.g. work and leisure, or between private and public goods, is an important and controversial one. With regard to the equity of distribution, there is the problem of what is meant by equity: is it personal, class or regional equity? In a discussion of the stabilisation of the economy, there exists the perennial problem of controlling unemployment and infla-tion and the trade-off between them. A consideration of administration must take into account the problem of efficiency versus practicality. Finally, there is the obvious conflict between the four criteria in that the achievement of one aim is usually at the expense of another; for example, what is most efficient in terms of collection may prove less (or more) equitable than what is considered to be socially desirable.

These complex considerations cannot be tackled here, given the level of generality of this chapter. The interested reader is, therefore, advised to consult the very extensive literature on 'public finance'.

The above relates to a discussion of the problems of fiscal policy in very broad national terms. When considering the EEC fiscal policy, there are certain elements of the international dimension that need spelling out and there are also some inter-regional (intra-EEC) elements that have to be introduced.

Very briefly, internationally, it has always been recognised that taxes (and equivalent instruments) have similar effects to tariffs on the international flow of goods and services — non-tariff distortions of international trade (Baldwin 1971). Other elements have also been recognised as operating similar distortions on the international flow of factors of production (Bhagwati 1969, Johnson 1965 and 1973).

In the particular context of the EEC, it should be remembered that its formation, at least from the economic viewpoint, was meant to facilitate the free and unimpeded flow of goods, services and factors (and the other elements discussed in Chapter 1) between the member nations. Since tariffs are not the only distorting factor in this respect, the proper establishment of intra-EEC free trade necessitates the removal of all non-tariff distortions that have an equivalent effect. Hence, the removal of tariffs may give the impression of establishing free trade inside the EEC, but this is by no means automatically guaranteed, since the existence of sales taxes, excise duties, corporation taxes, income taxes, etc. may impede this freedom. The moral is that not only tariffs, but all equivalent distortions, must be eliminated or harmonised. (See table 11.1 for the EEC tax structure in 1955.)

At this juncture it becomes necessary to emphasise that there are

Table 11.1 *Percentage Composition of Tax Receipts and Tax Burden in the EEC, 1955*

	Income and property taxes	Turnover taxes	Comsumption taxes	Tax receipts as percentage of GNP
Belgium	50.7	26.5	22.8	17.1
France	38.4	41.5	20.1	19.6
W. Germany	52.4	26.9	20.7	21.9
Italy	32.3	21.1	46.6	22.9
Luxembourg	66.4	15.4	18.2	23.6
Netherlands	60.0	20.1	19.9	26.6

Source: Balassa (1965).

at least two basic elements to fiscal policy: the instruments available to the government for fiscal policy purposes (i.e. the total tax structure) and the overall impact of the joint manoeuvring of these instruments (i.e. the role played by the budget). The aim of this chapter is to discuss the meaning of and the need for tax harmonisation and to assess the progress made by the EEC in this respect. The other element of fiscal policy, the general budget of the EEC, is discussed by Professor Brown in the following chapter. Hence, the two chapters complement each other in that, taken together, they cover the two basic elements of EEC fiscal policy.

The Tax Structure and Its Implications

In case it is not obvious why taxes should give rise to trade distortion (Swann 1978), it may be useful to examine the nature of taxes before the inception of the EEC, as well as to consider the treatment given at the time to indirect taxation on internationally traded commodities.

Before considering these aspects, however, it may be useful to state that there are two basic types of taxation: direct and indirect. Direct taxes, like the income and corporation taxes, come into operation at the end of the process of personal and industrial activities. They are levied on wages and salaries when activities have been performed and payment has been met (income taxes), or on the profits of industrial or professional businesses at the end of annual activity (corporation taxes). Hence, direct taxes are not intended to play any significant role in the pricing of commodities or professional services. Indirect taxes are levied specifically on consumption and are, therefore, in a simplistic model, very significant in determining the pricing of commodities, given their real costs of production.

Historically speaking, in the EEC there existed four types of sales, or turnover, taxes (Dosser 1973, Paxton 1976): the *cumulative multi-stage cascade system* (operated in West Germany until the end of 1967, in Luxembourg until the end of 1969 and in the Netherlands until the end of 1968) in which the tax was levied on the gross value of the commodity in question at each and every stage of production without any rebate on taxes paid at earlier stages; *value-added tax* which has operated in France since 1954 where it is known as TVA — Taxe sur la Valeur Ajoutée — which is basically a non-cumulative multi-stage system; the *mixed systems* (operated in Belgium and Italy) which were cumulative multi-stage systems that were applied down to the wholesale stage, but incorporated taxes which were applied at a single point for certain products; and finally, *purchase tax* (operated in the UK) which was a single-stage tax normally charged at the wholesale stage by registered manufacturers or wholesalers — this meant that manufacturers could trade with each other without paying tax.

Although all these tax systems had the common characteristic that no tax was paid on exports, so that each country levied its tax at the point of entry, one should still consider the need for harmonising them.

A variety of taxes also existed in the form of excise duties. The number of commodities subjected to this duty ranged from the usual (or 'classical') five of manufactured tobacco products, hydrocarbon oils, beer, wine and spirits, to an extensive number including coffee, sugar, salt, matches, etc. (in Italy). Also, the means by which the government collected its revenues from excise duties ranged from government-controlled manufacturing, e.g. tobacco goods in France and Italy, to fiscal imports based on value, weight, strength, quality, etc. (Dosser 1973, p. 2).

As far as corporation tax is concerned, three basic schemes existed and still exist, but not in any single country at *all* times. The first is the *Separate System* which was used in the UK — the system calls for the complete separation of corporation tax from personal income tax and was usually referred to as the 'classical' system. The second is the *Two-Rate System or Split-Rate System* which was the German practice and was recommended as an alternative system for the UK in the Green Paper of 1971 (HMSO Cmnd. 4630). The third is the *Credit or Imputation System* — this was the French System and was proposed for the UK in the White Paper of 1972 (HMSO Cmnd. 4955).

Generally speaking, corporation tax varied from being totally indistinguishable from other systems (Italy) to being quite separate from personal income tax with a single or a split-rate which varied between 'distributed' and 'undistributed' profits, to being partially integrated with the personal income tax systems, so that part of the corporation tax paid on distributed profits could be credited against a shareholder's income tax liability (Dosser 1973, p. 2).

The personal income tax system itself was differentiated in very many aspects among the original Six, not just as regards rates and allowances, but also administration procedures, compliance and enforcement.

Finally, the variety in the para-tax system relating to social security arrangements was even more striking. The balance between sickness, industrial injury, unemployment, and pensions was very different indeed, and the methods of financing these benefits were even more so (see tables 15.4 and 15.5 of the Statistical Appendix to Chapter 15).

In concluding this section, it is useful to discuss certain problems regarding these taxes. Since VAT is the EEC turn-over tax (see the section below on EEC progress on tax harmonisation), I shall illustrate the problems of turnover taxes in the context of VAT.

The first problem relates to the point at which the tax should be imposed. Here, two basic principles have been recognised and a choice between them has to be made: the 'destination' and 'origin' principles. Taxation under the destination principle specifies that commodities going to the same destination must bear the same tax load irrespective of their origin. For example, if the UK levies a general sales tax at 8% and France a similar tax at 16%, a commodity exported from the UK to France would be exempt from the UK's 8% tax, but would be subjected to France's 16% tax. Hence, the UK export commodity would compete on equal tax terms with French commodities sold in the French market. Taxation under the origin principle specifies that commodities with the same origin must pay exactly the same tax, irrespective of their destination. Hence, a commodity exported by the UK to France would pay the UK tax (8%) and would be exempt from the French tax (16%). Hence, the commodity that originated from the UK would compete unfairly against a similar French commodity.

The choice between the destination and origin principles raises a number of technical issues which cannot be tackled here. Those interested should consult the voluminous literature on the subject (Shoup 1966 and 1970, Musgrave 1969, Dosser 1973, Paxton 1976 and Pinder 1971).

The second problem relates to the range of coverage of the tax. If some countries are allowed to include certain stages, e.g. the retail stage, and others make allowances for certain fixed capital expenditures and raw materials, the tax base will not be the same. This point is very important, because one has to be clear about whether the tax base should be consumption or net national income. To illustrate, in a 'closed' economy

$$Y \equiv W + P \equiv C + I$$

where Y = gross national product (GNP), W = wages and salaries, P = gross profits, C = consumption and I = gross capital expenditure. If value-added is defined as $W + P - I$ (i.e. GNP minus Gross Capital Expenditure), then consumption will form the tax base. If instead of Gross Capital Expenditure one deducts only capital consumption (depreciation), then Net National Product will become the tax base. Obviously, the argument holds true in an open economy. It is therefore important that members of a union should have a common base.

The third problem relates to exemptions that may defeat the aim of VAT being a tax on consumption. For example, in a three-stage production process, exempting the first stage does not create any problem, since the tax levied on the second and third stages together will be equivalent to a tax levied at all three stages. Exempting the third stage will obviously reduce the tax collection, provided of course that the rates levied at all stages were the same. If the second stage is exempt, the tax base will be in excess of that where no exemptions are allowed for, since the tax on the first stage cannot be transferred as an input tax on the second stage, and the third stage will be unable to claim any input tax from items bought from the second stage. The outcome will be a tax based on the total sum of the turnover of stages one and three only, rather than a tax levied on the total sum of the value added at all three stages.

With regard to corporation tax, a proper evaluation of any system raises national as well as intra-regional (intra-EEC) questions. The national questions relate to the standard criteria by which a tax system can be judged: its effect on budget revenue and effective demand, on income distribution, on the balance of payments, on the rate of economic growth, on regional differences, and on price levels. It is obvious that what is very efficient for one purpose need not be so efficient for the other purposes.

The intra-EEC questions relate to the treatment of investment, since, if capital mobility within the EEC is to be encouraged, investors must receive equal treatment irrespective of their native country (region). Here, Dosser highly recommends the Separate System since it is 'neutral' in its tax treatment between domestic investment at home and abroad, and between domestic and foreign investment at home, provided both member countries practise the same system

(Dosser 1973, p. 95). Prest (1979, pp. 85–86) argues that even though a Separate System does not discriminate against partner (foreign) investment, it does discriminate between 'distributed' and 'undistributed' profits, and that the Imputation System, even though it is 'neutral' between 'distributed' and 'undistributed' profits, actually discriminates against partner (foreign) investment. Prest therefore claims that neither system can be given 'full marks'.

Again, at this level of generality, one cannot go into all the complications raised by such questions. The interested reader is therefore advised to consult Dosser (1966, 1968, 1973 and 1978), Paxton (1976) and Pinder (1971), or the vast literature on the subject.

Excise duties are intended basically for revenue raising purposes. For example, in the UK, excise duties on tobacco products, petroleum and alcoholic drinks account for about a quarter of central government revenue. Hence, the issues raised by the harmonisation of these taxes are specifically those relating to the revenue raising function of these taxes and to the equity, as opposed to the efficiency, of these methods.

Finally, the income tax structure has a lot to do with the freedom of labour mobility. Ideally, one would expect equality of treatment in every single tax that is covered within this structure, but it is apparent that since there is more than one rate, the harmonisation of a 'package' of rates might achieve the specified objective.

The Meaning of Tax Harmonisation

Having discussed the problems associated with taxes in the context of economic integration, it is now appropriate to say something about the precise meaning of tax harmonisation.

In earlier years, tax harmonisation was defined as tax coordination (Dosser 1973). Ideally, in a *fully* integrated EEC, it could be defined as the identical unification of both base and rates, given the same tax system and assuming that everything else is also unified. Professor Prest (1979, p. 76) rightly argues that 'coordination' is tantamount to a low-level meaning of tax harmonisation, since it could be 'interpreted to be some process of consultation between member countries or, possibly, loose agreements between them to levy tax on a similar sort of base *or* at similar sorts of rates'. Hence, it is not surprising that tax harmonisation has, in practice, come to mean a compromise between the low-level of coordination (the EEC is much more than a low-level of integration — see Chapter 1), and the ideal level of standardisation (the EEC is nowhere near its objective of complete political unity).

EEC Tax Harmonisation Experience

Article 99 of the Treaty of Rome specifically calls for the harmonisation of indirect taxes, mainly turnover taxes and excise duties. Harmonisation here was seen as vital, particularly since the removal of tariffs would leave taxes as the main source of intra-EEC trade distortion. However, given the preoccupation of the EEC with the process of unification, the Treaty seems to put very little stress on the harmonisation of its initial tax diversity. Moreover, the Treaty is rather vague about what it means by 'harmonisation': for example, in Article 100 it does not specify more than that laws 'should be approximated' with regard to direct taxation. Hence, the whole development of tax harmonisation has been influenced by the work of special Committees, informal discussions, etc., i.e., the procedure detailed in Chapter 2. This, however, should not be interpreted as a criticism of those who drafted the Treaty. On the contrary, given the very complex nature of the subject and its closeness to the question of political unification, it would have been short-sighted to have done otherwise.

Given this general background, it is now appropriate to describe the progress made by the EEC with respect to tax harmonisation.

In the area of indirect taxation most of the developments have been in terms of VAT — which the EEC adopted as its turnover tax following the recommendations of the Neumark Committee in 1963, which was in turn based on the Tinbergen Study of 1953 — particularly since it was realised that the removal of intra-EEC tariffs left taxes on traded goods as the main impediment to the establishment of complete free trade inside the Community. Between 1967 and 1977, six Directives were issued with the aim of achieving conformity between the different practices of the member countries. These related, apart from the adoption of VAT as the EEC sales tax, to three major considerations: the inclusion of the retail stage in the coverage of VAT; the use of VAT levies for the EEC central budget (see the following chapter); and the achievement of greater uniformity in VAT structure.

What then is the state of play? (See table 11.2 for information.) Having adopted the VAT system and having accepted a unified method of calculating it, the EEC has also acceded to the destination principle which, as we have seen, is consistent with free intra-EEC trade. It has been agreed by all member states that the coverage of VAT should be the same and should include the retail stage (now the normal practice), that crude raw materials, bought-in elements and similar components are to be be deductable from the tax com-

Table 11.2 *Taxes and Actual Social Contribution (% of Total), VAT and Corporation Tax 1977*

	Taxes and Actual Social Contributions (% of Total)				Effective Rates of VAT (%)			Corporation Tax	
	Taxes linked to production and imports	Current taxes on income and wealth	Capital taxes	Actual social contributions	Standard	Reduced rate(s)	Increased rate(s)	Rate (%)	System
Belgium	28.6	39.9	0.8	30.8	18	6–14	25	48	Imputation
Denmark	41.3	57.0	0.4	1.2	15	–	–	37	Separate
France	36.3	21.3	0.5	41.9	17.6	7	33.33	50	Imputation
W. Germany	31.3	34.5	0.2	34.1	11	5.5	–	56	Imputation
Ireland	53.7	31.4	0.6	14.4	20	10	35–40	35	Imputation
Italy	33.9	26.8	0.2	39.0	14	1–3–9	18–35	50	Separate
Luxembourg	27.0	41.7	0.4	30.9	10	2.5	–	40	Separate
Netherlands	27.4	34.1	0.4	38.1	18	4	–	48	Separate
UK	38.4	41.4	0.8	19.4	8	–	12.5	52	Imputation

Sources: Eurostat and Prest (1979).
Notes: (1) The effective VAT rate is that on the price net of tax.
(2) The Danish rate rose to 18% in 1978 and the UK rate to 15% in 1979.

putation, and that investment stock and inventories should be given similar treatment by all member nations. There is agreement about the general principle of VAT exemptions, but the precise nature of these seems to vary from one member country to another, thus giving rise to the problems concerning the tax base discussed earlier.

On the other hand, this similarity of principles is, in practice, contradicted by a number of differences. The tax coverage differs from one member country to another, since most seem to have different kinds, as well as different levels, of exemptions. For example, the UK applies zero-rating for foodstuffs, gas and electricity (zero-rating is different from exemptions, since zero-rating means not only tax exemption from the process, but also the receipt of rebates on taxes paid at the preceding stage — see Prest, Dosser and Paxton). There is a wide difference in rate structure.

With respect to corporation tax, the Neumark Report of 1963 recommended a Split-Rate system, the van den Tempel Report of 1970 preferred the adoption of the Separate or 'classical' system and the Draft Directive of 1975 went for the Imputation system. Moreover, the method of tax harmonisation which is accepted is not the ideal one of a single EEC Corporation tax and a single tax pattern, but rather a unified EEC Corporation tax accompanied by freedom of tax patterns. Hence, all systems have been entertained at some time or another and all that can be categorically stated is that the EEC has, at this stage, limited its choice to the Separate and Imputation systems.

As far as excise duties are concerned, progress has been rather slow and this can be partially attributed to the large extent of the differences between the rates on the commodities under consideration in the different member countries. This is a partial explanation however, because, as was pointed out earlier, these taxes are important for government revenue purposes and it would be naive to suggest that rate uniformity can be achieved without giving consideration to the political implications of such a move.

The greatest progress has been achieved in tobacco, where a new harmonised system was adopted in January 1978. The essential elements of this system are the abolition of any duties on raw tobacco leaf and the adoption of a new sales tax at the manufacturing level, combined with a specific tax per cigarette and VAT. Prest (1979) argues that the overall effect of this will be to push up the relative prices of the cheaper brands of cigarettes.

It has been suggested (Prest 1979) that the harmonisation of tax rates here is misguided, since the destination principle automatically guarantees fair competition. This is a misleading criticism, however, since the harmonisation of the tax structure should be seen in the context of the drive in the EEC for monetary integration and political unification, processes which become increasingly difficult without tax harmonisation.

Some progress has been achieved with regard to Stamp Duties. Harmonisation here is necessary for promoting the freedom of intra-EEC capital flows. The 1976 Draft Directive recommended a compromise between the systems existing in the member countries. This recommendation has been accepted, with the proviso that time will be allowed for adjustment to the new system.

Nothing has been attempted in the area of personal income taxation and very slight progress has been achieved in social security payments, unemployment benefits, etc. These are discussed in some detail in the chapter on the EEC Social Policy.

Conclusion

In conclusion, it must be emphasised that the lack of fundamental progress in EEC tax harmonisation should not come as a surprise. There are three basic reasons for this. First, lest it be forgotten, the EEC stands for the harmonised integration of some of the oldest countries in the world, with very diverse and extremely complicated economic systems, and this diversity and complexity is increasing with the enlargement (and potential enlargement) of the EEC. Secondly, tax harmonisation is intimately connected with the role played by the government in controlling the economy and since this role depends on a complicated package of taxes, it should be apparent that the separate harmonising of the different components of the package is extremely difficult and probably also misguided. Finally, and more importantly, tax harmonisation, or at least the complex and sensitive elements within it, is very closely linked with the question of monetary integration and political unification. It is argued in Chapters 9 and 10 that these matters are very closely related. It would therefore be naive to expect substantial progress in tax harmonisation, without similar progress in these other fields.

References

Balassa, B., *The Theory of Economic Integration*, Allen and Unwin 1965.
Balassa, B., *European Economic Integration*, North-Holland Publishing Co. 1975.
Baldwin, R.E., *Non-tariff Distortions of International Trade*, Allen and Unwin 1971.
Bhagwati, J., *Trade Tariffs and Growth*, Weidenfeld and Nicolson 1969.

Dosser, D., Economic analysis of tax harmonisation, in Shoup, C.S., *Fiscal Harmonisation in Common Markets*, 2 vol., Columbia University Press 1966.

Dosser, D., Taxation, in Pinder, J., *The Economics of Europe*, Knight 1971.

Dosser, D., *British Taxation and the Common Market*, Knight 1973.

Dosser, D., A federal budget for the Community, in Burrows, B., Denton, G. and Edwards, G., *Federal Solutions to European Issues*, Macmillan Press 1975.

Dosser, D. and Han, S.S., *Taxes in the EEC and Britain: the Problem of Harmonisation*, International Institute of International Affairs/PEP, London, 1968.

Johnson, H.G., Optimal trade intervention in the presence of domestic distortions, in Baldwin, R.E. *et al, Trade, Growth and the Balance of Payments*, North-Holland Publishing Co. 1965.

Johnson, H.G. and Krauss, M.B., Border taxes, border tax adjustments, comparative advantage and the balance of payments, in Krauss, M.B. (ed.), *The Economics of Integration*, Allen and Unwin 1973.

Musgrave, R.A. and P.B., *Public Finance in Theory and Practice*, McGraw-Hill 1976.

Paxton, J., *The Developing Common Market*, Macmillan Press 1976.

Peacock, A.T. and Wiseman, J., *The Growth of Public Expenditure in the UK*, Allen and Unwin 1967.

Pinder, J., *The Economics of Europe*, Knight 1971.

Prest, A.R., Government revenue, the national income and all that, in Bird, R.M. and Head, J.G., *Modern Fiscal Issues*, University of Toronto Press 1972.

Prest, A.R., *Public Finance in Theory and Practice*, Weidenfeld and Nicolson 1975.

Prest, A.R., Fiscal policy, in Coffey, P., *Economic Policies of the EEC*, Macmillan Press 1979.

Shoup, C.S., *Fiscal Harmonisation in Common Markets*, 2 vol., Columbia University Press 1966.

Shoup, C.S., Taxation aspects of international economic integration, in Robson, P., *International Economic Integration*, Penguin Modern Economics Texts 1972.

Swann, D., *The Economics of the Common Market*, Penguin Modern Economics Texts 1978.

European Commission, *Report on Problems Raised by the Different Turnover Tax Systems Applied within the Common Market*, ECSC, 1953 (The Tinbergen Report).

European Commission, *Report of the Fiscal and Financial Committee*, Brussels 1963 (The Neumark Report).

European Commission, *Corporation Tax and Income Tax in the European Communities*, Brussels, 1970 (The van den Tempel Report).

European Commission, *Report of the Study Group on the Role of Public Finance in European Integration*, 2 vol., Brussels, April 1977 (The MacDougall Report).

12

Fiscal Policy II: The Budget

A J BROWN

The general Budget of the Community makes provision for a somewhat miscellaneous collection of expenditures. First, it provides for the administrative expenses (official salaries, premises, etc) of the various Community institutions — the Parliament, the Council, the Commission, the Court of Justice, the European Coal and Steel Community (ECSC), the Social Fund, and the Regional Development Fund, described in Chapter 2. Secondly (and more important) it provides for the other operational expenditures of the Commission, the 'intervention' expenditures, which include the large grants made by the Agricultural Guarantee and Guidance Funds, described in Chapter 7 and also the payments made by the Social Fund and the Regional Development Fund. The former of these two funds provides grants to assist in promoting occupational and geographical mobility of workers, most particularly farmers leaving agriculture, workers displaced from the textile and clothing industries, and the young unemployed, both generally and in regions of particularly depressed activity. The Regional Development Fund, established in 1975 and described in Chapter 13, provides grants in support, within national quotas, of national regional policies and is in future also to support specific schemes intended to ease the structural difficulties arising from the working of Community policies. It should be added that the expenditure on food and some other aid for developing countries comes within the General Budget, whereas the operations of the European Development Fund are not yet included. The 'intervention expenditures' of the ECSC (as opposed to its administrative costs) also remain outside.

For the financial year 1978, the General Budget amounts to some 12,300 million European Units of Account (see table 12.1), or, very roughly, £7,000 million, of which agricultural expenditure accounts

218

Table 12.1 *Budgets Adopted by the European Parliament for 1977 and 1978 (in million European Units of Account (EUA))*

Commission	Approved for Payment	
	1977	1978
Intervention appropriations		
Agriculture	7289	9132
Social Sector	158	559
Regional Sector	319	525
Research, Energy, Industry, Transport	221	294
Development Co-operation	308	381
Sub Total	8294	10891
Administrative appropriations		
Staff	344	387
Administrative expenditure	98	106
Information	8	13
Aids and subsidies	36	45
Sub Total	486	551
Contingency Reserve	4	5
Repayment to Member States	629	690
Commission Total	9413	12137
Other institutions		
(administrative expenditure only)	186	225
Total	9600	12362

Source: Eleventh General Report of the Activities of the European Communities, Table 3.

for about three-quarters, administrative expenses (for all the institutions covered) for about 6%, and social and regional expenditures for about 5% each. The total is thus of the same order of magnitude as the expenditure under one of the larger United Kingdom departmental headings — Education and Science, or Defence, or the Health Service. To judge from data for previous years, it amounts to about 0.7% of the Gross Domestic Product of the Community members (at market prices) which, to place it in perspective, may be compared with the total expenditure of their national and other public authorities, amounting to about 45 per cent of total GDP. Even if the loans made by the ECSC and the Development Fund are included, the total outlay by the organisations concerned is not brought up to 1% of the member countries' aggregate GDP. By this measure, the weight of the Community within the European economies is small and, if they are regarded as the embryo centre of a federal system, then by this financial test the embryo is at an early stage of development.

The Budget may, however, be claimed to deserve more attention than its present size, in relation to the combined public or total expenditures of member countries, would suggest, first because in particular fields of expenditure it is already of significance, secondly because its financing raises the interesting problems that belong to federal and international systems, and thirdly because of the possibility that, in the course of its further growth, it may come to play a more substantial part in the European economy.

The purpose of this chapter is to discuss, briefly, each of these three grounds.

Community Expenditure[1]

It is plain, from what has already been said, that it is in agriculture that the Community expenditure is of the greatest significance, both absolutely and in relation to total public expenditure in this field. The greater part of the Community expenditure in question is on price support, mostly in connection with commodities where the Community's degree of self-sufficiency is high. The disbursements under this head between 1968 and 1972, before the enlargement of the Community and the rise in world prices, amounted to some 2 or 3% of the total expenditure on foodstuffs in the countries concerned. Where the Community is a considerable importer, however, much of the task of raising prices to a chosen height above world level is done by imposition of import levies. These matters are dealt with in Chapter 7. It is in milk and dairy products that the operation of the support-price system has been most expensive – about a quarter of the whole General Budget commitments in 1977. In most years in the 1970s, however, a very considerable extra expenditure has been incurred on 'monetary compensatory amounts' – payments made to offset discrepancies in costs of agricultural products from different countries in the Community which arise from changes in their cross-rates of exchange (see Chapter 7).

Expenditure from the Community budget on 'guidance' (that is to say, bringing about structural change in the agricultural industry, as opposed to 'guarantee', which is the raising of its product-prices) has generally run at only about one-tenth of the agricultural total. To a large extent it consists of grants in aid of projects to which the member government concerned also makes a contribution.

This is not the place to evaluate the economic results of the Community's heavy agricultural expenditure; that is done in Chapter 7. All that need be said here is that it amounts to rather over one-quarter of all the public expenditure directed towards agriculture in the Community countries, where, admittedly, such expenditure (at about 1.7% of GNP) is higher than in, for instance, the United States; it accounts for about 60% of total agricultural subsidies. A good deal of the Community expenditure may be regarded as transferred from national budgets in this continent of traditionally high agricultural protection.

Other headings under which Community budget expenditure is fairly substantial in relation to total public expenditure are regional aid within the Community (the Regional Fund), development assistance outside it, and industrial training. In the first, Community budget expenditure may be as much as one-eighth of the total, if that total is rather narrowly defined, but is probably less if one uses a definition that enables like to be compared correctly with like. Of the total official development aid to external countries from Community countries in 1975, that through the Community budget amounted to about 7½%, but this proportion was expected to increase substantially in later years, and, with the addition of amounts made available by the European Development Fund and the European Investment Bank, to rise to perhaps a quarter or a fifth of the Community countries' total official external aid. Social Fund grants in aid of adult training schemes and the like apparently amount to about a quarter of total public spending on them.

Under other headings where there is some Community budgetary expenditure, such as research, its importance in relation to national expenditure is generally much lower than in these instances, though it must be remembered that a considerable amount of research and development is financed by governments under *ad hoc* cooperative arrangements or through Community institutions operating outside the General Budget. Again, under the heading of Manufacturing, Mining, and Construction, the Community budget expenditure is small, but the loan expenditure of the ECSC and the sectoral moder-nisation and multi-country project loans of the European Investment Bank amount to perhaps 2 or 3% of all comparable national and local budgetary expenditures in member countries. It follows from what has been said earlier that Community budget expenditure as a whole is about 1½% of total member countries' public expenditure.

If one looks at the Community budget as that of an embryo federal government, however, it is what it lacks rather than what it contains that is most striking. Federations vary, of course, in the range of activities assigned to the Centre; federal expenditure, which is typically about half of total public expenditure (in Australia, Switzerland, and the United States, for example), can be as high as 56% of it (in Germany) or as low as 38% (in Canada). The functions that are always assigned to the Centre are external relations and defence; indeed, it was largely in order to obtain the benefits of united action in these fields that most existing federations were formed in the first place. In the countries of the European Community, these two headings account between them for about 9% of total public expenditure, though in federations elsewhere the proportion can be as high as 15% (Canada) or over 18% (the United States). If, therefore, these functions, on their present scales, were assigned to the central organs of the European Community, the General Budget would have to be some seven times as big as it is at present. In fact, also, existing federations take on large parts, at least, of other spending functions which would otherwise have to be performed by their member states. Social security is the most notable of these, partly because of the mobility of population within federal areas, and partly also because, within an established political entity (even a federal one), the appeal of pooled arrangements for meeting adversity which may affect one member state more than another is powerful — a consideration which has also worked to make a good many economic services federal in the chief existing federations.

What this amounts to, therefore, is that the development of the North Atlantic Treaty Organisation separately from the European Community prevented the latter from taking the classic route towards a federal structure, with at least important elements of defence as the first charges on the common budget, while the existence of highly-developed social security systems and many public economic services within the member states has pre-empted the area in which most of the old federations have most increased their central activities in the present century. What this implies for the prospective development of the General Budget is a question to which it will be necessary to return after considering the revenue side.

Community Revenue

Under the Treaty of Rome, the European Economic Community was to be financed mainly by contributions from its member states in a fixed, agreed proportion, it being provided that the Budget should be balanced. The Commission was, however, instructed to study the conditions under which these contributions 'may be replaced by other resources available to the Community itself, in particular by revenue accruing from the common customs tariff when finally introduced'. The results of this study were incorporated in a decision of April 1970, laying down a scheme for a gradual transition, beginning in 1971, to the final system of total reliance on 'own resources' of the Community, to be attained in 1978.

Apart from some minor items (e.g. taxes on Community officials' salaries) these 'own resources' in their final form were to consist of three parts: the customs revenue collected by member states under the common tariff, the levies collected on agricultural imports to bring them up to the agreed common price, and the proceeds of a tax assessed on a common Value Added Tax base in each country — the rate of tax not to exceed 1% of the base, and to be the variable for adjusting revenue to match the approved total expenditure (see table 12.2).

Meanwhile, Denmark, Ireland, and the United Kingdom, joined the Community in 1973, and provision was made for the contributions

Table 12.2 *Revenue Sources: Estimated Out-turn for 1977 (million EUA)*

Own Resources	
Customs Duties	4800
Agricultural and Sugar levies	1614
GNP-based contributions*	3030
Other Revenue	140
Total	9584

*   This was the interim source of revenue, to be replaced from 1978 by a VAT-based levy, which for that year was fixed at 0.64%.

The Triennial financial forecasts for 1977–9 gave the following estimates of resources (in Million Budgetary Units of Account** at 1976 prices) for the year 1978:

Miscellaneous revenue	72
Customs duties	3411
Agricultural levies	1180
VAT at 0.74%	5017
Total	9680

** The Budgetary Unit of Account was originally equal to 1 US Dollar, and was converted into member currencies at the fixed IMF parity rate. It has now been replaced for budgetary (as well as other) purposes by the European Unit of Account (EUA) which is based, like an index number, on a 'basket' of currencies, and therefore varies in value in relation to each of those currencies as their cross-rates change.

The financing of the 1979 Budget was expected to be as follows:

	Million EUA
Agricultural levies	1706.0
Sugar levy	467.0
Customs Duties	4745.5
VAT (0.77% of base)	6982.5
Miscellaneous	158.5
	14059.5

Source: Bulletin of the European Communities, Supplement 6/78: *Preliminary Draft General Budget of the European Communities for the Financial Year 1979.*

and transitional arrangements to be modified accordingly, so that definitive 'own resources' scheme would operate without restriction from 1980. In 1974, however, the new United Kingdom government entered into re-negotiations concerning terms of entry, including, in particular, the country's contribution to Community revenue. The Commission subsequently estimated that, had the post-1980 procedure been in force in 1974, the relative shares in the budget and in the Community's GDP would have been as follows:

	% of Budget	% of GDP
Denmark	2.4	2.8
W. Germany	30.2	33.6
France	18.2	23.2
Ireland	0.6	0.6
Italy	13.2	13.2
Netherlands	7.8	6.0
Belgium &		
Luxembourg	5.6	4.7
UK	22.0	15.9

(The shares were calculated at the then current market exchange rates)
Source: Bulletin of the European Communities, Supplement 7/74, Table XIV.

The Commission concluded from the discrepancy between GDP shares and Budget shares that 'it does appear that problems would arise in the future', and subsequently, in March 1975, agreement was reached on a 'financial mechanism' by which countries with relatively low levels of GDP per head, without relatively high growth-rates, especially if they were in balance of payments deficit, should receive reimbursement of 'excess' payments to Community revenue, on an agreed scale.

This has the effect which the UK Government sought, though it can hardly be denied that it is a clumsy system. The discrepancy which it is aimed at correcting arises from different degrees of dependence upon imports of food and dutiable goods from outside the Community, and so far as the VAT-based levy is concerned, from the (freely acknowledged) fact that VAT is not assessed on investment, which forms a quite widely varying proportion of different countries' Gross Domestic Products. Fixed capital formation in 1971–75 was about 17½% of GDP in the United Kingdom, 20% of it in Italy, 25% in Germany, and 27% in France. The doctrine that customs duty and similar receipts should go to central revenue is, however, well established in all federations. Once there is no control of trade across the frontiers between one member state and another, it becomes impossible to know how much of a commodity imported from outside the federation into member state A is consumed within it, and how much is passed on for consumption to other member states. To the extent that it is so passed on, an import duty on it levied by A will fall in part upon citizens of the other states. It therefore solves an awkward problem if the revenue from such duties goes to the federal government, for the benefit, in principle, of all the states of the federation. On the other hand, a part of a federation that, by virtue of its economic structure and geographical location consumes more dutiable merchandise from foreign countries than other parts do, may find itself contributing disproportionately to federal taxation — a particular case of the general truth that any tax not based on a generally accepted criterion of ability to pay will draw plausible complaints from some taxpayers, and perhaps from particular parts of the taxing authority's domain. If particular taxes raise these problems in a sufficiently acute form, the only remedy is either to diversify the tax structure, so that different taxes hit different member states in such a way as to achieve rough justice, or to introduce some sort of *ad hoc* compensatory mechanism, however clumsy this device may be. The fact that Community revenue is relatively small makes diversification difficult — hence the adoption of the second of these courses.

Impact on the European Economy

The relative smallness of present revenue and expenditure means, as has already been implied, that the Community Budget plays at present only a very minor part in the macroeconomics of member states — their activity and the distribution of activity among them — as opposed to the fortunes of particular sectors such as agriculture. There is a presumption that the tax system, by itself, has a systematic tendency to be slightly regressive, because of the extent to which it is indirect, because of the slightly regressive character of the VAT base (since investment is likely to be higher where incomes are higher), and perhaps also because peripheral member countries have a broadly systematic tendency to be among both the poorer and the more dependent on trade external to the Community. The financial mechanism goes at any rate some way towards offsetting this regressiveness. On the expenditure side, the Regional Development and Social Funds may be relied upon to tend towards diminishing international welfare differences within the Community, but the much larger Agricultural Funds are not so reliable. If (as one might expect *a priori*) the member states with the largest agricultural sectors, and the greatest needs for structural adjustment, were also the poorest, then the Funds would tend to diminish international disparities, but this is by no means uniformly the case — the United Kingdom with a smaller and more efficient agricultural sector than France or Germany (which have higher average incomes) is an outstanding anomaly. Thus, even in proportion to its small absolute size, the Community Budget is probably not very effective in diminishing welfare discrepancies between member states. By the same token, it does little to stabilise activity in particular member countries, while its present capacity to contribute to stabilisation in the European economy as a whole is negligible. Nevertheless, the possibility of its playing a larger part in all these respects has received attention, for reasons which must now be briefly stated.

Prospective Functions

The impulse to consider a possibly enlarged role for the Community budget arose from aspirations towards economic and monetary union. A study group, set up by the Commission in 1974 'to examine the future role of public finance at the Community level in the general context of European economic integration', (the group's report is published as *Economic and Financial Series*, 1977, A13 and B13) began its work by examining the part played by public finance in the working of the free market economy within existing federations and those unitary states for which regional data were available.

The role of public finance (essentially, of the national budget) in this connection is a very considerable one. In the first place, it generally tends to diminish differences of income and welfare not only between richer and poorer people, but (what is relevant for the present purpose) between states or regions with different average income levels, and it may be claimed that this is, on balance, a factor tending to promote and preserve the economic union in question.

The conditions in which this claim is valid are not hard to see. It is valid so long as residents in the richer states or regions which are called upon to bear the burden of assisting the poorer ones through the channels of public finance, are generally of the opinion that the working of the economic and monetary union is sufficiently to their advantage to make the burden of assistance bearable, and so long as those in the poorer areas are less convinced of the benefits of union — apart from the benefit of their public finance subsidy. If everyone is convinced of the benefits of belonging to a common monetary and market area, that institution will not, of course, need subsidies from the richer to the poorer regions to make it viable. Public finance transfers between states or regions may be desirable, but they will not be necessary to union. Equally, if residents in a richer region do not see their welfare as depending greatly on membership of an economic and monetary union, the fact that the union is accompanied by net transfers to poorer partners will make them still less inclined to enter into it. It does, nevertheless, seem to be broadly the case in Europe that the more prosperous members of the Community are more in favour of closer union, while some, at least of the less prosperous, more peripheral members, are more doubtful about the benefits of giving up the instruments of control over their own economic destinies. On balance, therefore, (as we have said) the prospective equalising power of a more developed system of Community public finance would be likely to promote — perhaps to be a condition of — closer economic union.

But the presumption that an enlarged budgetary function is a condition of economic and monetary union probably depends less on who is more and who is less prosperous now, than on a fairly general awareness that national fortunes can change — indeed, that participation in economic and monetary union is likely to promote quicker and more drastic change. A built-in system of net transfers from whoever is doing well at the moment to whoever is doing badly is an insurance against economic misfortune, which may well be regarded as essential to entering on a more dangerous (even if, it is hoped, generally more rapidly progressive) way of economic life.

The extent to which this kind of insurance operates within unitary countries or federations that constitute developed monetary and free market areas is, in fact, very substantial indeed. Direct information is lacking on the extent to which a region that suffers, say, a fall in its sales, is automatically compensated by paying out less in tax and receiving more in social insurance benefits and the like, but there is indirect evidence from the extent to which public finance, at any given time, renders average personal disposable incomes (including benefits in kind) less unequal between regions than average pre-tax factor incomes are. The Study Group found that, in the eight countries and federations examined, inequalities were reduced by about 40% on average (more in Australia and France, less in Germany and the United States). They also found that continuing regional balance of payments surpluses and deficits are financed mostly by net flows of public finance, commonly to the extent of 3–10% of Gross Regional Product, and in the case of inflows into poor regions, occasionally up to about 30% of it (Northern Ireland is an example of this). Other, less direct, lines of inquiry suggest that short-run relative falls in regional income may be cushioned by public finance to the extent of considerably more than half in some countries.

Large degrees of levelling and cushioning of regional income differences and fluctuations are thus normal features of modern economies within which there are single monetary systems and high mobilities of factors and products. As far as the levelling is concerned, it is relevant to note that without it, and without a considerable degree of uniformity in tax rates and levels of benefit from public services, interregional migration would be considerably greater than it is. Indeed, if regions were financially self-sufficient, those that fell on hard times would suffer from high taxation and/or inferior public services and the better-off would benefit correspondingly, so that migration of labour and industry would, up to a point at least, tend to be promoted cumulatively. Mobility of factors has virtues, but there is certainly a limit to the amount of it that is socially and politically acceptable, at least to communities with strong senses of corporate identity.

As far as fluctuations in income are concerned, modern communities have come to expect that they will be cushioned, in one way or another. A sovereign state cushions its population against, say, a fall in demand for its exports partly by running into deficit on its current external account, (to the extent to which it finds borrowing from abroad acceptable), or partly by using exchange-rate or trade barriers to deflect demand towards its own goods. A region in a country, or a state in a federation, cannot operate with exchange-rates or trade barriers, but in so far as its personal disposable incomes are maintained by social insurance or relief from national or federal sources, and by reduction in its tax bills, its inevitable balance of payments deficit is automatically financed for it by a net inflow of public finance. A country joining an economic and monetary union with little supra-national public finance would have to rely for cushioning on its ability to borrow, either from its partners in the union or outside.

This, then, is the relevance of the scale and pattern of the Community's Budget to its ability to develop towards a union in which member states had given up their power to shift demand towards their own products by exchange rate manipulations and trade barriers. What is the prospect of a development of the Budget that would be significant magnitude in this connection?

At first sight, the chance looks slight, short of a move to a federal system that would transfer, at least, defence and external relations into the General Budget from those of the member states, thereby giving the new federal Community control over perhaps 10% or more of members' total public expenditures, at least 4 or 5% of their GDP. The prospect of new Community activities, additional both to existing ones and to the public activities of member states, appears to be narrowly restricted, since the general opinion (partly conditioned by the slow growth of the years since 1973) is that public expenditure should not be substantially increased in relation to total product.

The Study Group referred to above saw, however, a stronger possibility of development — short of federation — than this would suggest. It noted that, while in the countries studied, public expenditure amounting to 45% of GDP goes with a 40% reduction in inter-regional inequalities (and presumably with corresponding, probably rather greater, cushioning of short-term fluctuations), the net transfer from richer to poorer regions is merely the difference between very large payments to and from the central government. In federal countries, schemes for sharing tax-revenue between the centre and the states, and central grants to the poorer states, serve to effect large parts of the total equalisation that takes place with much smaller portions of the total gross flows of funds. (Indeed, the total *net* transfer from richer to poorer regions is commonly only 2—5% of total GDP.) If, therefore, the extension of the Community's functions involved not giving rather more to the poor than to the rich, but giving to the poor only, a significant increase in the amount of equalisation and cushioning might be achieved with a Community budget that was still a small fraction of those of the member states. Even, indeed, with external relations and defence federalised, and 4 or 5% of Community GDP passing through the General Budget, it is clear that there would not be much scope for automatic income-equalisation between countries and regions, or for automatic offsetting of local income fluctuations, unless the basis of Community taxation became much more progressive. If the increased Community expenditure was met in the obvious way, by extending the present VAT based assessment from its limit of 1% to, say, 5% of that tax base, this source of revenue would dwarf the customs and agricultural levy sources, giving a total community tax burden distributed more nearly in proportion to private consumption — in relation to total income, a slightly regressive distribution. The chief distributional change would, in fact, be that arising from the present international non-proportionality of defence and external relations expenditure, which claims between 3½ and 4% of Community GDP. A considerable relief, perhaps over 1% of her GDP, would accrue to the United Kingdom, and possibly a very much smaller relief to France, at the expense of the rest — an expense which would fall, proportionately, most heavily on Ireland (perhaps to the extent of more than 2% of her GDP) and to a significant extent also on Denmark, Italy, and Belgiun. This, clearly, is very far from being a convincing measure of income equalisation, though it would, by definition, tend to equalise the burden of defence and external relations, and would also have a small stabilising effect on national or regional incomes through the Community tax relief that would accompany any reduction of private consumption. To achieve any substantial degree of income equalisation, it would be necessary either to introduce in place of the VAT base a progressive tax-base (say personal income tax) to which Community taxation would be related, or to extend the Community Budget still further by having it take over a portion of, say, unemployment insurance, as the Marjolin Report suggested. Some members of the Study Group on the Role of Public Finance thought that a Community budget handling about 10% of GDP including defence expenditure, or 6 or 7% without it, could, with a suitably progressive tax-base and a concentration of its non-defence expenditure on grants or benefits directed towards poorer regions, provide enough income equalisation and geographical stabilisation to make monetary and economic union feasible, although others were doubtful of this.

The Group recognised that any such development is still far off, and concentrated on the possible pre-federal expansion of the Budget to some 2–2½% of Community GDP – that is to say, something like a trebling of its present size. The main lines of expenditure envisaged were a transfer to the Community of most of the external aid undertaken by its members, a partial takeover of unemployment benefit and vocational training, and various forms of grant to weaker member states and regions. The programme was thought of as taking over national expenditure rather than adding to it, though a small increase in total public expenditure (of less than 1% of GDP) was recognised as a possible outcome. A further tranche of VAT was suggested as one means of financing, but in addition, a more progressive base (such as a measure of personal income tax capacity) was recommended.

Perhaps the most appropriate closing comment on the present state and prospects of the Community's General Budget is that a mistake was made in 1970 in pursuing the goal of dependence on 'own resources' rather than continuing to rely at least partly on contributions from member governments, and perhaps also another mistake (dating from 1963) in choosing VAT as the Community's main tax-base and, eventually (as was hoped), its own uniform tax. One objection to VAT – the fact that it is slightly regressive, whereas a public finance system aimed at holding the Community together probably needs a progressive tax-base, has already been explained. A second objection is that VAT is, in fact, a complicated tax, unsuited to a Community in which some member-states have stronger traditions of tax-evasion than of tax collection. (On this subject, see Dosser 1978.)

But to the present writer, at least, the whole search for 'own resources' rather than national contributions seems to be misconceived; perhaps based on a false analogy with existing federal systems, or perhaps merely premature in its ambitions. In any case, the Community does not collect its own revenue; that is done for it by national revenue services, and in this its situation differs from that of federal governments, which usually collect not only their own revenue, but (for reasons partly of efficiency and economy) also a good deal which they subsequently hand over to the member states. An obligation undertaken by a member state to hand over the proceeds of a hypothetical tax, not exactly corresponding to the VAT which it actually operates, is no different for any practical purposes from a similar obligation to hand over, say, a sum equal to 1% of its GDP, measured according to agreed conventions. Either of these contributions can be regarded as the Community's 'own' by virtue of the agreed legal entitlement to it. The real difference is that a contribution calculated from GDP, perhaps in such a way as to provide a degree of progressiveness, has more chance of being recognised as equitable than has the yield of a hypothetical VAT, or, indeed, any other practicable single tax. Especially while the General Budget is small, but to a significant degree even if it were much larger, a revenue made up of sums assessed on the member governments (which are in fact the tax-collectors) would seem to offer much better prospects of acceptability than one based on the fiction that the budgetary agents are in a position to collect certain taxes on their own account.

That the acceptance of this doctrine would be viewed as a regression to a more primitive stage of development is a fact likely to complicate the course of budgetary growth very considerably.

Notes

1 The relevant data on Community and national expenditures are largely assembled in *Report of the Study Group on the Role of Public Finance in European Integration* (The MacDougall Report), Vol II, Chapter 12.

References

Dosser, D., A federal budget for the Community?, in *Federal Solutions to European Issues*, Macmillan 1978.

European Commission, The Community's economic and financial situation since enlargement, *Bulletin of the European Communities*, Supplement 7/74.

European Commission, *Report of the Study Group on the Role of Public Finance in European Integration*, 2 vol., Brussels, April 1977 (The MacDougall Report). Vol I, General Report; Vol II, Individual Contributions and Working Papers.

European Commission, Preliminary draft (general budget of the European Communities for the financial year 1979), *Bulletin of the European Communities*, Supplement 6/78.

13

Regional Policy

E T NEVIN

The Nature of the Regional Problem

The expression 'regional policy' refers to the set of measures adopted by government, the primary aim of which is to influence the geographical distribution of economic activity. The object of the exercise is usually to increase output and incomes, in absolute and/or relative terms, in areas believed to be operating below their true potential, or to reduce them in areas considered to be over-congested or in danger of becoming so. Correspondingly, policy measures may be designed to encourage the growth of existing or prospective enterprises in 'depressed' regions or to restrict further expansion in congested ones. The regional 'problem', in other words, arises from the propensity of societies to spread their prosperity unevenly within their political boundaries and, in particular, to leave some of their regions noticeably behind others in terms of level and growth of income, population or environmental quality. Not everyone would describe this phenomenon as a 'problem'; there may be certain societies, after all, whose development positively requires some regional imbalance. It certainly becomes one, however — rightly or wrongly — if the political consciousness of any society declares it to be one. And most modern societies have in fact done so.

The origins of the phenomenon are closely bound up with four fundamental characteristics of a modern economy. First, the declining use of labour relative to capital in agriculture, and the corresponding urbanisation of society, has led to the continuing depopulation of (usually peripheral) regions whose only natural advantage is the availability of surface area for cultivation and whose environment is in other respects rather hostile to modern urban settlement.

The second element has been the decreasing reliance of manufacturing industry on natural materials, whether for processing or for

232

power, and the consequent emphasis on proximity to a final market, rather than to mineral deposits or cultivable areas, as a determining factor in industrial location — and thus in population distribution. This, again, has tended to militate against regions in which deposits of coal, ore, stone or slate underlay prosperity in an earlier stage of development, but whose exploitation has left a despoiled environment unattractive to contemporary settlement.

III   The third force at work has been the continuously increasing importance of service activities — as opposed to primary and manufacturing production — as income levels rise, and the apparently compulsive power of economies of scale in so many of those services e.g. transport, health, distribution and perhaps education and entertainment. To this, some might even add the service of government, whose addiction to both growth and proximity to the other cogs of its own machine explains much of the sprawl and congestion of the capital cities of the developed world.

IV   The fourth factor is the continuing displacement of the flexible prices and free markets of earlier stages of development (and the textbooks) by administered prices — fixed by unions or entrepreneurs — and imperfect markets. In such a market context, the response to disequilibrium tends to be expressed, at least in the medium run, in terms of quantity rather than price. In particular, a reduced demand for labour which arises when an industry is falling behind in the technological race results, not in a fall in relative wages and a rapid switch of capital, but in an increase in idle human and physical capacity. When the industry concerned is heavily concentrated in particular locations, as is the case with coal, steel or shipbuilding, the phenomenon of the 'depressed area' is automatically created.

All this is true, of course, at an international as well as a regional level but there is one crucial respect in which the regional adjustment problem is more intractable than the international. This is, of course, the fact that in the context of international trade it is comparative cost which determines the long-run viability of any industry; differences in the absolute costs of production in different countries can be largely, if not wholly, eliminated by one or both of two powerful perquisites of sovereignty: on the one hand, a tariff (or other restrictions on trade having a comparable effect) and, on the other, the rate of exchange of the national currency, both of which affect the relative prices of foreign and domestic products. As between sovereign countries the impact of differing rates of technological change can be qualified, to varying degrees, by these instruments of national economic policy. Within any individual country, on the other hand, by definition there can be neither tariffs nor significant differences in general price-levels; both product prices and wage-rates now tend to be determined by central decisions or national negotiating arrangements which make significant regional differences increasingly improbable (Buck 1975, pp. 368—9).

In theory, then, an uneven growth process within a country must lead to a movement of factors out of high-cost regions and into low-cost regions until cost differences are minimised. At first sight, any policy measures aimed at impeding this movement are bound to result in inefficiency in resource allocation. There are three reasons, nevertheless, why even the most laissez-faire government may be led to intervene. In the first place, given the quality-response referred to earlier, this factor-reallocation may work very slowly — too slowly to be tolerable to politicians who have to operate on the premise that in the long run we are all dead — or at least threatened with loss of office.

Secondly, it is not obvious that the process is a convergent one leading to a new equilibrium. Because of the operation of economies of scale, the movement of capital from A to B in search of relatively high returns may *increase* the efficiency gap between A and B rather than reduce it. Similarly, the migration of labour tends to be a highly selective business, drawing particularly on the younger, more able and more enterprising amongst the population; the population remaining behind in a declining region may be reduced not only in size, but in competitive ability, accentuating rather than correcting the initial cost disadvantage (Balassa 1975, pp. 259—60).

Thirdly, the movement of labour and capital in response to market forces will be determined by private rather than social cost; where the two differ significantly a serious misallocation of resources may result. In the context of the location of industry and population, such differences are in fact probable. On the one hand, factor movement into an already densely populated area is likely to impose serious external diseconomies of congestion on enterprises already in the area; such costs will not enter into the calculations of the decision-maker concerned. On the other hand, an opposite problem may be posed for the 'exporting' area where the usage of services may fall below the point at which their provision is viable: unused capacity is as much a recipe for increased costs as is excess pressure on capacity. Public transport or medical facilities are obvious examples.

All of this refers to the strictly *economic* aspects of regional development, but it would be unrealistic to ignore the fact that a regional 'problem' may be perceived to exist because of political and social, rather than purely economic, considerations. Regional policy is a particular manifestation of the general truism that overall prosperity enables countries to afford the luxury of a conscience regarding the less fortunate and the non-economic. This concern has been especially striking when the underprivileged groups involved have drifted from their place of origin to form congealed groups of squalid misery in the centres of increasingly congested cities, the centres themselves physically decaying as the more fortunate citizens retreat to the suburbs.

Hence, the motivation behind regional policy is a mixture of the political, social and economic. Underdevelopment has become a political issue within countries as well as internationally; like all such issues, it has tended to become a means of attack by 'them' and a necessity for defensive reaction on the part of 'us'. In the social context, the relative decay of particular regions frequently threatens (or is alleged to threaten) cultural patterns regarded by their defenders as being both valuable to society as a whole and irreplaceable. In some countries, the cultural patterns may involve language (as in Quebec, or Brittany, or Wales) or colour (as in the southern United States) or religion (as in Northern Ireland, or the Low Countries) or nothing more specific than a general lament about the passing of the rural way of life (a lament which, it has to be said, seems to increase in appeal as the familiarity of its audience with the realities of rural life grows weaker).

Leaving these rather elusive considerations on one side, however, the purely economic case for regional policy tends to reduce to the question of immobility of resources, although the external economies element (or diseconomies, as in the congestion issue) is an important one. Hence the case for regional policy can never be regarded as self-evident; in fact it rests on two crucial hypotheses concerning the real world. First, that these immobilities and external effects are of sufficient magnitude and of a sufficiently long-run nature to justify market intervention to deal with them. Second, that the costs of dealing with these factors by 'artificial' regional development at the losing end are less than the costs of eliminating them (by increasing mobility or removing external effects such as congestion) through action at the winning end.

There can be no *a priori* demonstration of the validity of these essentially empirical hypotheses; their validity will vary through time and from one society to another. The evidence, however, seems to suggest that the economic and social costs of the unrestricted gravitation of the population into a small number of large, densely populated conurbations are not only high, but rise rapidly as both the extent of urban concentration and the complexity of modern urban existence increase. One might add that as societies advance in affluence, their willingness to tolerate any given degree of environmental deterioration probably diminishes as steadily as the deterioration itself increases.

Integration and the Regional Problem

Put at its simplest, the effect of any movement towards a customs union, and *a fortiori* a common market, is to reduce the extent to which its member countries can conduct their affairs as sovereign, independent states and to increase the extent to which they acquire the characteristics of a single, unitary economy. On strictly *a priori* grounds, therefore, the likely consequences for the 'problem' regions of the participating countries are obvious enough.

In important respects, joining a customs union puts each individual member country in the position of a single region rather than that of a sovereign, independent state. The national power to levy tariffs against the rest of the union disappears; the power to vary exchange rates does not disappear necessarily or immediately, but it is inherent in the logic of most customs unions – and certainly in that enshrined in the Treaty of Rome – that one day it will. At first sight, therefore, economic theory would lead to two rather pessimistic predictions. First, that the mechanism of the EEC, i.e. increased specialisation, fiercer competition and the exploitation of the economies of scale, is of its nature likely to accentuate, rather than reduce, the adverse pressures operating on areas in decline or in which industrial growth is at only an early stage. Second, that any centripetal tendencies in evidence within individual countries must *a fortiori* exert themselves at the customs union level. There are, however, two rather important reasons why this pessimism must be significantly qualified. The first is that generalisations about 'industries' may prove to be hopelessly inoperable as the basis for predictions concerning the actual course of national or regional events. In the real world, there is no such thing as an industry or a sector; rather, there are individual producers and individual products. In other words, it behoves economists to beware of generalisations here as everywhere else; the evidence suggests that the range of productive performance *within* any given country, be it on the farm or in the factory, is at least as great as that *between* countries. Of course, this cannot entirely dispose of the proposition that the comparative geographical remoteness of the less prosperous regions are likely to be accentuated by the expansion of 'domestic' market horizons so as to take in the whole of a customs union, rather than merely the home territory. But it does suggest that broad generalisations concerning the regional impact on existing enterprises are on shaky ground.

The second reason why the pessimism of the predictions concerning regional consequences of integration needs to be tempered is certainly much more important. The simple (and rather obvious) lesson of experience is that policy intervention aimed at the improvement of the economic position of peripheral regions — certainly in absolute and possibly in relative terms — is invariably easier and more effective in the context of a national economy growing at a relatively high rate, than in that of a stagnant economy. The reasons are plain enough. In so far as policy relies on the use of bribery or cajolery to steer new development towards relatively depressed regions, it is obviously unlikely to work if industrial expansion generally is slow or zero. The most 'foot-loose' of industries must be faced with the need for expansion before it can be guided anywhere. Again, where regional policy takes the form of the direct use of public funds in the improve-ment of the infrastructure of depressed areas, or the active promotion of industrial development in them, the necessary intervention is liable to be politically easier, and present smaller fiscal problems in a relatively prosperous environment, than in recession conditions.

Given existing techniques of regional economic policy, in other words, it is axiomatic that a critically important factor in the deter-mination of the pace of regional development must be the growth rate of the surrounding economy. Hence it follows that the impact of the formation of the EEC on its problem regions during the 1960s was likely to be the outcome of two separate sets of forces: on the one hand, any special regional dimension it might or might not have had and, on the other, its consequences for the European economy generally — which means, predominantly, the prosperous central regions rather than the peripheral 'depressed' regions.

Such are the *a priori* predictions of theory. How far are they confirmed by the evidence of actual developments in the EEC during the formative years between 1958 and 1972? Such evidence is unfortunately difficult to obtain with any great degree of accuracy. In the first place, the definitions of the constituent regional areas did not remain constant over the period. Secondly, calculations of regional income and employment on a consistent basis are a relatively recent phenomenon and any attempt to measure movements over this earlier period of 14 years must necessarily rely on statistical series of some-thing less than complete comparability. The evidence assembled in table 13.1 can therefore be interpreted as giving only broad orders of magnitude.

Bearing these provisos in mind, the evidence of table 13.1 for the 'peripheral' regions of four major countries of the EEC — this in itself being only a rough approximation to their 'problem' regions, of course — suggests that the more pessimistic predictions concerning the impact of economic integration on the EEC periphery were probably not well founded; put alternatively, any adverse impact of integration itself seems to have been more than offset by the beneficial effects of the remarkably high growth rates experienced by the

Table 13.1 *'Peripheral Regions' of the EEC 1958–72*

Region	% of total national population		Per capita income: % of national average				Per capita GDP 1972 % of EEC average
	1960	1972	1958	1963	1968	1972	
A. France:							
(i) South East[1]	9.7	10.7	. . .	98.5	92.0	79.0	90
(ii) South West[2]	9.6	10.7	. . .	83.1	84.0	82.5	89
(iii) Massif Central[3]	4.4	9.0	. . .	80.9	85.0	104.1	119
(iv) West	13.8	13.1	. . .	78.4	85.0	75.2	86
(v) Normandy	5.6	5.5	. . .	. . .	90.0	87.2	99
(vi) Picardy	3.2	3.2	. . .	. . .	87.0	88.5	101
Total, France	46.3	52.2	(83.5)	85.2	87.2	84.5	95
B. W.Germany:							
(i) Schleswig-Holstein	4.2	4.1	83.7	85.6	84.0	82.6	106
(ii) Lower Saxony	12.0	11.7	86.8	89.8	88.0	84.6	108
(iii) Hessen	8.5	8.9	99.2	102.9	107.0	104.6	133
(iv) Bavaria	16.9	17.4	87.8	92.2	92.0	95.9	122
Total, Germany	41.6	42.1	89.5	93.1	93.2	93.3	119
C. Italy:							
North-East	11.8	11.4	. . .	97.2	99.0	104.2	70
South[4]	37.6	34.9	65.0	65.5	63.0	67.8	45
Total, Italy	49.4	46.3	73.0	73.1	71.6	76.8	51
D. Netherlands:							
North	11.1	10.9	85.5	86.4	87.0	98.5[5]	99
TOTAL[6]	43.2	44.0	(81.8)	83.6	83.7	85.4	90

Sources: Data for 1958–68 from *National Institute Economic Review*, No. 57 August 1971, Ch. III, p. 57. Data for 1972 from *Regional Statistics 1975*, Statistical Office of the European Communities, Brussels, 1977.

Notes

1   For 1972, the 'Mediterranean' region.
2   Excludes Limousin.
3   For 1972, the 'Rhone-Alpes' region.
4   Includes Sicily, Sardinia, Campania and Abbruzzi-Molise.
5   1973.
6   Totals for 1958–68 are weighted by population in 1960; for 1972, totals are weighted by the 1972 population. The overall total for 1958 is based on the assumption that the change in the total for France between 1958 and 1963 was equal to the (weighted) average change in the other three countries; the purpose of this is solely to 'neutralise' the distortion which would otherwise be introduced in the total by the absence of France in 1958 and its inclusion from 1963 onwards.

member countries during those years. The data are too imperfect to support any confident deductions, but if the evidence points in any direction at all, it indicates in general a slight narrowing of the relative income gap between the peripheral and central regions over the period as a whole.

That being said, two important qualifications must be expressed immediately. First, the final column of table 13.1 shows that being a 'peripheral' region can mean vastly different things in different countries in terms of average income; in the Hessen district of Germany, for example, average per capita income is roughly three times that of the south of Italy. Secondly, and following from this, the evidence, imperfect and approximate as it is, reveals a disturbing tendency for the relative income gap to close only very slowly in the poorest regions, and even to widen in some of them from time to time, as in the case of the south of Italy between 1958 and 1968 and in the west of France between 1963 and 1972. The problem of southern Italy, the Mezzogiorno, was particularly acute; for the region as a whole, average income was well below a half of the EEC average and in parts — Sicily and Sardinia — was barely a third, (McCrone 1969, pp. 201–3). In short, progress towards economic integration may not have aggravated the 'regional problem' as much as had been feared by some; equally, however, it had certainly not disposed of it.

The Regional Aid Debate 1958–72

In June 1977 the European Commission submitted to the Council of Ministers a report on regional policy which began, 'The time has come for the Community to define clearly an overall approach to Community regional policy . . .' (The European Commission 1977, p. 5). Since the member countries had then been arguing intermittently over regional measures for nearly twenty years, the phrase could fairly be described as a masterpiece of understatement.

The truth of the matter is that the Treaty of Rome contained no specific provision for a common regional policy comparable to that made for agriculture or transport. Indeed, it could reasonably be said that the spirit of the Treaty — and particularly its strong emphasis on the desirability of removing impediments to, or distortions in, trade between member countries — was inherently antagonistic to the sort of measures which have come to be associated with regional policy. Nevertheless, even the much-cited Article 92, which enunciated the basic doctrine that state aid which destroys competition should be deemed 'incompatible with the Common Market', immediately proceeded to admit the possibility of dispensation for 'aid intended to promote the economic development of regions where the standard of living is abnormally low or where there exists serious under-employment', (Article 92, section 3(a)).

Nor was this somewhat grudging dispensation from the perfection of undiluted market forces confined to the broad (and vague) generalisation of Article 92: it was repeated in several of the more detailed provisions of the Treaty. Title II enshrining the concept of the Common Agricultural Policy, contained, for example, in Article 49 the specific caveat that due account would have to be taken of the 'structural and natural disparities between the various agricultural regions', (Article 39, section 2(a)). Similarly, the common rules to be laid down as part of the transport policy enshrined in Title IV were stated to be subject to qualification if their application 'might seriously affect the standard of living and the level of employment in certain regions' (Article 75, section 3). The financial agencies established by the Community were also exhorted to pay due regard to regional problems. The 'guidance' section of the Agricultural Guarantee and Guidance Fund (FEOGA) was instructed to pay due regard to the regional impact of the CAP referred to in Article 39 and for this reason most of its finance of structural reform measures has been directed to Italy. This regional dimension of FEOGA received even greater stress in 1971, when the Council of Ministers approved the specific allocation of about £125 million from it over a period of five years to finance 'development operations' in priority areas (Stewart 1971, p. 36).

Similarly again, the European Social Fund was directed by Article 125 to assist workers whose employment had been reduced or suspended 'as a result of the conversion of their enterprise to other productions', an activity of direct and obvious relevance in the context of regional policy, (Article 125, section 1B). In 1971 a directive by the Council of Ministers provided that 60% of its resources should be devoted to increasing employment in 'problem' regions. Finally, the European Investment Bank was given, as its first task, the financing of 'projects for developing less developed regions' (Article 130(a)) and has in reality operated as a regional development bank; the great bulk of its lending has been concerned with development projects in the poorer regions, most especially in Italy. Between 1958 and 1973, in fact, 46% of its total lending related to projects in Italy (Woolley 1975).

This motley collection of qualifications, derogations and exhortations, however, in no way added up to an integrated and coherent regional *policy*, or anything remotely like it. It enabled actions to be taken by individual member countries unilaterally, giving positive financial support to some and moral condonation to others, but provided no mechanism for ensuring that these separate actions were consistent with those being pursued by other member countries, or indeed followed any rational pattern over time within any individual member state. Nor, even less, did it comprise any kind of framework within which the Community as a whole could formulate or initiate regional policy measures for itself — nor, for that matter, did it ensure that the regional dimensions of its own separate policies were consistent with one another.

The overall result was that while the 1960s and the early 1970s were sprinkled with a dreary succession of conferences, reports, recommendations and ministerial pronouncements, the Community was very long on grandiose generalisations embodied in the tortured prose of the international civil service, but very short indeed on action. A Community regional policy, to have any meaning, required an enforceable agreement on two separate matters:

(a) criteria against which actions taken by individual member countries to assist their own regions could be adjudged, so as to determine whether they were compatible or incompatible with the rules of the club; and

(b) a mechanism by which the Community collectively could formulate its own regional policy measures independently of (or at least in addition to) measures being adopted by member countries individually.

It was only after 1975 that some vestige of progress could be said to have been made on the second of these elements; before that time, such debate as occurred was in practice concerned only with the first.

It would be unduly tedious to attempt a chronological summary of the succession of reports and resolutions emerging between 1958 and 1973. (Excellent summaries are to be found in Balassa 1975 pp. 260–4, Flockton 1970, and McCrone 1969.) In essence, three questions formed the bulk of the subject-matter of the debate. First, what characteristics distinguished a 'problem' region (for which special measures of assistance were justified), from 'prosperous' regions (for which they were not)? Second, in assisting problem regions, which types of policy measure were to be deemed compatible with the principles of the Common Market and which not? Third, what, if any, was to be the maximum *level* of any such 'compatible' policy measures?

As far as the first question was concerned, it proved relatively easy to secure agreement on the matter in general, but less easy on matters in particular. As early as 1961, broad agreement was reached that 'problem' regions were those falling into one or other of four categories:

(a) those in which one or more basic industries were in long-run decline — the obvious examples being districts heavily dependent on coalmining, shipbuilding or (later) steel;
(b) those which had remained essentially rural and in which the infrastructure necessary to encourage industrial development did not exist — for example, Brittany or the south of Italy;
(c) those in which industry and population had become so congested that further expansion would generate serious diseconomies and/or environmental degradation; and
(d) those peripheral regions through which ran the border between two (or more) member countries — the so-called 'frontier zones'.

While this classification was adequate enough for distinguishing between different *categories* of problem region, unfortunately it did not in itself provide criteria by which a decision could be made concerning whether a particular region was or was not a problem in the first place. The fact that a region is predominantly agricultural does not in itself render it depressed or declining — far from it in the context of the CAP; nor does the mere presence of a border with another member country. Criteria of economic underprivilege were therefore needed in addition — a problem of particular delicacy when different national governments are involved, since criteria based on national averages (for example, of per capita income or unemployment) could result in identical situations being symptoms of regional underprivilege in one member country and regional prosperity in another.

It cannot be said that any real agreement had been reached on this issue prior to 1975 nor, indeed, that it has yet been attained. By common consent, the indicators of regional underprivilege included a level of income which was, by some standard, unduly low, an above-average (but which average?) level of unemployment and an excessive tendency towards population migration. The various member countries had very divergent ideas, however, as to other appropriate criteria, the supreme example being perhaps the Belgian Minister for Regional Economy who managed to accumulate a total of 35 criteria for designating areas to be assisted under his country's regional policy legislation (including 'commuting under unfavourable conditions', which would strike a sympathetic chord in the hearts of many Londoners). What is worse, no agreement has yet been reached concerning the relative weight to be attached to the different criteria especially when — as must inevitably happen — they point in different directions.

An answer to the second question, i.e. which forms of regional aid were to be permissible and which not, was in fact much easier to obtain, since it is in reality implicit in what might be called the theology of the Common Market. On the one hand, the commitment to market competition — and the conviction that all state aids to industry are *prima facie* an interference with it — led to agreement that to be permissible all regional assistance measures should be 'transparent' — that is to say, that they should be open in nature and precisely calculable in value. Hence grants of a specific value — say, $x\%$ of initial capital cost — are permissible, whereas special investment allowances against taxes on future profits are not. Secondly, anything amounting to a subsidy of current operations would be inadmissible; on the other hand, measures designed to correct an underlying deficiency in the general infrastructure — and which would hopefully result eventually in an ability to compete unaided on the open market — are acceptable. These general principles were agreed in 1971; since then, the Commission has proceeded on a case-by-case basis, challenging (usually with success) the validity of any measures which appear to it to conflict with one or other of these two principles.

The third question, i.e. what limits, if any, should be imposed on the magnitude of regional aid, was also resolved in 1971 through the rather simple expedient of fixing a ceiling so high as to cause discomfort to no-one. The Council of Ministers (conscious of the folly of competitive bidding by member countries for the favours of overseas, and especially American, investors) resolved that after 1973, investment incentives should not exceed 20% of the cash value of investments in the so-called 'central' — i.e. prosperous — regions of the Community. Provided that the concept of the 'central' area was not constricted so far as to be meaningless, this was neither an unreasonable nor in practice a restrictive limit. (That considerable elasticity is possible, is revealed by the fact that under its 1971 law, the Belgian government was proceeding to treat 41 of its total of 43 regions as eligible for aid — a practice which the EEC Commission sharply discouraged. See *The Economist*, 3 June 1972, p. 72.) For the frontier areas of Germany and some Danish regions, the limit was put somewhat higher, at 25%, for the main development areas of the UK, France and Italy, the ceiling was even higher at 30%, but even this limit could be exceeded in Southern Italy, Ireland and Greenland (Stewart 1976, pp. 35—6).

By the early 1970s then, some progress had been made towards the establishment of a degree of uniformity in the national policies of the Six with regard to regional assistance. In a sense this was the negative requirement for a community regional policy — it substantially reduced the degree of conflict between the regional and other aspects of EEC policy and between the efforts of one member country and another. But the positive requirements for a community regional policy were as lacking in the early 1970s as they had been in the early 1960s.

The Emergent Community Policy 1973 onwards

With the benefit of hindsight it is not difficult to see why, on the one hand, regional policy was pushed somewhat to the background during the first decade of the Community's existence nor, on the other hand, why it suddenly shot into prominence in the early and middle 1970s, a process which began with the celebrated declaration by the new President of the Commission before the European Parliament in May 1968 that an effective regional policy had become the *sine qua non* of further integration and should be in the Community 'as the heart is in the human body' (Flockton 1970, p. 46). The heart, as it proved, had a good deal of waiting still ahead of it before its beat became audible, but times were manifestly changing.

In the first place, the opening decade of the EEC was inevitably and necessarily dominated by the problems of what were unquestionably the crucial foundations of the whole edifice — the rapid movement to internal free trade, the establishment of a common external tariff and the creation of the common agricultural policy. Compared with these, questions of regional economic policy seemed a second-order triviality. By the end of the 1960s the situation was reversed: the foundations had been laid and, in a sense, the easy part was over. Further progress was likely to be politically very difficult, now that the first flush of enthusiasm was waning, if the interests of the hardest-hit regions within member countries were not visibly protected.

This was particularly the case once the Community had declared its intention of embarking on the path whose ultimate objective was the achievement of complete monetary union, a situation in which regional differences in output and income would be revealed most starkly (Stewart 1976, p. 35). The second holder of the office of Regional Policy Commissioner — a post originally created in 1969 — went so far as to declare in 1973 that monetary union in Europe was 'inconceivable' without a strong Community regional policy (Thomson 1973, p. 5).

Secondly, the 1960s had unquestionably been a decade of phenomenal growth in which, as the evidence given above has shown, even the regions whose relative position had worsened had nonetheless experienced a marked improvement in their absolute standards of output, employment and income. The early 1970s saw a sharp reversal of the fortunes of both old and new members of the Community and it was one which was to prove distinctly intractable. Between 1958–72, on the one hand, and 1973–76, on the other, the annual growth rate of the real GDP of the six original member countries fell from 5.2 to 2.5%, while that of industrial production fell from 6.0 to 2.3%; the total number unemployed rose from 1½ million in 1972, to well over 3 million by 1976.

As was argued in section 2 above, in such rather dismal economic circumstances, regional policy becomes both more necessary and more difficult. It is more necessary precisely because recession (like prosperity) tends to have an uneven impact and the distress of the worst-affected regions (for example, the older steel-making centres) was too obvious to be ignored. In the context of the integration of the Community, it would have been particularly unrealistic to suppose that further progress could be made while pockets of quite acute distress remained scattered through member countries. As the Commission was to remark in its 1977 report, the strengthening of Community regional policy was 'not only desirable; it is now one of the conditions of continuing European economic integration' (The European Commission 1977, p. 6). The pursuit of regional policy becomes more difficult, on the other hand, because measures aimed at attracting new development have little effect when no new development is occurring, while measures designed to improve regional infrastructure are more difficult to finance in a context of an economy growing only slowly or not at all. The co-ordination and strengthening of the Community's regional measures therefore took on a greater urgency.

The third stimulus to the development of regional thinking in the early 1970s was, quite simply, the political necessities of the prospective accession of three new members, in particular that of Britain. As the oldest of the industrial countries, British involvement in regional problems was far older and more extensive than in any other member country; Britain also had the longest acquaintance with a problem which the other member countries were now encountering for the first time – regional policy in the context of near-zero growth. What is more, this greater awareness of the regional problem had accentuated in British political thinking the potential threat to its already depressed regions implicit in their becoming even more peripheral than before as a result of membership of the EEC.

Like God, therefore, even if the inclination towards a Community regional policy had not existed, it would have been necessary to invent it. Some prize had to be offered to the British (and Irish) and part of this took the form of the appointment as Regional Policy Commissioner of Mr George (later Lord) Thomson, together with the promise of resources for him to work with; this resulted, in 1973, in a report with which his name is customarily associated and which can fairly be described as the beginning of a genuinely collective regional policy in the Community.

The proposals of the Thomson Report, which were substantially adopted by the Council of Ministers in 1975, were subsequently replaced by 'new guidelines' set out in another Commissioner report in 1977 which was in due course approved by the Council of Ministers in 1978; hence there is little point in rehearsing its contents in detail. (For excellent summaries and comments see Balassa 1975, pp. 267–271 and *The Economist* 1973.) It opened a new era in the regional policy debate by establishing the concept of a comprehensive Community policy, with a Regional Development Committee to develop and apply it and a new financial source, the European Regional Development Fund (ERDF) through which Community resources, as contrasted with the budgetary allocations of individual member countries, were to be channelled into regional development programmes in the form of grants and rebates on loan interest charges. Certainly, it could be argued that a Community policy in the true sense had not yet emerged, since the resources of the ERDF were to be used only to contribute towards the cost of projects submitted by individual member governments – in general, to a maximum of 50% of the amount of aid provided by the member government itself; the role of the ERDF, in other words, was wholly passive and the initiative in regional development remained with member countries. Nevertheless, an important principle had been established: Community resources were being allocated specifically to regional policy, rather than as a by-product of the application of other policies.

The activities of the ERDF over the four years 1975–78 are summarised in table 13.2. The first point which has to be made concerns the relatively modest scale of the operation. The assistance provided by the Fund averaged little more than the equivalent of £250 million a year, although it has to be conceded that the running-in phase of 1975 makes this something of an understatement; for 1978 the actual total of grants approved was about £375 million. Even this latter total, however, represented less than 5% of the Community budget for the year (compared with 74% for agriculture) or somewhat less than 0.05% of the total Gross Domestic Product of the Nine. For the three years 1975–77 the Commission itself sought a total ERDF budget of 2,250 million EUA; the principal prospective beneficiaries – Britain, Ireland and Italy – had proposed a total of 3,000 million, while the likely principal contributor, Germany, suggested 1,000 million. In the final outcome, the agreed total of 1,300 million was far closer to the latter than to the former.

Secondly, it is clear that the allocation of the Fund's resources by a national quota (shown in column 2 of table 13.2) ensured that there was relatively little relationship between the total allocated for regional projects in any given country and the actual demand for such finance in that country – or at least its capacity to absorb it. The grants *approved* for any country (column 3 of table 13.2) could of course considerably exceed that country's quota in any one year, or even a period of years, because of varying lags between the approval

Table 13.2 *Operations of the European Regional Development Fund, 1975–78*

(1)	Quota allocation (EUA million) (2)	Assistance approved (EUA million) (3)	% distribution of (2) (4)	(3) (5)
Belgium	27.4	30.1	1.5	2.0
Denmark	23.8	23.4	1.3	1.5
France	291.1	268.8	15.5	17.6
W. Germany	117.3	151.1	6.2	9.9
Ireland	121.4	90.1	6.5	5.9
Italy	748.4	528.2	39.8	34.6
Luxembourg	1.8	2.1	0.1	0.1
Netherlands	31.1	36.7	1.7	2.4
UK	517.7	394.8	27.5	25.9
TOTAL	1880.0	1525.2	100.0	100.0

Source: Col. (2) from European Communities Commission *Background Report* ISEC/B60/78; col. (3), European Commission, *Twelfth General Report on the activities of the European Communities*, Brussels, February 1979, Table 11, p. 146.

of a project and its completion. (In the period 1975–78 as a whole, the grants actually paid out by the ERDF amounted to only 53% of the commitments entered into.) The marked differences between the pattern of the quota and that of approvals, as shown by columns 4 and 5 in table 13.2, suggest that the quota system was far from realistic. Italy, for example, had about 40% of the quota total, but less than 35% of the approvals; Germany, by contrast, had 6% of the quota, but nearly 10% of the approvals.

Thirdly, the relatively small contribution made by the ERDF made it unlikely that it was having any significant influence on the majority of regional development projects being initiated. Its activities during 1975–78 involved some 6,300 projects, but its contribution towards them amounted, on average, to only 11% of their total value – although this average conceals a variation between 6% in Germany and 16% in Italy. (The quota for the UK of about £65 million a year over the period 1975–78 compares with an official estimate of about £430 million spent on 'regional' support and regeneration by the British government in 1974/75.) There was more than a suspicion, therefore, that the ERDF was being used by member countries as no more than a means of recovering part of the cost of projects which would have been undertaken in any event. This is scarcely what is meant by a positive and dynamic *Community* policy.

An awareness of these underlying weaknesses led to the 1977 Commission report on revised guidelines for regional policy referred to above (The Commission 1977) and which embodies current Community regional policy.

The first major change introduced by the revised guidelines involved the redefinition of 'problem' regions not so much in terms of the nature of the source of their weakness, but rather in terms of the appropriate level of policy action. The four categories are now defined as:

(a) underdeveloped regions which require long-run aid in order to acquire an economic and social infrastructure amenable to sustained growth — the Mezzogiorno, Ireland, Greenland and the French overseas territories;

(b) regions requiring short- or medium-term assistance in order to 'adapt' their structure (through productive investment) in order to replace declining industries or reduce dependence on agriculture — the typical 'depressed' regions of the highly industrialised countries;

(c) 'regional impact areas' — that is to say, those on which the changing world economic environment or, more importantly, other Community policies are having, or are likely to have, an unusually marked adverse effect; and

(d) frontier regions, where national boundaries divide what are in fact natural economic unities and where an integrated and coherent policy involves the actions of two or more separate member governments.

The essential proposition advanced by the 1977 report was that while (a) and (b) represent regions for which sensible remedial action can and should be taken by and through individual member governments, (c) and (d) do not. Inherently, their situation calls for *Community*, not national, action.

Secondly, and following logically from this, the resources available to the ERDF had to make separate provision for (a) and (b) on the one hand — complementing but not displacing, it was stressed yet again, member government action — and, on the other hand, for cases falling under (c) and (d). Hence the funds of the ERDF were henceforth to be split between a 'quota' section, financing projects in (a) and (b) regions, and a non-quota section reserved for projects in (c) and (d) regions. While no precise figure was put on this 'non-quota' element in the 1977 Commission report, it was clearly envisaged that it would be allocated a fairly substantial fraction of the total ERDF budget; further, the specific recommendation that the approval of grants from the non-quota element should require only a 'qualified majority' among the Council of Ministers was a crucial element in establishing a *Community* policy as distinct from one dependent on the consent of every individual member country. In the event, both items received a severe mauling by the Council of Ministers before its approval was forthcoming. For the initial three-year period, 1978–80, the non-quota section was allocated only 5% of the total ERDF budget — scarcely an overwhelming start. What was worse, a provision was inserted specifying that every project financed from non-quota funds would need unanimous approval by Ministers — which meant, of course, that every ingredient of regional policy remained totally under the control of each member country concerned. This inevitably gives the apparently supranational character of the policy framework a somewhat superficial quality.

The third feature of the 1977 proposals — accepted by the Council — was the increased stress given to the co-ordination of the regional policy measures at both national and Community level. As far as the former was concerned, the Commission recognised the need to provide what had always been lacking — a system by which, through improved statistical information, the analysis and assessment of the state of the regional economies of the Community as a whole could be continuously undertaken. A two-yearly report on the state of the regions is proposed with the aid of this strengthened analytical system; this in turn, it is proposed, will form the basis of comparison between the regional programmes of individual member countries, also to be prepared on a continuous and systematic basis. It is also noteworthy that the 1977 guidelines spelled out in more detail than hitherto the relevant indicators of 'regional imbalance' to be used in applying the resources of the ERDF and, by implication, in determining the regional policies of individual member countries. These were (a) the trend in regional unemployment rates over the preceding five years; (b) the proportion of the working population engaged in agriculture and in 'declining industrial sectors'; (c) the net regional migration rate during the preceding five years; and (d) the level of, and trend in, regional GDP totals.

So far as the co-ordination of Community Policy is concerned, the 1977 guidelines emphasised the need to assess and take due account of the 'spatial dimension' of all major policies of the Community. To this end, the Regional Development Committee is to be supplied with reports on the regional impact of Community policies and, in the light of these, to advance recommendations to the Council of Ministers concerning measures to be adopted to offset them when necessary — including, of course, projects to be financed from the non-quota section of the ERDF.

All this sounds impressive enough: what it will amount to in reality only time will tell. At the risk of excessive cynicism, however, it has to be recorded that the 1977 report on 'new guidelines' was merely the latest in a long series of reports and recommendations whose operational impact has so far been confined to a relatively minor (although not trivial) modification of national policy measures, so as to eliminate the grosser contraventions of the rules of competition. The insistence on the rule of unanimity in allocating even the vestigial resources of the non-quota element of the ERDF is not a good omen: a genuinely independent Community regional policy is still far distant.

British Regional Policy

Two large questions are raised by membership of the European Community for the future of British regional policy. First, what are likely to be the effects of membership of the EEC, in so far as they can be foreseen, on the nature and magnitude of Britain's regional 'problem' in itself? Secondly, what impact is the EEC likely to have on the policy measures which can be adopted to deal with that problem?

The first question has been extensively discussed in general terms in the preceding sections and little can or need be added to what has already been said. The general theoretical prediction has been stated as being that the net outcome will depend on the balance between, on the one hand, the centripetal tendencies inherent in the integration process and, on the other hand, the stimulus to regional growth provided by the overall expansionary consequences of integration. The evidence suggests that for the Six in the 1960s and early 1970s, the latter probably tended to outweigh the former, but there are two factors likely to qualify severely this rather comforting conclusion in the particular context of Britain in the late 1970s and the 1980s.

The first of these is the obvious fact that the immediate growth prospect is far less favourable than in the 1960s. Between 1958 and 1972 the annual growth rate of real GDP averaged 5.2% in the Six and 3.0% in the UK; by contrast, between 1972 and 1977 the corresponding averages were only 2.7% for the Six and 1.5% for the UK. It would obviously be rash to project this rather depressing deceleration indefinitely into the future, but it would be less than realistic to assume that the growth context in the 1980s is likely to be as favourable as in the 1960s.

The second qualification arises from the simple proposition that while expansion in the EEC as a whole provides an *opportunity* for the British regions to share in and benefit from it, opportunity is not the same thing as achievement. If the overall expansion of the

Community is concentrated predominantly outside Britain — and, indeed, is based partly on the failure of the British economy to participate fully in it — the consequences for the regions take on a very different character. So far from offsetting the adverse effects of integration in a larger economic unit, the rate of growth in the expanded market becomes merely a manifestation of those effects. Once again a simple projection of the trends during four or five years immediately succeeding British accession would be ingenuous in the extreme, but equally the evidence of those years cannot be ignored. During the first five years after its entry to the EEC, Britain's annual rate of increase in industrial output-per-man hour averaged 1.3% compared with 11.6% in the EEC Six. Over the same period, Britain's overall foreign trade in manufactured goods rose by 46% in real terms, whereas such trade with the rest of the EEC rose by 66% — a clear indication of the trade diversion effects of membership. It was rather ominous, however, that over those five years the volume of UK imports of manufactures from the rest of the EEC rose by 75%, whereas its exports of manufactures to the rest of the EEC rose by only 58%. The implication is clear: if the growth of productivity in the British economy persistently lags behind that of the other EEC countries, the growth effects of integration are minimised, while its adverse competitive effects are maximised. And if the relative productive efficiency of the peripheral regions of the UK remain below that of Britain in general, the impact of those competitive effects must inevitably be greatest in those regions least able to accommodate them.

A corollary to this is, of course, that if relative growth rates continue to diverge between Britain, on the one hand, and continental member countries, on the other, the regions are not only likely to face more severe competitive pressures than hitherto, but are also likely to suffer as potential sites for development in comparison with the remainder of the EEC area. Policy measures previously designed to reduce the unattractiveness of the peripheral regions relative only to the remainder of Britain, now have to enable them to stand comparison with the whole of the EEC area, equally, the use of negative controls over factory and office development in the relatively prosperous regions of Britain can no longer be presumed to divert that development to less favoured regions of Britain — the diversion may well occur to more attractive sites in continental Europe (Buck 1975). Clearly the greater the divergence between growth rates in Britain and the rest of the Community, the greater the erosion of the effectiveness of existing policy measures must become.

This must bring into question even more sharply than before any strategy which seeks to reduce regional inequalities of *income* rather

Table 13.3 *The UK 'Problem Regions', 1958–76*

| | UK = 100 | | | | GDP per head, 1972 EEC = 100 |
	1958	1968	1972	1976	
A. GDP per head					
(i) S.W. England	—	92	95	91	81
(ii) North England	—	85	89	95	75
(iii) Scotland	90	90	92	97	77
(iv) Wales	90	86	89	90	76
(v) N. Ireland	61	70	72	78	60
Average	87[1]	87	90	92	76[2]
B. Personal income (before tax) per head[3]					
(i) S.W. England	88	90	90	100	
(ii) North England	87	78	90	99	
(iii) Scotland	87	78	81	92	
(iv) Wales	84	75	89	93	
(v) N. Ireland	64	64	71	73	
Average	85	79	85	94	

Notes:

1   In order to neutralise the absence of data for S.W. and North England in 1958, the growth of GDP in these regions between 1958 and 1968 was assumed to be equal to the weighted average of the three other regions.
2   The UK average in 1972 was 86.
3   The figures shown for personal income per head in the 1958 column relate to the fiscal year 1959–60.

Sources:
GDP and personal income: 1958 and 1959 from G. McCrone, *Regional Policy in Britain*, Allen and Unwin 1969, Chap. VI, Tables IV and VIII; 1968–76 from *Regional Statistics*, HMSO; GDP per head 1972, *Regional Statistics 1975*, Statistical Office of the European Communities, Brussels 1977.

than the inequalities of *productivity* from which those income differences arise. That British regional policy, as so far applied, is open to this criticism, is clearly implied by the evidence summarised in Table 13.3, incomplete and ambivalent as that evidence unquestionably is. It indicates that during the 18 years between 1958 and 1976, the relative *income* position of the 'problem' regions has improved a great deal more than their relative *efficiency* — the former, in fact, improved by 10.6%, whereas the latter improved by only 5.7%. In a closed economy, the appraisal of regional policy by its capacity to redistribute income rather than improve efficiency is a matter of political choice; in an increasingly open economy, however, the ability to exercise such a choice is constrained by the over-riding need to preserve competitiveness. The evidence so far suggests that entry into the EEC will force British governments to reconsider both the fundamental aims and the techniques of future regional policy. Membership of the Community, in other words, seems likely on present evidence not only to accentuate the severity of the regional 'problem' in Britain, but also to narrow the limits of the range of possible solutions.

This consideration leads on naturally to the second issue of the consequences of membership for the nature of British regional policy itself. At least it can be said at the outset that two fears expressed in this context during the negotiations of the 1960s can now safely be laid to rest. The first of these was that once the regions of Britain had to be compared with what were then the much poorer regions of continental member countries, any special regional policy measures would be hard to justify at all; Scotland and Wales and so on, it was argued, could plausibly be said to be meritorious of special assistance when judged against the standard of the rest of the UK, but the same would hardly be true when they were judged by comparison with the poorer regions of the whole of Western Europe. The evidence shown in Tables 13.1 and 13.3 demonstrates, unhappily enough, how far events have moved since then. Only in the south of Italy can it be said that per capita GDP is further below the EEC average than it is in the peripheral regions of Britain. In other words, there may be many reasons for criticising regional measures in the UK, but an unduly high relative wealth in the regions is certainly not one of them.

The second fear was that major instruments of British regional policy would be adjudged incompatible with the rules of the Community, a fear concentrated especially on the Regional Employment Premium introduced in 1967 and regarded by some as probably the most effective policy device ever applied in Britain (Balassa 1975, pp. 270–1). That such a device would fall foul of the fundamental objection to 'operating subsidies' referred to in section 3 above is virtually certain, but the matter became one of only historic interest with the decision to phase out the REP system after 1977. That decision may have been influenced by this belief that the device fell foul of the Community rules; more probably the operative factor was its rapidly rising cost. Equally arguable is the real significance of its abolition; while in theory it constituted something approaching the equivalent of a regional devaluation, it can be argued with some force that it was an instrument whose effect was precisely the redistribution of income without stimulus to increased efficiency, as referred to above. Whatever the merits or otherwise of the arguments, the fact is that it no longer represents an element in contemporary British regional policy.

The REP issue apart, it is difficult to see why Community rules should prevent future British governments from doing in the future anything which they have done in the past. It is true that the guidelines currently applicable restrict the total amount of permissible aid for UK regions to a maximum of 30% of the investment projects concerned, but the fact is that the scale of British regional aid has seldom approached such a figure: for development areas the standard grant is currently 20% of capital costs (22% in Special Development Areas). It is also true that the insistence in the Community rules on both the 'openness' and the non-continuing nature of regional assistance may make it more difficult for future governments to camouflage as regional aid operating subsidies adopted more often than not for political rather than economic ends. It is doubtful if any such constraints on government action would represent any real loss : as has been argued above, the logic of the situation in any case is such as to impose on future government action a much greater concern with economic efficiency, rather than with open or concealed subsidies designed essentially to redistribute income.

On the positive side, membership of the EEC should in principle increase the effectiveness of British regional policy in three separate respects. First, and most obviously, the existence of the ERDF ensures the availability of resources over and above those extracted from the pockets of inevitably reluctant national taxpayers. Admittedly, the total funds at the disposal of the ERDF are small in comparison with the aspirations of both the UK government and the European Commission, but even a small budget is greater than zero — and small budgets have a habit of growing. Admittedly, too, the British government has shown a marked inclination hitherto to treat ERDF grants as substitutes for, rather than complements to, its own regional allocations, but this is a practice which is certain to become more difficult with the passage of time. If and when it disappears, the magnitude of the British regional effort must necessarily increase.

Secondly, the steady development of the Community regional policy mechanism will involve the British government in an experience with which it has been unhappily unfamiliar for many decades — the necessity of formulating coherent statements of intent and forward plans concerning its regional policy, and of explaining and defending those statements to the representatives of other member governments in the Regional Development Committee. Nothing but benefit can spring from this enforced framework of rational analysis, so sharply in contrast with British government practice throughout the post-war period — a practice characterised by a Parliamentary Committee, acidly but accurately, as 'empiricism run mad, a game of hit and miss, played with more enthusiasm than success ... efforts ... not sustained by a proper evaluation of the costs and benefits of policies pursued' (Manners 1976, p. 36).

Thirdly, the insistence by the Community on the avoidance of operating subsidies, open or concealed, and on the essential aim of reducing or eliminating relative productive inefficiencies, may well help to bring a long overdue element of economic reality into British regional policy. The inescapable fact that after 30 years the 'problem' regions of Britain were still the same regions as at the beginning demonstrates that in seeking to compensate for regional income disparities rather than to remove their causes, British policy has been trapped in a never-ending blind alley, if such a phenomenon is architecturally feasible. If the moral has to be imposed from the outside, this is at least several degrees better than not having it applied at all. This is not to deny that it would be a catastrophe if the concept of commercial viability were to be elevated to the total exclusion of considerations of social cost, or at the price of losing sight of the crucial distinction between things which are desirable in the very long run and those which are feasible in the medium run. But the enforced shift in emphasis away from the repair of income disparities and towards the removal of their basic causes cannot be other than welcome; the ultimate condemnation of British regional policy is not that it has been unduly motivated by social and political expediency, and dominated by short-run immobilities, but rather that, after decades rather than years of application, it has failed to become one degree less necessary than on the day it began.

The overall assessment must thus be a distinctly mixed affair. On the evidence of the first six or seven years of membership of the Community, the British regional problem must necessarily appear more, rather than less, serious and difficult than before. At the root of that conclusion lies the fundamental cause of so much of Britain's economic difficulties at the end of the 1970s — the failure of its productivity to keep pace with that of its neighbours and competitors. Associated with that, in turn, is the tendency to believe that short-run redistributive measures are sufficient to deal with — or indeed are consistent with the cure of — the long-run weaknesses which called them forth. The primary ground for optimism concerning future regional policy in Britain is that both the changed economic environment and the policy attitudes imposed by the EEC will force upon British policy a degree of realism which, left to itself, its own political machinery has proved unable, or unwilling, to embrace.

References

Balassa, B. (ed.), *European Economic Integration*, North-Holland Publishing Co, 1975.

Buck, T., Regional policy and European integration, *Journal of Common Market Studies*, vol. 13, 1975, pp. 368—78.

Button, K.J. and Gillingwater, D., *Case Studies in Regional Economics*, Heinemann 1976, Chapter 5.

Flockton, C., *Community Regional Policy*, Chatham House London, November 1970.

Manners, G., Reinterpreting the regional problem, *Three Banks Review*, no. 3, September 1976.

McCrone, G., Regional policy in the European Communities, in Denton, G.R. (ed.), *Economic Integration in Europe*, Weidenfeld and Nicolson 1969, Chapter 7.

National Institute of Economic and Social Research, Entry into the EEC: a comment on some of the economic issues, *National Institute Economic Review*, no. 57, August 1971, Chapter III.

Stewart, J.A. and Begg, H.M., Towards a European regional policy, *National Westminster Bank Quarterly Review*, May 1976.

Thomson, G., European regional policy in the 1970s, *CBI Review*, no. 10, Autumn 1973.

Van Doorn, J., European regional policy : an evaluation of recent developments, *Journal of Common Market Studies*, vol. 13, 1975, pp. 391—401.

Woolley, P.K., The European investment bank, *Three Banks Review*, no. 105, March 1975.

The Economist, *Europe and Britain's Regions*, 21 April 1973, pp. 55—60.

European Commission, Community regional policy: new guidelines, *Bulletin of the European Communities*, Supplement 2/77, June 1977.

14

Energy Policy

Y-S HU

Does the European Community have, or has it ever had, a common energy policy? What have been the difficulties hindering progress? In an attempt to answer these questions, we shall review the Community's achievements and failures in the coal, nuclear and petroleum sub-sectors.

Coal

The European Coal and Steel Community (ECSC), established by the Treaty of Paris in April 1951, is the oldest of the three European Communities. It is also the most supranational in inspiration, vesting the High Authority with considerable powers of intervention. As stated in the Treaty, the aims of ECSC are to ensure, within a common market for coal and steel, orderly supply; equal access for consumers; low prices; the removal of intra-Community import and export duties, quantitative restrictions, State aids and subsidies, and restrictive practices; to promote modernisation and expansion; and to promote improved working conditions and living standards for the workers. The High Authority is empowered to obtain the information it requires; to impose fines on firms evading their obligations; to raise revenue by imposing levies (normally not to exceed 1%) on the production of coal and steel; to contract loans for the purposes of financing or guaranteeing investments; and finally to impose production quotas and other necessary measures in the event of a *manifest* crisis. The consent of the Council is necessary only in certain important matters, and unanimity is required in even fewer instances. These supranational powers reflected the mood of the time. Thus, whereas under the Treaties of Rome (EEC and Euratom) the Council decides on the Commission's proposal, under the Treaty of Paris the Commission decides with the Council's endorsement (see Chapter 2).

After World War II, the control of the coal industry in West Germany lay with the Allies in the International Ruhr Authority. By 1950, however, the East—West conflict, the American view that West Germany should become a full member of the Western alliance, and the extent of German economic recovery, combined to make this direct foreign control of an important part of the German economy increasingly untenable. France became fearful lest her traditional enemy regained full national control of the two industries that were considered to be the basis of military and economic power. Under the inspiration of Jean Monnet, Robert Schuman, the French Foreign Minister, proposed the pooling of German and French coal and steel resources in a complex arrangement with supranational features that were meant to make war between the two countries impossible. The other European countries were then invited to join, and the Americans supported the venture. The UK refused to join.

Apart from these considerations of high politics, however, the negotiations leading to the signing of the Treaty and the early life of ECSC benefited from a convergence of national interests: the desire of France, the Benelux countries and, to some extent, Italy, to obtain secure and non-discriminatory access to coal from the largest producing country on the continent outside the Iron Curtain, and the desire of West Germany to be recognised as a full member of the international system (Lantzke 1976). During the 1950s, this convergence of national interests was made much easier by the combination of rising demand for, and production of, coal. It seems much easier for nations to agree on the distribution of benefits in an environment of growth, than to agree on the distribution of costs at a time of recession and/or contraction (Lucas 1977).

It is sometimes argued that the major factor inhibiting European integration or the development of a common policy in any sector is the lack of policy instruments at the level of the Community; in other words, just as the Community now has its 'own financial resources', so it needs to have its 'own policy instruments'. There is, however, a vital difference between the legal provision of certain powers and instruments, and the ability to actually use them. We have seen that, under the Treaty of Paris (Article 58), the High Authority disposes of considerable powers of intervention in the event of a manifest crisis being declared. Such a crisis did indeed develop in 1958—1960, due to a combination of falling demand for energy as a whole and rising imports of oil and coal. Stocks of coal at the pithead in ECSC countries rose from 7.3 million tonnes in 1957, to 24.7 million tonnes in 1958 and to 31.2 million tonnes in 1959. Despite repeated attempts by the High Authority which proposed to introduce production quotas and import restrictions, a state of manifest crisis could not be declared because the Council withheld its consent. In the May 1959 vote, the Benelux countries supported the High Authority, but France, Germany and Italy opposed it. The French and Italian position can be understood with reference to their interest in cheap, imported sources of energy, but why did Germany, with its important coal industry, oppose the High Authority? In fact, both Germany and France were reluctant to transfer important powers to the supranational level. Thus, the episode clearly established the precedent that supranational powers, even where they are specifically provided for in a legal sense, can be activated only with the consent of member states. This may be a cause for great lament by the supranationalists, but we would see it as inevitable in view of the nature of the real world.

In 1958, first Belgium, then Germany, took national measures to limit coal imports from third countries. France had already done so. It remained for the High Authority to 'approve' these measures and to 'harmonise' them in a Community framework. From the end of the 1950s onwards, the advent of abundant and cheap Middle Eastern oil changed the energy situation dramatically. In the Europe of the Nine, coal output fell from 436.9 million tonnes in 1960 to 270.2 million tonnes in 1973, and its share of total energy consumption fell from around 75% in 1950 to 21% in 1973. The nature of the problems facing policy-makers in the coal subsector changed; it was now a question, in coal producing countries, of easing the process of contraction. Again, ECSC could not agree on a real common policy, because of the divergent interests of Germany, with its important coal mining industry, and France and Italy who were poor in indigenous resources. The Community system of state aid involves no Community protection (through quotas and tariffs) and no Community financing; it simply means that the national aid is 'authorised' by the High Authority according to Community rules which give the system an appearance of a common policy. For coking coal, however, a system of Community subsidies for intra-Community trade in coking coal and coke produced in the Community was instituted in 1966, whereby the burden was shared 40/60 between the producing country and a Community common fund.

The ECSC has, however, played a useful role in the redeployment of miners by encouraging the creation of new jobs in mining regions. It has also helped to promote safer working conditions and to finance social housing.

Since the 1973—74 oil crisis, the Community has formally adopted a set of Energy Policy Objectives for 1985 (by the Council Resolution of 17 December 1974) which envisage, *inter alia*, arresting the decline of coal and maintaining Community production at the level of 250 million tonnes. The means available at the Community level for achieving this include: (1) Community subsidies on the production or stockpiling of coal; (2) Community subsidies on intra-Community trade in coal, to offset transport costs; and (3) Community subsidies to encourage the burning of coal in Community power stations and to finance the conversion of power stations from oil-burning to coal-burning. None of the Commission proposals in these directions has been adopted to date (December 1979), mainly because of divergences between the member states. The proposals would have benefited mainly the UK (the largest Community producer) and Germany (the second largest), but the UK, with an avowed anti-European Energy Minister under the last Labour government, would not make any concessions in the energy field (and in many other fields too) to induce the other countries to accept the costs involved. For these countries, there is always the option of importing cheaper coal from Poland, South Africa, the US etc. In 1978, extra-Community imports of coal represented 16% of coal consumption in the Community. Moreover, British coal is not only more costly, but, because of strikes, is not considered on the Continent as a secure source of supply (Lucas 1977, p. 124).

Despite the Community's objectives for 1985, Community coal output has continued to decline year by year since 1973, under the impetus of rising costs, depressed demand (especially from the steel sector which is in a state of crisis), and competition from other fuels and imported coal. From 270.2 million tonnes in 1973, it had fallen to 238.1 million tonnes in 1978. Thus, although ECSC attempts to maintain equitable conditions of competition in the coal market, there is no common energy policy in coal in the sense of a genuine Community solidarity and a common approach to encouraging Community coal production and utilisation.

Nuclear Energy

The treaty establishing the European Atomic Energy Community (Euratom) was signed in Rome in March 1957, at the same time as the treaty establishing the European Economic Community (EEC). Euratom was created to develop the civilian use of nuclear energy at a time when the Suez canal crisis (1956) had cast doubts on the reliability of Middle Eastern oil. Euratom was to pool together the member states' research and development (R&D) efforts in nuclear reactors and fuels. The Treaty was very ambitious, and provided for:

(a) the coordination of research and investments, the latter to be notified obligatorily to the Commission;

(b) pluri-annual common research programmes to be executed by a Common Research Centre (CCR);

(c) a common system for the dissemination of information;

(d) a common supply policy for ores, source materials and special fissile materials, on the principle of equal access for Community users. The *Supply Agency* was to have a right of option on all fuels produced in the Community and an exclusive right to conclude contracts relating to the supply of fuels coming from inside or outside the Community;

(e) a status of 'joint undertaking' to facilitate inter-country industrial cooperation;

(f) 'association contracts' which would allow the Community to participate financially in research undertaken by member states and to disseminate the results.

In 1956, the French were very enthusiastic about the idea of Euratom and saw it as a support for their military nuclear programme; they were, however, much less interested in the idea of a common market than the Germans and the Benelux countries, and less interested in the free circulation of workers and the regional policy than the Italians. Fearing that the French Parliament would only ratify the Euratom Treaty, the Five insisted on the link between the two treaties, which were signed on the same day.

Compared to its ambitious goals, Euratom was a failure. Part of the reason was that nuclear energy lost much of its urgency with the changed international energy situation, the Suez crisis being followed by abundant oil supplies from the Middle East. Another major reason was the divergence of interests and strategies of the member states. From the beginning, there was little sharing of information, research, or investment by France and Germany. With its considerable advance at the research level, France pressed ahead with its national military and civilian programme, and exploited the escape clause in the Treaty which suspended the obligation to share information if defence interests were involved. Germany, with its powerful industrial base and weakness in basic research, preferred to cooperate with the large American firms (e.g. General Electric, Westinghouse). This divergence of interests was reflected in the dispute over whether Euratom should develop the natural uranium system (French) or the enriched uranium system (American). Despite the existence of four establishments under the Common Research Centre, at Ispra (Italy), Geel (Belgium), Petten (Netherlands), and Karlsruhe (Germany), the activities of the CCR were marginalised, as the member states entrusted the most promising research to their own, national laboratories. As for the Supply Agency, the Commission has for a long time contented itself simply to authorise, retrospectively, the contracts signed by the member states, but in November 1978, at the demand of Belgium in Connection with an International Atomic Energy Agency (IAEA) conference in Vienna on the 'physical protection of fissile materials', the European Court of Justice reaffirmed the competence of Euratom. This provoked a furore in France which, in September 1979, asked for a modification of Chapter 6 of the Treaty dealing with supplies. The French argument is that there cannot be the same free circulation of dangerous materials (e.g. plutonium) as of potatoes, unless there is a common position on non-proliferation.

Although the French abandoned the natural uranium system around 1970 and went for the enriched uranium, light water systems developed by the Americans (Westinghouse's pressurised water reactor and General Electric's boiling water reactor), there is still no Community reactor construction industry. In the enrichment of uranium, however, there are two European groups: EURODIF led by France (and which groups together France, Italy, Belgium and Spain) and using the gaseous diffusion technique, and URENCO, grouping together the UK, West Germany and the Netherlands, and using the centrifuge technique. Both groups are outside the legal framework of the European Communities, and neither has the status of a 'joint undertaking' under the Euratom Treaty. In the development of the next generation of 'fast breeders', France, the UK and West Germany are in competition with each other, but the electricity boards of West Germany, France and Italy have a cooperative agreement to build in common the first few large-scale plants. Looking still further ahead to the concept of nuclear *fusion* (the phenomenon occurring in a hydrogen bomb explosion and in the sun), after years of hard bargaining between member states an agreement was reached in October 1977 to site an experimental prototype, the Joint European Torus (JET), at Culham in England. The JET is a joint undertaking under the Euratom Treaty, and is financed, to the extent of 80% by the Community (148 million Units of Account for the period 1976–80), 10% by the UK, and 10% by the other participants including Sweden and Switzerland.

Owing to environmental and safety concerns, the nuclear energy programmes have been slowed down or indefinitely postponed in all countries in the European Communities, with the sole exception of France. For 1985, the expected contribution of nuclear energy is less than half of the level (200 GWe, or 17% of total Community energy consumption) envisaged in the December 1974 Resolution. It is clear that this shortcoming cannot be laid at the Community's door; the obstacles lie in each of the countries, and even a real federation like the US is having the same problems.

Petroleum

It is in the area of oil policies that two questions arise acutely: is the European Community a community at all? And is it an appropriate forum for dealing with global problems?

During the 1973–74 oil crisis, the Netherlands was specifically subjected to an Arab embargo because of its professed sympathies for Israel. The European Community was not able, at least publicly, to manifest its solidarity with the Dutch, for fear of Arab reprisals, and France and the UK adopted what was seen as a *sauve-qui-peut* attitude and sought bilateral deals with individual Arab states. Whatever sharing of oil supplies that did in fact take place was implemented by the oil majors (the large multinational oil companies).

Although there has been a Council Directive since 1968 (Directive 68/414/EEC) requiring member states to maintain 65 days of oil stocks, which were subsequently increased to 90 days (Directive 72/425/EEC), and although Article 34 of the EEC Treaty clearly states, 'quantitative restrictions on exports, and all measures having equivalent effect, shall be prohibited between Member States', the European Communities do not have a semi-automatic oil-sharing scheme comparable to that of the International Energy Agency (IEA) which includes most OECD countries with the notable exception of France, and which was set up in November 1974 under American leadership. Under the IEA agreement, in the event of a shortfall in supplies of 7% affecting any or all participating countries, the oil-sharing scheme would be automatically activated unless members decided otherwise by a special majority. The most that the European Community has been able to agree on, to date, is contained in the Council Decision of 7 November 1977, adopted after many wranglings:

> Where difficulties arise in the supply of crude oil or petroleum products in one or more member states, the Commission . . . may set a target for reducing consumption . . . up to 10% of normal consumption . . . The quantities of petroleum products saved . . . shall be shared out between the member states . . .

Thus, not only are the provisions vaguer than in the IEA agreement, but there is no automaticity: the Commission may propose, but the Council does not have to agree. As between national policies and international cooperation at the OECD level, the European Community risks losing its relevance and specificity.

One way of encouraging more oil exploration in the IEA or EEC area is to set a minimum support price (MSP). While the IEA was able to agree to an MSP in 1976, within the EEC the subject has caused bitter arguments between the UK and other countries, agreement was never reached, and the UK eventually dropped the proposal. In the context of rising oil prices, an MSP at the levels originally envisaged has become increasingly irrelevant, but the disputes nevertheless succeeded in creating a great deal of ill-feeling in the EEC.

With the advent of economic recession, excess capacity began to develop in oil refineries in the EEC. The rate of capacity utilisation, which had been 85% in 1963–73, fell to 58% in 1975, 62% in 1976, and 63% in 1977 (Bacchetta 1978). In March 1977, the Commission proposed a reduction of capacity and a temporary suspension of national aid to the construction of new refineries. Agreement was blocked by the UK, which was opposed to any interference with the planned expansion of UK refining capacity in respect of North Sea oil. It is arguable whether such a policy was in the best interests of the UK: a refinery brings few jobs, and the value-added is rather low and has to be weighed against the loss of the price premium that North Sea crude commands because of its being of light quality. The UK's position, not surprisingly, led to retaliation by Italy and France, who vetoed the Commission's proposals for subsidising Community coal (see above). The UK has also rejected all suggestions that it should maintain normal supply flows in times of crisis. Whether this is because the UK refuses to 'do any deal' on North Sea oil, or because the potential deals are not considered attractive enough, remains to be seen.

Between 1973 and 1978, while EEC net oil imports declined from more than 500 million tons of oil equivalent (toe) to 472 million toe, under the impact both of reduced consumption and increased North Sea production, net oil imports by the US increased by 42.6%, from 287 million toe to 409 million toe. The impact on the oil market and on the value of the dollar has been highly negative. At the Tokyo summit of the major seven Western countries at the end of June 1979, the US, Japan and the EEC agreed to limit their oil imports for 1985 to given quantitative targets. The question arose of dividing the overall ceiling for the EEC between individual member states. This must have been a most difficult negotiating task, but the need to make the US stick to its part of the agreement forced the EEC countries to reach agreement by the end of September 1979. They were helped in this by the prospect that the UK's imports will become negative (the UK will be a small net exporter), which will allow other countries to import more within the overall ceiling.

Finally, the fact that, in times of short supplies, prices on the Rotterdam free market tend to shoot up to a much higher level than OPEC contractual prices, has been blamed as a factor encouraging or enabling general price rises, the argument being that OPEC producers use these prices to justify raising their contractual prices. France has been leading a move to make the Rotterdam market more 'trans-parent' in an effort to stabilise prices. Germany and the UK have, however, been less than enthusiastic, Germany because its economic strength and the value of the Deutsche Mark enable it to buy its way out of trouble and because it relies to a large extent on the Rotterdam market, and the UK because it hosts a number of oil majors and does not like controls.

To summarise this section on oil, there are a number of factors that undermine solidarity between the Nine:

(1) an attitude of *sauve-qui-peut* in times of crisis (solidarity works best when there is growth and hence something for everyone);
(2) differences in energy resource endowments;
(3) differences in economic strength, in ability to buy one's way out of trouble;
(4) differences in relations with the oil majors;
(5) differences in foreign policy attitudes, in relations with the US and the Arab countries.

Other Measures

A number of directives and recommendations have been adopted relating to energy savings in industry and in domestic heating. Community financial aids are provided for the development of new sources of energy (solar energy, geothermal, liquefaction and gasifi-cation of coal) and for hydrocarbon exploration. The amounts involved are, however, very small. Total subsidies by the Community for hydrocarbon projects amount to 36.7 million European Units of Account (EUA) for the period 1978–80, and Community spending on energy research amounts to less than 1% of the total Community budget. In March 1977, the Council authorised the Commission to borrow up to 500 million EUA on behalf of Euratom to be re-lent for nuclear energy investments in the Community. But the largest financial contribution from the Community has come through European Investment Bank (EIB) loans and guarantees. In 1978, loans for investment in the energy sector amounted to 721.3 million EUA, or more than a third of all financing within the Community; this was almost double the 1977 total for energy projects of 373 million EUA. Within the energy sector, the largest beneficiary in 1978 was the nuclear subsector, followed by thermal power stations, gaslines and oil pipelines.

Conclusions

At the beginning of this chapter, we raised the question of whether the Community has a common energy policy. The answer depends partly on what is meant by a 'policy' and partly on what constitutes a 'common' policy. If by a policy, one means a combination of a clear vision of the future, a coherent set of principles, a range of policy instruments adequate to the objectives that are set, and the existence of sufficient legitimacy and authority to carry the measures through, it follows by definition that Europe does not have an energy policy. But is this surprising, when even a full political union and a real common market, the US, with its vast resources, does not have an energy policy in this sense? As for a 'common' policy, if one adopts the supranational or integrationist view of what constitutes a common policy, it is clear that there is no common policy, since much of the conception and implementation of energy policy remains with the member states. Again, this is not surprising in view of the importance and sensitiveness of the issues involved. Nor is the Community entirely devoid of 'own' policy instruments (e.g. the EIB), but the coal crisis of 1958–60 clearly showed that, even where such dispositions exist legally, it would be difficult to activate them without the consent of the member states. If one abandons the Procrustean mould of integration theory and recognises the reality of national policies, the question is no longer one of a common policy, but of a convergence of national policies towards the common good. Such a convergence is facilitated or made difficult by the environment (we have argued that increasing resources make cooperation easier, and that finite or contracting resources tend to create a zero-sum game situation), but it also presupposes a convergence of national interests, which depends on perceptions, material circumstances, mutual trust, and the arrangement of package deals. In any case, negative integration (the common market in oil) is not viable without positive integration (effective oil-sharing in times of crisis).

It may be asked: why should the European Community have a common energy policy? If this question is accepted, the answer must be sought in economies of scale, increased bargaining strength, decreased vulnerability, or the need to maintain certain other common policies. In fact, however, the justification for a common energy policy depends on the vision that one has of the Community and of what it should become. If one believes in the ever closer working together of the peoples of Europe, the question becomes: why should the Community not work together in this vital area? It becomes a question, not of strict separation of powers, but of combining national and Community initiatives towards common goals. An analogy may be useful here. In the UK, there is a tendency to reason in terms of the public sector *versus* the private. In many other countries, however, the question is posed in terms of how best to use the 'two wheels of the chariot' to pursue national objectives.

References

Bacchetta, M., Oil refining on the European Community, *Journal of Common Market Studies*, December 1978.

Lantzke, U., International cooperation on energy, *The World Today*, March 1976.

Lucas, N.J.D., *Energy and the European Communities*, Europa Publications for the David Davies Memorial Institute of International Studies, London, 1977.

Pinder, J., Positive integration and negative integration, *The World Today*, March 1968.

15
Social Policy

C D E COLLINS

The Meaning of Social Policy

The term social policy, as used by the European Community, has rather a different meaning from that attributed to it in discussions of British governmental activity and this has led to considerable mis-understanding about the nature of Community social policy. In the context of the Community, attention is focused on problems of employment, industrial health, wages and the social costs of industry, labour mobility and the role of social spending in economic manage-ment, whilst activities which lie outside the economic field have been of less immediate concern. This was particularly so in the early years of the European Community, when the main task was the removal of tariff barriers to which social welfare seemed little related. Thus the Spaak Committee, whose report laid the basis for the Treaty of Rome, believed that there was a limited need for common policies in the social field, that the effect of social costs and state subsidies on the competitive system was a valid concern, but that social aid to individuals and social systems such as education and health lay outside the sphere of interest of the new organisation (Spaak Report, p. 58). In short, the Community has always been concerned with the impact of economic change, and in particular of integration, on the broad issues of living and working conditions, rather than with detailed consideration of the needs of particular individuals and the operation of personal social services. Thus its interests have only partially coincided with those of national governments which have become increasingly involved since 1957 in services for social security, health care, education and personal welfare.

Nevertheless, over time, the overlap of interest in social policy has grown. The development of social security schemes in both coverage and cost has been a major concern of both national governments and the Community. The rapid increase in expenditure for which these schemes are responsible has made them an ingredient in economic management and the growing participation in them of the public sector has made it more important to consider them as an issue in public spending. Furthermore, the desire for increased political legitimacy has led the European Commission to press for a steadily increasing social role for the Community, so that it can be seen to be responding to the needs of the ordinary citizen. At the same time, there are signs that the concept of social policy is broadening out in the current British political debate so that it more readily embraces the broad process of redistribution through incomes, property holding and working conditions and as it becomes clearer that the simple principles of the Beveridge social revolution have to be reconsidered as the post-war society recedes. Thus, interest in social policy is coming to be shared by national governments with the Community, although at the present time responsibility remains primarily with states and the prerogative is jealousy guarded by all national governments. They are far more important as sources of finance than the Community and the legitimacy of the Community interest is constantly challenged. Nevertheless, there is a growing number of matters in which states recognise that the Community has an interest and the process of 'concertation' of national and joint views and policies is becoming more familiar in British circles. There remain some policy matters such as education, personal health care and housing provision where the Community has little to say. Although Ministers of Education meet from time to time, and the Ministers of Health have done so once, they are still at the stage of discussion of common problems and of sharing experiences rather than of establishing a Community policy in these fields. One consequence of this position is that it is still possible for Community activities and policies, which seem so important from the Community point of view, to appear marginal in interest and priority from the vantage point of national social policy.

The Basis of Social Policy

Community social policy is shaped by two factors. The first consists of the provisions to be found in the respective treaties of which the Treaty of Rome creating the European Economic Community is most general in scope — see Chapter 2. The discussion in this chapter is primarily concerned with this treaty, but the Treaty of Paris creating the ECSC and the Treaty of Rome setting up Euratom are also significant in their respective spheres. The social policy clauses of the treaties differ in their legal significance. Some provisions are specific, but some are general statements of intent and many express only the will of states to collaborate in certain matters. However, such intentions may subsequently give rise to legally enforceable acts. Thus at any given moment there will be a wide variety of activity in the social field which stems directly from the treaties, but which will carry variations in state commitment.

Secondly, however, there is nothing to prevent the members of the Community from taking a new political initiative in the social field and from time to time they do so. The most well-known example is the Paris summit conference of 1972 (see p. 273). Some of these developments may be quite novel to the European Community, such as the opening of certain grant-aid provisions to help services directed to migrants from outside the Community, whilst others may be based upon the existing modes of work and simply require its greater effectiveness as in the re-emphasis on the policy of equal pay. Social policy is a mixture of acts deriving from the treaties and from subsequent political developments.

It is plain, therefore, that an understanding is required of the social provisions of the treaties and of the extent to which they can be used for novel developments, as a first step for this reveals both the formal commitments and the likely methods to be used for further development.

The charge that the Treaty of Rome is weak on the social side stems from the fact that there are relatively few precise commitments and that the Treaty did not contain a definite timetable for action as had been characteristic of the introduction of the common market. Since, however, it was believed that social policy had little direct relevance to this immediate goal, it was logical to limit the Treaty to the general co-operative sphere and to confine the more forceful parts of social policy to questions of immediate import. The curiosity is that, starting from a limited base, the Community has evolved a wide ranging social policy whose impact in certain spheres has been considerable.

In the first instance, the Treaty of Rome has general objectives of a broadly social character. These include an accelerated raising of the standard of living, the free movement of people and a social fund to help with employment problems. Furthermore, the social policy section of the treaty is placed within a recognition by members of the need to improve living and working conditions and of their expectation that policies will gradually align under the impact of the new system. Thus, it was not the Community itself which was given the task of direct improvement, although the future processes of social, economic and political change brought about by the existence of the Community were expected to have a particular effect which would be both beneficial and would bring about the alignment of national policies. Whilst the phraseology of Article 117 gave reassurance to members that their welfare role was not to be usurped, it also reaffirmed the commitment of members to the cause of social betterment (for more detailed analysis see Collins Vol. 2, pp. 21–2). State supremacy was reinforced by the agreement to collaborate in specific fields such as labour legislation, working conditions, vocational training, social security, industrial health and welfare, and trade union and collective bargaining matters where the Commission was given the responsibility to promote such collaboration in various ways such as study activities and the expression of views. Thus, scope for joint action was left open for the future, should the evolution of the Community require it as the common market, and later, economic union developed, but it was not considered inevitable that common policies would be required.

A much clearer issue in 1957 was the classic one of the effect of social costs on competition within the single market. Whatever the economic truth of the matter, the sensitivity of French industry as a whole to the possibility of European competition made it politically imperative for the French government to insist upon certain Treaty provisions. The most important of these, both at the time and subsequently, was the equal pay obligation (Article 119). Other Treaty clauses concerning holiday and overtime pay, although in the Treaty for the same reason, were less stringent in form and have been overtaken by events.

A special point had been made in the Spaak Report of the lack of effective utilisation of manpower in the West European area. It stated the belief that the lack of opportunities for the entrepreneur resulting from the restrictive nature of the economies, the refusal to substitute capital for labour, the lack of appropriate education and training so that the workforce could become more skilled, the wholesale overmanning on peasant farms, the existence of areas of considerable unemployment were all evidence that a much more effective use of manpower was urgently necessary. Furthermore, the process of economic change which the common market was itself designed to encourage would make better labour utilisation more compelling. These arguments resulted in the creation of a social fund through which the Community might help increase both occupational and geographical mobility, although it must be said that the fund has never been on the scale which would be necessary if it were to be allocated the tasks so graphically described by the Spaak committee. In addition, the treaty included the agreement to establish the common principles of vocational training, and although this seemed a logical necessity from the analysis, it has not in practice led to more than general guidelines of a relatively undemanding nature.

Of far greater significance, and the great prize gained by Italy, was the adoption of the principle of the free movement of wage-earners, together with rules to give it practical effect and to ensure the equal treatment of migrants with indigenous workers. The firm intent was expressed to agree on rules for the free establishment of the self-employed, including professional people and although that has been a separate programme of great complexity, it has been equally pursued. The free movement policy, together with its supporting policies of employment exchange collaboration, maintenance of social security provision and protection of equal working rights for migrants must be considered as a major Community success, although it also owed much to the buoyant economic conditions of the time. Subsequent attempts to move the policy into the much more difficult area of social integration and social equality and to evolve a policy towards migrants from outside the European Community have not been so successful. This can probably be accounted for both by changed economic circumstances and the fact that there is no Treaty commitment for such development which makes it possible for members to resist Community intrusion into matters of great domestic sensitivity.

Special protective measures exist in the coal and steel industries and antedate the social policy of the Treaty of Rome. These relate, in particular, to the payment of cash benefits to workers losing their jobs, needing retraining, or having to move home for work elsewhere and to the payment of grants to firms taking on workers from these two industries. A second novel feature of the work of the ECSC has been the use of Treaty provisions to aid investment to help with housing construction and this programme continues. Grant aid is also used for specific health and safety measures in the coal and steel industries. In the same way, Euratom has its own special concerns notably in the obligation to establish basic health and safety standards, both for workers in the industry and for the general public.

Development of Social Policy

Given this rather incoherent guidance, it is not surprising that the development of social policy was rather patchy. It was characterised by reluctance on the part of states to allow the Community's responsibilities to develop beyond the strict legal commitment of the treaty and even this was often fulfilled more in the letter than the spirit, as the early years of the equal pay policy and of the operation of the social fund clearly show. Although the Commission could initiate collaborative efforts, it had to accept that it was for individual states to put the results into operation since the Treaty did not provide procedures for this. Employers, too, tended to be cautious about the extension of specific measures for fear of extra costs. Support for the development of social policy came from Italy who was strongly behind the rapid implementation of the labour movement policy and who gained from the cash grants operated by the social fund for the migrants moving north; from the Commission which was anxious to establish its position and the credibility of the Community in the eyes of the general public; from the enthusiasts for European integration and a somewhat variable support from trade union representatives depending upon how they saw their interests affected. The first ten years of the European Economic Community saw the major steps taken to implement the policy on labour movement, a formal adoption of the equal pay policy, a narrow exploitation of the social fund and considerable discussion, study and research into labour questions, but it is difficult to avoid the conclusion that social policy hung fire.

A new impetus can be detected by the end of the 1960s which gave a new spurt in the field of social policy. The reasons for this are not hard to seek. The essential elements of the transitional period had been completed by 1968. A recommitment to the existence and importance of the Community was necessary to fill a possible political vacuum and an emphasis upon the non-material aims of the group was in accord with the new concerns of Western Europe. A widespread unease was evident over such issues as environmental pollution, the problems of disadvantaged groups and social inequalities. The lack of involvement of ordinary citizens in public processes, the difficulties of the old and handicapped and the stress problems of the cities were issues which were of concern to all member states, but where the Community's social policy seemed to make little impact and where political capital might readily be built. The claim to a social conscience was the more appealing to governments as the time of first enlargement came nearer, for this revealed a considerable public hostility to the Community in Norway, Denmark and Britain on the grounds of its social insensitivity. The West German Social Democrat government, too, was anxious to see the Community present itself in terms acceptable to its supporters at home and the Brandt memorandum on social policy development was a major source of inspiration for the summit meeting of October 1972.

The first sign of greater seriousness in social affairs was expressed at the Hague Conference in December 1969 when the existing six members accepted that the Community would go further towards the pursuit of common political and economic goals. They spoke of the need for a closely concerted social policy which would include a reformed social fund (*Bulletin of the European Communities* 1/70). This forward look was continued by the Paris summit conference of

1972 which asserted the importance members attached to vigorous action in the social field (*Bulletin of the European Communities* 10/72). The communiqué referred specifically to the need to widen participation in decision-making and action to lessen inequalities and to improve the quality of life. It called for the formulation of a social action programme to include both concrete measures and the corresponding resources, particularly in the framework of the social fund. The guidelines for the programme referred to matters such as the need for a co-ordinated policy on employment and vocational training, the improvement of living and working conditions, the closer involvement of workers in decisions taken by their firms, the encouragement of collective agreements at the Community level and greater consumer protection.

Two more technical matters were considered indicative of the new seriousness of social purpose. The agreement referred to the possibility of using Article 235 in the social field. This states that if the necessary powers to fulfil the objectives of the Community are not to be found in the treaty, the Council may take the necessary measures on a basis of unanimity and the recognition of this possibility appeared to fill the acknowledged gap in Community procedures mentioned earlier. Secondly, it was agreed that the Council, contrary to its previous practice of constant procrastination in social affairs, should take a decision on Commission proposals within nine months of their submission.

The Social Action Programme

The resulting Social Action Programme (SAP, *Bulletin of the European Communities*, Supplement 2/74) has formed the structure within which subsequent action has been taken, although it must be realised that the hopes of rapid development were quickly dashed by the onset of recession and the burden of large-scale unemployment against which the measures of the SAP seem small-scale and which have thus not been able to retain the sense of urgency and excitement engendered in the heady days of the Paris summit. States have been less ready to support those measures which require financial aid and which in prosperous years they might have been willing to accept. Nevertheless, it was a programme designed to give social policy more bite and push than hitherto.

The SAP was formulated by the Commission and adopted by the Council in January 1974. In practical terms it was very much of a rag-bag of projects, ranging over wide areas of social policy which, it hoped, would strengthen three themes which the document wished to emphasise. The first was the goal of full and better employment and reflected the belief that economic growth had been excessively based on the provision of unsatisfying forms of employment, on the encouragement of movement into over-crowded cities and on the import of large numbers of unskilled workers whose social integration was conspicuously lacking. It argued the case for much greater attention to vocational training in order to fill skilled vacancies, to vocational guidance to match individuals to appropriate jobs, the need to concentrate effort in declining or under-developed areas and to give wider opportunities to especially disadvantaged groups such as the young, the handicapped and women workers.

The second theme was the need to act to improve living and working conditions, a goal which was used to group a wide range of suggestions. These included a recognition of the patchiness of affluence and the necessity to devote special care, and money, to certain geographical areas. It also included measures to respond to the growing concern about income distribution in modern society, where the Commission suggested it could be helpful in research and information collection as a basis for state action. It included a small-scale programme to allow the Commission to aid directly pilot projects looking for new ways to combat poverty. Equal pay and opportunities for women also found their place and here the Commission was on stronger ground in view of the legal position in the Treaty and since the Council had already agreed that older women seeking to return to work should be a special group to be grant-aided from the social fund. Other suggestions included help with housing schemes for the under-privileged, with the encouragement to asset ownership and with improving social security schemes, the developmemt of studies on social budgeting and the continuance of work in the field of industrial health and safety.

The third theme was that of encouraging the participation of workers and employers in Community decision-taking in addition to that of a greater involvement of workers in decisions affecting their own firms. The first element led to the re-activation of the Standing Committee on Employment and the strengthening of the advisory committee structure, whilst the second has been handled in the wider context of the attempts to establish a legal framework for a European Company (see p. 285).

The programme itself laid down a timetable for the introduction and application of measures and this has been partially adhered to. Rather than provide a list of achievement and non-fulfilment, it is more helpful to discuss certain provisions in relation to those sections of social policy which have been pursued during the last five years. Space prevents the discussion being entirely comprehensive, but it is hoped that enough detail is given to illustrate the coverage of European Community social policy today.

The Social Fund

By 1971, the Council of Ministers had taken a decision on the reform of the social fund and this was put into practice the following year, (*Official Journal of the Community*, L28, 4 Feb. 1971). The intention was that the fund should be larger than in the past and operate from a more flexible base. Instead of being seen as a simple transfer system whereby *ex-post facto* cash grants were automatically paid to reimburse half of permitted costs, it was intended that the fund should become far more of a Community mechanism which could help with the employment needs involved in more positive Community policies for agriculture or for the regions and make a more positive contribution to labour training generally. Above all, a move was made towards giving Community institutions a hand in shaping policy. Such objectives required greater operational flexibility through on-going powers of decision for the Council and Commission concerning the groups to benefit and the ways of helping them. It was also expected that aid given should contribute far more than in the past to the priorities and objectives of the Community itself, should be available in a wider range of circumstances, and include aid to the private sector as well as to government directed schemes.

Underlying the complexity of the structure and rules was a definite conflict of view concerning the priorities for aid which led to the definition of two broad objectives respectively formulated in Article 4 and 5 of the decision. The first formula was designed to help in circumstances where Community policies adversely affect employment, or are seen to require assistance for other reasons relating to positive economic change. Article 4 was seen as the forward-looking article enabling the Community to fit its aid to the process of socio-economic change and the development of Community schemes. The second principle was to be found in Article 5 which provided aid in cases of difficulty, whether in regions, industrial sectors, or individual firms, such problems being only directly related to the development of the Community, or which could be held to impede its harmonious development. This approach is of more interest to countries with severe problems of regional unemployment, whether industrial or agricultural, whereas the philosophy of Article 4 is that of the furtherance of Community action and the integrative process, so that the Commission originally hoped to emphasise this heading.

The financing of the fund altered so that it became part of the overall Community budget and therefore its size and purpose became far more matters for political discussion than before. It had reached 617 million EUA by 1977, or about 6% of the total budget, but 1968 saw a cut-back to 568 million EUA. Within this total it has been necessary to determine the relative importance of schemes under Article 4 against those under Article 5. The original intention was for a roughly equal division, but over time to allow Article 4 to become the more important. So far this has not happened and half the budget is still used for the regions, with a concentration upon the most disadvantaged areas such as Northern Ireland and Greenland. Further changes included the possibility of grant aid to non-governmental agencies on the basis of joint financing between the Community, the national government and the providing institution, whilst public agencies were to continue to be financed on a 50% basis. However, the Council guidelines for the processing of applications are more concerned with public sector schemes, the slow repayment procedures prevent many small organisations participating and application must be channelled through public departments. All these factors have led to a rather disappointing situation for voluntary organisations who may be strong in special fields, such as training for the disabled, and new rules concerning the speedier payment of grants may help them (*Official Journal of the Community*, C141, 15 June 1977). The vexed question of 'additionality' whereby, so it is charged, the arrangements enable states to pass over to the Community costs they would otherwise have carried for themselves and therefore do not result in a real increase in help given, still remains.

Decisions on particular applications are now taken by the Commission and its advisers drawn from national governments and from representatives of employers and unions who together have the task of marrying Council policy guidelines, the respective merits of the schemes in question and pressure from governments to obtain their 'fair share'.

In theory, all groups of wage earners, including non-nationals, are eligible to benefit from the schemes, but in practice specific groups are designated by Council decision. Clearly, eligible groups, and the industries in which they work, may change from time to time. Groups under Article 4 include people leaving agriculture for other forms of employment or self-employment, workers in textile firms, handicapped people, migrants, young workers under 25 and women over 25 years of age. The types of activity eligible for grant aid are also laid down by the Council. At present, these include reception facilities, language courses and travelling expenses for migrants, building costs and teachers' salaries at vocation training centres as examples.

Until recently, groups eligible under Article 5, where aid is confined to specific regions, were also defined, but since 1977 only the handicapped have been so mentioned and general provision is made for the unemployed or those threatened with unemployment, experiencing short-time or stand-off arrangements (see above). Here, help with training or wage subsidy may be provided.

Generally speaking, there has been an emphasis upon the costs associated with training, other than those for immediate school leavers, resettlement costs for people moving home, help for migrants and their families, with a special mention for particularly disadvantaged groups, but there is some argument at the present time whether grants should be diverted away from vocational training towards job creation and income maintenance (*Agence Europe,* 2 March 1977, Reg. 2893/77 and *Official Journal of the Community*, L 337, 27 Dec. 1977). A small study and pilot scheme programme is also carried on the social fund budget.

The procedures are still complex and aid is on a small scale compared with the current problems of unemployment, but the reforms did represent an attempt to make the Community a more significant influence on employment opportunities. This may not always be welcome to states preoccupied with their own problems of regional unemployment or the return they receive for their budget contributions.

A particular problem for the Community is to try to integrate the work of the social fund with other Community policies and notably to align grants with those from the regional and agricultural funds, since they may all be working in the same area. Lack of co-ordination prevents the Community from making the maximum impact with its assistance which in any case has to fit into the programme of a receiving state. It is true that President Roy Jenkins made one Commissioner, Mr Giolitti, responsible for all funding operations as well as for regional policy, but a more radical reform is required if they are truly to be part of an overall rehabilitative programme for areas requiring a great deal of economic assistance and stimulus in addition to the specific help with employment which the social fund can give.

Current Social Issues

Women Workers

Although an equal pay policy had been written into the Treaty of Rome, there was a noticeable lack of enthusiasm concerning its application until the 1970s. Certain publicity had been attracted to the problem by the case of the Sabena air hostess who had lodged a complaint in Belgium concerning the inequality in her conditions of service. The question of her pay, which was less than that of male stewards on the airline, led ultimately to a consideration by the European Court of Justice in the light of the application of Article 119. The Court, which by now was feeling greater confidence in its role as a positive interpreter of the Community treaties, made clear its view that Article 119 was intended to be taken seriously and properly applied. One result of this episode was to spur the Commission on to produce a directive on equal pay which became operative in 1975 (Dir. 75/117/EEC; *Official Journal of the Community*, L45/19). This included a definition of equal pay to include both identical work and that of equal value, established certain controls and insisted upon an effective appeal system as a means of giving a stricter framework within which states were to apply the policy. By this time, the Community was clearly anxious to respond to the increasingly vocal demands made by women for greater consideration in employment matters and one result was the creation in 1976 of a small bureau for questions relating to women's employment. Equality of treatment between men and women on the labour market and a need to pay more attention to the balance between employment and family responsibilities had received a modest priority in the social action programme and the policy was further pursued by a directive to establish equal opportunity in relation to employment, in job recruitment, promotion and training (Dir. 76/207/EEC; *Official Journal of the Community*, L 39, 14 Feb. 1976). This was followed by the directive on equal treatment for men and women in social security schemes (*Official Journal of the Community*, C 34, 11 Feb. 1977). Although this aims at the ultimate elimination of all differences based on sex, implementation is in stages and questions of the retirement age, which often favours women at the present time, and of widowers' benefits, still remain outstanding.

Labour Migration

The original provisions of the Treaty of Rome concerning the free movement of wage-earners were largely implemented by 1968. A few outstanding matters were settled not long afterwards. These arrangements protected the right to move for working purposes and to remain in a country where one had worked, gave rights of entry to families and had elaborated a complex system for the maintenance of social security benefits, although there were still certain gaps in coverage. Attempts had been made to give effect to the concept of equal treatment at work through the protection of union membership and the holding of union office, as well as access to vocational training and employment services generally. However, whilst opinion had become aware of the difficulties facing migrants in relation to social integration and of the great difference between the formal possession of rights and the assumption of a full place in society, the Community lacked the power to develop a comprehensive policy.

Efforts to create a single labour market in order to aid migration through effective notification of job opportunities and labour offers had also been initiated in the early years, but has proved an extremely difficult problem to handle. The newest system of inter-state notification of job vacancies (SEDOC) is still only in the teething stage. Nevertheless, despite its imperfections, the broad outline of a policy enabling the working population and dependants to move reasonably freely within the EEC had been established by the 1970s. The same principle of free movement has been applied to very wide categories of the self-employed, although these may contain special rules to ensure professional competence, as in the case of doctors and lawyers.

Subsequent developments have been concerned with measures to strengthen the existing structure. These include matters such as the extension of social security cover to the self-employed, the need to fill gaps in social security cover for wage earners which relate to family benefits and to try to get action for wage earners which relate to family benefits, but which are not covered by the regulations. The identification of migrants as a group eligible for aid from the social fund may well have helped to make states more sensitive to the problems involved in ensuring equality of opportunity for migrants.

The great influx of people into Western Europe from outside the Community itself which took place during the flourishing years of the 1960s was an unexpected phenomenon. A recent estimate suggests that there are now about six million migrant workers in the area and twelve million people if families are included. In this group, non-Community workers outnumber Community nationals by approximately four to one (see Appendix for certain labour statistics). Not only were the social problems of integration, housing and employment opportunities increased by the growing cultural gap between host country and the newcomers, but the scale of the movement produced social tensions and pressure on services in the congested urban areas. Unfortunately, the Community lacks a legal base for effective policies towards migration generally and the attempts of the Commission to establish more wide-reaching activities met with very limited success. It is only fairly recently that policies have been put forward in terms, but they do not carry a definite obligation towards this group. The experience demonstrates once again the unwillingness of governments to surrender control in a sensitive political area.

By the early 1970s, the Commission had begun to question the value of such large-scale, uncontrolled migration, when its drawbacks were taken into account against the contribution which migrants were making to economic development. Stress began to be laid on the ill-effects for the regions losing manpower, the pressure on the urban social infrastructure and the slowing down of capital development in industry as well as the uncertain benefits derived for countries sending migrants (*Bulletin of the European Communities*, Supplement 3/76, pp. 11–12). Reliance upon unskilled labour reserves delayed recognition of the need to improve labour skills and eroded a major advantage Italy had received from the Treaty. It is not surprising that she has been particularly anxious to secure a Community policy to control clandestine immigration (see above). The moral strength which the Community derived from its policy of equality of treatment of migrant workers was rapidly diminished as it became obvious that the bulk of migrants could not benefit from the policy. The situation became further confused as unemployment grew, states began to ban recruitment from outside, claims were made that migrants were the first to lose their jobs, work permits for third country migrants expired and many workers decided to stay in the Community area illegally rather than join the queue for re-entry. Both illegal entry, and employment, with consequent exploitation by employers and unscrupulous employment agencies, resulted.

It is thus not surprising that the Commission made a more effective policy towards migrants a major element in the emerging SAP and this, in turn, gave rise to an action programme for migrants of which the Council 'took note' in February 1976 (see above), but against this difficult background the main lines of action are making somewhat uncertain progress. Minor improvements in social protection have been made. There are the gaps in the coverage of Community workers to which reference has been made and where studies progress, but non-Community migrants do not receive the benefits of these regulations and their position is generally less favourable, depending on bilateral arrangements. The stress laid upon the importance of vocational training as a means of improving the socio-economic position of the migrant has indeed led to the inclusion of migrants, including the third country category, as an eligible group for aid from the social fund. A special effort has been made, too, in relation to the education of the children of migrants which led to the directive of July 1977 (Dir. 77/486/EEC; *Official Journal of the European Community*, L 199, 6 Aug. 1977). This stemmed from a recognition of the relatively unfavourable employment of young migrants which could be traced to a less than sound educational base, including persistent language difficulties and erratic school attendance. The directive committed states to measures such as more effective reception facilities, tuition in both the language of the host country and the special training for teachers and including the possibility of employing teachers from the country of origin. The emphasis seems to be on the belief that such children will ultimately return home and, of course, its legal force only applies to the children of Community nationals.

Underlying these provisions are contrasting views about whether a migrant should be considered as likely to remain indefinitely in a host country and increasingly become merged into its society, or whether he is to be regarded primarily as a short-term visitor whose children must have the tools to enable them to resettle in the country of origin.

Considerable argument continues concerning policy to curb illegal entry into and employment in the Community, problems which, by definition, can apply only to non-Community nationals. Growing unemployment made public opinion more sensitive and alarmed many migrants. A rapid growth of illegal residents resulted, with consequent difficulties for the people involved including exploitation at work and lack of access to public services, even extending to a reluctance to send children to school for fear of detection. At the same time, since work and residence permits were no longer being issued, work seekers were thought to cross the frontiers illegally in increasing numbers. Thus by 1976, it was widely assumed that there were about 600,000 illegal workers in the Community (*Bulletin of the European Communities*, Supplement, 3/76 p. 21).

Community policy has been concerned both with attempts to curb illegal entry and to curtail abuses of employment by checking at places of work. So far, these efforts have not resulted in any formal agreements. States are in conflict over the advantages of a common policy on entry restriction and see disadvantages in surrendering to the Community a control which would limit their own freedom in employment policy. Checks on illegal employment may be in part humanitarian, but could easily be used to effect tighter control over migrant populations.

The question of how migration is to be handled, the extent to which the concentration of people in central areas and away from the peripheries is to continue, the social tensions which have resulted from the migration are all likely to become even more serious issues for the Community as enlargement occurs, for the new applicants have traditionally supplied the Community with significant numbers of working people.

The action programme contained an interesting development in the pursuit of civic and political rights. It pointed out that it was inconsistent with the spirit of the free movement policy, and indeed with the evolution of a Community in any understandable sense, that Community nationals should be deprived of political rights unless they became naturalised and that they usually had no voice in local politics, although much affected by educational, housing and personal services which are often controlled at local level. So far, no progress has been made to allow participation in local elections after a short period of residence, a Community passport is equally slow to appear and the idea that Community nationals should have a vote in elections for the European Parliament wherever they live received short shrift from most member governments in 1979. All such non-events suggest that states remain unwilling to accept migrants as full citizens and will resist Community pressure to achieve such a policy. Handling the manifold problems connected with migration remains very much a shared responsibility for the Community and the member states and an effective, overall Community policy in this field is a long way off.

Unemployment

The sensitivity of the migration issue was not caused by the onset of widespread unemployment, but antedated it. Falling employment prospects ensured that migration remained a political problem, but the continuing high unemployment rates have overshadowed all other issues as the most pressing problem for Community social policy. The Community is ill-equipped to provide significant measures and the last few years have shown the extent to which many policies were predicated upon the assumption of economic growth. Thus, much of Community social policy was seen as a means of helping people take advantage of expanding opportunities which, it was expected, would absorb the unemployed and allow an effective return to working groups in a context of generally improving standards. The social instruments through which it can help to alleviate unemployment consist of the grant aid that can be provided through the social fund, the improvement of measures to make the Community labour market operate more effectively, research projects and similar small-scale activities. To the list must be added the grants available for retraining and income maintenance to workers in the coal and steel industries which, at the present time, are concentrated upon the latter. A number of measures have tried to ensure that loss of job is handled as sympathetically as possible. Directives have been passed on procedures to be followed in the case of collective dismissals and the maintenance of rights when companies merge (*Agence Europe*, 1655, 19 Dec. 1974;

Bulletin of the European Communities, 12/76, p. 47). Protection of rights when a firm becomes insolvent is under discussion. The Commission has stressed the particular employment problems of the young, the elderly and women workers but, apart from the young, states have shown little response. Neither have they taken up the Commission's suggestions for Community action for the young unemployed. These have included job creation schemes and European youth service activities and the importance the Commission attaches to vocational preparation for young workers has led to no more than a Commission recommendation (*Official Journal of the European Community*, L 180, 20 July 1977). The problem is that, in times of considerable unemployment, it seems rather less compelling to single out the needs of particular groups of the workforce.

The Anti-Poverty Programme

A small-scale, but eye-catching, element of the SAP was the anti-poverty programme. This was the result of an Irish initiative and includes grant-aid to projects concerned to help groups in poverty and to research studies. The former category has attempted to concentrate on small projects with new, and sometimes unorthodox, procedures and thus forms some contrast to the grant-aid from the social fund. Its scale is such that the programme can hardly be expected to do much to alleviate a great deal of poverty and it must therefore be considered more as a means of expressing the interest of the Community in the conditions of some of the most disadvantaged groups. It also enables the Commission to remain in direct, close contact with one form of social movement and this must be considered a significant gain for a body so often considered, however unfairly, as remote and bureaucratic.

In 1975, a two year programme was adopted by the Council to allow financial aid to be provided for schemes which could be shown to be of value to the Community as a whole and which are, as far as possible, carried out with the participation of the recipients (*Official Journal of the European Community*, L 199, 30 July 1975). A cross-national poverty study was also financed and the programme has been extended at least until 1980 with a current annual budget of 5.7 million EUA.

Industrial Relations

Collective bargaining remains very much a matter for national arrangements, although it might have been expected that the creation of a single market, greater mobility and the growth of the multinational company would by now have required greater adaptation than has occurred in negotiating structures. Today, Community policy in industrial relations does not seem primarily concerned with this issue, despite reference to it at the Paris summit, but rather with the encouragement of active employer and union involvement in the Community decision-making process. Although certain formal structures such as the ECSC Consultative Committee and the EEC Economic and Social Committee explicitly require representation from both sides of industry, consultation has become far more widespread. It is normal for the various advisory committees to contain such representation, joint committees meet to deal with problems concerning a particular industry and in recent years a Standing Committee on Employment has been reactivated with attempts to give it greater prestige. This is an advisory committee which acts as a forum for the discussion of many questions; youth employment, work sharing and employment premiums are recent examples. From time to time, the members of the Committee meet with the Finance and Social Affairs Ministers to form the Tripartite Conference which has a wide ranging discussion of socio-economic issues and one advantage of these discussions is to keep the Community institutions in touch with industrial opinion and to elucidate problems to which the Community may have to respond.

A second major concern of the Community is to promote the notion of worker directors and this is an interesting example of the connection between social goals and other aspects of policy, for it is an essential ingredient of the move to launch a European company which is considered necessary as an alternative legislative base for companies encompassing the West European market, but which do not find national legislation suitable. Such a proposal has perforce to include provisions concerning worker representatives on supervisory boards in order to prevent national legislation being undermined. This, in turn, leads onto the argument that, for competitive reasons, it is necessary to require such arrangements to be incorporated into national legislation where they do not yet exist. Attempts to achieve this ran into considerable opposition, particularly in countries like the UK where there is no great interest in such a move and, indeed, is one which not all union opinion supports. It demonstrates the great sensitivity of the concept of harmonisation in the social sphere which at first sight can appear appealing.

Two other long-standing policies of the Community in the field of industrial relations should be mentioned. One is the attempt to promote a policy of asset holding amongst employees and the second the promotion of industrial health and safety. The latter was established from the start as an important function of the ECSC and an active programme of research and standard setting has existed since 1951. Special Commissions exist for the steel industry and for mining — the latter now includes offshore oil wells and a large number of recommendations have been issued by the Commission.

Industrial health and safety figures in the Treaty of Rome as one of the matters where the Commission can encourage collaboration. It has an active programme and may propose directives to the Council. However, over the years, Community interest has included more general issues such as the pollution of the environment through smoke, the dumping of waste, the fouling of seas and rivers, the effect of modern industrial life styles on human beings, the social costs of industry such as the effects of night work and the incidence of alcoholism. Its span of interest has extended greatly and in 1977 the nine Ministers of Health held their first (and so far only) meeting under Community auspices. Although there is no direct mention of health in the Treaty of Rome, it has in fact arrived on the agenda for its own reasons. The environmental issue is one which clearly cannot be controlled in a national context alone, whilst the interest the Community displays in social security, and its cost, has always included questions of access to personal health care. The experience suggests that, as social matters come to be seen as requiring consideration at Community level, they will find their way there even if there is no clear mandate in the Treaty.

An Overall View

Whilst it can fairly be claimed that the Community is active in the social field, the measures comprise a miscellany rather than a coherent social policy informed by a few compelling themes. Great efforts have gone into the creation of a positive programme despite a rather uncertain Treaty base. One disadvantage of this legal position is the corresponding lack of a sound financial base. Resources for social policy are derived in several ways. The social fund has its own funding through the budget, whilst research into industrial safety in coal and steel, housing programmes for workers in these two industries and work in the collaborative field are all funded separately, so there is little financial incentive for the overall consideration of social policy as a unity. Lack of coherence between the use of social, agricultural and regional funds was to be cured by placing them under the responsibility of a single Commissioner, but the price of this is the continued atomisation of the social field itself. It has to be remembered, of course, that social policy does in fact deal with a wide variety of circumstances and that too much coherence cannot be expected even from a developed national policy.

It is useful, nevertheless, to try to pull some general themes out of these activities albeit at the risk of pressing the evidence too far.

A considerable range of work can be described as *minimum standard setting*. The precision of these standards is, however, variable. A directive such as that on basic standards of protection against ionising radiation is very specific in its rules (Dir. 76/579/Euratom; *Official Journal of the European Community*, L 187, 12 July 1976). Other directives which fall into this group allow greater flexibility of procedure. It includes the directive on the arrangements to be followed in the case of mass dismissals, which provides a definition of the term variable according to the size of the firm, establishes the principle of prior discussion with representatives of the workforce and insists upon prior notification of the public employment services. The equal pay directive also falls into this category.

This approach appears to have replaced the earlier, heated discussion of the harmonisation, or even equalisation, of social standards which appeared implicit in Article 117 of the Treaty of Rome. The impracticability of such an aim, the problems of definition and of comparability, the difficulty of deciding what was to be compared and the lack of conviction that it was a particularly useful objective, were all obstacles to its pursuit in the early years. During the 1960s, there appeared some evidence that, in broad terms, social security expenditure was naturally aligning both in the sense of a steady expansion and in the sense of the percentage of national income devoted to it, although the trend of expenditures on various ends such as retirement pensions or family allowances showed no such feature. During the 1970s, however, this trend does not seem to have been continued, no doubt reflecting the lack of convergence in the economic fortunes of the members (see Appendix for some social security statistics).

A second feature is the *support of investigatory activities, research and pilot schemes*. In financial terms this is modest, but it enables a wide range of projects to be supported either entirely or in part and whilst some of these may be no different in kind from work supported by other bodies, it helps promote cross-national studies and work which entails a fresh approach to old problems. The anti-poverty programme is a good example of this category, as is also the small budget of the social fund for the support of pilot projects.

A recent tendency has been to create 'European Institutes' for study and research in cities other than Brussels. It remains to be seen if these perform functions different from those that are carried out by the Social Affairs Directorate itself. In December 1974, the Council decided to establish a European Centre for the Development of Vocational Training to give new impetus to the creation of a common policy through trying to harmonise national systems and promote new initiatives. This began work in 1977 in Berlin. In 1975, a Foundation for the Improvement of Living and Working conditions was set up in Dublin and, again, is primarily a study unit. The third venture has been slower, but Council agreement has been given to support a project of the European Trades Union Confederation to set up a European Trades Union Institute for the study of trade union affairs.

Such work merges into the *general promotional field*. A body like the social fund only provides a small amount of assistance in comparison with the costs borne by national governments, so that its value must depend upon the influence this grant aid carries. The fact that certain costs can be shared with the social fund is intended to stimulate national governments into activity in certain directions rather than others. However, since the main decisions about the fund's objectives are taken in the first place by governments, this influence is hardly likely to produce very startling changes in national schemes.

However, a great deal of the social policy of the Community can be described as a stimulation to governments, whether through grant aid, discussions of social policy issues at international level, or through support to non-governmental agencies. Fresh ideas, new ways of handling problems, perhaps a slightly quicker response to changing problems and their identification, comprise the sort of advantages to be looked for in this category.

Some consideration must be given to the role of social policy in the *wider context of Community policies.* It is now a long time since the Commission began to argue that, as the Community developed positive policies in the economic field, so it would increasingly influence social conditions and, for this reason alone, it required a more active social policy (Lévi-Sandri 1968). Since the time of the Paris summit conference, it has been formally recognised that a goal such as economic and monetary union cannot be pursued without adequate consideration to the social consequences and this view has been strongly argued by the Commission. It has attempted to demonstrate the connection between economic and social policies through its work on the social budget. This is not, as might be supposed, an assessment of the money required by Community social policies, but the aggregation of national estimates of current and future social spending so that its importance in economic development may be discussed. Article 4 of the social fund is motivated by the same concept of the necessary inter-relationship between social and economic goals.

However, the history of social policy, whether in general or in particular subjects, shows how strong is the grip of national states and how unwilling they are to allow the development of policy at Community level. Thus the real brake on development is the lack of political will, rather than the uncertainties of the treaties. The new initiatives that occurred during the period 1969–74 depended upon the willingness of members to support them and for political reasons they were prepared to do so. At the Hague conference in 1969 they were anxious to show the Community as a developing entity for the future, at Paris in 1972 to capitalise on the mood of 'disenchantment with growth' and to mobilise opinion behind a Community seen to be socially responsible. Subsequent faltering results from the current preoccupation with unemployment and inflation which are not matters that Community social policy as such can greatly influence.

The main lesson of developments so far seems then to be that the Community is likely to edge forward very slowly in the social field, dependent on occasions when, for their own reasons, states see it as opportune to allow a new initiative. The history of attempts to develop a social policy shows states as reluctant to allow changes which cost money and this makes any Commission proposal very vulnerable in the absence of a Community social budget. States have shown that they dislike too many direct contacts to grow between the Commission and non-governmental agencies and have managed to retain a grasp on channels of communication as in the case of social fund grant aid. There remains a dormant conflict between the Commission and the Council concerning how far collaboration under Article 118 can be insisted upon and whether the Council has an obligation to activate Article 235 to ensure action when no other means exist. At the present time, specific, concrete initiatives making for an incremental social policy seem more likely than grand policies.

A reflection on how far social policy has developed since 1951, or even since 1957, leads to a realisation that there is now a Community dimension to be considered on matters of health, social security and working conditions. Change does occur, albeit slowly. Broad social issues such as the migration of workers, the pollution of the environment, industrial welfare and democracy, issues of competitive cost, consumer protection and regional subsidy have all now to be considered on a wider than national basis. Issues such as lower, or more flexible retirement ages, a shorter working week and job creation schemes as means of alleviating unemployment are now freely discussed at Brussels level. When it is remembered, however, that the next major political act of the Community is the enlargement of the group, with countries whose per capita income is lower than the existing average, then states will doubtless consider that any necessary aids to make enlargement possible constitute the maximum they are prepared to offer to make possible new initiatives in the social field.

Thus the main theme of social policy in the near future is likely to be the contribution that can be made to the support of financial policies.

There is a curious duality about Community social policy which makes it hard to assess. It contains large, inspirational goals along with work of the utmost detail and highly specialised content. It is difficult to trace the path towards the former by immersion in the latter and the lack of instant appeal from which so much of the work suffers can lead to the assumption that the detail is insignificant.

The Community institutions, and particularly the Commission, can however claim a great advantage, for they are in a better position than governmental institutions to identify the broad processes of social and economic change occurring in Western Europe and to consider the extent to which the social policy response must be one which is taken in concert rather than independently. It is clearer today than was once the case that there are indeed such issues, but their consideration only requires a standardisation of policy in discrete circumstances.

Statistical Appendix

Table 15.1 *National and Foreign Employees in Employment 1976 (thousands)*

	Total employees (1)	Foreign employees (2)	Community nationals (3)	(2) as % of (1)	(3) as % of (1)
Belgium	3,092	250	148	8.1	4.8
W. Germany	19,939	1,937	403	9.7	2.0
France	16,963	1,900	300	11.2	1.8
Italy	13,759	59	24	0.4	0.2
Luxembourg	136	49	31	35.6	22.9
Netherlands	3,857	175	55	4.5	1.4
Denmark	1,965	39	13	2.0	0.7
Ireland	722	2.6	0.9	0.4	0.1
United Kingdom	22,491	1,665	632	7.4	2.8
Total Community	82,924	6,077	1,607	7.3	1.9

Source: European Commission, *Foreign Employees in Employment V/512/77 EN (fin)*. For necessary qualifications of above figures, consult this document.

Table 15.2 *Unemployment at End of Fourth Quarter 1976*

	Total	Foreign	Rate total	Rate foreign
Belgium	260,590	36,680	9.8	—
Denmark	144,600	—	7.0	—
W. Germany	1,089,935	95,042	4.8	4.6
France	1,036,889	95,679	6.0	—
Ireland	114,433	—	10.2	—
Italy	1,212,440	—	6.2	—
Luxembourg	696	—	0.5	—
Netherlands	217,611	10,317	5.3	—
United Kingdom	1,316,000	—	5.7	—

N.B. Denmark, Ireland, Italy and UK are unable to return unemployment amongst foreigners.

Source: As for Table 15.1

Table 15.3 *Social Protection Expenditure as % of GDP 1976*

W. Germany	France	Italy	Neth.	Belg.	Lux.	UK	Irel.	Denmark
27.4	23.1	23.8	28.3	25.1	23.7	19.6	19.2	25.3

Table 15.4 *Sources of Receipts for Social Protection 1976 (%)*

	W. Germany	France	Italy	Neth.	Belg.	Lux.	UK	Irel.	Den.
Enterprises	33	46	55	28	36	27	27	—	6
Central government	32	26	23	22	38	37	41	84	56
Local government	7	4	4	7	2	4	7	—	32
Households	27	22	13	34	21	25	17	15	3
Social Institutions	2	2	3	9	2	7	8	0	3
Other	0	0	2	0	1	1	0	0	0

Table 15.5 Social Protection Benefits 1976 (%)

	W. Germany	France	Italy	Netherlands	Belgium	Luxembourg	UK	Ireland	Denmark
Sickness	29	28	25	30	24	24	26	35	30
Invalidity, physical and mental disability	8	5	20	17	7	9	9	5	10
Industrial injury and disease	3	4	2	–	4	6	1	1	1
Old Age	28	37	31	31	38	37	44	33	32
Survivors	15	6	6	5	incl. in Old Age	15	3	incl. in Old Age	1
Maternity	1	2	1	0	1	1	2	2	1
Family	9	13	9	10	14	8	9	11	11
Placing, vocational guidance	2	0	–	–	1	–	0	–	1
Unemployment	3	4	2	6	8	0	6	10	10
Housing	1	–	–	–	–	0	–	–	–
Misc.	1	1	3	0	4	0	1	2	3

Source: Tables 3—5, Eurostat, Basic Statistics of the Community. Taken from tables 126, 125, 124. It will be appreciated that nil returns may result from e.g. late national returns or definitional problems which prevent isolation of expenditure on particular items. They should not be taken to mean no service is provided.

References

Collins, D., *The European Communities: The Social Policy of the First Phase*, Martin Robertson 1975.

Fogarty, M., *Work and Industrial Relations in the European Community*, PEP/ Chatham House, London, European Series No. 24, 1975.

Lévi-Sandri, L., 'Pour une politique sociale moderne dans la Communauté Européenne'. Reprint of speech to European Parliament, 13 March 1968.

Shanks, M., *European Social Policy, Today and Tomorrow*, Pergamon Press 1977.

Agence Europe, for various years.

Comité intergouvernemental créé par la conférence de Messina, *Rapport des Chefs de Délégation aux Ministres des Affaires Étrangères*, Brussels 1956 (The Spaak Report).

European Commission, Action programme in favour of migrant workers and their families, *Bulletin of the European Communities*, Supplement 3/76.

European Commission, Guidelines for the management of the European Social Fund, *Official Journal of the Community*, C 141, 15 June 1977.

European Commission, *Bulletin of the European Communities*, for various years.

European Commission, *Official Journal of the European Community*, Legislation series (L), Information series (C), for various years.

Eurostat, for various years.

16

Factor Mobility with Specific Reference to the Accounting Profession

A M EL-AGRAA and
P S GOODRICH

It was established in Chapter 1 that the EEC is more than just a customs union, since it allows for free intra-EEC movement of all factors of production and for the harmonisation and coordination of economic, social and other policies. The aim of this chapter is to examine the implications of free factor mobility inside the EEC, giving particular emphasis to the accounting profession. Accountancy is singled out because it is one of the few areas in which the EEC has made some progress. However, special aspects of capital and entrepreneurship mobility are discussed in the chapters on European monetary integration and competition policies respectively.

Labour Mobility and Economic Theory

According to basic economic principles, labour as a factor of production would tend to move to where it can fetch the highest possible 'net advantage' or reward. This reward would usually comprise two essential elements: 'transfer earnings' and 'economic rent'. Transfer earnings refer to the amount the factor needs to earn in order to stay in existing employment and economic rent refers to any sum exceeding transfer earnings.

The relative magnitude of these two elements depends on the elasticity of supply of the factor being considered. If the factor is specific in nature (can only perform one function) and is completely inelastic in supply, what it would earn (which would depend entirely on the demand for the factor's services) is entirely economic rent. If the factor is non-specific (can perform more than one function) and has a perfectly elastic supply, its entire reward will be transfer earnings. Factors which are not very specific in nature and are neither less than perfectly elastic, nor infinitely inelastic, in supply would tend to have rewards which are partially transfer earnings and partially economic rent.

The distinction between transfer earnings and economic rent is of great significance when factor mobility is under consideration. A factor of production will not remain in the same occupation if its reward is less than in an alternative job, i.e. its reward falls short of its transfer earnings. It follows therefore that free factor mobility can be encouraged only if factors are offered rewards in excess of their transfer earnings.

However, this does not mean that factors of production can easily be induced to move freely by the adoption of a system of differential tranfer earnings. There are two basic reasons for this. Firstly, the transfer earnings of a factor are not purely pecuniary in nature. For example, apart from wages and salaries, a host of considerations enter into the calculations regarding the employment of labour: housing provision, medical care, income tax, social security payments, pension schemes, proximity to 'social grouping', the need for further training, and so forth. Hence the concept of a 'net advantage' referred to at the beginning of this section includes both pecuniary and non-pecuniary elements. The sum of these two elements ultimately determines labour mobility.

Secondly, even if labour possesses perfect rationality and foresight and can therefore be induced to move according to differential advantage, it will still be necessary to make a trade-off between the extra reward and the disutility of movement (Meade 1955, pp. 358 and 372). Hence, differential rewards could exist if the disutility of movement exceeds them.

In very general terms, given the above considerations, labour is more mobile within the same occupational category within the same proximity. It is less mobile, even within the same proximity, between occupational categories, since the cost of *retraining* has to be taken into consideration. Moreover, within the same occupational category, labour is less mobile between proximities and is even less so between occupational categories *and* proximities. Professor Brown (1972, p. 253) writing in the context of regional mobility within the UK states:

> ... mobility in the sense of propensity to change address is quite high; households move, on the average, more than once in ten years, making about six million changes of address by individuals annually. Three-quarters

of all moves within the country are, however, over distances of less than ten
miles, and only about one-eighth of the total, involving in England and Wales
about 1½% of the population (three-quarters of a million) each year, are
interregional. The Labour Mobility Survey shows most short-distance moves
to be motivated by housing considerations, long-range moves to be connected mostly with change of employment, or, to a smaller extent, with
retirement.

It is no surprise therefore when Adam Smith noted that 'man is of all
sorts of baggage the most difficult to be transported'.

If factors of production were perfectly mobile, what would be the
economic implications? If labour could move to the location of the
highest possible 'net advantage', then areas of relatively high marginal
productivity would attract the most efficient labour. This would
result in certain regions of the economy being depressed and depopu-
lated — see the chapters on the EEC regional policy and European
monetary integration. Provided no conscious regional policy exists,
the overall results of this tendency would be to increase efficiency and
therefore national and, in this case, Community product and income.

Labour mobility has implications for trade too. According to
orthodox international trade theory, the international (interregional)
exchange of commodities, where there exists complete lack of international (interregional) factor mobility, would, under extremely
restrictive assumptions,[1] eliminate any factor reward differentials
that initially prevailed between nations or regions — the Factor-Price
Equalisation Theorem. Hence the exchange of commodities would
produce results similar to those achieved through factor mobility.
This tends to imply that free international (interregional) factor
mobility would tend to discourage trade.

In reality this need not be true. Firstly, neither process is ideal:
commodities are exchanged, but are subject to impediments and
transport costs and factors do move, albeit in a minor way. These
two considerations taken together would tend to suggest the weaker
proposition that factor-prices would *move* towards equality. It should
be emphasised, however, that factor prices alone are not synonymous
with 'net advantage'.

Secondly, migration may change the total preferences of the
adopting population, since the immigrants may have preferences for
commodities from their area of origin. More trade may therefore
result, particularly if immigration leads to increases in productivity as
a result of exchanges of technical skills, greater expertise and experience (Balassa 1961, pp. 84–5). Balassa does warn, however, that
labour migration may result in an absolute deterioration of living
standards at the place of emigration, if those left behind are the least
skilled, their age structure is deteriorating and their per capita burden
of taxation is increasing (Balassa 1961, p. 85).

For our purposes, it should be emphasised that the Treaty of Rome specifically calls for the adoption of inducements for factor mobility, assuming that this mobility would increase productivity and encourage Europeanisation. If labour mobility is to be encouraged, it would be necessary to ensure *equal treatment* of labour across the entire EEC. Equal treatment means that both elements of 'net advantage' – the pecuniary and non-pecuniary – must be considered. This, however, does not mean that the EEC must harmonise *every single* element that enters into the calculations; the harmonisation of a sufficiently large 'package' of the elements should produce the desired effect. Eventually (in a complete political union) the harmonisation of *all* elements may become essential. Moreover, unless qualifications are recognised or harmonised across the EEC, factor mobility will not be forthcoming; the real world does not have homogeneous factors of production.

The Provisions in the Treaty

Title III of the Treaty of Rome addresses the problem of the free movement of persons, services and capital. Article 48, which addresses the general question of labour mobility, states that 'freedom of movement for workers shall be secured within the Community by the end of the transition period (1970) at the latest' (Sweet & Maxwell 1972, p. 87).

In addition to the general need for free movement of labour in a common market as an incentive to increased efficiency, there also exists the requirement to provide comparable professional services throughout the Community. The EEC has long recognised this need with respect to the mutual recognition of professional qualifications. Articles 48–66 of the Rome Treaty indicate this as a European Community goal.

Let us first consider briefly the history of the trends in the development of general labour mobility within the EEC, in order to have a general sense of perspective.

In the 1960s, there were three stages in the development of free labour movement (Swann 1978, pp. 144–5). From September 1961 to May 1964, Council Regulation 15 of 1961 applied. Workers needed a permit from the destination member state. After three years on the job, they could renew the work permit for any other occupation in which they were qualified. After another four years, workers could enter any paid work. In addition to the work permit requirements during this 1961–4 period, domestic workers received preference. Jobs had to be advertised for three weeks in the home nation before other member states were notified. Only if an employer asked for a particular worker specifically by name would national preference be waived.

The second phase in the increasing freedom of labour movement within the European Community was from May 1964 to June 1968. Permits continued, but foreign Community workers needed only two years in regular employment before they could compete equally with domestic nationals. Still, the home nations retained a preference outlet. If a member state could justify a need to the European Community, that nation could exercise a 15 day reinstatement of national preference whenever, for example, there was a surplus of workers in a particular field. During this 1964–1968 period, Community workers received preference over non-Community workers.

By July 1968, a year and a half prior to the end of the transitional period, national preferences and work permits had been abolished. The only requirement was a five year residence permit, but these were automatically renewable. Community over non-Community preference was retained.

In order that freedom of labour movement might be feasible as well as permissible, it was generally recognised that workers needed to be informed of job openings and able to transfer social security benefits from one member state to another (Swan 1978, p. 146). Furthermore, one should not underestimate the importance of political policies in the perversion of the intensity and direction of factor movements as predicted by economic theory. Should governments adopt certain wage, fiscal, monetary, and social security policies, these may counter-balance and indeed offset the expected labour movement by changing the 'net advantage'. In addition, political instability and uncertainty may mean that labour moves in an unexpected direction.

The Rome Treaty explicitly addressed the need to harmonise professional rights of establishment and service provision. Article 52 states that:

> restrictions on the freedom of establishment of nationals of a member state in a territory of another member state shall be abolished by progressive stages in the course of the transitional period. Such progressive abolition shall also apply to restrictions on the setting up of agencies, branches or subsidiaries by nationals of any member state established in the territory of any member state.

(Sweet & Maxwell 1972, p. 89)

Article 59 calls for the progressive abolition of restrictions to provide services within the European Community. Nationals of one member state should be free to provide services in member states other than the one in which they are established. Article 60 defines 'services' in general as 'normally provided for remuneration'; in particular to include 'activities of the professions'. Furthermore, conditions imposed by a member state on service providers within its own territory should apply equally to citizens of other member states as well as its own citizens (Sweet & Maxwell 1972, p. 91). In line with these stated objectives of the European Community, there has been significant progress in recent years with respect to the following professions: architects, doctors, footballers, lawyers, nurses, and veterinarians. These are discussed in the *Bulletin of the European Communities*. (For architects – 11/1977, p. 21 and 12/1978, p. 33. For doctors – 11/1977, p. 21; 2/1978, p. 29; 11/1978, p. 23. For footballers – 2/1978, p. 29. For lawyers – 3/1977, p. 17. For nurses – 6/1977, p. 32. For veterinarians – 4/1978, p. 32; 12/1978, p. 33.)

The Accounting Profession

Let us now consider specifically the case of the accounting profession with regard to EEC policy. Accountancy especially illustrates the problems inherent in trying to harmonise standards and training in a European profession characterised by great diversity. The accountancy profession in the nine member states of the European Community varies considerably in structure, quality and scope. Harmonisation, therefore, requires considerable deliberation and skill. Thus, it presents a significant challenge to the EEC policy-makers. The manner in which the Community has proceeded with these delicate negotiations is a measure of the patience and skill of the Common Market.

Article 2 of the Treaty of Rome had set forth ambitious goals in terms of economic integration:

> The Community shall have as its task, by establishing a common market and progressively approximating the economic policies of member states, to promote throughout the Community a harmonious development of economic activities, a continuous and balanced expansion, an increase in stability, an accelerated raising of the standard of living and closer relations between the states belonging to it.
>
> (Sweet & Maxwell 1972, p. 72)

In order to accomplish this 'harmonious development of economic activities' with relation to accountancy, certain company law 'professional' directives were to be addressed to how accountants performed their work, and where they could establish themselves and offer services (Reydel 1976, p. 256).

One of the crucial problems that the European Community faced was to overcome the great diversity of accounting quality in Europe. Table 16.1 indicates the divergent assessments given to the quality of reports and accounts within the European Community. This difference was partially due to the different levels of training and status accorded

Table 16.1 *Assessment of Quality of Reports and Accounts, by Country**

Country	Very high	High	Fair	Poor	Total
Belgium-Luxembourg	—	2	10	7	19
France	—	3	15	11	29
West Germany	2	8	19	2	31
Italy	—	1	2	20	23
Netherlands	9	20	2	—	31
Switzerland	1	1	7	15	24
United Kingdom	12	17	1	—	30

* Figures refer to the number of managers and analysts reporting

Source: Corner and Stafford 1977, p. 113.

the accountants in different member states. This diversity of accounting quality could adversely affect the confidence of investors in certain areas of the Community. Accordingly, in the early 1960s, the European Commission started the 'professional' directives to encourage consistency and harmony through free establishment and free service provision within the EEC. Presumably, the best qualified accountants would migrate to areas of higher marginal productivity, thereby harmonising professional standards and increasing overall efficiency.

On 18 December 1961, a general programme of the European Commission was inaugurated to reduce restrictions both to freedom of establishment and of services provision. Nearly ten years later, on 6 July 1970, the Commission published a draft proposal for the liberalisation of the accountancy profession and submitted this proposal to the European Parliament. On 28 July 1970, the Council consulted the Parliament with regard to two items:

(a) the rights of establishment and to provide services for financiers, economists and accountants, and
(b) the qualifications of these professions.

On 11 August 1970, the Parliamentary Committees for Legal Affairs and Economic Affairs started to examine the proposal.

The EEC Accountants Study Group of the European Union of Professional Accountants, Economists, and Financiers (UEC) rendered its opinion on the Parliamentary directive on 21 January 1971. The UEC noted that the proposal applied to the auditing activity handled by a wide range of professions including not only accountants, but also economists and financiers. While the proposed Eighth Directive does list the activities it envisages should be covered, the text of the 1970 proposal used the word 'especially' (*notamment*) in introducing this list of activities. This indicated that the scope of the EEC intervention might prove to be limitless.

The 3 March 1971 opinion of the Economic Affairs Committee deplored the excessive delay in the harmonisation and liberalisation of the financial, economic and accounting professions (European Parliament, *Documents de Séance*, 30/1971, p. 67). The Economic Committee felt that the activities of auditors were of crucial importance to the functioning of the Common Market and the pursuit of economic integration. The Committee argued that by freeing accountants from restrictions inhibiting the performance of their duties outside their own domestic jurisdiction, the vital mutual international confidence in accounting activities would be enhanced. The current situation undermined the creation of a harmonious economic ensemble carved from the economic integration of the member states of the European Community. Thus, the Economic Affairs Committee recommended the greatest possible relaxation of restrictions while, at the same time, safeguarding national controls. The Committee noted with regret that the proposition failed to include provisions for harmonising certification procedures among the member states. No provision was made for harmonising the required service in the face of a nation's legal, administrative or regulatory constraints. In the long term, the Committee argued that professional profiles and study programmes as well as harmonisation arrangements should be drawn up *for* the accounting profession. The Economic Affairs Committee obviously hoped to take up the leadership in the coordination and harmonisation of such qualifications. Direction and guidance was to come from the institutions of the European Community. On 8 April 1971, noting the comments of the Economic Affairs Committee, the Legal Affairs Committee unanimously adopted the proposal (European Parliament, *Documents de Séance*, 30/1971, p. 2).

Since the acceptance of the report by the Legal Affairs Committee in 1971, there was a significant time span during the 1970s when no further formal action was taken. Ultimately, the *definitive* 1971 Directive was found to be too difficult to implement and was withdrawn. What has emerged as the Eighth Directive Proposal is a *transitional* Directive still in the process of negotiation between the Council, Commission, and Parliament in autumn 1979.

During this gap in the activities of the Community institutions between 1971 and 1978, the *Union Européene des Experts Comptables Economiques et Financiers* (UEC) has continued its attempts to unify the European accountancy profession (Reydel 1978, p. 30).

Professor Gerhard Mueller has called the UEC, 'probably the most effective international accounting organisation' (1967, p. 242). The UEC is often consulted on accounting matters by highly placed European decision-makers. The European Commission has always been willing to listen to the EEC Accountants Study Group of the

UEC on matters that have no political consequences. Professor Robert Parker has observed the irony that 'all that is required is agreement among the professional representatives from nine member states!' (1977, p. 70). The UEC recognises that much work remains to be done, not only to harmonise the procedures, techniques and principles of accounting, but also to harmonise the qualifications of accountants to enhance the movement of its members throughout the European Community. The UEC, like the EEC, has adopted a policy of 'low profile', non-antagonistic, incremental progress towards change. It recognises that national interests must always be respected. Technical arguments in favour of change must often yield to political realities.

On 24 April 1978, the European Commission submitted to the Council of Ministers a proposed Eighth Directive on Company Law in accordance with Article 54(3)(g) of the Treaty of Rome:

> The Council and the Commission shall carry out the duties devolving upon them . . . by coordinating to the necessary extent the safeguards which, for the protection of the interests of members and others, are required by member states of companies or firms . . . with a view to making such safeguards equivalent throughout the Community.
>
> (Sweet & Maxwell 1972, p. 90)

This directive deals with the approval of persons who are concerned with the carrying out of statutory audits of the accounts of limited liability companies (*Bulletin of the European Communities*, Supplement 4/78).

This proposed Eighth Directive is essentially a building block and corollary to the Fourth, Fifth and Seventh Directives on Company Law.

The Fourth Directive, adopted by the Council on 26–27 June 1978, obliges limited liability companies to have an audit of their annual accounts by persons so authorised by their own national legal systems to carry out such audits (*Official Journal of the Community*, 14 August 1978). The proposed Fifth Directive will require auditors to be independent of the company, to be nominated and approved by judicial and administrative authority. The proposed Seventh Directive will augment the Fourth Directive with relation to group accounts (*Official Journal of the Community*, 13 December 1972 & 2 June 1976).

The Eighth Directive postulates that a high level of theoretical knowledge would be necessary for accountants to audit the financial accounts of limited liability companies and states that 'member states will be able to approve only those persons who pass an examination of professional competence at graduate level' (*Bulletin of the European Communities*, Supplement 4/78). The Directive allows member states to set forth their own transitional provisions with auditors who had been trained under the old system and could not therefore easily comply with the conditions of the new directive. It also recognised that those who have lengthy practical experience in the fields of law, finance and accountancy might be exempted from the need to prove their theoretical expertise.

The Eighth Directive establishes provisions for those persons who could be approved to carry out statutory audits of the annual accounts of various types of limited liability companies throughout the European Community. These persons would be approved 'only after having attained university entrance level, followed a course of advanced training and passed an examination of professional competence at graduate or equivalent level which is organised or recognised by the State' (*Bulletin of the European Communities*, Supplement 4/78, pp. 7–8).

The proposed directive outlines the requisite curriculum for the test of theoretical knowledge in Article Five. It allows university graduates in any of the subjects contained in the statutory curriculum to be exempted from those tests of theoretical knowledge which were covered by the degree. This, of course, has implications for the freedom of universities teaching accounting and finance. Ultimately, they may be pressured into conforming to the European Community curriculum as proposed by the Eighth Directive in Article Five. Theoretical accounting knowledge must cover the following subjects – auditing, critical evaluation of balance sheets and income statements, general accounting, group accounting problems, cost and management accounting, internal auditing, company law (tax, general, criminal). Theoretical auditing knowledge shall encompass – principles of civil, commercial, social law; information systems and computer science; general, business and financial economics; mathematics and statistics; and the basic principles of the financial management of business enterprise (*Bulletin of the European Communities*, Supplement 4/78, p. 8).

In addition to this theory test, there would be be a practical exam which would take place after a minimum of three years' practical training with an auditor who had been approved in accordance with the directive. This practical training could take place after the examination of professional competence had been passed.

Like the 1971 proposal, the Eighth Directive is widespread in its scope. It includes the fields of law, finance and accountancy. It allows generous transitional exemptions for current practitioners in the member states.

The member states are required to publish lists of those qualified to carry out audits. This list is to be amended regularly and published annually. Each member state must supply the Commission with a list of exams that are deemed equivalent to the state-run exams of professional competence.

In relation to the free movement of labour, Article 10 of the proposed Eighth Directive states that 'member states *may* approve, to carry out the statutory audits, persons who have obtained qualifications outside the EEC which are deemed to be equivalent if approval has already been granted in this latter state according to the provisions of this directive' (*Bulletin of the European Communities*, Supplement 4/78, p. 9). In addition to these qualifications, prospective auditors were to prove that they have *sufficient* legal expertise in the member state in which they are to practice.

When the Commission forwarded the Eighth Directive to the European Parliament in the spring of 1979, several important modifications were made to Article 10 — see table 16.2.

The important statement that qualifications from another member state would always be considered equivalent was deleted. In addition,

Table 16.2 *A comparison of the text of the Eighth Directive proposed by the European Commission and amended by the European Parliament*

Commission Proposal	Parliamentary Amendment
Article 10	
1. A member state, where necessary by way of derogation from Article 4, may approve to carry out the statutory audits referred to in Article 1 persons who fulfil the following two conditions:	1. A member state, where necessary by way of derogation from Article 4, may approve to carry out the statutory audits referred to in Article 1 persons who fulfil the following two conditions:
(a) they have obtained, elsewhere than in that member state, qualifications which are deemed by the competent authorities to be objectively equivalent to those required under this directive. Qualifications obtained in another member state are however always to be considered equivalent if approval has already been granted in this latter state according to the provisions of this directive;	(a) they have obtained, elsewhere than in that member state, qualifications which are deemed by the competent authorities to be (*1 word deleted*) equivalent to those required under this directive (*30 words deleted*):
(b) they have proved that they have sufficient legal knowledge to carry out statutory audits in the member state in which approval is sought.	(b) they have proved that they have *the stipulated* legal knowledge to carry out statutory audits in the member state in which approval is sought.

Source: European Parliament, *Working Document* 173/79, p. 13.

the required legal knowledge was to be *stipulated* by the member states. These two changes stopped the proposed directive short of direct harmonisation. Member states could still preclude certain other member states' auditors from practising within their boundaries if they wished.

It should also be noted that Article 10, unlike the other provisions of the proposed Eighth Directive, is not time-bound. While the other provisions all envisage a transitional period for the implementation of the auditing proposals, Article 10 does not.

Furthermore, Article 10 does not facilitate the new arrangements for statutory audits. Auditors may be approved to practise in two ways – first, the auditor may have attained his qualifications outside the European Community and these qualifications are deemed equivalent by a member state; or second, the auditor may have attained his qualifications in another member state. Thus, the Directive allows people trained outside the Community to continue practising within the Community (subject to the approval of the relevant member state). But one of the original aims of the Eighth Directive was to allow intra-Community labour mobility for those who had been trained in accordance with the directive. But the Parliament's objections were such that member states were accorded protection 'so that a member state is not forced to recognise the qualifications of another member state when such recognition is not reciprocated' (European Parliament, *Working Document* 173/79, p. 25).

The Legal Affairs Committee of the European Parliament essentially held that the aim of the proposed Eighth Directive is to increase the level of professional training within the Community and set forth uniform conditions within the member states. It would seem that, given the differences in the qualifications in a number of the member states and the resulting jealousy and conflict between those states with regard to their qualifications, that Parliament has been reluctant to concede that 'qualifications obtained in another member state are . . . *always* to be considered equivalent'.

In the explanatory memorandum published by the European Commission, it was stated that the purpose of the Eighth Directive proposal was to harmonise the minimum qualifications required in the member states for persons performing 'statutory audits of the annual accounts of limited liability companies' (Blanquet 1978, p. 302).

In a study of comparative legal accounting requirements in the European Community, Françoise Blanquet, a Principal Administrator to the EEC Commission declared that:

> the level of qualifications for persons responsible for carrying out . . .
> (limited liability company) audits is very different between the various
> countries making up the European Economic Community . . . People are,

> after all, entitled to expect that, throughout the Community, companies
> subject to statutory audit are in fact properly audited by experts fully
> qualified to carry out such assignments — which is in fact far from the
> truth.
>
> (Blanquet 1978, p. 302)

By rectifying these faults in the present system, the proposed
Eighth Directive would protect the interests of shareholders and investors by ensuring a training scheme for auditors that would upgrade
the present standards. This would promote confidence in European
Community investments as a whole. Thus, outside capital would be
encouraged to invest in the Community and intra-Community capital
would have more mobility through better confidence in financial
reports. This would ultimately increase the overall efficiency of the
allocation of resources throughout the European Community.

The purpose of the Eighth Directive was:

> not to establish a system for the mutual recognition of the degrees, dip-
> lomas, and other qualifications required to carry out this activity, nor does
> it aim to bring about the effective exercise of freedom to provide services
> or the freedom of establishment of a person authorised in one member
> state who wishes to practise in another member state. However the fact
> that this proposal for a directive will already have harmonised the qualifi-
> cations required for authorisation to be obtained in a member state will
> certainly facilitate the effective attainment of freedom of establishment
> and freedom to provide services with regard to the carrying out of statutory
> audits of company accounts.
>
> The purpose of this directive is not to harmonise the qualifications required
> of members of a particular profession nor to lay the conditions governing
> entry to a particular profession.
>
> (*Bulletin of the European Communities*, 4/78, pp. 12–13)

Conclusion

With characteristic understatement, the European Commission minimised the goals and objectives of the proposed Eighth Directive. After
all, the Commission is a political animal — and politics has been called
'the art of the possible'. Thus outwardly, the Commission states
attainable objectives (even if they desire more) so as to minimise
its risk of failure and continue its incremental progress toward
economic and political integration.

Yet, the goal of increased labour mobility remains unresolved with
regard to the European accounting profession. The European Community, through its directives on company law, has attempted to
resolve the inherent contradictions of diversity and harmonisation.
European accountancy and financial reporting remain nationalistic in
spite of the efforts of the UEC and the true internationalism of the

'Big 8' accounting firms (Parker 1977, p. 71 and Lafferty pp. 373 & 374). It would appear that much remains to be done before unity, uniformity and mutually recognised qualifications become the norm in Europe.

By the introduction of minimum qualifications, at least the EEC will correct the present situation where auditing in Europe may be deemed as comprising *different* occupational categories because of the great differences in quality and training. By harmonisation, it will effectively become one occupational category. The need for retraining would be eliminated if an auditor desired to migrate from one member state to another. This would reduce the costs of the move to that auditor and thus increase the propensity to move. Therefore, labour mobility should be increased even though the proposed Eighth Directive stops short of the mutual recognition of qualifications.

Thus, this minimal progress – a harmonisation of minimum qualifications rather than the mutual recognition of degrees and qualifications – may in fact represent a significant accomplishment.

Michael Lafferty has identified an increased trend toward increasing barriers and restrictions to labour mobility in the EEC countries on the part of local accounting professions. These local groups often seek to impose 'short-sighted restrictions with meagre gains' instead of seeing the 'long-term benefits of mutual co-operation' (1975, p. 376). Perhaps the proposed Eighth Directive of the EEC will force the selfish, short-sighted nationalists to become more perceptive. Then, the economic advantages and efficiencies of free labour mobility may have a good chance of success.

Notes

1 The theory (Samuelson–Hechscher–Ohlin) is based on five main assumptions: international trade free from any trade impediments and transport costs, perfect factor mobility nationally and perfect immobility internationally, perfect competition in both product and factor markets, commodities produced under the same production function everywhere, linear and homogeneous production functions (i.e. factors are rewarded according to their marginal productivities) etc. – see Samuelson (1948, 1949), Bhagwati (1967), Johnson (1961) and Batra (1973).

References

Balassa, B., *The Theory of Economic Integration*, Allen and Unwin 1962.
Batra, R.N., *Studies in the Pure Theory of International Trade*, Macmillan Press 1973.
Bhagwati, J., The pure theory of international trade, *Economic Journal*, vol. 74, 1964.

Blanquet, F., Proposed eighth directive concerning the approval of persons responsible for carrying out statutory audits of the annual financial statements of limited liability companies, *Journal UEC*, June 1978.

Brown, A.J., *The Framework of Regional Economics in the United Kingdom*, Macmillan Press 1974.

Corner, D.C. and Stafford, D.C., *Open-End Investment Funds in the EEC and Switzerland*, Macmillan Press 1977.

Johnson, H.G., *International Trade and Economic Growth*, Allen and Unwin 1961.

Lafferty, M., *Accounting in Europe*, Woodhead-Faulkner 1975.

Meade, J.E., *Trade and Welfare: the Theory of Economic Policy*, vol. 2, Oxford University Press 1955.

Muller, G.G., *International Accounting*, Macmillan New York, 1967.

Parker, R.H., Accounting in Europe, in Carsberg, B. and Hope, A., *Current Issues in Accounting*, Philip Allan 1977.

Reydel, A., The accountant and the Community texts, *Journal UEC*, April 1976.

Reydel, A., Harmonisation of accounting and auditing practice in the last five years, *Journal UEC*, no. 1, 1978.

Samuelson, P.A., International trade and the equalisation of factor prices, *The Economic Journal*, vol. 58, 1948.

Samuelson, P.A., International factor-price equalisation once again, *The Economic Journal*, vol. 59, 1949.

Swann, D., *The Economics of the Common Market*, Penguin Modern Economic Texts 1978.

European Community Treaties, Sweet and Maxwell 1972.

European Commission, *Bulletin of the European Communities*, for various years.
European Commission, *Official Journal of the European Community*, for various years.

European Parliament, *Documents de Séance*, 30/71, 1971.
European Parliament, *Working Document*, 713/79, 1979.

17

External Trade Relations

A M EL-AGRAA

Even though most of the policies so far considered have international implications, particularly those with respect to European monetary integration, they basically relate to the harmonisation and coordination of intra-EEC elements. The purpose of this chapter is to discuss those EEC policies and attitudes which specifically relate to its dealings with the outside world.

The external trade relations of the EEC comprise three basic issues. The first deals with the extent to which the EEC has been able to adopt a common stance in the area of multilateral tariff negotiations (MTN) which were conducted under the auspices of GATT in the Kennedy and Tokyo Rounds and in UNCTAD — the United Nations Conference on Trade and Development. The second relates to the progress made with regard to the association of other countries. The third is concerned with the attitude of the EEC towards new membership, even though this issue relates to more than just trade relations as the discussions so far have clearly indicated — refer to Chapter 1 in particular.

International Negotiations and Agreements

According to the Treaty of Rome (Articles 110—116), the common commercial policy of the EEC was to be based on:

> uniformly established principles, particularly in regard to tariff amendments, to the conclusion of tariffs and trade agreements, to the establishing of uniform practice as regards measures of liberalisation, to export policy and to commercial protective measures including measures to be taken in cases of dumping or subsidies.
>
> (Article 113)

What are the EEC achievements with regard to these principles and expectations, particularly in the area of international commercial negotiations?

As the opening paragraph of this section clearly indicates, the commercial policy of the EEC includes various subjects, one of the most important of which is non-tariff distortions on international trade. These were discussed in some detail in the other policy chapters and, in theoretical terms, in Chapter 4.

As far as tariffs are concerned, negotiations regarding the level of the CET for the EEC were of crucial importance. The original Six were expected to present to GATT in 1960 the CET that would replace their tariffs at the time. According to GATT regulations, the average incidence of the CET should not exceed that of the average incidence of the tariffs of the individual members of the original Six. In 1960 the average incidence of the individuals' tariffs was 9.3% and the average incidence of the CET was 8.2% (Swann 1978, p. 307), so members of GATT were readily accommodating. That was not all, however, since the EEC, in anticipation of the forthcoming Dillon Round (Douglas Dillon was the US Under-Secretary of State at the time) of negotiations (see below), decided to make a provisional tariff reduction of 20%. Hence the initial alignment of the 1960 individual tariffs was made with regard to only 80% of those tariffs. In short, the CET was lower on average not only because of its lower average incidence, but also because the tariffs were aligned at a lower level.

The Kennedy Round of negotiations, which opened in Geneva in May 1964 and concluded in May 1967, was the first opportunity for the EEC to try and adopt a common stance in international tariff bargaining. However, although these negotiations were supposedly international in character, the real hard bargaining was mainly between the US and the EEC, particularly since the latter decided to adopt a more aggressive attitude than during the earlier Dillon Round of negotiations in 1960–2, see Coffey 1976, p. 23.

The US publicly declared that her relationship with the EEC should not be seen as one of rivalry, but of equal partnership — see the text of the speech delivered by President Kennedy in Philadelphia in July 1962 in which he made his famous Declaration of Interdependence. In reality, however, the US basically sought to maintain any industrial advantages it had, but simultaneously wished to make the EEC accessible as a market for her agricultural products — at the time, $1600 million of the US total receipts ($5500) from sales to the EEC were attributable to agricultural commodities (Swann 1978, p. 308).

In any case, the US Congress passed the Trade Expansion Act in October 1962. This Act was intended to extend and to replace the 1934 Act concerning international trade negotiations. The 1962 Act vested in the US President the power to conclude commercial agreements with other countries and to amend US restrictions on imports for a five-year period. The Act also bestowed on the President the power to reduce tariffs by up to 50% and, in products where the EEC and the US together accounted for about 80% of (the non-Communist) world trade, by up to 100%, i.e. to restore free international trade. As a result, the US proposed a 50% *global* tariff reduction, on both industrial and agricultural products, for five years.

The proposal was certainly an improvement, particularly since it amounted to a policy of equal 'linear' tariff reductions accompanied by the adoption of a specific procedure for tariff harmonisation; the previous negotiations under GATT were conducted on the most-favoured nation clause on a commodity by commodity basis, although in the Dillon Round 'partial linear' reductions were introduced (Coffey 1976, p. 24).

Although the EEC expressed a sympathetic attitude to the proposal, it had certain reservations. First, the EEC was not sympathetic to the suggestion that certain commodities should be completely excluded from tariff reductions — certain 'sensitive' products. Secondly, the EEC wanted assurances regarding negotiations about commodities on which the US tariff level was so high that even a 50% tariff reduction was still not very impressive — these were textiles, chemical products and plastics. Thirdly, the EEC sought negotiations about certain US impediments to international trade: the US American Selling Price (ASP) system (applied to chemicals and rubber shoes), whereby the price subjected to a tariff was not the EEC price, but the price of import-substitutes produced in the US — this system resulted in tariffs of up to 170% *ad valorem* for some products; and anti-dumping legislation. Finally, the EEC wanted to negotiate and conclude agreements for agricultural products at the international level for the purpose of protecting and giving international respectability to her newly emerging Common Agricultural Policy.

Given these conflicting interests, the bargaining was hard and agreement was not likely to be reached. Moreover, the proposal of aiming at free international trade in commodities where the EEC and the US conducted between them about 80% of trade was a non-starter since, because the UK was not a member of the EEC at the time, there were not many products in that category. Also, for certain elements (a general agreement for cereals, a system of international grain prices and the organisation of an international food aid programme), the ultimate negotiations took place outside the general framework of GATT (Coffey 1976).

In spite of these drawbacks, certain progress was made. First, 50% tariff reductions were agreed for many products. Secondly, the number of commodities which originally were either totally excluded from tariff reductions or were subject to less than 50% reductions, was reduced. With regard to tariff reductions, the actual information on

Table 17.1(a) *Distribution of the Tariff Rates of the Principal Industrial Countries Before the Kennedy Round Negotiations*

Rate of duty	CET	USA	UK
Duty free	6.2	6.9	8.0
> 0 − ⩽ 5.0%	5.5	5.4	0.8
> 5.0 − ⩽ 10.0%	26.7	15.0	24.9
> 10.0 − ⩽ 15.0%	34.8	17.2	12.7
> 15.0 − ⩽ 20.0%	22.2	17.7	26.1
> 20.0 − ⩽ 30.0%	4.3	20.4	17.4
> 30.0 − ⩽ 50.0%	0.2	15.4	9.8
> 50.0%	0.1	2.0	0.3
Total	100	100	100

Modal tariff class* > 10.0 − ⩽ 15.0% > 15.0 − ⩽ 20.0% > 15.0 − ⩽ 20.0%

Table 17.1(b) *Distribution of the Tariff Rates of the Principal Industrial Countries After the Kennedy Round Negotiations*

Rate of duty	CET	USA	UK
Duty free	8.2	8.7	12.4
> 0 − ⩽ 5.0%	23.2	23.1	21.2
> 5.0 − ⩽ 10.0%	55.6	29.9	34.7
> 10.0 − ⩽ 15.0%	10.7	14.6	16.1
> 15.0 − ⩽ 20.0%	2.0	11.2	12.7
> 20.0 − ⩽ 30.0%	0.3	8.6	2.6
> 30.0 − ⩽ 50.0%	−	3.4	0.3
> 50.0%	−	0.5	−
Total	100	100	100

Modal tariff class* > 5.0 − ⩽ 10.0% > 5.0 − ⩽ 10.0% > 5.0 − ⩽ 10.0%

Source: Coffey 1976, p. 31.

* Modal tariff class is defined as the tariff class below which 50% of the tariff levies lie.

tariffs before and after the Kennedy Round is given in tables 17.1(a) and 17.1(b) — the most obvious conclusion is that tariffs were cut more or less across the board, but that tariff reductions on average were about 35% (Swann 1978, p. 308) and that the quantity of international trade involved was just about one-quarter of the total.

Detailed agreements were also reached with regard to: the abolition of ASP (discussion of this is unnecessary since the ASP was in fact not abolished); a higher world price for wheat; and the donating of 'food aid' to poor countries — 4.5 million tons of grain per annum financed by the US (42%), the EEC (23%), Canada (11%), and Australia, Japan and the UK (5% each).

As far as this section is concerned, it can be argued that the Kennedy Round enhanced the 'unity, strength and common personality' of the EEC, and this despite the fact that members of the EEC did not always stand or participate together; indeed, Coffey (1976) argued that the major credit for reconciling the disparate interests of the members of the EEC must go to the EEC Commission and to M Jean Rey in particular. The EEC was able to negotiate on equal terms and the negotiations were described as a 'dialogue between equals', particularly since it is quite clear that the final outcome of the negotiations was a compromise of the initial positions.

The EEC, Japan and the US agreed in February 1972 to the opening of a further round of international trade negotiations under the auspices of GATT. This round (initially referred to as the Nixon Round) was extremely difficult, particularly since it aimed at considering not only tariffs on industrial commodities, but also those on agricultural products, as well as non-tariff impediments on trade.

Just before the official commencement of the Tokyo Round the spirit of 'equal partnership' was subjected to severe strains. On the one hand, the US stood firm with regard to securing certain concessions from the EEC for agricultural commodities and expressed a preference for commodity agreements to be reached by the producer nations to be conducted outside the GATT negotiations. Moreover, the US wanted to link the granting of the most-favoured-nation clause to the USSR with the politically sensitive issue of the emigration of Soviet Jews. On the other hand, the EEC wanted to see a link between trade and monetary progress in the belief that trade liberalisation was meaningless without a monetary system which protected the world economy from 'shocks and imbalances'.

Against this background, leaving out minute details, a conference was held in Tokyo on 12–14 September 1973 which was attended by about one hundred nations. It was a Ministerial conference of the contracting parties which were prepared to participate in the forthcoming negotiations; also present were delegates from about twenty countries which were not party to GATT. The Conference unanimously adopted a declaration — the Tokyo Declaration, the full text of which is appended to this chapter — officially launching the negotiations and outlining their guidelines. These, basically, were:

(a) the progressive dismantling of all obstacles to trade and improving the international framework for the conduct of world trade;

(b) the securing of additional benefits to developing countries by improving the conditions of access for their exports and by ensuring equitable prices for primary products.

The ministers declared their intention to conclude the negotiations in 1975. In reality, the negotiations did not get properly under way until February 1975 when the US Congress passed the Trade Act required for giving the US Administration the necessary negotiating powers. Moreover, the hard bargaining in these negotiations was in reality between the US and the EEC only.

Before proceeding further, let us consider specific details of the background to the actual negotiations. These can be clearly shown in terms of what each side set out to achieve. The EEC position was discussed in great detail in the Council in July 1973 and that discussion influenced the details of a document sent by the Commission to the Council in October 1974 which was to form the basis of a strategy for the negotiations. The main points of this document were:

(a) to ensure that all nations participating in the negotiations should not have tariffs higher than 20% on average, hence tariff reductions of 25–50% were to be proposed, with the 50% applying particularly to the very high tariff levels;

(b) impediments on imports should be carefully examined and co-operation between consumers and producers should be sought and encouraged;

(c) the market for certain essential raw materials should be stabilised by encouraging international agreements;

(d) three types of agreement were proposed for seeking international cooperation on agricultural products, particularly butter, maize, milk powder, rice, sugar and wheat (which form 25% of EEC trade) — these were: price agreements for dairy products, storage agreements for cereals under the management of main world producers, and similar storage arrangements for sugar and rice (but here the management should be under the appropriate international organisation);

(e) for other agricultural products, particularly meat, a 'code of conduct' should be sought between exporters and importers to ensure continuity of both supply and demand.

The US position was not so clearly set out, but it demanded tariff cuts of up to 60% *ad valorem*, sought agreements among producers and consumers, demanded concessions for agricultural products, and, of course, set out to protect its particular brand of trade impediments like ASP and anti-dumping legislation.

After a lengthy period of discussions and many 'substantive' phases, seventeen participants including the EEC signed the 'procès-verbal' authenticating the overall results at the end of April 1979. Official ratification is still to come, even though the process of implementing the agreed outcome commenced on 1 January 1980.

The agreed results of this very lengthy round of negotiations can be summarised in the following points:

(a) the US industrial tariffs are to be reduced by about one-third and very few products will be subject to more than 20% *ad valorem*; Japan's will be reduced by about one-quarter and the EEC's by slightly less than a quarter (from 9.8 to 7.5%);
(b) the EEC can grant export restitution on agricultural products provided this practice does not result in unfair expansion of the EEC world market share;
(c) the agricultural package includes an international agreement on meat and dairy products, but no agreement was reached regarding cereals;
(d) the EEC was granted better access to certain markets including those of Canada, the US and New Zealand for products such as biscuits, cheese, cognac and whisky in return for concessions by the EEC for dairy products, meat, rice, tobacco, etc., but these concessions are not to affect either the principles or mechanisms of the CAP and any adversely affected EEC producers are to receive 'adequate compensation';
(e) the reductions on tariffs on tropical products granted before the conclusion of the negotiations (1977) are, as a special gesture towards developing countries, not to be reciprocated;
(f) in the field of non-tariff measures, substantial results were achieved; for example, the ASP system is to be abolished under the Customs Valuation Code.

Hence the Tokyo Round has resulted in deals with regard not only to tariffs, but also to non-tariff barriers, agricultural products, safeguard clauses and the developing countries.

The outcome is described with the particular viewpoint of the EEC so that, in concluding this section, an evaluation can be made with regard to the success or failure of the EEC in this round of negotiations. Comparing the final outcome with the points of negotiations set out in the 1974 document, it seems, firstly, that the tariff reductions achieved were not out of line with those desired by the EEC; secondly, that the EEC has managed to secure the principles and mechanisms of its CAP system and has at the same time secured international agreements for certain agricultural products; thirdly, that the US has been persuaded to discontinue certain practices like the ASP system; and finally that certain concessions, albeit very minor, were granted to the developing countries. On the face of it, therefore, the EEC has been very successful, so it is not surprising that Mr Roy Jenkins 'praised the example that the negotiations had given of the way in which the Community could work and act together in a spirit of mutual trust and cooperation. The Commission itself had great reason for satisfaction in that the final settlement was very much on the lines it had proposed' (*Bulletin of the European Communities*, No. 4. 1979, p. 10).

No one can deny that the Tokyo Round has demonstrated that the EEC has benefited from its size and unity in international negotiations, but it should be obvious that the concessions made in the agricultural field are insignificant since they relate only to the selling of surplus products, which is the most inefficient element of the CAP — see the chapter on the CAP. Therefore, such achievements are in direct contradiction to the statement that the 'Council's approval of the final result of the MTN offered a real chance of a *fairer* and *freer* world trading system in the 1980s' (the emphasis is not in the original text) — Roy Jenkins quoted in the *Bulletin of the European Communities*, *op. cit.*, p. 11. In short, the EEC has succeeded in becoming a very strong bargaining opponent to the US, but it seems that this power is being used to protect its own interests, particularly its inefficient CAP system. However, lest it be forgotten, that inefficient system seems ironically to be the very foundation of the unity of the EEC at this stage in its development.

Association Treaties

The original signatories of the Treaty agreed to associate to the EEC those 'non-European countries and territories'[1] which had special relations with Belgium, France, Italy and the Netherlands, with the purpose of promoting their economic and social development and establishing close economic relations between them and the EEC as a whole (Article 131). The Treaty claimed that the association is meant to promote the interests and prosperity of the citizens of these countries, so as to take them to the 'economic, social and cultural development to which they aspire'.

The following were the aims of associations as stated in Article 132:

(i) the EEC partners will treat imports from the associated countries on the same basis as they treat intra-EEC imports, i.e. preferential access into the EEC is granted to these countries;

(ii) the associated countries will treat imports from other EEC countries on the same basis as they treat imports from the EEC country with which they have a special relationship, i.e., the so-called 'reverse preference';

(iii) the EEC countries will provide aid towards the capital investments which are required for the development of the associated countries;

(iv) the capital investments which are financed by the EEC will be open for competition to all citizens of the EEC on an equal basis;

(v) the provisions on the right of establishment will be extended on a non-discriminatory basis towards the associated countries.

Moreover, the EEC had definite attitudes regarding its relationships with the countries of Eastern Europe and the Mediterranean — see Shlaim and Yannopoulos (1976). The EEC made precise recommendations concerning these relationships. Articles 110—116 read together indicated that by the end of the transition period, the EEC would negotiate as a single entity with Eastern Europe. This single entity was obviously meant to counteract the unity of Eastern Europe as reflected in COMECON — Council for Mutual Economic Assistance. Also, in September 1972, the Commission sent a document to the Council asking for an EEC 'global' strategy towards the Mediterranean countries. The document was accepted on principle at the Paris Summit in October 1972 and was officially accepted on 7 November of the same year. The main points of the document were: the establishment of a free trade area in industrial goods between the EEC and each individual country of the Mediterranean; the granting of certain concessions to agricultural products provided the CAP is not jeopardised; the promotion of industrial and technical collaboration and the granting of aid to the poorer Mediterranean countries; and, finally, of course, the promotion of access to EEC agricultural products to the markets of these countries.

How successful has the EEC been in concluding association agreements? The EEC has signed Association Agreements with: Greece in July 1961; eighteen African States and Malagasy[2] (the Yaoundé Convention) on 20 July 1963 for five years with the object of regulating trade and aid (this was renewed in 1969 and in 1975 a wider agreement, the Lomé Agreement, was signed, originally with forty-four African, Caribbean and Pacific — ACP — countries; this was renewed in July 1978 and the number of countries became 57 in 1979); Turkey in September 1963; Nigeria in July 1966; Kenya, Tanzania and Uganda (the Arusha Convention) in July 1968 — this expired in 1969 before it was actually ratified, but was renewed and ratified in 1969 and 1975; Malta in April 1971 for five years; and Cyprus in 1972. The EEC has also signed Trade Agreements with Iran in September

1963; Israel in October 1970; and Spain in October 1970. In addition, Partial Association Agreements were signed with Morocco and Tunisia in 1969 and in September 1975. In March 1970, a three-year non-preferential Agreement was signed with Yugoslavia and this was later renewed and negotiations for a new agreement commenced in late 1979. Finally, in the context of the global Mediterranean policy, agreements were signed with the Maghreb countries (Algeria, Morocco and Tunisia) in 1976, for an unlimited period; with the Mashrek countries (Egypt, Jordan, Lebanon and Syria) in 1977; and with Israel in 1977 (this treaty covers trade, aid and industrial cooperation); and Malta in 1976 (this was a wider re-arrangement of the earlier treaty).

Before discussing the economic implications of these associations and their overall significance, it is necessary to examine briefly the factors that determined them.

The original impetus for the EEC to enter into special agreements with particular developing 'countries and territories' was due to the fact that one of the most important considerations for drawing up an acceptable Treaty of Rome was that the preferences granted by Belgium, France and Italy to their respective colonies in Africa should be made secure (Kreinin 1975 and Coffey 1976), particularly since these countries were anxious to maintain and/or to evolve special connections with their African 'countries and territories'. Hence in May 1956, at the Venice Foreign Ministers' Meeting, France made it quite explicit to her future partners that French membership of the EEC hung largely on the acceptance of the future 'economic integration of her overseas territories' (Coffey 1976).

France had two reasons for this insistence. First, the French regarded their overseas territories as a 'natural extension' of their country and French membership of the EEC without a special provision for them would undermine that natural extension. Secondly, the French, in assisting these territories by granting them aid and higher prices for their raw materials, felt financially burdened and wanted the EEC to share this burden particularly since West Germany, by investing in commercial enterprises in these territories, was indirectly benefiting from French expenditure in infrastructures in these territories.

The enlargement of the EEC in 1973 introduced a new dimension. The UK had operated a system of preference — 'imperial preference' — with a large number of her former colonies and the UK, like France, wanted these countries to have certain commercial links with the EEC. This became an important consideration in negotiating the terms of entry and was partly responsible for the negotiation of the Lomé Agreement in 1975.

Another consideration was that certain Mediterranean countries conducted about 50% of their international trade with the original

Six and this encouraged them to find ways and means of by-passing
the CET. This was not the only consideration, however. Apart from
conducting about 12% of its trade with them (Shlaim and Yannopoulos
1976) the attitude of the EEC towards the Mediterranean countries
has 'evolved out of an array of conflicting political pressures, coupled
with a need to preserve an economic and/or diplomatic balance between Greece and Turkey, between Spain and Israel, between Israel,
Egypt and the Lebanon, and between Morocco, Tunisia and Algeria'
(Kreinin 1975, p. 332).

A final consideration is that the evolution of a united policy towards
Eastern Europe could arguably be attributed to an EEC effort to
encourage the 'relationships' between West and East Germany and
to counteract the influence of COMECON on Eastern European
solidarity.

The specifics of these arrangements and the analysis of their costs
and benefits for the EEC and the countries concerned cannot be
tackled here, since an adequate treatment would require a book in its
own right. One could, of course, give details regarding the financial
arrangements made; for example, the aid given through the European
Development Fund (EDF) in 1964 was $581.25 million for five years,
the financial expenditure of the European Investment Bank (EIB)
with regard to the 1975 Lomé Convention was 390 million European
Units of Account, the total amount of aid provided under the Lomé
Agreement (the STABEX Fund) was 3466 EUA allocated for a
four-year period, and in the latest agreement this was revised to 5607
EUA for a five-year period. One can also give details regarding the
mutual concessions stated in the different agreements; for example,
the special agreements contracted with Greece in 1962 and Turkey
in 1964, apart from providing for a customs union and eventual full
membership of the EEC once the economies of these countries
became 'comparable' with those of the members of the EEC, allowed
for reductions in EEC industrial tariffs and specified periods of tariff
cuts by Greece and Turkey of 12–22 years depending on the commodity in question. However, such details cannot be adequately
treated here and, moreover, a useful discussion is provided by Cosgrave
(1969), the Curzons (1971), Kreinin (1975), Coffey (1976) and
Shlaim and Yannopoulos (1976).

As far as broad generalisations are concerned, there are two points
which are worth mentioning. Firstly, as far as the Third World is
concerned, a link between them and the EEC was provided through
the introduction of a General System of Preferences (GSP) on 1 July
1971. The GSP was meant to ensure that manufacturing goods
exported by the developing countries are allowed to enter the EEC
free of duty. Since similar goods coming from developed countries are

subject to the CET, this amounts to granting a 'margin of preference' to the developing countries. It is, of course, arguable how significant these margins have been.

Secondly, estimates of the trade creation and trade diversion of these arrangements have been attempted. Given the reservations expressed in Chapter 5, these estimates suggest (see Kreinin 1975, p. 363) the following conclusions:

(a) the formation of the EEC has resulted in trade diversion in both agricultural and manufactured products and this has been detrimental to developing countries;

(b) in the case of the AASM, 'the decline in their share in the French market has been more than compensated by preferences granted in the markets of the other EEC countries and they have generally gained at the expense of non-associated countries';

(c) the 'reverse preferences' which resulted in the associated countries paying higher prices for their imports from the EEC are an obvious cost to the former countries, although Kreinin suggests that these costs have decreased since the formation of the EEC;

(d) although Greece and Portugal have expanded their exports to the EEC as a result of association, there is no such evidence for Turkey;

(e) the enlargement of the EEC is 'expected to further increase trade diversion at the expense of the developing countries, with the Asian Commonwealth countries being the main losers', and the benefits expected from the Generalised System of Preference are 'likely to remain small'.

UNCTAD

One of the most sensitive areas of international and multinational cooperation is that between the developed countries and the Third World. This cooperation has a formalised existence in the form of the United Nations Conference on Trade and Development — UNCTAD. At this juncture it is appropriate to ask about the attitude of the EEC towards UNCTAD.

Again, an adequate treatment of this subject is certainly not possible without devoting a whole book to it. There are at least two reasons for this. Firstly, there have been five meetings: the first UNCTAD was held in 1964, the next three were held at four-year intervals and the last, UNCTAD V, was held only three years later between 7 May and 3 June 1979. Secondly, each meeting was preoccupied with a major but different topic: the first two made their major concern the EEC preferential treatment and considered the possibility of a Generalised System of Preference (GSP) and the last three were preoccupied with the questions of trade, aid and the oil crisis. The reader is therefore advised to consult the UNCTAD Reports for detailed information and the *Bulletin of the European Communities* for summaries and progress reports.

In this section it suffices to state that the EEC conceded the demand by the Third World for adopting the GSP instead of its preferential treatment via Association Agreements particularly to former colonies – see the previous section. However, the question of aid is still a national matter within the EEC (see Chapter 3 for detailed information) and this partly explains why the EEC attended UNCTAD V as an 'observer' and probably also explains why UNCTAD V ended in failure.

New Membership

Strictly speaking, the Treaty of Rome specifically stated that *any* European country may apply for membership of the EEC. The Treaty also specifically declared that no membership would be granted unless a unanimous decision by the Council is obtained.

That is as far as one can take this issue. However, one should recall that despite the French veto of UK membership, the UK was finally admitted, her terms of entry were re-negotiated and the EEC has recently promised to reconsider the UK's 'unfairly high' contribution to the Central Budget — for a discussion of these costs the reader should consult Pinder (1971), Young (1973), Paxton (1976), Morris (1979) and the various publications on the work carried out by the Cambridge Economic Policy Group at the Department of Applied Economics. Moreover, a Treaty of Accession has just been signed with Greece for commencing membership by 1 January 1981, and applications for joining have been received from Portugal and Spain. These considerations suggest, on the one hand, that the EEC is genuine in encouraging the 'democratic' countries of Europe to join and this is indirectly substantiated by the EEC–EFTA Free Trade Treaty signed in 1977 which is 'progressing satisfactorily', and on the other, that certain European countries *are* interested in joining. The costs and benefits of membership still remain wide open and subject to the ingenuity of the negotiators!

Conclusion

The overall conclusions of this chapter are the following:

First, the EEC has proved capable of acting as a unit in international trade negotiations and has negotiated with the US on equal terms; it has pursued and has succeeded in concluding Association Treaties; and it has succeeded in attracting new membership.

Secondly, these successes should be viewed with considerable caution, particularly since the results of the international negotiations have strengthened the protectionist elements in the EEC.

Thirdly, the Association Treaties have had a very marginal impact, and it could be argued that they were detrimental to the Third World.

Fourthly, the EEC does not only seem reluctant to have a clear policy on aid to the Third World but, in spite of conceding to the GSP, it has remained basically selective and this selective nature has been basically for its own benefit.

Finally, the terms negotiated for new membership have been, albeit marginally, at the expense of the newly contracting parties.

Notes

1 French West Africa including: Senegal, the Sudan, Guinea, the Ivory Coast, Dahomey, Mauretania, the Niger and the Upper Volta; French Equatorial Africa including: the Middle Congo, Ubangi-Shari, Chad and Gaboon; St. Pierre and Miquelon; the Comoro Archipelago; Madagascar and the French dependencies, the French Somali Coast, New Caledonia and dependencies, the French Settlements in Oceania, the Southern and Antarctic Territories; Togo; the French Trusteeship Territory in the Cameroons; the Belgian Congo and Ruanda-Urundi; the Trusteeship of Somalia under Italian administration; Netherlands New Guinea; and Netherlands Antilles.

2 These are Chad, the Central African Republic, Gabon, Cameroon and the Congo Republic, which formed the Central African (Customs) Union, Dahomey, the Ivory Coast, Mali, Mauritania, Niger, Senegal and Upper Volta, which form the West African Union, and Togo, Somalia, Zaire, Madagascar, Ruanda Urundi and Mauritius. They are usually referred to as the Associated African States and Malagasy (AASM).

References

Balassa, B. (ed.), *European Economic Integration*, North-Holland Publishing Co. 1975.

Cambridge Economic Policy Group, various publications, mainly in the *Cambridge Economic Review*.

Coffey, P., *The External Relations of the EEC*, Macmillan Press 1976.

Cosgrave, C.A., The EEC and developing countries, in Denton, G.R. (ed.), 1969.

Curzon, G. and V., Neo-colonialism and the European Community, *Yearbook of World Affairs*, Institute of World Affairs, London, 1971.

Denton, G.R. (ed.), *Economic Integration in Europe*, Weidenfeld and Nicolson 1969.

Kreinin, M.E., European integration and the developing countries, in Balassa, B. (ed.), 1975, Chapter 9.

Matthews, J.D., *Association System of the European Community*, Praeger 1977.

Morris, V., *Britain and the EEC — the Economic Issues*, Labour, Economic, Finance and Taxation Association, London, June 1979.

Paxton, J., *The Developing Common Market*, Macmillan Press 1979, Chapter 2.

Pinder, J. (ed.), *The Economics of Europe: What the Common Market means for Britain*, Knight 1971.

Shlaim, A. and Yannopoulos, G.N. (eds), *The EEC and the Mediterranean Countries*, Cambridge University Press 1976.

Swann, D., *The Economics of the Common Market*, Penguin Modern Economics Texts 1978.

Young, S.Z., *Terms of Entry: Britain's Negotiations with the European Community, 1970—1972*, Heinemann 1973.

European Commission, *Bulletin of the European Communities*, for various years.

Appendix

The Tokyo Declaration

The complete text of the Declaration adopted by the Ministers in Tokyo on 14 September is as follows:

1. The Ministers, having considered the report of the Preparatory Committee for the trade negotiations and having noted that a number of governments have decided to enter into comprehensive multilateral trade negotiations in the framework of GATT and that other governments have indicated their intention to make a decision as soon as possible, declare the negotiations officially open.

    Those governments which have decided to negotiate have notified the Director-General of GATT to this effect, and the Ministers agree that it will be open to any other government, through a notification to the Director-General, to participate in the negotiations.

    The Ministers hope that the negotiations will involve the active participation of as many countries as possible. They expect the negotiations to be engaged effectively as rapidly as possible, and that, to that end, the governments concerned will have such authority as may be required.

2. The negotiations shall aim to:
    - Achieve the expansion and ever-greater liberalisation of world trade and improvement in the standard of living and welfare of the people of the world, objectives which can be achieved, *inter alia*, through the progressive dismantling of obstacles to trade and the improvement of the international framework for the conduct of world trade.
    — Secure additional benefits for the international trade of developing countries so as to achieve a substantial increase in their foreign exchange earnings, the diversification of their exports, the acceleration of the rate of growth of their trade, taking into account their development needs, an improvement in the possibilities for these countries to participate in the expansion of world trade and a better balance as between developed and developing countries in the sharing of the advantages resulting from this

expansion, through, in the largest possible measure, a substantial improvement in the conditions of access for the products of interest to the developing countries and, wherever appropriate, measures designed to attain stable, equitable and remunerative prices for primary products.

To this end, coordinated efforts shall be made to solve in an equitable way the trade problems of all participating countries, taking into account the specific trade problems of the developing countries.

3. To this end the negotiations should aim, *inter alia*, to:

   (a) conduct negotiations on tariffs by employment of appropriate formulae of as general application as possible;

   (b) reduce or eliminate non-tariff measures or, where this is not appropriate, to reduce or eliminate their trade restricting or distorting effects, and to bring such measures under more effective international discipline;

   (c) include an examination of the possibilities for the coordinated reduction of all barriers to trade in selection sectors as a complementary technique;

   (d) include an examination of the adequacy of the multilateral safeguard system, considering particularly the modalities of application of Article XIX, with a view to furthering trade liberalisation and preserving its results;

   (e) include, as regards agriculture, an approach to negotiations which, while in line with the general objectives of the negotiations, should take account of the special characteristics and problems in this sector;

   (f) treat tropical products as a special and priority sector.

4. The negotiations shall cover tariffs, non-tariff barriers and other measures which impede or distort international trade in both industrial and agricultural products, including tropical products and raw materials, whether in primary form or at any stage of processing including in particular products of export interest to developing countries and measures affecting their exports.

5. The negotiations shall be conducted on the basis of the principles of mutual advantage, mutual commitment and overall reciprocity, while observing the most favoured-nation clause and consistently with the provisions of the general agreement relating to such negotiations. Participants shall jointly endeavour in the negotiations to achieve, by appropriate methods, an overall balance of advantage at the highest possible level. The developed countries do not expect reciprocity for commitments made by them in the negotiation to reduce or remove tariff and other barriers to the trade of developing countries, i.e. the developed countries do not expect the developing countries, in the course of the trade negotiations, to make contributions which are inconsistent with their individual development, financial and trade needs. The Ministers recognise the need for special measures to be taken in the negotiations to assist the developing countries in their efforts to increase their export earnings and promote their economic development and, where appropriate, for priority attention to be given to products or areas of interest to developing countries. They also recognise the importance of maintaining and improving the generalised system of preferences. They further recognise the importance of the application of differential measures to developing countries in ways which will provide special and more favourable treatment for them in areas of the negotiation where this is feasible and appropriate.

6. The Ministers recognise that the particular situation and problems of the least developed among the developing countries shall be given special attention, and stress the need to ensure that these countries receive special treatment in the context of any general or specific measures taken in favour of the developing countries during the negotiations.

7. The policy of liberalising world trade cannot be carried out successfully in the absence of parallel efforts to set up a monetary system which shields the world economy from the shocks and imbalances which have previously occurred. The Ministers will not lose sight of the fact that the efforts which are made in the trade field imply continuing efforts to maintain orderly conditions and to establish a durable and equitable monetary system.

The Ministers recognise equally that the new phase in the liberalisation of trade which it is their intention to undertake should facilitate the orderly functioning of the monetary system. The Ministers recognise that they should bear these considerations in mind both at the opening of and throughout the negotiations. Efforts in these two fields will thus be able to contribute effectively to an improvement of international economic relations, taking into account the special characteristics of the economies of the developing countries and their problems.

8. The negotiations shall be considered as one undertaking, the various elements of which shall move forward together.

9. Support is reaffirmed for the principles, rules and disciplines provided for under the general agreement.[1]

Consideration shall be given to improvements in the international framework for the conduct of world trade which might be desirable in the light of progress in the negotiations and, in this endeavour, care shall be taken to ensure that any measures introduced as a result are consistent with the overall objectives and principles of the trade negotiations and particularly of trade liberalisation.

10. A Trade Negotiations Committee is established, with authority, taking into account the present declaration, *inter alia*:

   (a) to elaborate and put into effect detailed trade negotiating plans and to establish appropriate negotiation procedures, including special procedures for the negotiations between developed and developing countries;

   (b) to supervise the progress of the negotiations.

The Trade Negotiations Committee shall be open to participating governments.[2] The Trade Negotiations Committee shall hold its opening meeting not later than 1 November 1973.

11. The Ministers intend that the trade negotiations be concluded in 1975.

Notes to Appendix

1 This does not necessarily represent the views of representatives of countries not now parties to the general agreement.

2 Including the European Communities.

18

Concluding Thoughts

A M EL-AGRAA

Originally, I intended here to put together all the conclusions reached in this book as a result of the analysis and discussion of the various theoretical, empirical and policy aspects of the EEC. I was dissuaded from this by the realisation that some readers might be tempted to come straight to this note and commit (as often happens) the dangerous error of failing to appreciate the reservations and qualifications on which such conclusions are based. Moreover, readers who so wish can, in any case, refer to the concluding sections of the various specific chapters. I have therefore decided that this final chapter should contain two brief sections: the first deals with two issues which are not specifically discussed elsewhere in the book, while the second considers the conclusion that emerges from the book as a whole and speculates about the future prospects for the EEC.

Fisheries Policy, Capital Mobility and International Investment

The first point to make in this section is that the EEC has a common fisheries policy, agreement on which was reached in October 1970, and which came into force in February 1971 — a very opportune time considering the imminent membership of Denmark, Ireland and the UK! The policy has two elements: market organisation and structural aspects. The market organisation covers fresh fish and frozen and preserved products and its main aim is to apply common marketing standards and to facilitate trading between the member nations of the EEC. The structural aspects are basically concerned with equal access to fishing grounds for all EEC nationals, with provisos for certain kinds of offshore fishing. Overall, it can fairly be stated that this policy is far from common, since so far it has been based on *ad hoc* compromises and concessions for *individual* member nations.

The second point to make relates to capital mobility and international investment, subjects which are not discussed in specific chapters of their own. The mobility of capital is more complicated than that of labour (Chapter 16), particularly since it is very much interconnected with the questions of monetary integration (Chapters 9 and 10) and the common regional policy (Chapter 13). Here it can be pointed out that capital mobility (the technical problems of which were discussed in the Segré Report which was presented to the Council in January 1967) has been inhibited by the fluctuations in the rates of exchange of the member countries. In addition, the practice of controlling the convertibility of domestic currencies into foreign currencies for international transactions (for short-run balance of payments equilibrating purposes and for protecting job-creating investments) and the imposition of restrictions (for the purposes of effective control of the money supply and inflation) on non-member nationals seeking to acquire short-term securities have been further inhibiting and distorting factors.

Internationally, there has been no evidence of increased foreign investment in the EEC, particularly with regard to investment coming from the USA — it was generally believed that discrimination against the outside world would attract more investment from abroad, i.e. foreign firms were expected to avoid the discriminatory trade impediments erected against them by working within the Community (Scaperlanda 1967, Bergesten and Krause 1975 and Corner and Stafford 1977). Of course, the Japanese have made successful investments, but the overall picture is far from clear.

Overall Conclusion and Future Prospects

Before speculating about the path the EEC will follow in the future, it is necessary to state the overall conclusion of this book. It is that the EEC has been very successful in achieving *negative integration* (defined as the removal of mutual tariff barriers between member nations — see Chapter 1); indeed, the formal achievement of the removal of intra-EEC mutual tariffs and quota restrictions was accomplished ahead of schedule in July 1968, one and a half years ahead of the original target date. Moreover, the new partners have had no difficulties in accommodating themselves to these measures within the periods of transition that were mutually agreed. The EEC has also been successful in adopting some elements of *positive integration* (defined as the act of introducing common external relations, policy harmonisation, etc.), for instance the introduction of common external tariff rates (also achieved ahead of schedule), the common agricultural policy and the progress towards monetary integration. However, in the latter area, and that is where true integration is really tested, progress has been very slow and in some instances altogether lacking. This is, of course, not meant to suggest that there have been no apparent signs of strength in the forces pushing the EEC towards more positive integration. Indeed, the opposite is the case; it is only that progress has been slow because true positive integration is very much connected with the sensitive issue of sovereignty. Moveover, lest it be forgotten, the EEC stands for the harmonised integration of some of the oldest countries in the world with very diverse cultures and extremely complicated economic systems.

On the face of it, it seems that the EEC is set to take one of two alternative courses: either to become a more diluted arrangement (the implications of which are discussed in El-Agraa and Jones 1980, Chapter 3) so as to accommodate more members who are jealously guarding their sovereignty, or to take a 'quantum leap' (Ingram 1973) in terms of a political commitment to a United States of Western Europe. There does not seem to be a middle ground (though some commentators have predicted that the EEC will become a two-tier organisation, with the original Six minus Italy going ahead with complete political integration and the remaining four, plus new members, forming a diluted and less committed second tier), because that is the area where principles are diluted and temporary disadvantages become a permanent reality. However, one cannot help feeling, despite the quarrel between the British government and the rest of the EEC over the British net contribution to the Community budget, that political commitment is on the way. The feeling is justified by the recent progress towards the European Monetary System. All member nations except Britain are now full participants and the UK has taken two steps that indicate imminent membership: it exchanged 20% of its dollar and gold reserves against European Units of Account (which is an indication of positive participation in the European Monetary Co-operation Fund) and in October 1979 it abolished all foreign exchange restrictions.

References

Bergesten, C.F. and Krause, L.B. (eds), *World Politics and International Economics*, The Brookings Institution, Washington DC 1975.

Corner, D.C. and Stafford, D.C., *Open-ended Investment Funds in the EEC and Switzerland*, The Macmillan Press 1977.

El-Agraa, A.M. and Jones, A.J., *The Theory of Customs Unions*, Philip Allan 1980.

Ingram, J.C., The case for European monetary integration, *Essays in International Finance*, Princeton University Press, International Finance Section, No. 98, April 1973.

Ingram, J.C., Discussion of Corden's contribution to *European Monetary Unification and its Meaning for the United States*, Krause, L.B. and Salant, W.S. (eds), The Brookings Institution, Washington DC 1973.

Scaperlanda, A., The EEC and US foreign investment: some empirical evidence, *The Economic Journal*, March 1967.

Author Index

Subject Index